"What is a Special Interest Car?"

The term Special Interest in automotive jargon has been reasonably well defined in the past, but not within the hardbound parameters as such categories as Horseless Carriage, Antique, or Classic cars. Because a Special Interest car will largely qualify for the title only in the eyes of its beholder, it might just as easily be a '25 model as a '65 depending on several basic factors, including the numbers of them originally produced or the quantity of survivors today. But on the other hand, a particular plain-jane car can be considered of Special Interest if it has had a memorable history, or if it played a significant role in a famous event. In fact, there are an almost infinite number of reasons why a car is of Special Interest, but to make some broad generalizations and bring our own qualifications into some kind of focus, permit us to establish some rules.

A Special Interest car becomes worthy of that august appelation if it: A) was originally manufactured in relatively low numbers as, say, nearly any mid-'30's convertible sedan in relation to a closed 4-door of the same model; B) is in restorable condition considering its age; C) embodies distinctive mechanical innovations as, say, a first-year HydraMatic model; D) has styling that is noteworthy by way of either a great advancement for the time (as the Chrysler and DeSoto Airflows), or by virtue of its homeliness (the '35 Hupmobile with its odd, 3-pane windshield).

To cite additional limitations, the term Special Interest is earned if a car has a reasonably low cost *today*. This weeds out models that are far, far beyond the average restorer's or collector's purse, as the great Duesenbergs, Auburns, Cords and others, most of which are proven Classics but which might also be defined as Special Interest in some circles. The senior Packards are a part of this group, as are some of the '30's Cadillacs, the big Franklins, a Reo or two, and some others. All of these cars, even if discovered unrestored and available for *just* a few thousand dollars, are well worthy of restoration by a professional and hence would have such a high rebuilding price tag, that we must shun them here.

Another limitation; we've opted to confine our coverage to cars built between the exciting automotive years of 1930 and 1960—more accurately, through the '59 model year. Further, limited-production models as the six stainless steel '36 Fords, the special Chrysler Thunderbolts and Newports (each of which was also built in a quantity of six), and others of the ilk, while indeed of Special Interest to the affluent collector, have all been accounted for and hence are no longer available except when a rare exchange is made between moneyed collectors or museums.

But despite the omissions outlined above, there are many more cars that can be proclaimed as Special Interest than a cursory first thought would bring to mind. Virtually every make of car built in America between 1930 and 1959 offers models that are now collectable, and this holds true for the major makes that survived the entire era as well as those that went out of business shortly after 1930, were introduced not long before 1959, or came and went somewhere between these years. Chevrolet, Ford, Pontiac, Plymouth, Cadillac, DeSoto, to name a scant handful, all offered cars that are now both collectable and affordable. The short-lived marques such as King Midget, Keller, Davis, Tucker, and the almost-giant Kaiser-Frazer, as well as many others, also produced noteworthy automobiles that today have a large following of buffs. Some of these companies, of course, have been since proven to be little more than stock issues to help line the pockets of their developers, but most are included on the following pages since not all the cars that resulted from these devious rip-offs have been accounted for.

Here we go, then, with what we have decided are Special Interest cars. If *your* favorite is missing from the following pages, we would be happy to hear from you.

Spence Murray

SPECIALTY PUBLICATIONS DIVISION

Erwin M. Rosen/Executive Editor
Spencer Murray/Editor
Al Hall/Managing Editor
Jay Storer/Feature Editor
Jim Norris/Associate Editor
Richard L. Busenkell/Associate Editor
Eric Rickman/Special Assignments
Dick Fischer/Art Director
George Fukuda/Artist, Design
Angie Ullrich/Editorial Assistant

PETERSEN'S SPECIAL INTEREST AMERICAN CARS (1930-1960)

Edited by Spence Murray and the automotive editors of Specialty Publications Division. Copyright© 1976 by Petersen Publishing Co., 8490 Sunset Blvd., Los Angeles, Calif. 90069. Phone: (213) 657-5100. All rights reserved. No part of this book may be reproduced without written permission. Printed in U.S.A.

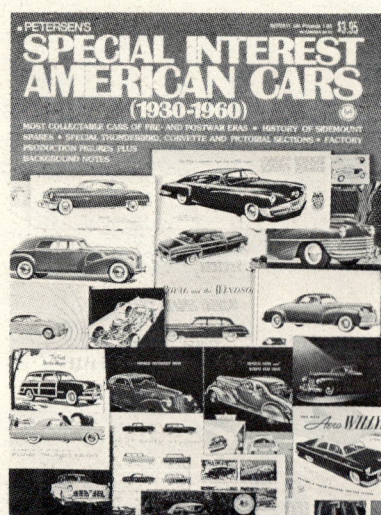

Library of Congress Catalog Card No. 75-27123

ISBN 0-8227-0116-2

COVER

A potpourri of Special Interest cars grace our cover, an assemblage of automotive greats via their original brochures. But these, and those sketched on the inside covers by artist Steve Amos, are only a part of the Special Interest story which will unfold for you, make by make and model by model, as you leaf these pages. Here are keylines of our inside covers to help you identify the cars. Cover photo by PPC Photographic. Cover design by Dick Fischer.

PETERSEN PUBLISHING COMPANY

R. E. Petersen / Chairman of the Board

F. R. Waingrow / President
Philip E. Trimbach / V. P., Finance
Herb Metcalf / V. P., Circulation Marketing
William Porter / Director, Circulation
Jack Thompson / Assistant Director, Circulation
Spencer Nilson / Director, Administrative Services

Alan C. Hahn / Director, Market Development
James J. Krenek / Director, Purchasing
Thomas R. Beck / Director, Production
Al Isaacs / Director, Graphics
Bob D'Olivo / Director, Photography
Maria Cox / Manager, Data Processing Services

Contents

CHRYSLER CORPORATION
  Chrysler/Imperial
    The cream of Chrysler's crop, by Jim Norris............................4
  DeSoto
    For a market that disappeared, by Spence Murray................12
  Dodge
    Dependability through the years, by Spence Murray............18
  Plymouth
    In the wake of the Mayflower, by Jim Norris......................22

A HISTORY OF THE SIDEMOUNT SPARE
  The most glamorous accessory, by Robert F. Mehl, Jr........26

FORD MOTOR COMPANY
  Edsel
    Destined for a quick failure, by Jim Norris............................40
  Ford
    The king of special interest cars, by Jay Storer....................44
  Lincoln/Continental
    FoMoCo's leading stars, by Buddy E. Holiday........................58
  Lincoln-Zephyr
    Plugging a marketing gap, by Jim Norris..............................64
  Mercury
    Edsel Ford's gift to the world, by Spence Murray................66
  Thunderbird
    Special cars of special interest, by Bob Leif........................74

THE WONDERFUL WOODIE
  One jump ahead of the termites, by Spence Murray..............80

GENERAL MOTORS CORPORATION
  Buick
    Some special interest sleepers, by Bob Kovacik..................86
  Cadillac
    GM's highest line, by Rick Busenkell....................................94
  Chevrolet
    The bread-and-butter line, by Tom Clark............................104
  Corvette
    Bringing sports cars to Americans, by Chuck Koch............112
  LaSalle
    Cadillac's profitable back-up, by Rick Busenkell................118

  Oldsmobile
    GM's "experimental" cars, by Bob Kovacik........................124
  Pontiac
    The years of the Indian, by Bob Kovacik............................130

PICTORIAL OF MINOR MARQUES
  The not-so-triumphants, by Spence Murray........................136
    American Bantam..136
    Checker..136
    Cunningham..137
    Davis..137
    Franklin..138
    Jeep..138
    Keller..139
    King Midget..139
    Muntz..140
    Playboy..140
    Reo..141
    Tucker..141

SPECIAL INTEREST CAR CLUBS
  Join up with the car of your choice..................................142

THE LEADING INDEPENDENTS
  Those who gave the "biggies" a run for their money........143
  Crosley
    A little car that almost made it big, by Paul Dexler............143
  Graham
    Down the Depression tube, by Spence Murray..................148
  Hudson
    One of the almost-made-its, by Al Hall..............................152
  Hupmobile
    Another Depression-era fatality, by Spence Murray............158
  Kaiser-Frazer
    The major manufacturer's biggest scare, by Bob Kovacik..162
  Nash
    Tracing mergers and diversity, by John Conde..................170
  Packard
    The one who shouldn't have failed, by Rick Busenkell........178
  Studebaker
    The oldest line in the world, by Jay Storer........................184
  Willys
    Who went on to greater things, by Spence Murray............190

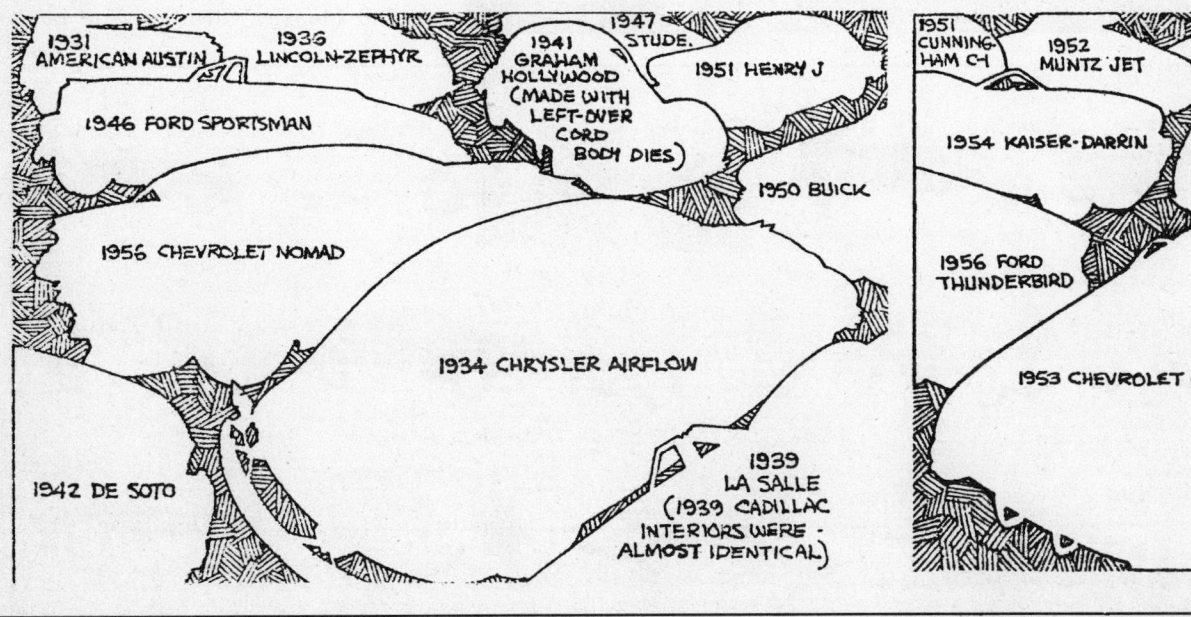

Chrysler Corporation

Chrysler/Imperial

The hallmark of engineering excellence

Never before in automotive history had a new automobile so completely whetted a nation's appetite for power and speed as the high-compression six of Chrysler. To be sure, there were names of glamour and speed; the Duesenbergs, the Marmons, and others, but the trouble was they all *cost* more than the Chrysler. At $1395, the 201-cu.-in. Chrysler "Red Head" engine could propel its model 70 body at 70 mph, and in 1924, it was an act of big proportions. Almost 32,000 Chryslers were built that year, and sold by Maxwell dealers—a record for first year sales. The Chrysler name conjured up visions of engineering excellence from its birth, a heritage that would stand it in good stead during the years of questionable artistic merit; the years of the *Airflows*, and the design dinosaurs of 1937 and '38.

The first Chrysler straight 8 entered in 1931, and set industry standards for smoothness and power. The car was a jewel that contained fully automatic spark advance, and sold for $1565. In 1932, a breakthrough was made with Chrysler's revolutionary new engine mounting system, dubbed "Floating Power." An already excellent ride was further enhanced, as the engine mounts hung the engine high at the front, and low at the rear to minimize inertial rocking and vibration.

By 1932, sales of Chrysler cars slid to 32,000 in the wake of the Great Depression, and by 1933, all Chryslers but one were powered by straight 8's.

Walter Chrysler had the unwavering faith in engineering to maintain the research department, even though, in the early Thirties, his plants were operating at only 40% of capacity, and operations were being slashed constantly. It was a decision that could allow production of the most advanced automobile in the world in 1934.

Unquestionably, the most advanced and revolutionary automobile in the world in the '30's was the Chrysler Airflow. It had cost years, and millions of dollars to work out the details of the futuristic, streamlined automobile.

The Airflow was produced in 1934 Chrysler, Imperial and DeSoto models, and would continue to roll from production lines for four years, from 1934 to '37. It was reported that about 26,500 Chrysler Airflows were built

during its lifetime—that's not including the DeSoto and Imperial cars.

Today, special interest car enthusiasts have cradled unto their own, *all* Airflows, regardless of make or body style. It is a record nearly unmatched among special interest cars; and is a reflection of the enormous impact of the Airflow. Not only do some people say that the Airflows provided the cornerstone for the special interest cult, but there are others who rate the Airflow as the finest example of a special interest car ever built. Perhaps that is because the Airflow ridicule lasted well into the next generation, was bridged by a World War, and as such doubled the mysterious aura of the car even further. The engineering and styling approaches of the car are without doubt modern, even today, especially to those who must drive a car while restoring it. And, too, it often follows that a car most ridiculed can be resurrected with an extra amount of desirability. Such is the case with the Airflows.

The Airflow embarrassed the Chrysler Corporation, and became the butt of many cruel jokes, but no other car changed the thinking of Detroit any more. And, when one considers the advances in areas of body engineering, engine placement, roominess, ride and seating, the Airflow's influence can be rightly applied world-wide.

People laughed at the Airflows wherever they appeared, and yet the ironic thing is that the Airflows were part of a 1935 corporate profit of $35 million. Although the Airflow was a money-loser, the 1935 Chrysler and DeSoto Airstreams gave the company a healthy return. Plymouths and Dodges also did well; and by 1937, the corporation remained well in the black, easily absorbing the Airflow's drain. The only losses were incurred in 1934—due especially to the Airflow—but in 1936 the company could pay a whopping $2.3 million in bonuses to its employees.

One thing to remember, is that the conventional Chrysler Airstream models, although smartly rushed into production, did have a siphoning effect on potential Airflow sales. And, by the time the bugs had been ironed out, and the Airflow was indeed a solid and dependable car, the car had lost out in the marketplace.

The man who was head of experimental engineering at Chrysler, Carl Breer, told a story to *Automotive News* in 1964, that reflected his creative impetus for the Airflow. One day in 1927, Breer and his wife "were spending the summer at Gratiot Beach, 60 miles from Highland Park. Many evenings I drove the straight and partly paved road to Gratiot Beach. It took about an hour if everything was okay.

"One late evening as dusk closed in, I noticed what I thought was a flock of a dozen or so geese flying across the road in the distance. To my surprise, this flock was really a group of airplanes heading for the Air Force's nearby Selfridge Field."

Breer decided that automotive design, with its concept of high center of gravity and boxy shapes, was far from the efficiency that should go easily through the curtain of air that exists. He wondered how much air his own Chrysler sedan must be pushing back at 50 mph, and more experimenting led him to construction of a wind tunnel at Chrysler's research center in Highland Park. Since Breer was Chrysler's head of research, he became involved personally in a totally new concept in automotive design—one that was surely destined to stagger the imaginations of stylists the world over. It may have been the most auspicious design thinking to hit the motor city.

Walter Chrysler, a man with firm faith in his engineers' ability, gave

1. This 60-lb. metal casting of original Chrysler Corporation symbol bore lightning bolts of connected "Z's" for Chrysler's first chief engineer, Fred M. Zeder. Giving replica to Detroit restaurateur Jim Constand is Corporate Historian John Bunnell.

2. Parade of Chrysler special interest cars lists some, but not all, desirable Chryslers to own today.

3. Car that started the special interest car craze is the 1934 Chrysler Airflow, an advanced, well-built machine, yet doomed by initial bugs and bad publicity.

4. Elisabeth Ann Tegtmeyer of Atlanta, Ga., and a 1935 Airflow C-1 4-door sedan. Overdrive-equipped Airflow was facelifted for '35; used bigger 323.5-cu.-in. 8; cruised at 80 mph.

5. Imperial Airflow for 1936 featured forward-opening windshield, seats between axles, interchangeable doors, engine over front axle, tubular-type frame; unusually quiet, comfortable ride, and high reliability.

6. Robert J. Wood of Red Hill, Pa., keeps his 1937 Airflow in immaculate condition, as do most owners in the fiercely dedicated Airflow cult.

Chrysler Corporation
Chrysler/Imperial

Breer the go-ahead for the Airflow's development.

Originally planned as a rear-engined prototype, the Airflow suffered, because Breer found that the car would have to use existing Chrysler and De-Soto engines which made the Airflow tail-heavy. Handling, therefore, with such great loads of weight transfer, forced Breer to abandon the rear-engine idea and concentrate instead on front placement for a 298-cu.-in. straight 8.

A new slope in order to erase the conventional box-bodied rear deck, meant that Breer had to move the rear seat forward to give rear passengers enough head room. In a very unorthodox move for that day, Breer was able to do just that. Until then, the rear bench had stood directly over the rear axle, because the front seat was placed in the center of the wheelbase. By moving the back seat off the rear axle, Breer found that passengers were given a much better ride.

What this did, though, was to shove the front bench farther forward, a move that affected the cowl, toeboard and engine. No one knew at the time just exactly what such a situation would do to ride and general handling.

At this point, the knotty problem of engine placement arose. There was now no choice but to put the engine directly over the front-axle centerline, a thing very nearly as unusual as placing it in the rear. No one knew what would happen to the car's balance, and there was lots of trial and error before the engine was finally set in—the front third of the block ahead of the axle and the rear at an angle of some 5 degrees, with a special oil pan to accommodate axle travel. More innovations followed, due to the shape and layout. These included a low-placed cooling fan which was mounted directly to the vibration damper, and a wide, low radiator that would clear the radically sloping hood.

But it remained for body engineering to provide the most fascinating engineering challenge. The Airflow used all steel, which was still uncommon in the day. Most bodies were wood frames covered with steel. What the engineers came up with was a light, cage-like steel girder network that carried body panels. It was to become the most advanced body structure of its day, and a direct precursor of today's automobile manufacture.

Although it could be argued that the American public didn't want the Airflow anyway, such a statement, even at the time, tended to ignore, the unit-body construction and the "boulevard ride." With all the Airflow's innovations in construction and engine layout, plus a whole host of engineering introductions. Things not overly tout-

ed, but nevertheless a part of every Chrysler included roller bearing universal joints, introduced in 1932, and followed matter-of-factly by valve seats and all-helical-geared transmissions in 1933. But the prudent Airflow buyer was aware of much more.

It was no secret that the standard Airflow horizontal frame was much lighter and not as deep as conventional frames. Main body sections were built to consist of three large stampings, with a one-piece rear roof/deck/bumper pan. DeSoto and small Chrysler 8's used the same right and left side panels, with difference only in front-end dimensions. On sedans, an interesting situation existed, with the right-front door interchangeable with the left-rear door,, and vice versa. Originally, Breer wanted to taper the rear body line, which would have meant a 2-passenger rear seat in the Airflows. Walter Chrysler nixed the idea, and perhaps rightly so.

The introduction of the Airflows took place at the 34th Annual National Automobile Show in New York, on January 6, 1934. It was a time of consternation by Walter Chrysler who became enraged when a 3-wheeled Dymaxion car had been selected to occupy center stage in the big Grand Central Palace. By the well-tested mixture of straight talk backed by dollars, Chrysler squeezed out the 3-wheeler from center stage, and the Airflow became somewhat a muted sensation, because Buckminster Fuller, creator of the Dymaxion, parked the vehicle at the curb by the front door to the show. Even so, Chrysler picked up several thousand orders on the spot, and things looked rosy, indeed. Trouble was, that Airflow production didn't get into high gear until April, and many orders were cancelled. Worse, rumors—stirred up chiefly by the opposition—flew hot and heavy that the Airflow was nothing but junk. Breer and others felt that the Airflow could have held on for a fantastic success if only the car's production could have coincided with the introduction. When letters were received from early Airflow owners that serious problems were developing, it was clear that the car had been premature. Bugs hadn't been worked out. One concern became of a serious nature. Reports were heard that engines were breaking loose at 80 mph. The problems were soon ironed out, but public disillusionment was much too widespread to reverse. Owners, however, after the problems had been corrected, soon came to realize that the Airflow was an extremely fine automobile.

With the overdrive transmission and either the 298.6-cu.-in. or 323.5-cu.-in. straight 8, a 1934 to '37 Airflow could sustain an easy 65-mph cruising speed. Reliability, when things got ironed out, was high, and the passenger ride was extremely smooth and comfortable, more closely approaching the cars of today. The car is softly sprung, but corners with unusual ease for a car its size.

The Airflow wasn't slow, either; as reflected in a host of speed records early in its short life. In 1934, it set 72 national and international AAA speed records at Bonneville, by Wilbur Shaw, Harry Hartz, and Billy Arnold. The three were able to average 84.43 mph for 24 hours of flogging, including 95.7

1. Realizing sales mistake, Chrysler countered in Airflow's last production year with more conventional bodies, as this '37 Imperial C-15 convertible sedan—a car for strange tastes.

2. Glory years of the Thirties was unmistakably at high point with this 1933 Custom Imperial 8—to some a classic, to others a special interest.

3. Good example of a non-classic in a conventional-bodied 2-door sedan line is a 1933 Chrysler Imperial 8.

4. Still offering an alternative—even in the years of the Airflow—was this 1934 Chrysler CA convertible sedan; now a collectible selection.

5. There was nothing more chic in 1941 than a Chrysler Windsor C28W convertible; today it's likewise attractive. Coming off a rather nondescript year in 1940, the Windsor still offered the 241.5-cu.-in. 6—a little slow in the convertible body style because of weight.

6. Next to the Airflows, the Town and Country is without doubt the most desirable Chrysler today. There were about 100 4-door sedans in the 8-cyl. New Yorker series from 1946-48; and some 3994 built on the 6-cyl. Windsor chassis.

SPECIAL INTEREST AMERICAN CARS/7

Chrysler Corporation

Chrysler/Imperial

mph for the flying mile. It was a staggering performance for 1934, yet wasn't given a nod by a wary, Depression-ridden public, even though the Airflow's records were to stand for 23 years, and were not broken until 1957! But the Airflow was fighting for its economic life in a time of appalling ignorance. If a large portion of any group of people can take to the streets in panic at a 1937 "War of the Worlds" broadcast ala the "famous" Orson Wells adaptation, it stands to reason that a car as unusual-looking, as the Airflow and cloaked in bad publicity to boot, could not succeed. The public was, to put it bluntly, literally afraid of the Airflow. All in all, a case could be made that the Chrysler and DeSoto Airflows—but especially the Chrysler Airflows—have withstood the infamy surrounding them to become the most desirable "special interest" American cars of all time.

Best examples, today, are the 1934-35 Airflows, with their well-balanced, round-faced dashboards. In 1936 square gauges appeared, and the chromed steel seat frames came off as well. By 1937, Airflow grille and headlights were changed for the second time, into sort of a prow-like appearance. A small, not especially good-looking trunk was added in 1936, and an all-steel turret top the same year. With the Airflow, though, it was a simple matter of replacing the old fabric insert with a bolt-in metal one. In 1937, the Airflow was rolling off the line in its final form, the C-17, even though many other automotive designs were freely using its advances; among them the Lincoln-Zephyr, the aerodynamic Hupmobile. Even conventional cars, such as the 1937 Ford and Chevrolet were offering many innovations and styling touches which were pioneered by the Airflow.

Total Chrysler production in 1934—including Airflow lines—was 36,929 units; for 1935, 50,010; 1936, 71,295; and 1937, 107,872. Of these, about 26,500 were Chrysler Airflows, not counting DeSoto and Imperial models. In 1934, the last word in luxury from Chrysler was the Imperial CV Airflow Coupe. Only 185 were made. Try finding one now. Today's prices on an Airflow depend on what the market will bear. But if you have a chance to find

1. The Custom Club Coupe was the industry's first modern hardtop; made from '46 to '48 and in 1950. Until 1950, only 7 were built, due to heavy custom work needed on the top for the metal-to-wood combination.

2. The 1948 Town and Country 4-door sedan was a dazzling expression of "status." Other production figures to end of 1948 for all models were: 1941—996 station wagons; 1942—1000 wagons; 1946-48—8300 convertibles. 1941 and '42 T&C were wagons only.

3. In 1949, Chrysler built 993, 8-cyl. Town and Country convertibles, but in 1950 closed out the entire Town and Country line by building 693 of the pleasing 8-cyl. 2-door hardtop; today a much-wanted gem.

4. A rare Chrysler convertible, and a sought-after item for its name, is the 1950 Highlander convertible.

5. Where it all started for Chrysler's modern onslaught is in 1951 with the Hemispherical head V-8. This engine started a revolution by setting off a horsepower race. It was an expensive engine to build.

6. The 1952 Chrysler Imperial Newport is heavy and fast. With the Hemi and a plush interior, the specially grilled Imperial Newport has become a collector's sleeper.

one at a good price, grab it. Owning a Chrysler Airflow is perverse satisfaction in its finest form.

Quite apart from the highly individual and tainted historical pasture of the Chrysler Airflow, the corporation as a whole has been active in producing a long list of automobiles that, solidly in their own right, have become desirable special interest acquisitions. A representative list would have to include the following:

1930—Chrysler "77" Roadster and Phaeton.
1934—Chrysler Airflows, also, the Custom Imperial Airflow "CW" with curved glass windshield.
1939—Chrysler, Hayes-bodied coupes.
1941—Chrysler Highlander, with Highland Fling Musical Horn.
1946—Chrysler Town and Country 2-door hardtop.
1946—Chrysler Town and Country Convertible.
1950—Chrysler Windsor and Town and Country 2-door hardtop.
1951—Chrysler New Yorker, or any of the Hemis.
1951—Chrysler K310 Sport Coupe.
1955—Chrysler 300 Sport Coupe.
1956—Chrysler 300-B Sport Coupe.
1957—Chrysler 300-C Sport Coupe.
1958—Chrysler 300-D Sport Coupe. Last of the Hemis.

Next to the Airflows, and the two intriguing Chrysler dream cars of 1940—Newport dual-cowl phaeton and Thunderbolt—the great, lumbering Chrysler Town and Country series provide a lucrative reservoir for special interest car collectors.

Chrysler had first applied the Town and Country label to what might be called a streamlined wagon, introduced in 1941. This particular car broke away from the traditional square shape of a wagon with a rounded, semi-fastback rear end not unlike that of a Chrysler sedan of the same year.

The 1941 Town and Country, curiously enough, was a 6-cylinder car. It was built on the 121½-inch wheelbase Chrysler Windsor chassis, with a 114-hp, 250-cu.-in. engine.

Most of the modifications to the hardtop's roof were done by hand. That's probably why so few of this body type were ever produced.

From a styling point of view, the Town and Country idea should never have worked. The 1946-48 Chryslers, like the 1941-42 models from which they derived, were soft, rounded-looking cars that wouldn't seem suitable for the blunt squareness of wood trim.

It's hard to avoid the word audacity once more, for the Town and Country was truly audacious in its contradiction of form and material. And somehow, it *did* work. The paneling was shaped smoothly into the car's flowing lines and enhanced the basic Chrysler styling rather than conflicting with it.

In 1949, Chrysler came out with its first truly postwar cars. These were of a functional, square-cut design that was promoted as being smaller on the outside but bigger on the inside.

There was a Town and Country convertible in 1949 and a hardtop in 1950. But even though the more nearly square lines of the new models might seem more compatible with wood paneling, they weren't as successful as the 1946-48 models. In emphasizing functional packaging, Chrysler had produced an ungainly-looking car, and wood trim only served to emphasize its awkwardness.

Chrysler itself seemed to lose interest in the whole thing. By 1950, it had dispensed with the mahogany veneer and was merely bolting ash trim to the steel bodies of ordinary New Yorkers. The door and deck panels were no longer wood-finished at all. They were metal, painted the same color as the

SPECIAL INTEREST AMERICAN CARS/9

Chrysler Corporation

Chrysler/Imperial

rest of the car. The real Town and Country had ceased to be.

In 1951, the Town and Country nameplate was transferred to a station wagon, which, ironically, had an all-steel body, without any wood trim whatever. The name has been used on wagons only ever since.

There was a brief revival of interest in simulated wood paneling on convertibles and hardtops in the mid-1960's. Chrysler offered such a treatment in its Newport series, for example. It wasn't especially well received, though, because it *was* simulated and possessed nothing of the appeal of the real wood on the 1946-48 Town and Country.

Those paneled convertibles and sedans and that prophetic hardtop of the first postwar years, improvised though they were from prewar designs, provided a rare moment of grace and elegance in an age of austerity, when most other automobiles were uninspired in appearance. That earned them a niche in motoring annals.

But their appeal is more than historic. They happen to be damned fine-looking cars in spite of themselves. And we aren't apt to see anything quite like them ever again.

Condition of particular Town and Country models today is a bit more critical than most, due to the nature of construction. That, of course, is obvious. Equally obvious to a collector is that average market values fluctuate against what the market will bear. In this area, the condition of a car is nearly the whole ballgame, period.

But a rough figure for all '46 to '50 Town and Country's is around $1500 to $4500 and still climbing. Some sources say that a Town and Country will appreciate faster than the slowest, but slower than the hottest.

Perhaps it's exactly as it should be, for the great lumbering beauty is dignified, but in its own specially quiet way.

Not only are the Airflow and Town and Country series much sought after today, but the recently ill-fated Imperial is certain to become a special interest car. It is a natural, since from the beginning, the Imperial was an expensive and well-made automobile.

The big Imperial joined the Chrysler line in 1926, and remained a 6-cyl. engine until 1931, when a long, 125-hp straight 8 was mated to a 4-speed transmission. The 1931 Custom Imperial roadster employed a low, slanting windshield and an exceptionally long hood. At $3220 from the factory, the Imperial was anything but cheap, making several models today true classics. Condition, however, is the true determinant, and it behooves the special interest car enthusiast to look long at the senior Chryslers, as well.

By 1932, Chrysler Imperials had "floating power," a movement-oriented, yet vibration-free engine mount system, and, also, "Oilight" bushings between the rear spring leaves. These bushings used a porous bronze material containing 40% oil, to quiet spring action and enhance smoothness.

Also during this period, Chrysler was gaining a reputation for solid steel bodies, at a time when much of the competition used steel/wood combinations. Such stunts as leading a 10,000-lb. elephant atop a wooden platform on a Chrysler sedan; or pushing a 1934 Airflow off a cliff, showed the world a toughness seldom matched.

Chrysler used elephants in several succeeding stunts, and recently, too, with the aim to show a solid construction that has always been a Chrysler trademark. Not only did the original elephant fail to crush the Chrysler sedan like a beer can, but there was

1. By 1954, Chrysler had increased the Hemi's gross power output to 235. Note the factory touch stock dual exhaust, a hot-rodder's dream. The '54 New Yorker Convertible is a desirable special interest car.

2. If a '54 Chrysler New Yorker can be bought (or found), it should be available at a good price. The 4-door was among the least popular, but with wires, is a stunning machine.

3. No discussion of the Chrysler name is ever complete without the mention of the 1955 "300." Attention was given to suspension, steering, engine and design to make a higher-priced collector's car, even when new.

4. This is the view to which most lesser disposed mortals were treated. The Chrysler "300" is a special interest car at its finest.

5. The 1955 Chrysler "300" featured special cast iron cam followers for the tappets. The factory re-worked Hemi put out some 300 horses at 5200 rpm. There were two 4-bbl. carbs, a great torque converter, and five axle ratios: 3.36, or optional 3.54, 3.73, 3.91, and 4.1:1's.

6. Any of the "300" series are today excellent special interest cars to and including 1959. Another sleeper among beautiful collectibles, though, is this 1957 New Yorker Convertible. By 1959, the Hemi would be gone.

2

3

4

5

claimed hardly a dent; and in the case of the Airflow, the car reportedly was driven away from the fall down the 100-ft. cliff, none the worse for wear. In both cases, the cars were subjected to the punishment in order to silence critics of the all-steel bodies. Any buyer of a special interest car would do well to study the solidity of a Chrysler product when making a choice.

Any of the conventional Chrysler Airstream models of the middle Thirties would be a desirable special interest car. The '35 Chrysler Airstream, for example, shared its basic body shell with Plymouth, in a move to counter the Depression. What has been called by some "the rock bottom of Chrysler styling" was the offering in '37 and '38, and would obviously take a collector of great courage. The '39 and '40 Chryslers came with Fluid Drive, column-mounted shift and graceful bodies with flowing fenders. In 1941, the switch was made to heavy-looking square designs, and the same in 1942, but with a record number of chrome strips, especially on the big New Yorker. The evolution of Chrysler was of engineering solidity and styling conservatism, until well after the war, with the flamboyant tail fins hitting the country in 1957. 🐞

6

Chrysler Corporation

DeSoto

Engendered to fill a marketing gap.

History little notes or remembers the individual who, in 1928, actually chose the name DeSoto as the appellation for a new Chrysler Corporation car. It probably wasn't Walter P. Chrysler. He most certainly had grander things on his mind, such as how this new car, named after the 16th-Century Spanish explorer and discoverer of the Mississippi River, would form the perfect marketing bridge between the larger, more expensive Chrysler 6's and the lower-priced 4-cylinders.

It has to be a tribute to Walter P. Chrysler the automotive entrepreneur that, without so much as even seeing a prototype model, 500 prospective DeSoto dealers took out franchise options. They even paid their own way to Detroit to get their first look at the new car. It was unveiled at a private showing on July 7, 1928.

A comtemporary automotive writer described the initial dealer reaction: "The DeSoto Motor Corp. has done a really remarkable job in securing suitable dealers...At this writing, in only four months, 460 excellent dealers have been secured, and the remainder will be obtained in a very short time. What surprises even factory officials is that this record was made with nothing to sell except the DeSoto name, backed by the Chrysler reputation. Not only were there no sample cars to show or demonstrate but no specifications whatever were given out... It stands as a remarkable feat, due apparently to just one thing—confidence in the Chrysler product."

The dealers left Detroit with visions of record orders dancing in their heads. Walter P. Chrysler didn't let them down. Production had begun in July of 1928, and by the year's end, 34,518 DeSotos had been shipped to a dealer force which now numbered 1500. The 100,000th vehicle was on its way 14 months after initial shipments had begun. It wasn't long before enough DeSotos were in the hands of owners (and testers) to provide a good line on their performance.

In reality, there was nothing particularly revolutionary or innovative about this new car; in appearance and engine design it was much the same as the Chrysler Six. What set it apart was the degree of workmanship it was able to deliver for so low a purchase price. Car buyers then, as now, had a highly developed sense of value for their dollar, and it was the "bargain" aspect of the new DeSoto which brought them to the dealers in record numbers. (The fact that the country was in the midst of an economic boom didn't hurt sales either.)

As it turned out, the year 1928 was a momentous one for the Chrysler Corporation. The Plymouth was also put into production that year, and Dodge was brought into the fold. By the beginning of 1929, you were not only able to put a Chrysler in your garage, but a Dodge, Imperial, DeSoto or Plymouth as well. (Initially, the DeSoto shared production facilities with Plymouth at Chrysler Corporation's Highland Park plant in Detroit. However, in 1936 it would get its own plant on Wyoming and Warren Avenues.)

Thus was the stage set for DeSoto's entrance into our era of Special Interest cars; an era, in DeSoto's case at least, of solidly reliable transportation but wrapped in relatively nondescript sheet metal. A few models, like the open cars are, of course, attractive and desirable from today's point of view. But as far as producing anything of an extremely outstanding nature is concerned, DeSoto in the '30's are pretty

1

1. The 1930 DeSoto was the first of the make to boast an 8-cyl. engine, and though it shared the powerplant with sister Dodge, it preceded the senior Chrysler line's use of the new engine by a year. The 8-cyl. cars were the CF series, while the smaller 6's were relegated to the CK lineup.

2. DeSoto was never one to offer particularly outstanding styling (until the Airflows) but yet, there's something definitely appealing about this pair of '32's, especially the Custom Roadster at left. The marque had lost the 8-cyl. engine by now, but offered eight separate body styles and abounded in engineering "firsts." Twin horns, among other items, identify both these cars as high-level Deluxes.

3. DeSoto put all its '34 eggs into this basket. A true engineering and styling innovation, the Airflows were quick to bomb yet are desirable collector's cars today. The Division was fast to announce the more contemporary looking Airstreams the following year, no doubt helping save Chrysler Corp. from probable disaster.

4. The queen of the '36's had to be the Airstream convertible sedan. As one of the Deluxe models it was stuck with the flat windshield while the higher-level Customs went to the Vee. But the marque did boast many mechanical innovations, for which the Corporation has always been well-known.

much ho-hum. Chrysler Corp., though, was extremely innovative in this period, and has continued to be so throughout its history, and DeSoto naturally shared in some fairly radical, for the time, engineering advancements. It is obvious, then, that today's collectable DeSotos feature mechanical innovations rather than appearance advances—with a notable exception being the Airflows.

For 1930, DeSoto (along with Dodge) was available in an 8-cylinder version. This was the first time an 8 had been fitted to a Chrysler product, and ironically, it brought the DeSoto's price to within a few dollars of the Chrysler 66, which was still using a 6-cylinder powerplant. The DeSoto was still available as a 6 that year, having received a bore increase up to 3.125 ins. Bore and stroke of the initial model had been 3.00x4.125 ins.

Following along with the trend of the times, DeSoto added 5 ins. to the standard 109-in. wheelbase to accomodate the inline 8-cyl. engine. This resulted in two distinct series of cars bearing the DeSoto nameplate. The stretch, however, was accomplished forward of the cowl. Two notable models for the year are the 6-cyl. Victoria-styled 3-passenger cabriolet, and the 8-cyl. phaeton. DeSoto followers aren't nearly as legion as other marque buffs, hence such early DeSotos as these may yet turn up at affordable prices. Searching out missing mechanical and sheet metal pieces, however, is a problem for swap meet goers.

DeSoto carried through 1931 with basically the same models as the previous year, with the 6 getting an increase in bore and the 8 an increase in stroke. By this time it was pretty obvious that the DeSoto had been a good idea (maybe even a better one). However, the economy was now becoming as bad as it had been good in 1928 at the time of DeSoto's introduction. The country was slipping deeper into the Depression. It was becoming harder and harder to sell cars. In an effort to entice buyers, DeSoto's prices were cut and new models began to be announced twice a year. All this was pretty much a case of trying to get blood from the proverbial stone, however. It wasn't that people didn't *want* to buy DeSotos (or any other car, for that matter); they just couldn't *afford* to do so.

A look at DeSoto new car registrations in the period just before and during the Depression gives an idea of the downward sales slide which was being experienced by most carmakers:

1930......................................35,267
1931......................................28,429
1932......................................25,311
1933......................................21,260

It's noteworthy, however, that despite

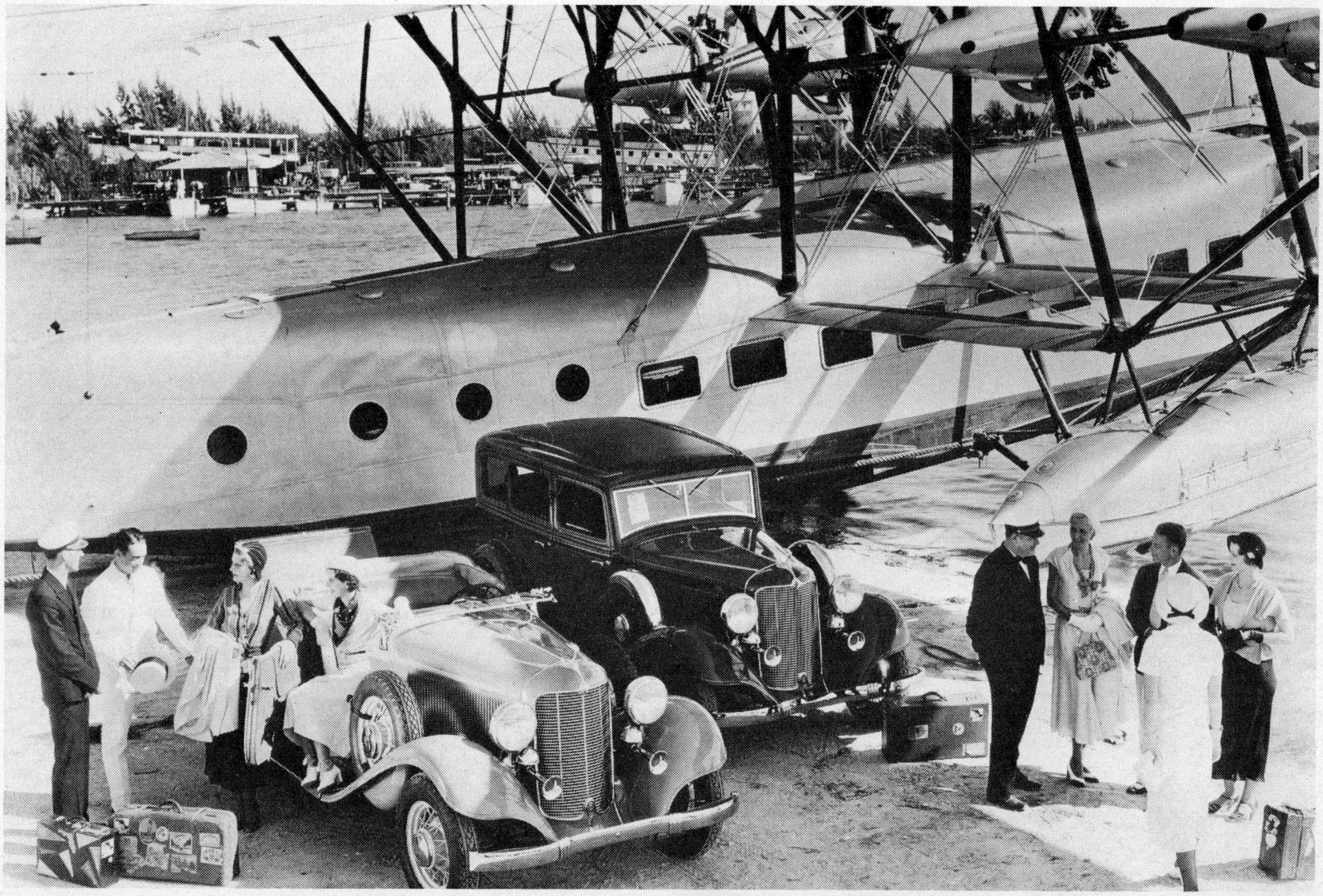

3

4

SPECIAL INTEREST AMERICAN CARS/13

Chrysler Corporation
DeSoto

this steady drop in registrations, DeSoto was able to move from 15th to 12th in sales, passing such established marques as Graham and Hudson.

The bad times were probably responsible for the dropping of the DeSoto Eight after the 1931 model run, although it might also be argued that Chrysler Corporation was merely using the DeSoto as a test bed for the new 8-cylinder design. The Chrysler models didn't actually appear with an 8 until 1931. This engine, with many improvements, of course, would continue to be used in Chryslers through 1950, after which it was replaced by the new V-8. DeSoto, however, never used the straight-8 again after '31.

It wasn't a period of affluency and the 8-cyl. DeSotos didn't enjoy the popularity of the 6's, making the 8 the more desirable car for the collector. Production of the larger-engined cars ran from Dec. '29 to Nov., '30 (for the '30 models) and from Dec. '30 to Feb. '32 for the 1931's.

If a word to the wise is to be deemed sufficient, then the acquirer of a basketcase '30 or '31 should be alerted that few of the major mechanical and body components can be interchanged between the two years. The 6-cyl. '30 wheelbase of 109 ins. grew 3/8ths-in. for '31, and both the bore and stroke of the 8-cyl. engine were increased for '31 to raise the displacement from '30's 207.7 cu. ins. to 220.7 cu. ins. for '31.

The DeSoto Six of 1932 was an exemplary automobile, despite the loss of its 8-cylinder version. It was all-steel, available in eight body styles and featured innovations such as an optional freewheeling, vacuum-operated automatic clutch and Chrysler Corporation's famed Floating Power engine mounts. The latter, patented in 1928, located rubber engine mountings along the natural rocking axes (at the front, above the timing chest and at the rear, below the transmission).

A DeSoto ad of the period described Floating Power as "not a mere refinement (but) a basic improvement in automobiles that must inevitably affect design from now on." A little bombast never hurts. In the case of Floating Power, it was probably justified.

The 1933 DeSotos were offered in two versions, the Standard and the Custom. Displacement of the L-head 6 was now up to 217.8 cu. ins. from the 174.9 cu. ins. of the original 1929 engine; the compression ratio was up to 6.0:1 from 5.2:1. New for '33 were automatic choke, automatic manifold heat control and a coincidental starter operated from the accelerator pedal.

Despite the loss of the 8-cyl. engine, or perhaps because of it, DeSoto offered two distinctively different models for '33; the Standard and Custom. The difference, though, was in trim levels and bodies were shared throughout both lines.

The year 1934 saw the introduction of the now legendary Chrysler/DeSoto Airflows. These cars had been on the drawing boards for several years, but it was obvious to the powers-that-were at Chrysler that the middle of a nasty Depression was hardly the time to introduce so earthshaking a design. As an example of just how much production was being hurt during those years, American car output went from a peak of 4,794,898 in 1929 to a low of 1,186,185 in 1932—a decrease of 75%. In fact, such a radical design would have been risky even in the best of times, simply because it was so radical.

Chrysler, however, decided to take the risk. As a result, DeSoto offered only a single model for 1934—the Airflow. Despite its wind-cheating lines (the ads described it as being able to "bore a hole in the wind"), structural steel unit body, wide-angle windshield with DuPlate safety glass, rust-proofed body, chrome tubing seat frames, flush-mounted headlamps with "asymmetrical passing beam," super-efficient ventilating system and "Bonderized" fenders and sheet metal, the 1934 DeSoto Airflow bombed. To say that it met with consumer apathy would be rash understatement. What it amounted to was that DeSoto had the worst sales year in its short history. New car registrations amounted to only 11,447, down from 21,260 the previous year.

Perhaps because of the public's unwillingness to accept the odd-appearing (for the time) Airflows, resulting in a relatively low number of them being produced, or maybe because hindsight being what it is we have lately come to accept the peculiar lines of the models, Airflows are high on the col-

1. A milestone of a sort was achieved in '37 when DeSoto was picked to provide the Indianapolis 500 pace car, despite the mild 93 hp of its 6-cyl. engine. Car buffs were quick to appreciate the ribbed bumpers, used this year only, making the items scarce today.

2. As solid, troublefree and long-lasting as DeSotos were during the late '30's, their overall styling was anything but outstanding. Nevertheless, this '39 S-6 model has a quiet charm about it. Custom and Deluxe series was carried forward for the year, but all rode on the same 119-in. wheelbase.

3. DeSoto bowed for the short-lived '42 model run with "Airfoil Lights" with electrically-driven panels that raised to reveal the headlights. The feature was gone in '46 even though the models (and through '48) were more markedly similar during this period than most other cars. Production of the '42's halted after only 24,771 units had been completed.

4. DeSoto received its true postwar restyling with the advent of the '49's though it continued to labor under the power of the self-same 6-cyl. engine introduced so long before. Its output, though, was now up to 112 hp.

lector's desirable list. Examples in virtually any condition command a steep price at swap meets and auctions. Luckily, the higher-level Chrysler Airflows are much more in demand making a DeSoto Airflow somewhat easier on the collector's purse but still allowing him to be "into" an interesting era in automotive technology and design.

A man as shrewd as Walter P. Chrysler was not about to risk the reputation (and finances) of his corporation on a single divisional model for long, so in 1935, the DeSoto Division along with the Chrysler Division) introduced the Airstream as a hedge against another poor showing by the Airflow. This proved to be a wise decision. The aerodynamic cars had another bad year, while the more conventional Airstreams sold like there was no tomorrow. Out of 26,952 DeSoto new car registrations for 1935, the Airflows accounted for only some seven thousand units. The engines were both 6's with cubic-inch displacements of 241.5, so it wasn't the engine which was affecting people's decisions as to which car to buy. What probably did affect buyers, though, was the fact that a 4-door Airstream could be had for $795 f.o.b. Detroit—$220 below a comparable Airflow. Besides, the Airstreams had the all-steel body and numerous other features offered by the Airflows. But they didn't *look* like Airflows, and apparently that was the crucial difference.

Partly because of the current interest among Chrysler Corp. buffs in the Airflow models, and partly because the more sedate Airstreams outsold the higher priced "swoopy" models and are thus more readily available, the Airstreams today may be the investment sleepers of DeSoto's '34-'35 period.

In 1936, another Airstream model was added to the DeSoto line to further bolster the slumping Airflow. Of about 45,000 new car registrations that year, only about five thousand were Airflows. The last of the DeSoto Airflows was produced in September of 1935.

Sales took a giant surge upward in 1937 with the introduction of the DeSoto S-3 and its "safety-styled" interior. Instrument panel knobs were recessed and gauges were mounted flush against the dash. The S-3 was the work of Ray Dietrich, who headed the Chrysler design staff at the time. New car registrations totaled an impressive 74,421 for the year.

A mini-depression rolled over the country in 1938, and sales of the new S-5 fell to less than 40,000 units. The 1938 DeSoto was not a particularly innovative automobile. Except for the fact that it produced four more lbs.-ft. of torque, its engine specs were identical to those of the '37. Its new, oversize cowl ventilator did mark the death of the long-used crank-open windshield, however.

The 93-bhp 6 of the previous year was carried over unchanged to the 1939 DeSoto S-6. Business had turned for the better and Chrysler decided it was time for a styling change. Ironically, much of the inspiration for the changeover seems to have come from the Airflow. The 1939's had an undeniably sleeker look about them than the '37's and 38's. The headlamps were now fully recessed into the bodywork. Passengers assigned to the middle front seat position also got a bit more leg room with the transfer of the shift lever to the steering column. The 1939's also anticipated Nader's Raiders with their "safety-signal" speedometer, which featured a green light up to 30 mph, an amber one from 30 to 50 mph and a red one over 50.

During all this time, nothing very much was being done with the venerable DeSoto L-head 6. Horsepower had reached its zenith (100 bhp) way back in '34 with the first Airflow, and since that time the only change had been to destroke the 3.375-in.-bore engine to 4.25 ins. (from 4.50 ins.). The bore itself was not destined to be enlarged until the very last prewar models (3.438x4.25 ins.).

But then, the DeSoto Six had proven itself a very satisfactory powerplant, and it had not yet reached the limits of its displacement. (What gains were made after the demise of the Airflow came as the result of playing around with carburetion, cams, timing, etc.) In contrast to the absence of development on a new engine, however, DeSoto was doing a good deal of work in the field of safety- and comfort-related equipment. The 1940 S-7 came fitted with sealed-beam headlights and had as an option the All-Weather Air Control system, which featured dual blower/heater units. The 1940 model also had the distinction of having the longest wheelbase of any DeSoto up to that time: 122.5 ins.

In the waning months of 1940, the effect of the war in Europe was becoming increasingly evident in the U.S. The majority of the automakers were gearing down from passenger car production and gearing up for war production. The demand for new cars began to increase sharply. One reason for this demand was that people simply had more money to spend. Industry was going to a longer work week and the workers were taking home a bigger paycheck. In addition, no one was real-

3

4

SPECIAL INTEREST AMERICAN CARS/15

Chrysler Corporation

DeSoto

ly sure when automobile production would have to shut down altogether because of war pressures. People wanted a new car while there still *were* new cars. As a result of this semi-hysteria among the car-buying public, sales figures in 1940 and '41 took huge leaps upward. DeSoto was no exception. Their new car registrations in 1940 totaled 71,943 (20,000 more than in '39) and in 1941 they jumped nearly another 20,000 to 91,004.

By the time the 1941 model run was over, things were really getting tight for the American car buyer. The necessities for making a car were getting awfully sparse; witness the fact that the first '42 DeSotos had chrome grilles, while those which came off the line a few months later had painted grilles. In addition, the chrome side and fender moldings were soon replaced with painted strips. DeSoto production for 1942 only lasted about five months, with 24,771 cars leaving the factory before the machinery of peacetime ground to a halt.

The post-Airflow, prewar period in DeSoto's history did not produce any particularly noteworthy models; they remained mundane in appearance though with marked reliability as basic transportation. Unless a '36–'41 DeSoto can be found in essentially complete condition, and thus require only superficial clean-up as opposed to total restoration, they are not a good buy for the investor/collector. Interest in models of this period remains low indeed.

The '42's however are interesting in several ways, and if any example of the immediate prewar era is desirable today it might be the convertible DeSoto in view of its low production run. Because DeSoto, like other manufacturers, was forced to switch to "black-out models" not long before assembly lines shut down for war production on Feb. 10, '42, a few convertibles with painted trim were produced. Many of Chrysler's records were destroyed by fire late in the war, so a count of convertibles in either standard or "black-out" trim cannot be estimated. But with a total '42 model production run of less than 25,000 units, and with the war-urged concentration on the lower-level body styles as 4-door sedans, ragtops in '42 guise are rare indeed—but in all probability not worth the expense of restoring a virtual basketcase acquisition to pristine condition.

The '42's were interesting in that they featured disappearing headlights. These so-called "Airfoil Lights" had lids which lifted up and into the fenders when the lights were switched on. Fluid-drive coupled with (are you ready?) "Simplimatic" transmission was also used on the '42 DeSoto (to be followed by Gyrol Fluid Drive/Tip-Toe Hydraulic Shift in '46—'48; PowerFlite in '54 and TorqueFlite in '57).

Chrysler had used fluid couplings on some models as far back as 1939, under a license from the European concern Vulcan-Sinclair. The first fluid coupling had been built in America by the Radcliffe Turbine Company and was fitted to a Studebaker chassis about 1920 for exhibition purposes. However, it apparently was never used on a production model. The DeSoto fluid drive had four speeds: two high and two low, with shifts controlled by the accelerator pedal. The clutch pedal was retained as a safety measure.

The 1942 models also got a bore increase, the first since the days of the original Airflow. The displacement of the DeSoto 6 now stood at 236.7 cu. ins., where it would remain until 1951.

DeSoto Division began making non-military conveyances again in November of 1945. The 1946-48 models didn't stop coming off the production line until February of '49. These cars were not much more than a carry-over from the postwar models (the disappearing headlights had themselves disappeared, however). In fact, the only way to tell '46/'47/'48 DeSotos apart is by the serial numbers.

The 1949 model was the first brand-new, postwar DeSoto automobile. It had all-new sheet metal (the modern "boxy" look), but the engine compartment was still occupied by the now hoary 236.7-cu.-in. 6. DeSoto's sales figures for the years right after the war were nothing short of phenomenal.

New car registrations went from 54,000 in '46 to 115,000 in 1950. DeSoto went over the 100,000 mark in registrations for the first time in 1949, with a total of 103,311.

Help finally arrived for Chrysler Corporation's engine lineup in 1951 in the form of the new hemispherical-combustion-chambered V-8. This was an event which could only be judged as pure Progress. Chrysler Division immediately took the V-8 as its own, fitting it to the Saratoga and New Yorker models. DeSoto, however, had to wait another year, until 1952, to receive the gift of the Hemi. Chrysler called it the Firepower V-8, DeSoto called it the Firedome.

Since the Chrysler line pioneered the introduction of the Hemi, a first-year DeSoto Firedome cannot be considered much of a milestone car today.

The name Firedome didn't much matter...it was a V-8, and a Hemi at that. How much of a giant step the

1. Face-lifting was mild for '50, but this Custom series station wagon rates fairly high with collectors. Gone now were the all-wood station wagons and this was the height of the wood-over-steel era. Soon, though, the industry was to discover wood-grained applique materials that could be applied over regular sheetmetal and the true wagons would disappear.

2. The stretched wheelbase sedans saw high sales to taxi fleets, while a few went to buyers who desired the interior space without having to opt for a full-fledged limousine. This is the 1950 edition.

3. If a postwar DeSoto is to be singled out as a Special Interest car, it has to be the '56, 320-hp Adventurer Sport Coupe. The muscle car was in direct competition with senior Chrysler's 300 series, which had bowed the year before. Extended rear fenders and the bold exterior trim were a herald of the approaching finned fender period.

V-8 really was can be seen by examining the power gains it offered over Chrysler's previous Straight-8, namely: 33% in maximum bhp, 15.5% in torque and 30% in specific output. DeSoto unquestionably needed a new powerplant—at 250 cu. ins. and 116 bhp, the old 6 was certainly nearing the end of its usefulness in propelling a modern 4000-lb.-plus automobile.

Ironically, though, it may have been the Hemi which started DeSoto on its way to dusty automotive death. For with the adoption of the V-8, the DeSoto began to move closer to the bigger, more costly Chryslers. What had always made the DeSoto so attractive in the past was its quality coupled with its reasonable price. With the last of the 6's appearing in 1954, both Chrysler and DeSoto now had V-8's across the board. Nevertheless, it would have been difficult to predict the ultimate demise of the DeSoto back in 1952. In fact, new car registrations would prove the DeSoto to be in the best of health for the next five years.

At any rate, Chrysler Corporation embarked upon the V-8 project in the biggest possible way. They even built DeSoto its own Hemi engine plant. The new plant began operation in November 1951. Of 322 machines used, about 20 were of the transfer type, which meant that numerous operations could be carried out without any human assistance at all. The relative complexity of the operation is borne out, for example, by the Heald Bore-Matic, which, at one of its stations, automatically fed valve seat inserts directly from a refrigeration cabinet located above the line and pressed them in place without operator attention. This new DeSoto engine plant had 367,192 sq. ft. of floor space and the capacity to produce one engine per minute.

As mentioned previously, the last DeSoto 6 (the Powermaster) was turned out in 1954, after which time the V-8 proliferated in both the Chrysler and DeSoto lines. Subsequently, the cars of the two divisions began to draw closer and closer together in both appearance and price. The mid-Fifties found Virgil Exner in charge of the DeSoto styling section, and it was not long before tailfins were being tacked onto experimental DeSotos. "Flite-Sweep" styling was about to be born.

The appearance of the fin was of questionable value to DeSoto's individuality, since Chrysler and Plymouth were also getting the upswept rear treatment at the same time. However, the buyers did not really react negatively to the DeSoto Flite-Sweep concept, as evidenced by the fact that new registrations continued to run above the 100,000 mark through 1957, the year of the most radical fin treatment.

The 1956 model year had seen the introduction of the DeSoto Adventurer, a 320-hp, limited-production hardtop. DeSoto now had its own Fifties muscle car (the Chrysler 300 had been introduced in 1955), and the horsepower race was on. The V-8 fitted to the 1957 Adventurer was a square one (3.80x3.80 ins.), and from then on bores got bigger, compression ratios got higher and bhp ratings shot skyward. After 1957, all the DeSoto series V-8's were oversquare, just as they had all been undersquare since the V-8's inception in '52.

For 1958, an optional version of the Adventurer came equipped with fuel injection. Its impact upon the buying public seemingly couldn't have been more minor, however, and it never appeared again. Another-high performance option, Ram Induction Manifolding, was tried on a version of the '60 Adventurer, but by that time DeSoto's fate had been sealed.

The year 1958 was a disastrous one for DeSoto. It was also a mildy disastrous year for the whole economy. New car sales figures slid all the way down the side of Mt. Everest. Total registrations showed a decrease of more than 56,000 from 1957 figures. Ironically, 1958 was also the year in which DeSoto celebrated its 30th birthday, with glowing praises and high hopes for the future. Things got worse still in '59 and '60. Obviously there is not much point in making cars if you can't sell them, and DeSotos were not selling. The final cars came off the line in the first week of December, 1960., with just a few '61's having been delivered.

Two DeSotos of the postwar period might be culled out and considered of Special Interest; the '50 Traveler Sedan and the '56 Adventurer Sport Coupe noted above.—unless one wants to add "stretched" 139.5-in. wheelbase sedans offered for several years that made a try at being 9-pass. "limousines" as well as taxicabs. Though produced in low numbers, Adventurer Sport Coupes could probably be considered a relatively wise investment; they, along with Chrysler's 300's, presaged the age of the real muscle cars, yet are not so elderly that any missing bits and pieces from a relatively intact acquisition would be too difficult or expensive to come by.

Chrysler Corporation

Dodge

Coining the word *dependability*

Although 146 different new makes of American cars were introduced during the banner year of 1914, only one of them is alive and healthy today. When brothers John and Horace Dodge announced that they would turn from supplying the automobile industry—especially Ford—with engines, transmissions, axles, and other components—and begin producing a car bearing their family name, no fewer than a record 22,000 potential dealer applications swamped their still-carless enterprise. Anyone who had been somehow involved with a car's intricacies at the time knew of the Dodge's reputation and it was widely held that anything the brothers produced would be troublefree and long-lived. An entire *car* of Dodge-built parts would, indeed, be a sure-fire winner—a fact which we all know now to be true.

Through the late Teens and Twenties Dodge prospered in its line of reliable though somewhat visually unexciting automobiles, despite the brothers' unfortunate deaths in '20 and the takeover of the sprawling empire by family heirs. In '25 the estate sold the auto holdings to the banking firm of Dillon-Read & Co., for $146,000,000.

Walter P. Chrysler had founded his own automobile company in 1924, and now he was looking for ways of expanding his marketing base. One way to do this would be to get into the low-priced field (an area in which Ford and Chevrolet had held a stranglehold for the past several years). However, Chrysler found himself in a difficult position. He desperately needed a lower-priced entry in the market, but his fledgling corporation barely had the facilities to produce a single make—the Chrysler. In addition, all cast iron and forged parts had to be bought from outside suppliers. It was estimated that building its own parts facilities would have cost the corporation at least $75,000,000—a figure which it could scarcely afford at that early stage in its development.

Walter Chrysler saw in Dodge a possible answer to both his dilemmas. The Dodge automobile would provide his entry into the low-priced field, while the Dodge factory at Hamtramck (which included a huge forge and foundry) would enable him to produce his own parts. Thus in 1928, the company founded by John and Horace Dodge came under the aegis of the Chrysler Corporation. (The purchase price paid the New York bankers, Dillon-Read and Co., amounted to $170 million in stock and the assumption of notes totaling another $59 million.) Under the leadership of its newly hired president, K.T. Keller, Dodge soon became a front-runner in the low-priced marketplace (along with the concurrently introduced Plymouth).

With the exception of a line of 6's in 1927, all of the cars produced by the Dodge Brothers had been 4-cylinders. However, the popularity of the smaller-engined cars was on the wane, and Chrysler chose to drop them in favor of the L-head 6 models. The first car which could really be called a "Chrysler" Dodge was the 1929 Dodge Brothers Six. (The term "Dodge Brothers" was used through the 1930 model year, even though Dodge was now owned by Chrysler Corporation.)

The car was a carryover from the Dodge Brothers Victory Six in its use of that car's 58-hp, 208-cu.-in. engine. The styling influence, however, was pure Chrysler, as evidenced by the grille-bar-mounted headlamps. An L-head 8 appeared in 1930, and for the next three years both a 6 and an 8 were available as a powerplant for the Dodge. In 1932, Dodge was fitted with the famous Chrysler Floating Power engine mounts, along with free-wheeling and 13-in. brake drums. At this point in time (it was then the bottom of the Depression) Dodge stood seventh in the market in sales.

Prewar Dodges all used the same basic powerplant, following the discontinuance of the straight-8 in 1933. It was the standard Chrysler Corporation L-head 6 and displaced 217.8 cu. ins. It had a compression ratio of 6.5:1 and a horsepower rating of 87 at 3600 rpm. Dodge's sheetmetal got its first really "modern" look with the introduction of the 1939 Luxury Liner model. The headlamps were now integral with the fenders, and lines in general looked much smoother all around. The 1941 version of the Luxury Liner had the distinction of being the first lower-priced Chrysler to be offered with Fluid Drive. Dodge was able to assemble 68,552 cars before Pearl Harbor brought a halt to all civilian vehicle production.

Even though Dodge styling during the '30's failed to produce anything as exciting as senior Chrysler's dual-cowl phaetons, roadsters, convertible coupes, and others, the corporation was an innovator in the engineering sense and Dodge's "firsts" make a number of interesting, but not necessarily milestone, models which are at least worth scruti-

1. Dodge Brothers Senior Roadster for 1930 offered extra-cost, dual fender-mounted spares. The division dropped the "Brothers'" appellation after this model year.

2. Dodge 6's for '31 featured a 4½-in. wheelbase stretch over the '30's, bringing this 4-door out to 114⅜-ins.

3. Another wheelbase stretch occurred for '32, but it amounted to less than an inch—confounding restorers trying to piece together one car from an assortment of various-year components. Sidemount spares added flair to what is otherwise somewhat uninspired styling.

ny as potential Special Interest cars.

Chrysler Corp.'s new L-head 8-cyl. inline engine was first offered for the '30 model year, as noted above, but this wasn't an exclusive to the Division since DeSoto debuted it simultaneously. Again paralleling DeSoto, Dodge had to offer two wheelbase variations of its body styles in order to accomodate the longer engine. In '30, the 6-cyl. cars rode on a wheelbase of 109 ins., while the 8-cyl. versions stretched to 114 ins.

Styling and chassis revisions for '31 again produced two wheelbase variants; 113-⅝ ins. for the 6's and 118 for 8's. Further changes for '32 saw additional increase between front and rear axles; to 114-⅜ ins for 6-cyl. cars and 122-⅜ ins. for 8's.

The resulting scramble of various-engined, various-wheelbased cars (which continued for '33) prevent the restorer from intermixing many components between years and models to assemble a particular car. He is faced with the dilemma (and necessarily high price) of unearthing bits and pieces for the car of his choice.

The year 1933 found DeSoto minus the 8, but Dodge was allowed to keep it for this final year. Once again, apparently as ride and handling were undergoing concentrated study, wheelbases were altered; to 115 ins. for 6's and 122 for 8's. It seems peculiar that the short wheelbase models would grow, albeit ever so slightly, and the long ones would be shrunk. It seems attempts were being made to eventually produce the 6's and 8's on identical chassis, but the 8 was dropped from the Dodge line at the end of the '33 model run and the division wouldn't offer this many cylinders again until the "V" configuration appeared in the Coronet series for 1953.

Freewheeling was a strong selling point added to the Dodge line beginning in '32, and synchromesh transmissions were adopted for '33. Automatic overdrive appeared in '34. While these innovations are hardly worthy of providing us with Special Interest category cars, they were much-advanced innovations at the time and serve to show that Chrysler Corp., was a true pioneer within an industry laboring to provide the motoring public with easier-riding, less effort-requiring automobiles.

Dodge followers today may bemoan the fact that the highly controversial Airflow styling did not reach this division, but corporate decision to introduce the advanced concept in only the higher-level DeSotos and senior Chryslers may have been an important factor in the company's salvation. The millions poured into the Airflow were at least partly recouped by Dodge (and Plymouth) during the mid-'30's period which saw DeSoto and Chrysler output plummet to all-time lows while Dodge and Plymouth rose to new highs. We're not knocking the Airflow cars for at this point in time they have a legion of followers and are much sought-after as collectibles. But it is a strange fact that the shape that almost did Chrysler Corp. in is today greatly prized, while the firm's salvation models were so unassuming appearance-wise and produced in such large quantities that they are largely shunned by restorer/collectors. If a single segment of the body styles offered are noteworthy, however, it is the open cars—as it is for nearly any U.S. make of the '30's.

An automatic transmission with the appelation Fluid Drive came to the senior Chrysler line in '39, and by '41 found its way down to the Dodge Luxury Liner series; the lowest price American car to offer this transmission advancement. Even though the Dodge was equipped with a conventional clutch pedal, the car could be driven all day without left foot usage (unless the car had to be reversed).

Postwar Dodges from 1946-48 were basically similar in appearance to the last prewar cars. However, in 1949 the Dodge, along with the whole Chrysler line, got its first postwar restyling. Motive power was the old L-head 6, now up to a displacement of 230.2 cu. ins. and referred to as the "Getaway" 6. Neither the engine nor the basic styling of the Dodge automobile would see any significant changes until October of 1952, when production began on the all-new 1953 Dodge Coronet.

When the first true postwar Dodges bowed in December of '48, they were offered in four series on three wheelbases; the Wayfarer with 115-in. wheelbase, the Coronet and Meadowbrook with 123.5 ins., and the Kingsway with 118.5 ins. One collectable model to come out of this total model overhaul was the Wayfarer Sportabout, though it was discontinued—or, rather, modified—in mid-'51. This was a postwar effort to produce true roadster styling, where by definition a roadster has no door windows (as compared to a convertible with roll-up glass). Discontinuation of this now seldom-seen Wayfarer model was by virtue of the addition of roll-up windows. Apparently the postwar car buyer wasn't interested in a full stream of fresh air in the face and was becoming more conscious of creature comfort. A Sport-

2

3

Chrysler Corporation
Dodge

about easily fits within our Special Interest parameters, though how many survive is unknown but they must certainly be low in number.

Dodge bowed for '53 with its now-famed Red Ram V-8, a 241.3 cu. in. engine rated at 140 hp. This was the Division's own version of the Hemi engine and, unlike sister division DeSoto's Firedome V-8 which had been introduced one year previous, it was of over-square design. Bore was 3-7/16 ins. and stroke was 3-¼ ins. The 140 hp was attained at 4400 and it boasted a compression ratio of 7.1:1.

Floyd Clymer road-tested a new Coronet V-8 for the March 1953 issue of *Popular Mechanics* and commented, "I put the V-8 Dodge through every conceivable kind of driving test. It is a well-engineered car with a surprising amount of acceleration, power and speed." *Consumer Reports* magazine also carried out an extended test of a Coronet V-8 in 1953, and although somewhat critical of the car's body, was high in its praise of the new engine: "This new 241-cubic-inch Dodge engine, which reaches maximum horsepower (140) at 4400 rpm, puts out a lot of power, especially at the higher car speeds; equipped with it, the 1953 car is a far cry indeed from the stodgy Dodge of yore."

So with the benefit of the V-8, Dodge, like the other models in the Chrysler Corp. line, was able to take a giant step into the modern automotive era... the era of the V-8. The L-head 6 was retained by Dodge as their bread-and-butter engine through the 1959 model year, after which it was replaced by the new slant-6.

For the next several years after the introduction of the V-8, Dodge's styling and engineering tended to follow the general pattern laid down by Chrysler Corp. The 1954 V-8's came

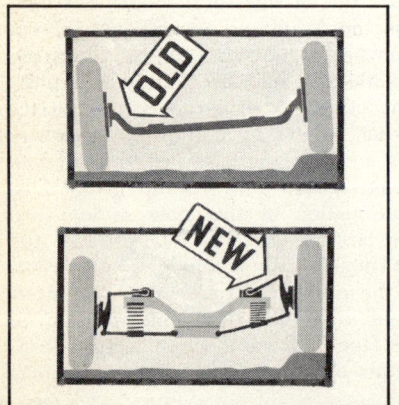

20/SPECIAL INTEREST AMERICAN CARS

with optional PowerFlite automatic transmission (Dodge's first full automatic). "Magic Touch" push button automatic was used in 1956, the same year that Dodge offered its famed D-500 engine option. This was a 260-hp, 315-cu.-in. V-8 and came with dual 4-bbl. carburetion. A D-500-equipped car won its class that year at the Daytona Speed Trials, clocking a flying mile at 130.577 mph.

1. Dodge unveiled its synchromesh transmission for '33, and this was the final year for its 8-cyl. engine until the post-war V-8. Chrysler Corp. styling was recognizable between all of its car divisions.

2. Dodge continued to offer two wheel-base versions for 1934, although the 6-cyl. engine was the only available powerplant. This version measured 121-ins. between axles, distinguished by long hood with closely-spaced vertical side louvers. The shorter 117-in. wheelbase models had horizontal air vents.

3. Sketches like these were used in '34 advertising and promotional literature to reveal the difference between the previous beam-axle front suspension and the new independent arrangement.

4. Newly styled Luxury Liner series had bowed for '41, pioneered Dodge's use of Fluid Drive automatic transmission, and looked like this after '42's front sheet metal facelifting.

5. The mild facelifting after the war resulted in a series of cars that would remain virtually unchanged until '48. Hardly outstanding, they were still good cars—and look even better today.

6. Dodge strived for both a low cost car and one with sporty flair by bringing out the Wayfarer Sportabout along with its other fully restyled models for 1949. This is a true roadster without rollup door windows, but sales were low and the line was dropped in mid-'51. Folding top frame was of aluminum to ease operation, which was by hand since top motors were not included.

7. A new, optional transmission was brought to Dodge's lowest-level models in 1951; these are Wayfarers leaving the assembly line at Detroit plant.

8. The '53 Diplomats brought wire wheels (optional) back to Dodge, and hardtop styling wore the continental spare well. Line-up also introduced the first Dodge V-8, and the first 8-cyl. engine since 1933. Motive power was via 140-hp Red Ram.

9. Dodge Custom Royal for '55 could be ordered with 3-tone paint. A step up from this was the specialty model known as Dodge La Femme that came with rain cape, umbrella, boots and handbag, all in matching colors, for "her." "His," was in the form of more cubic inches, now out to 270, and 193 hp, via a Special Equipment Power Package (Custom Royals only).

10. In May of '59 Dodge began producing a limited quantity of Silver Challengers. All were silver-painted outside with silver metallic vinyl and black fabric upholstery.

The tailfin made its appearance at Chrysler Corp. in 1957, and it continued to sweep off Chrysler Corp. drawing boards for the next two years. Dodge got its full share of swoopy rear fenders in those two years. A Dodge Division brochure urged the prospective buyer to "Step into the Wonderful World of AUTODYNAMICS." It went on to describe the new Dodge as unleashing "a hurricane of Power" and taming "a tornado of Torque."

Another milestone was reached in 1958, with the introduction of the first Dodge big-block V-8. These were brand-new engines in that they had wedge-shaped combustion chambers, as opposed to the hemispherical ones used on the original V-8's. With the introduction of the new 361-cu.-in. wedge engines, the older Hemi types were dropped from the Dodge line (although the older 325 was still being offered in '58).

For 1959, Dodge offered a 383-cu.-in. wedge engine which developed 345 hp at 5000 rpm and came fitted with dual 4-bbl. carburetors, special cam and heavier valve springs. This was the so-called "Super" D-500 and, in effect, marked the transition from the earlier, more mundane Hemi engines to the real blood-and-guts V-8's which were to follow in the '60's.

There emerged no particularly noteworthy styling innovations from this period, since the wildly upswept rear fender design introduced in '57 was shared by all of Chrysler's divisions. Dual headlamps were also first offered for '57, but again this was not a Dodge exclusive. A now-rare electronic fuel injection option became available on a limited number of Dodges for '58, providing a rarity today worth seeking. Convertibles of any of the late '50's may not provide a wise investment if the acquisition is a basketcase, but if one is available running and generally complete, for a price in keeping with its age, it will surely become increasingly valuable in light of the automobile industry's dropping of this configuration after 1975. 🎬

Chrysler Corporation

Plymouth

Synonym for solid dependability and value

By 1959, Plymouth had earned a strong reputation among automobiles for dependability. It was only with the beginning of the Fury series in 1956 that the marque began "cloaking its skin with fire." Most Plymouths available as a special interest car must therefore appeal to conservative reliability and not so much to out-and-out speed. The Superbirds and the muscle cars were to come later.

One thing that worked against Plymouth for much of its life was the reputation that it was stodgy transportation from the stone age—lacking flash and dash of cars with a V-8. In 1955, Plymouth introduced their first V-8, which came in a 270-cu.-in. version the next year. From that, of course, there was a whole new era of a car that for most of its life had depended, not on brute speed, but on rock-ribbed durability. Back in 1937, the rugged 6-cyl. Plymouth engine came from a process called "super-finishing," which was a precise metal-conditioning process, eliminating all scratches over a millionth of an inch deep on all engine and chassis parts subject to friction wear. By 1956, that same engine had been pumped out to some 250-cu.-ins., with a 3.44-in. bore and a 4.5-in. stroke. It had long featured full-pressure lubrication with an oil filter, and was known to many the world over as a product of precision American engineering. In 1959, a Plymouth brochure called the engine " . . . probably the most efficient . . . powerplant of its size ever built." The Six arrived in 1933; and therefore a long look at Plymouth's history is mandatory.

In 1930, Chrysler decided to sell the Plymouth through all his 7000 dealers, including Dodge and DeSoto dealers, instead of just through the Chrysler dealers, giving his low-priced model more outlets than any other car. There were a few more engineering refinements, and the sales doubled the '29 total.

But 1931 was the real banner year for Plymouth. The famous "Floating Power" system of engine mounting was introduced, along with vacuum-controlled spark advance. The mounting system, which consisted of a rubber-isolated mount high at the front of the engine and another at the rear of the transmission with a steel leaf spring under the transmission, evenly divided the engine's weight so it pivoted about its center of gravity. The system prompted the advertising slogan "smoothness of an 8, economy of a 4" which became the Plymouth dealers' watchword.

The car was finally priced to be really competitive with the "Big Two" at $535, and as a result of the engineering, the lower prices and a 2½-million-dollar improvement and research program, Plymouth jumped up *five* places in the production race to take over third place, a position Chrysler held every year (except for 1945) thereafter until 1954. It cost some nine million dollars just to retool the factory to keep up with needed production.

A restyled front end appeared on the Plymouth for 1933, and the beginnings of custom-to-order car buying were apparent in the variety of optional colors, accessories and body styles. The biggest news of the year, though, was the introduction of the new 6-cyl. Plymouth engine. This came at Depression time, when other manufacturers were just treading water, and it sold for only $495, the lowest price a Plymouth was ever to sell for. Another nine million dollars went into retooling for this new 70-hp machine. This 6 was enlarged to 201 cu. ins. in the next year and "individual wheel springing" (independent front suspension) was introduced. The one-millionth Plymouth proudly rolled off the assembly line on Aug. 10, 1934. Production for the year ran to 351,113.

1. The 1932 Roadster was bigger and heavier than its competition; featured a rigid X-member chassis, was well accepted, even then.

2. The 1935 Plymouth Deluxe convertible coupe was traditional in styling, used a suspension stabilizer bar, and had a 201-cu.-in. 6-cyl. engine; a desirable find today.

3. By 1936, Plymouth was solidly in third place among all car sales, and followed the next year with a bigger body. The 1937 coupe had a cavernous trunk; but this windshield bar is strictly after-market.

4. To clarify '37-'38 Plymouths, a collector must be courageous to seek one, even though, in 1938, Plymouth completed most successful first decade in automotive history. A '38 4-door is not desirable; yet experience teaches that many special interest "no's" can become "yes's." One man was heard to remark that a '38 Plymouth reminded him of "a lobster in a tide-pool."

5. The 1939 Plymouth 4-door convertible sedan was easily the best design to date (for Plymouth). Everything had been redesigned. Note the windwings in this pleasing special interest automobile.

6. The 1941 Plymouth Deluxe was among the most reliable and desirable of all time (for Plymouth). Pleasing of stature, the Plymouth became a durability champ second to none.

Continuing the tradition of introducing features to the Plymouth that had been successfully used on the more expensive Chrysler, 1935 saw new weight distribution for better ride, "Chair Height Seats," stabilizer bar, horsepower increased to 85 and water jackets in the engine which extended to the bottom of the cylinders. Still in third place in production in 1936, more than half a million Plymouths were built with new insulated body mounts, and there were 10 different body styles to choose from.

Safety in automobile design was considered important early in Plymouth's history. The '37 models saw the introduction of a safety-styled dash without protruding knobs and safety glass installed as standard equipment in all windows. Their forward thinking earned the company the Eastern Safety Conference award in both 1939 and 1940 for even more new safety features, such as the "safety-signal" speedometer (1939) and standard equipment sealed beam headlights (1940). The speedometer dial (when lighted) would change colors to warn of speed changes. It flashed green up to 30 mph, amber from 30 to 50 mph and was red above 50 mph! Two other features of the '39 models were an optional power top for convertibles and a new column shift referred to as "perfected remote control gear shifting." Just for reference, it took Ford another year to offer column shift, and Ford was just then introducing hydraulic brakes, which Plymouth had had for over 10 years.

The next decade brought few major changes, mechanical or stylistic, to any of the Detroit automakers. Most of them were involved in some way in producing material for the war effort. Features for 1941 included the oil-bath air cleaner, battery under the hood instead of under the floor, door check straps and a counterbalanced deck lid for easy opening. Plymouth made only minor changes to their 1942 models and rushed them out to the marketplace. There were, of course, engineering refinements like low-pressure, softer-riding tires, a fuel filter in the gas tank and an improved fuel pump, but basically the 1946-48 Plymouths were the same as the '42's.

The first big change was in 1949, as it was for the other auto manufacturers, who had all been building up to where they could afford to retool for a new car. The Chrysler Corp. spent some $90 million retooling for the brand new look of Plymouth, Dodge, DeSoto and Chrysler, but it paid off in the best year that the corporation (and Plymouth, with 574,734 produced) had ever had. The new cars had much smoother styling. The biggest news was Plymouth's wagon. They had had a 9-passenger wagon with exterior wood trim, but in 1949 they introduced a Deluxe Surburban 6-passenger wagon *without* the trim, making it the first all-steel-bodied station wagon. The year 1950 brought with it a new war, and while the public wasn't denied cars totally, many of the auto plants were back to making military hardware, with the Chrysler Corp. producing about a third as much as during the Second World War. This additional war insured that the 1951-53 years would be good ones for the entire auto industry. Plymouth remained firm in its number three position.

The 1954 Plymouth was a short, rounded-slab, practical car. This was not, however, what the buying public wanted. Always fickle, the public was beginning to look beyond practicality and yearn for the fancies that would speak more of postwar prosperity. The figures show that in 1954, people were buying Buicks and Oldsmobiles, more expensive cars than Plymouth, and Chrysler's foremost arm slipped from its traditional third place to fifth, with only 399,900 Plymouths assembled.

What was a bad year for Plymouth may have worked in its favor in the end, for '54 showed management that they needed a new look in a hurry. The corporation's new president, Colbert, speeded up the normal procedures of a model changeover, and "The Forward Look" cars were brought out next fall, a full year before anyone expected they could have them completed. It cost the corporation some $270 million to retool for the new-look cars, but Plymouth hit its all-time high of 742,991 cars sold that year.

What made these new cars so great in the eyes of the public? First, there was the all-new, ohv V-8 engine. The sleek styling was also all new, as it was for the other manufacturers that year. The Forward Look encompassed new trim, two-tones, "a hint of fin" on the rear fenders, and forward-slanting eyebrows over the headlights. Both the fins and the headlight eyebrows were to be the distinctive styling features of Plymouths for the next six years. The new engine and new sheetmetal of the '55 Plymouths were enough to displace Oldsmobile and put them up a notch in the production race to fourth. A minor facelift and 1956 saw them retain

3

4

5

6

COURTESY AUTOMOTIVE CLASSICS, SANTA MONICA

Chrysler Corporation
Plymouth

this position, although sales were down considerably from the previous banner year.

The next year was another highlight for the company, as the fins had now fully bloomed, sales were up again and Plymouth was finally back again in its place as one of the Big Three. One of those cars that rolled off the line that year was the ten millionth Plymouth, and the new "suddenly it's 1960" styling helped the corporation to a fifth of the automobile market and almost $120 million in profits!

The next two years marked pleasant restylings of the car and sales good enough for Plymouth to retain its production position, but the country was suffering an economic recession that hit the whole auto industry and stalled sales. Such is the up-and-down nature of catering to the public with a product that changes yearly.

In order to understand which Plymouths are of special interest appeal, one must back-track for a moment to a reiteration of the special Plymouth mystique. The 1940-41 Richardson Pan-American Expedition demonstrated that a Plymouth 6 sedan was capable of deeds almost beyond human imagination. On the one hand, then, the Plymouth became a hallmark for reliability. It was a primary goal of Walter Chrysler's from introduction of the very first Plymouth back in 1928.

But also, the reputation of reliability, and that (as far back as 1931) the Plymouth had the "smoothness of an eight and the economy of a four," led it into position as the third-best selling car in the country in only its fourth year on the market. This was as startling as it was true. On the other side of the picture, it should be noted that in 1931, race driver Lou Miller piloted a Plymouth across the U.S. and back to set a new non-stop speed record of some 6237 miles in a little over 132 hours and 9 minutes. The Plymouth, therefore, was a balanced product, with tremendous flexibility, and as such, should be looked at through clear eyes by any erstwhile *aficionado* of special interest cars.

Any of the 1930 Plymouth Roadster models are highly desirable to a collector, for the simple reason that the quality construction and close resemblance to the Model A Fords act as inducements. Obviously, however, the pickings are thin in such an age bracket. To a history freak, the 1932 Plymouths offer great inducement, in the success of Chrysler's "Look at All Three" advertisement that swept the country. It was a straight, no-nonsense pitch in the Depression-shaken economy, and resulted in improved sales, Plymouth being the *only* car that year to do so. Again, the roadsters of Plymouth were very attractive packages, heavier and more economical than the Model 18 Ford V-8's. Plymouth also had an all-steel body which has weathered time well. The 1934 Plymouth added a massive look to its front cowl, with hood-mounted collapsible door vents to augment its louvers. That year, advertisements were hitting favorably the preference that salesmen apparently were having for the car—a function of extra weight and economy, which, if you can get them, are always preferred on long drives.

The 1935 Plymouth convertibles began searching for the more pleasing design combinations, especially in the side of the hood department. With a rumble seat, the particular design found many adherents among the young set. Cars then were still affordable by them, and Plymouth's "solid" reputation had already begun to take a firm hold.

The 1936 and '37 Plymouths began to show the Chrysler expression of late-Depression conservatism—a thing that placed a blight on Chrysler design reputation. Many Chrysler products appeared inflated, as giant balloons, yet with absurdly tiny taillights and other appendages. That plus the blatantly vertical grilles, allowed the more venturesome imaginations to think of the long teeth of a Tyrannosaurus Rex, with its absurdly small, almost withered front claws. Actually, a Plymouth of those years had nothing to do with a large, carnivorous dinosaur; in fact, the Plymouth, by its shorter dimensions, looked less carnivorous than other Chrysler products. Some owners even went so far as to install 2-piece windshields in their '37's, in an effort to make their car closer to a Chevrolet in appearance. But underneath the controversial skin, every Plymouth was an ambassador for

1. The 1948 Plymouth Special Deluxe 4-door was essentially a warmed-over '42—which, it may be noted, was in great demand as an Army staff car, due to a comfortable ride, superior brakes, cooling, and general toughness. Quality control generally was of a high order in these Plymouth models.

2. The 1952 Belvedere hardtop club coupe reflected increased buying influence of feminine drivers. Mint green with a black top was popular.

3. Highest production year in Plymouth's history to date was the 1953, with 662,510 units. In '54, production was down, but the factory-installed Continental Kit on the Belvedere hardtop is a collector's choice, at a relatively low price.

4. The 1955 convertibles, with Plymouth's V-8 and optional Power-flite torque converter, remain today a car of solid appeal. A record 742,990 Plymouths were built in '55.

5. Perhaps the most desirable Plymouth since the war remains the 1956 Fury. Its 240-hp, twin carb V-8 and stiff suspension made it a performer of a high order.

6. The 30th Anniversary of Plymouth was underscored by the gold upward tailsweep of the '58 Fury. Engine was 290-horse wedge-head V-8 with two 4-bbl. carbs, hot cam, dual points, and choice of seven rear-end ratios.

engineering superiority. For this reason, it behooves a special interest collector or restorer to look closely at the Plymouths.

By 1939, the Plymouth lines had been smoothed, and the curves given more fluidity. It was the first of two years running that Plymouth received the Eastern Safety Conference Award for safety-minded automotive design. As if to atone for the bulbous headlights of the previous few years, Plymouth did something unusual: it designed nearly rectangular headlights, and buried them in the fenders.

A car of great value today is the 1939 Plymouth 4-door convertible—a very good-looking vehicle. Plymouth, of course, was in solid command of engineering respect by this time, as well.

The Deluxe Plymouth 4-door touring sedan could be purchased in certain 1940 Southern California towns for $1042.71. More refinements were made in the 1940 suspension, and a new power top mechanism was available on the good-looking Deluxe Convertible Coupe, complete with wind-wings and more chrome. There was new rust-proofing, a new ventilation system, and what was called "the year's big advancement in brake efficiency—'superfinished drums.'" Ford, by this time, had gone, finally, to hydraulic brakes; Plymouth, therefore, was trying to go the competition one better. Of definite interest, and no doubt rare, was the 1940 Plymouth Deluxe 7-passenger sedan. A typical statement in Plymouth advertising in 1940 was that "of 'all three' low-priced cars, Plymouth is like the high-priced cars."

There are those who say that the 1941 Plymouth was the "best ever built," and it certainly was a durable automobile. A particular example of Plymouth thoroughness was found in the Deluxe Station Wagon, Plymouth by this time matching its running gear excellence with an improved quality of ash and oak construction.

By 1942, Plymouth's L-head legend had been upped to 95 hp., and of note to the magnifying-glass diehards—the new car catalogs measured 10x14-ins. (How many new car catalogs are *that* big?) Production for 1942 puts available examples today as among the rarest of the lot, since the great War held final year units to 25,113, down more than 400,000 cars from the year before. It's a pity, too, because the early '42's were among the best chromed Plymouths ever built. The entire line was exemplary. Of special note was the Special Deluxe Convertible, with the factory installed optional fender skirts, the latter bearing a horizontal chrome ornament of nearly the emotional *pizazz* of Ford's legendary Ripple-Discs.

A 1942 Plymouth, especially in light of its widespread reputation as a comfortable and rugged Army staff car, makes it among the most desirable to own as a special interest example.

By 1946, the cars were too little, too late for a car-hungry public, and it wasn't until 1949 that Plymouth received its first facelift since the War. By merely sticking on a couple of reduced taillights from a 1941 Dodge Luxury Liner, the overall lower and boxier body has failed to convince a majority of special interest enthusiasts.

The 1950 to '52 models were the same way. Convertibles, however, continue to bring the highest prices today.

The '52 Plymouth came in the Cambridge and more expensive Cranbrook. It was a neat car, with a soft ride. A *Motor Trend* test revealed 23.2 mpg at 30 mph, and 17.3 mpg at 60. Its 97-horse 6, with a 3.73 axle ratio, took it from zero to 60 in 22.54 secs. This demonstration of conservatism belied the plucky engine's refinements, however. There were four rings per piston, two oil rings and porous-chromed top compression ring. Exhaust valve seats were likewise of high-durability metal. It's a pity that, with all these strong points, the '52, and the even stubbier '53's and '54's that followed, few special interest examples from those years exist. The '53 Cranbrook Belvedere was a pillarless 2-door coupe—the top-of-the-line—and when equipped with optional overdrive, was efficient transportation. The '54 Plymouth sported optional wire wheels, and a semi-automatic trans called "Hy-Drive," which did its work well, only was slower than most. Some of the Belvedere models, especially the '54 convertibles, are desirable today.

The 1955 "big sales year in Detroit" featured a Plymouth, with a futuristic dash and a V-8. Big news in 1956 was the 240-hp., twin-4-bbl. V-8 Plymouth Fury coupe. A sought-after special interest car, the Furies, clear up to '59, are desirable cars almost without peer, although the '56-7's and 8's are worth more, with the '56, the best of the lot; as Plymouths, like fine wines, get better with age.

A history of the sidemount spare

Perhaps the one accessory that denotes a car of special interest.

Probably the most popular extra equipment ever offered on automobiles the world over was the sidemounted spare wheel. Why this is so defies practical explanation. It is true that early tires had a habit of blowing out frequently and that having two spares was a hedge against being stranded. Yet the appeal of the sidemounted spare goes beyond this simple explanation and may well be rooted in Freudian psychology. From an aesthetic point of view, the artist will readily point out the beauty of the wheel, an example of perfect symmetry and unity of design, and it might be concluded that the visual appeal is the simple explanation.

Whatever the underlying explanation of the appeal, the popularity of the 6-wheel option is undeniable, and universally shared. Nash was the first manufacturer to offer a spare tire and rim as standard equipment in 1909 in a factory-designed mounting; other makers followed shortly thereafter, although some did not make the change until the 1920's. Spares were not usually seen prior to that time except as something tied to the car. The spare presented a problem in terms of aesthetics as well as mechanics—what did you do with it? Initially the extra tires were mounted on the left running board as seen on the 1905 Rambler. By 1908 the Rambler spare had moved to the right running board, and for several years thereafter this was the mounting, and it effectively blocked the right front door, if it was not merely a dummy anyway. Some tires were fabric covered, but more often they were bare. About 1911 the first tire well appeared, an indentation of a few inches in the running board. A 1913 Hudson had two tires on the right running board. Probably the ultimately equipped car was a 1916 Hudson with double dual sidemounts—four tires in all! Or maybe it was the 1925 Locomobile made for cartoonist Sidney Smith which had dual sidemounts and dual rear-mounted spares!

The year 1914, or thereabouts, seems to have marked the beginning of the sidemounted spare in a position beside the hood and cowl, clearing the front door, and mounted against the curve of the front fender, no well being yet utilized. In a sense, then, sidemounted spares represent a natural evolution from running board placement to fender mounts where they were out of the way. Well into the '20's sidemounts, which began to appear on almost all cars here and abroad, continued in the position in the curve of the fenders. Actual fenderwells made their appearance in the late teens as did dual sidemounts generally. As fender design in the late 20's moved from cycle fenders to the long sweep fender, wells became deeper and the spares nestled more deeply, yet generally they were placed between the plane of the running board and the belt line on the hood. About this time wheel design changed significantly; the demountable rim was gone and tires were mounted directly on drop-center wheels. This made wheel changing easier and sidemounted spares then included a complete wheel instead of only the tire and rim. From an aesthetic point of view this configuration was much more handsome; the complete wheel with tire was simply more attractive as well as interesting when compared to the hoop appearance of the tire and rim. At this time, the term "6-wheel car" came into being, although a few cars never used this nomenclature. Several makes continued the demountable rim into the first years of the 1930's, and their 6-wheel cars look somehow barren.

Early automobile design lent itself to sidemounted spares easily, but developments and changes in the early 30's spelled the end of this equipment. After the horseless carriage became an automobile, the design became fixed in the format we know today—engine in front, hood, fenders and the body. Until the early 30's the automobile chassis remained basically unchanged. The radiator was mounted directly above the front axle providing a long expanse of hood and front fenders which facilitated the sidemounted wheel easily. Bodies were only two passengers wide in the front seat, and running boards made up the remaining width of the front end. Hood and fender length, of course, varied according to engine size, yet as long as the radiator remained placed over the front axle there was ample fender length for the sidemount, even on most short-hooded 4-cylinder cars.

Two design changes occurred in the '30's that spelled the end of the side-

1. General automotive styling of the early '30's practically demanded sidemounts; long hood and fender lines, narrow body with wide runningboards. This is a '30 Franklin.

2. DeSoto for '30 showed typical Chrysler Corp. sidemount treatment.

3. Sidemounts were almost always in evidence on the luxury cars, such as on this awesome '30 Lincoln. Sharp down-sweep of fender line, though, prevented the spare from being deeply imbedded.

4. Author Mehl once owned this 1930 Packard 733 whose spares mounted rear vision mirrors.

PHOTO BY AL SWEIGERT

mounted spare. The first was the fundamental chassis modification which progressively moved the engine forward over the front axle. As this happened, hood and fender length diminished and the room available for a fender-mounted spare wheel shrank and eventually disappeared. The problem was further compounded by front-opening doors which required clearance past a sidemount. The leading edge of the front door that stylishly slanted like the windshield further reduced the space for a sidemount. At this point some makers dropped sidemounts, but most continued this equipment which was easier when front doors were almost all changed to rear-opening.

The other change, primarily a styling change but also a basic passenger compartment modification, produced wider and wider bodies which diminished the width of both front fenders and running boards. As fender width became very narrow at the leading edge of the running board (when there was one), sidemounted wheels could no longer be placed parallel with each other and the side of the car (on a line between the front and rear wheel). Thus, in the late '30's sidemounts were often mounted on an angle, paralleling the hood line. As fenders got shorter, spare wheels had to be mounted higher in the fender. No longer were they positioned between the level of the running board and the belt line; on many makes in the late '30's wheels were mounted unusually high, extending above the belt line and even above the level of the hood.

Eventually both running boards and front fenders disappeared, yet the sidemounted spare persisted even into the running board less era of the late '30's and early '40's. By 1942 slab-sided styling had spelled the end of the sidemount forever. The popularity and demand for the sidemount option caused manufacturers to listen. Even though their cars were becoming wider and wider, Studebaker, Cadillac and Buick continued to offer 6-wheel equipment until 1941 and Packard continued through their 1942 year. Buick redesigned the front fenders of the small series 40 and 60 for the 1940 models so as to afford a neater sidemount than the 1939 cars had provided which was quite awkward due to the curve and lack of width of the fender where it met the door line. Cadillac originally had planned on dropping sidemounts on the 60 Special when it was introduced in 1938, but continued them through 1940 due to customer demand.

Yet the number of cars after 1934 that came equipped with sidemounts was a small percentage compared to the number produced in the last halcyon days of the late '20's and the first few years of the depression. In the second half of the '30's, cars with sidemounts became increasingly rare; by the end of the decade most motorists regarded them as anachronistic. The intense interest, or, the fad if you will, of the sidemounted spare lasted for a relatively short time; the high point was 1928-29, but by 1936 it was really over. Eight years is indeed a brief period in the history of the automobile.

One of the fascinating ramifications of the intense interest in the sidemounted option was the evolution of the tire cover and related accessories. Early cars, and even some through the early '30's, had no tire covers of any kind. The first covers were fabric, often matching the top material in open cars. In the late '20's two-piece metal covers appeared; one piece covered the sidewall, leaving the spokes and hubcap exposed, and the other, serving as a clamp, covered the tread and held the side panel in place. The tread cover was often chrome plated on anything from a Ford to a Duesenberg. In

2

COURTESY CHRYSLER·HISTORICAL COLLECTION

3

PHOTOS BY THE AUTHOR UNLESS OTHERWISE NOTED

4

PHOTO BY ROBERT H. RAND

SPECIAL INTEREST AMERICAN CARS/27

A history of the sidemount spare

the middle '30's covers concealed the entire wheel, but often included a regular hubcap in the middle of the side panel, suggesting the wheel was no longer visible. These followed the contours of the wheel. By 1938 Cadillac had offered the one-piece tire cover that hinged to the fender and covered the entire wheel front and back. The sides were smooth and no hubcap was added, although on some models medallions or trim were. Other makers also went to the smooth-sided cover, but the covers slipped off and on and were held by clamps. Occasionally miniature hubcaps were used to decorate the side panels.

The jewels adorning the sidemounted spares were round rearview mirrors either attached with chains or straps to tires with canvas covers or no covers, or bolted to the metal covers. In the late '20's and early '30's buyers often added this dress-up accessory. It is somewhat doubtful as to how useful these mirrors actually were unless they were convex glass, but nevertheless they looked very sporty and were the crowning touch.

Even though the last sidemounted production car was made over 30 years ago, interest continues even in popular culture. Ads, cartoons and comic strips still depict 6-wheel cars when the purpose is to indicate affluence, swank, class and elegance. Owners of 5-wheel cars often have converted their prizes into 6-wheelers in those rare instances when parts were available, thus increasing their total value when the option was a factory offering. We've seen a 1941 Packard 160 sedan converted to a 6-wheeler using parts from a hearse; the frame had been made with the necessary mounting holes. One ingenious collector made a 6-wheeler out of his 1937 DeSoto convertible sedan (DeSoto dropped sidemounts after the '36 model) when he determined that his car was identical to the 1937 Chrysler Imperial convertible sedan which did offer sidemounts. The DeSoto body, shared with the Chrysler, had the necessary holes for mounting; he simply obtained Chrysler fenders, covers and mounting hardware and now has a car that, although not genuine, is nevertheless quite original looking. One Cadillac owner installed homemade wells in the fenders of his 1939 convertible coupe. Other homemade sidemounts have been seen occasionally, a further tribute to this obsessive interest. We've seen a 1940 Chevrolet convertible with false covers (possibly taken from a Cadillac) mounted on the fenders. Several 1939 Plymouths including a convertible sedan have been seen with somewhat crude sidemount installations, and a very well done sidemounted Bantam was recently advertised.

Of added interest is the fact that at the outset of World War II the federal government ordered civilians to turn in excess tires over five per car, which meant that all 6-wheel cars lost one sidemount for the duration and had to drive around with one empty well.

Almost all American makes offered sidemounts at one time; some came as standard equipment, but most were optional at extra cost. Prices varied in relationship to the total cost of the car, anywhere from 2% of the cost to as high as 18%. In terms of dollars, an early Chevrolet could be equipped with dual sidemounts for $20 while a 1939 Chrysler Custom Imperial cost an additional $145 for six wheels. Most buyers of the cheaper cars were not prepared to spend more money on extras, particularly after the 1929 crash and this explains the scarcity of 6-wheel equipment on most of the cheaper cars. The luxury cars often came with six wheels as standard; in any event the added cost meant little to the affluent buyer of such a car and hence many more higher priced cars had sidemounts. Of course, in terms of total numbers of cars, far fewer expen-

1. Demountable wheels were still in evidence in '31 as on this Hudson.

2. Metal covers on the '31 Nash left tire sidewall exposed.

3. Ford was in on the sidemount fad for a short time. This is their version on a '31 station wagon.

4. Ford's push on sidemounts began to wane even as the rest of the industry began to emphasize them. Though they were commonly seen on '32's, they saw limited application for '33-'34 and then disappeared.

28/SPECIAL INTEREST AMERICAN CARS

sive cars of any description were sold.

Car makers varied considerably in their promotion of this option; early sales literature almost always mentioned the option as extra equipment along with a trunk rack, or pictured an open luggage compartment on later cars suggesting greater capacity when spares were sidemounted. Many catalogs showed sidemounted cars or included smaller illustrations of a fender and sidemounted wheel as an available option along with heaters, radios and other extras.

FORD

In the low-priced market Ford offered sidemounts for the shortest period of time. No sidemounts appeared on Fords until 1928 and the last Fords so equipped were a few 1933-34 models. More Model A's were made with one sidemount than two and commercial cars had only one. Deluxe or sport models usually had two, but some notable exceptions—the 2-door phaeton and the convertible sedan—had one left-hand spare. Ads and factory photos and sales literature illustrated many cars with sidemounts. Apparently many Model A's had either one or two sidemounts added after delivery to the dealer. No production figures for sidemounted Fords are available nor is there any precise information available on the cost of this option. Parts books which list prices are a partial help in determining what this option probably cost the new car buyer. Wheels cost $5, wheel carriers cost from $1.25 to $1.95, and welled fenders at $8.50 cost only $1 more than straight fenders. By inference, then, we may guess that one sidemount cost the buyer almost nothing extra, and that dual sidemounts cost from $8 to $10 extra. Tire covers were optional and cost $1.50 for fabric. In 1930-31 metal covers could be had for $2.25 painted black or for $4.50 chromed. Options in 1931 included covers with rustless steel molding at $4.50 and covers with a chrome outer ring at $7. In 1932 prices rose to $2 for fabric and $6 for the rustless steel molding covers.

By 1932 and the V-8, sidemounted Fords began to be seen less and less. One new model for 1932, the Deluxe 3-window coupe, the only 1932 model with front-opening doors, could not be equipped with sidemounts because the doors would not open. The factory finally issued a service letter requesting dealers to stop ordering them that way. Of course, all other 1932 Fords could be equipped with six wheels and many were. By the 1933-34 model only a very few sidemounted cars, usually utility vehicles, were produced. Front-opening doors, short hoods and fenders due to the short-block V-8, and the location of engines further forward, ended sidemounts for Ford by 1935.

PLYMOUTH

Plymouth went two years more; the last car with six wheels was the 1936 model. Chrysler brought out the Plymouth in 1928 and by 1929 sidemounts were available and appeared somewhat regularly through 1934 when they had handsome metal covers. Factory photos often showed 6-wheel cars. In the 1935 catalog, a deluxe rumble seat coupe is shown with sidemounts, yet nowhere in the remainder of the catalog is this option mentioned. The wheels were mounted high, extending above the belt line due to the relatively short fenders. Either one or two sidemounts could be had and quite a few 1935 Plymouths had only one right mount. Chrysler apparently offered either a single or a double sidemount option on all corporation cars in the '30's. The 1936 models were exactly the same, and apparently used the same fenders and covers. The 1936 catalog showed no sidemounted cars but does illustrate an open trunk with a wheel inside and the notation that, "When spare tire is mounted in fender-well the shelf can be left out." The 1936 Plymouth sidemounted is probably one of the very rarest of all—the author has seen only one in 39 years.

The 1939 station wagon on the Deluxe chassis named the "Sportsman" had a right-hand sidemount. This spare was very handsomely placed snugly in the fender and below the top of the hood but had no cover. The wheel was not crowded by the door and the total effect was very pleasing; what a bit of dash this would have added to the 1939 passenger cars! Ads showed the wagon, usually the right side view. Plymouth parts books list both right- and left-hand welled fenders in 1939.

CHEVROLET

Chevrolet adopted the sidemounted spare in 1929 as standard equipment on commercial cars in the left fender and as an option on passenger cars at an additional $20 for dual mounts. Either one or two sidemounts could be ordered, but if only one was desired, it came in the left fender. Few cars were produced with sidemounts and factory promotion was minimal. The same conditions prevailed in 1930 although more often factory publicity included sidemounted cars. Advertising in 1931 featured the "Special Sedan" illustrated with sidemounts and a note that stated, "Six wire wheels standard." The price was listed as $650. The "Standard" sedan with rear-mounted spare was listed in other ads at $635; one might infer, then, that the 6-wheel equipment therefore cost the new car buyer an extra $15, but apparently, as an option, the cost was $20 from 1929-1932. It is not precisely clear that 6-wheel equipment was a factory option on models other than the "Special Sedan." A factory service letter of January 1931 contained detailed information and diagrams for installing sidemounts on other Series AE passenger cars as well as on 1930 cars. In addition to replacing the straight fenders with welled fenders (at a cost of $12.50 each), a series of five holes had to be drilled in the cowl, and a hole in the dash. Some 27 parts, mostly nuts, bolts and washers were required, none costing more than a few cents. The tire rested against the fender and was secured by a rod attached to the frame at the bottom and the cowl at the top; a screw clamp held the tire securely. The same dealer option may have been operative in 1929-30 as well, but definite information is not at hand.

The 1931 Chevrolet accessory catalog listed several items for the owner of a sidemounted model; locks for sidemounts cost $5, canvas tire covers $2.50, and metal covers $6. Rearview mirrors for mounting on the spares were listed at $2 if metal covers were used and $5 if canvas covers or no covers were used.

A history of the sidemount spare

By 1932 Chevrolet really promoted 6-wheel cars in publicity photos, magazine ads and sales literature. Many sidemounted cars were made and this year was probably the peak of Chevrolet production of 6-wheel cars. Probably a single mount was still available although this is not certain. Ads always showed cars with either canvas or metal covers in place although both were extras. In 1933 ads and literature 6-wheel cars continued to be featured in the Master series (the Standard series did not offer sidemounts). A very stylish full metal cover appeared this year, with a hubcap mounted in the center of the side panel. Many other makers adopted this design, too. For some unknown reason, this sleek design was dropped after 1934. Sidemounts cost an additional $22 in both 1933 and 1934.

The year 1934 included ads promoting sidemounted cars, but the sales catalog did not illustrate any 6-wheel cars although it was noted that, "Six wire wheels and fender wells are available at slight extra cost." By 1935 factory interest in sidemounts was definitely dead, and consequently so were sales of cars with 6-wheel equipment. Neither ads nor sales literature illustrated cars with sidemounts. Only in small print on the back cover of the catalog was the 6-wheel option noted.

One could, however, order either one or two sidemounts on Master series cars. If the new car buyer ordered sidemounts from the factory the cost was $34, but if he decided he wanted sidemounts on a car already delivered, the dealer would install said equipment for $48. The last year for factory installed sidemounts was 1936, and apparently they were available only on the 3-window coupe and the sport sedan at $34 extra. Why Chevrolet reverted to the strange practice of earlier years is not known. This practice certainly did nothing to stimulate sales of sidemount equipment and must have cost the company a fair number of sales, although sidemounts could apparently be installed on any other model by the dealer for $48 extra.

Although both the 1937 and 1938 Chevrolets had fenders of sufficient length to handle a sidemounted wheel handsomely, the factory did not offer the option although all other GM divisions did. However, others felt sidemounts would be attractive, and in 1938 a number of 6-wheel Chevrolets appeared.

Some low-priced cars such as Austin and the Willys 77 never had sidemounts, but the medium-priced makers all offered sidemounts for a time, including the numerous small independents and lesser known makes such as Durant, Gardner and DeVeaux. Willys adopted the sidemount option and both ads and sales literature promoted this equipment until the introduction of the depression-motivated small model 77 in 1933 when sidemounts disappeared due to the small dimensions of the car.

REO

By 1929 Reo had adopted wire wheels and sidemounted spares; cars so equipped were called "Sport" models. The Flying Cloud could be had with six wheels for an additional $125 and the junior model, the Mate could also be equipped for an additional $100 on all body styles. Again in 1930 sidemounts were offered but at prices of $85 and $75 on the two lines, clearly a depression price cut. The hallmark year for Reo was 1931 with the introduction of the magnificent Royale, a luxury line which included sidemounts and metal tire covers as standard equipment on all models. The Royale continued for the next few years although its luster was somewhat dimmed by naming a lesser model Royale also; this one did not have six wheels as standard. On the other lines for 1931, the Flying Cloud (8-30) offered 6-wheel equipment at $85, including fabric covers. Oddly, the Flying Cloud 6-21, a lesser model, cost $115 extra if equipped with six wheels. The 1932 Model S offered optional sidemounted wire wheels at $75. In 1933 Reo adopted, for one year, the term "Elite" to signify a 6-wheel car; by 1934 the term was again "Sport." The 1934 sales catalog showed, among others, a Flying Cloud Sport Coupe with sidemounts and noted, "The two fender-mounted spare wheels add to its smart appearance." Full metal covers were used and indeed added a bit of style.

The 1935 Reo offering continued one line of larger cars closely resembling the 1934 design, and a new model Flying Cloud with a streamlined Hayes body and fenders. This latter model offered the buyer an option of either one or two sidemounts, apparently an option never previously possible.

For 1936, the last year for Reo passenger cars, the Hayes-bodied small Flying Cloud was the only offering, and sidemounts were again offered. Since production for the last year only reached 2700 (only 2-and 4-door sedans), probably very few 6-wheelers were produced and those made must have been the rarest sidemounted cars of all.

HUPMOBILE

Hupmobile, in its early years, often included a spare tire and rim lashed to the right running board. Sidemounted

1. Oldsmobile rode with the tide for '32, but didn't push the option which resulted in only 219 of this choice model being produced.

2. Sweeping front fender line of this '32 Studebaker permitted good placement of sidemount without it crowding the door or front wheel.

3. Many an otherwise mundane car was nicely upgraded by use of sidemounts, as on this '33 Dodge.

4. Ever see a 7-wheel Ford? We hadn't, but the photo is from Ford Archives. Possibly it was a special-order '33 Tudor.

spares in fenderwells seem to have been adopted for the 1928 model. Much Hupp advertising and sales literature included illustrations of 6-wheel cars from 1929 until 1934. An ad in *House and Garden* for the 1930 Century Six showed a 4-door sedan with sidemounts. Listed under "Highlights" is the notation that, "Custom equipment—six wire or disc wheels, two spares sidemounted in fenderwells...available at slight extra cost." A *Saturday Evening Post* ad for 1932 showed a 6-wheel roadster; a notation stated that, "Deluxe equipment (i.e. six wheels) on any model $55 extra." For 1934 Hupp introduced its "Aerodynamic" series in three lines. The smaller cars (417 series) might have had six wheels as an option since the fender design and length was sufficient, but a definitive answer is not at hand. It is certain that the highly streamlined, slab-sided larger series could not have mounted spares in the fenders. By 1935, then, 6-wheel cars were gone as an option on Hupmobile since the company concentrated on the highly streamlined models until the end, including the Cord-bodied cars.

GRAHAM

Graham, too, apparently adopted the 6-wheel option in 1928 along with many other makes. Beginning in 1928 many ads and the sales literature featured sidemounted cars, usually with trunk racks, too. The catalog of the startlingly new 1932 streamlined Graham, the one that introduced skirted fenders, showed all cars with sidemounts, although five wheels were listed as standard. The 1933 and 1934 Grahams, a minimally altered continuation of the glamorous 1932 styling, continued to feature sidemounts and sales literature showed many cars so equipped. In 1934 full metal covers added a bit of dash. The Deluxe 1935 sales brochure showed the Sport Coupe and the Convertible Coupe with sidemounts and noted under options for the 8 and Special Six, "Available at extra cost; side mount and fenderwell for fifth wheel with rear luggage rack. Six-wheel equipment with side mounts, fenderwells, rear luggage rack, wheel locks and metal tire covers." Apparently you got no tire cover with one sidemount. An additional illustration showed two open trunks, one with a spare inside and the other minus the spare.

Sidemounts were still available in both 1936 and 1937 on all models; a 6-wheel deluxe sedan was featured each year. In 1937, and probably for 1936, too, 6-wheel equipment cost $51 on Cavalier models, $53 on Supercharger models and $55.50 on the Custom Supercharger cars. The sensational new 1938 Graham "shark-nose" was too streamlined to permit mounting wheels in the fenders; the Hollywood models of 1940-41 did not offer this option either (the Cord bodies again).

NASH

The great independents in the medium-priced bracket also promoted sidemounts vigorously for a time and then ignored them. In 1935 Nash presented the new "Aeroform" design which was highly streamlined, and that ended sidemounts for Nash. The LaFayette, introduced in 1934 as a small Nash, continued virtually unchanged in 1935 and may have offered sidemounts but definite information is not at hand. Many sidemounted Nashes were seen from 1928 through 1933, with both fabric and metal covers.

HUDSON

Hudson used sidemounts intermittently from 1914 until 1929 when all cars came with one right sidemount as standard equipment; the left one was listed as an option. This was also true in 1930, but in 1931 sidemounts were optional except for the sport roadster and the long wheelbase sedan. The 1929 Essex literature neither illustrates nor mentions sidemounts, but in 1930 and 1931 a right fenderwell was available, yet apparently no left was offered. The last Essex, the 1932 model, offered dual sidemounts. The Terraplane sported sidemounts in 1933, after being introduced in 1932 without any, at $10 per fender. Tire covers on both Hudson and Terraplane for 1933 were of two pieces, including full contour side panels with a hubcap mounted in the center, a design continued until the end in 1939. Most earlier cars had fabric covers which exposed the wheel, or none at all. The 1934 Terraplane literature showed no sidemounted cars nor was the option mentioned, although factory photos showed such cars. The 1935 literature for both cars showed no cars and made no mention of the option. Single sidemounts continued to be seen on some Hudson-built cars until the end in 1939. The 1936 and 1937 catalogs returned to promoting sidemounts, proclaiming 23½ cu. ft. in Hudson trunks when spares were sidemounted—otherwise only 16½. The 1937 dealer's price sheet listed dual sidemounts available at a cost of $53 to $58 depending on the model; 1936 prices were probably the same as the cars were very similar.

By 1938 the trunk with sidemounted spares had shrunk to 20½ cu. ft. but six wheels were still available on all Hudson and Terraplane models. The termi-

3   COURTESY CHRYSLER HISTORICAL COLLECTION

4   PHOTO COURTESY FORD ARCHIVES (BY PERMISSION)

A history of the sidemount spare

nal year for sidemounts on Hudsons was 1939 (Terraplanes ceased after 1938), and by then the wheels were mounted high, extending above the belt line and pointed slightly inward, paralleling the hood. After 1935 sidemounts were very seldom seen on Hudson-built cars.

STUDEBAKER

Studebaker, the other great independent of the medium-priced field, also began including spare tires and rims mounted on the running board by the right door about the same time that Nash (Rambler) did. Sidemounts evolved over the next few years from this mounting into the mountings in fenderwells with occasional Studebaker models including a number of LeBaron customs seen in ads. These were on the Big Six series. By 1927 the first President models began to feature sidemounts and in 1928 Studebaker really began promoting 6-wheel equipment in ads and sales literature. The cars so equipped were referred to as "State" models in the President series, "Regal" models for Commanders and "Royal" models for Dictators and Erskines. The 6-wheel equipment came in a package deal along with bumpers, trunk rack, extra windshield wiper and spring covers, at a cost of about $100. The cost went to $105 in 1932 and down to $94.50 in 1936. Many cars had six wheels as standard equipment in 1929-30, and sidemount options were also available on the Rockne when it was introduced. A variety of tire covers was used, including fabric and metal which always showed the wheel and hubcap even on the last cars in 1940. After 1933 sidemounted cars began to disappear generally; 1934-35 models were shown in sales literature and ads with sidemounts and were listed in catalogs under Specifications. In 1936, promoting trunk space, the catalog showed an open trunk, noting 15½ cu. ft. of space when the spare was sidemounted, but no cars were shown with sidemounts and we've never seen one, although several exist today. In 1937 literature a President sedan is shown with sidemounts, and a picture of a trunk with a notation stating that 19½ cu. ft. were usable with sidemounts. In 1937, 850 Presidents were 6-wheel equipped; 13% of the sedans were dual sidemounted and 12 sedans had only one sidemount. Studebaker pickups and station wagons had a single sidemounted spare through 1938. Although sidemounts were available on 1938 through 1940 Presidents, no mention was made in sales literature and these cars are very rare; we've seen only a 1939 with six wheels. The 1937 sidemount was a very handsome fitting, but by 1938 and through 1940 the wheels were of necessity mounted very high, and like the 1939 small Buick, almost totally exposed although a good deal more attractive than the Buick version. Wells were quite small. The 1941 Studebakers were of such dimensions that sidemounts were precluded even on the President.

PONTIAC

In the GM group, Pontiac (and Oakland) joined the 6-wheel fad in 1928 and sales literature through 1935 illustrated cars with sidemounts. There seem to have been two different sidemountings in 1935, one for the 6 and one for the 8. On the 6 the wheel was mounted higher than on the 8, and although the fenders looked exactly the same, the fender used on the 6 must have been shorter, due to a different wheelbase. By 1936 no cars were shown with sidemounts but the sales catalog noted along with each illustration that the cars were ". . . available with two spares in fender wells," on both the 6 and 8; apparently the front fenders were the same this year. The 1937 catalog followed the pattern of 1936—no cars were shown with sidemounts and only a note beneath each model indicated that they were available. A *Saturday Evening Post* ad showed a 6-wheel 6-cylinder sedan. In 1938, the last year available, sidemounts were identical to the 1937 mounting, except the wheel style and hubcap had changed. The 1938 catalog seemed to state that only on certain models of the 8 could sidemounts be ordered; a brief note by some of the illustrations stated, "Available with two spare wheels in fenderwells . . . ." The last 2 years had very handsome mountings, whereas the 1935 and 1936 sidemounts were rather high and seemed a bit bulky. Very few Pontiacs after 1934 were seen with sidemounts. One final sidemounted Pontiac appeared in 1940, the station wagon with one right mount including a metal cover. After 1932 fabric covers were replaced by metal which covered the entire wheel and were contoured to match the shape of the wheel. For some reason in the last 2 years wheels were again exposed. No price information is at hand, but 6-wheel equipment must have been about $75. There is no evidence that Pontiac offered a single mount.

OLDSMOBILE

Oldsmobile, which has to be the most on-the-ball GM division for the historian, has complete records by years and models. The first year of sidemounts on Oldsmobile (and Viking) was 1929, and 1938 was the last year. In 1929 32% of the cars came with sidemounts and 38% of the Viking models; 1931 figures—63% had sidemounts (no more Viking); 1932—63% (6

COURTESY CHRYSLER HISTORICAL COLLECTION

1. Plymouth styling for '35 demanded high placement of sidemount and probably was hated by service station attendents when groping to unlatch the hood.

2. Oldsmobile continued to offer the sidemount but still did little to encourage sales, resulting in only 31—thirty one!—of these '35 coupes being manufactured.

3. Though the sidemount would continue to survive for several years in the luxury field, medium-priced cars like this '35 Pontiac gave the stylists fits. High mounting looked awkward.

4. Larger cars, like Oldsmobile, had enough physical bulk to handle the sidemount from a styling standpoint, but again this marque refused to push the option and for '37 only 95 of this 8-cyl. convertible were sold.

and 8); 1933, 17%; 1934, 11%; 1935, 3%; 1936, 4%; 1937, 5%, all on 8's, none available on the 6; 1938, 6%, all 8's again. From 1929 through 1938 Oldsmobile produced 86,222 sidemounted cars including Viking and export models. These figures show the peak of popularity and trace the declining interest in the 6-wheel option, although a slight upswing is seen in the last 3 years, perhaps reflecting the improved economy. A similar downward trend in interest can be seen in most other makes, although the peak years may have varied. Some makers, like Buick who really promoted this option, sold a higher proportion of 6-wheel cars rather consistently. Olds sales literature and ads illustrated cars with sidemounts through the 1934 models both on the 6 and the 8. In 1935 no cars were shown with sidemounts, but the catalog pictured a covered wheel in a fender with the notation, "... all models available with six wheels and fenderwells at slight added cost." Two trunks were shown, one with a spare inside and the other without. Tire covers for 1935 were two-piece contour full covers; hubcaps and wheels were no longer visible as in the previous years. In 1936 sidemounts were exactly the same as 1935; the same catalog illustration was used to illustrate the covered wheel in the fenderwell. No comments or pictures of trunks were included, but under "Specifications" sidemounts were listed for both 6's and 8's. Prices were $85 for the 6 and $95 for the eight—why the difference is a mystery since they were identical. Prices in 1935 must have been the same. Apparently in 1935 and 1936 Olds shared fenders with Pontiac, and both sidemountings appear similar. In 1937 and 1938 only 8's were available with six wheels, and the mountings were the same for these 2 years. Tire covers were smooth sided, replacing the contour-shaped covers of 1935-36, and included three short trim strips. Wheels were pointed slightly toward the front of the car rather than being parallel to the side of the car. In 1937 sidemounts cost $95 and this included bumpers, bumperguards, two tires, two welled fenders, two metal tire covers, two wheel locks, two side tire carriers, rear spring covers and extra wheel. In 1938, the last year, the price dropped to $65, but this price no longer included bumpers and spring covers. To determine the actual cost of a 6-wheel car over that of a 5-wheel car, one would have to subtract the cost of all that equipment listed that was not directly related to 6-wheel mounting as well as subtracting the cost of one spare. The 1938 catalog showed a 4-door smooth back with six wheels, noting that, "Six-wheel equipment as illustrated here is offered on all 8-cylinder models at extra cost," but no mention of the option is made under accessory groups. Olds clearly was not really promoting six wheels any longer, and cars for the last few years are fairly rare.

DODGE AND DESOTO

Chrysler's medium-priced cars, Dodge and DeSoto, both carried 6-wheel equipment quite often after 1927 until the 1937 model dropped them. Apparently Dodge, DeSoto and the small Chrysler shared bodies and fenders for most of these years and hence looked very similar. Dodge sales literature consistently showed many models with six wheels. In the 1933 Dodge sales folder, several cars were shown with sidemounts and the newly adopted two-piece metal covers which exposed the wheel. Under "Note," was included the statement," ... six, wire or demountable wood wheels mounted in fender wells ... are available at extra cost." The 1935 Dodge catalog showed three cars with sidemounts and included pictures of the trunk with and without an inside spare; the caption stated, "Here you see the built-in trunk of the Dodge Touring Sedans, opened to show the capacious space available for baggage when spare tires are carried in fenderwells." The 1936 Dodge sales literature showed several cars carrying sidemounts and also included a view of the trunk with a spare, noting," ... generous luggage

A history of the sidemount spare

space... When spare tire is carried in fenderwell, capacity is even greater." This seems to imply the availability of either a single or a double mount. DeSoto literature seemed not to have promoted 6-wheel equipment to the same extent; the 1935 DeSoto catalog showed no cars with sidemounts and made no mention of their availability. Even pictures of open trunks showed spares within but no suggestions of increased creased capacity with sidemounts was made.

CHRYSLER

Chrysler itself featured sidemounts from the very first model in 1924, and continued through the 1939 Imperial models when the mounting was very handsomely executed—a smooth-sided cover adorned by a small medallion and very stylishly set in the fender. All other Chrysler covers showed the wheel and hubcap; the two-piece metal cover adorned by a small medallion and very stylishly set in the fender. All other Chrysler covers showed the wheel and hubcap; the two-piece metal cover had been adopted by 1931. Both small Chryslers as well as Imperials were available with sidemounts, but after 1936 only the Imperial carried six wheels as an option. Either one or two mounts were available on Imperials from 1937 through 1939, an odd option for the top-of-the-line models. Sales literature and ads as well as factory photos often showed sidemounted cars. Ads in high-brow magazines showed sidemounted cars consistently through 1933 when the larger models were featured. A particularly effective series of ads appeared in *Fortune* in the early 1930's; they were not as faultless as the Packard ads of the same time, but they were perhaps Chrysler's best.

The year 1934 marked a turning point for Chrysler, or so they hoped, when the new "Airflow" models were introduced (on the DeSoto too). These cars from 1934 through 1937 were so wide that there was no question of sidemount equipment. Other 1934 Chryslers could be had with six wheels. The 1935 "Airstream" catalog showed one 6-cylinder model with sidemounts, but did not mention the equipment; it was nevertheless available on all 6 and 8 models. The 1936 catalog showed no cars with six wheels and did not mention the option, but ads often showed cars sidemounted and quite a few were seen on the streets. The mounting was identical to the 1935 design and used the same fenders and covers. By 1937 only the Imperial models could be ordered with sidemounts, either one or two. Occasional ads showed sidemounted Imperials in both 1937 and 1938. The 1938 sales catalog showed only the Imperial Custom sedan with sidemounts, and the 1939 catalog neither showed a car nor mentioned sidemounted spares. The 1939 Special Equipment price list showed the single sidemount group, fenderwell, wheel lock and metal cover listed for $55 on the Imperial and $75 on the Custom Imperial (dealer's net: $41.25 and 56.25!). The difference is hard to understand as the mounts seem to have been identical. The dual mount included the same equipment plus another tire and wheel and listed for $125 for the Imperial and $145 for the Custom Imperial. These high prices perhaps explain why so few 1939 Chryslers were seen with sidemounts. The company was somewhat irratic in its promotion of this equipment and no records survive to indicate production of sidemounted cars.

BUICK

Buick, GM's junior luxury car, was perhaps the major purveyor of 6-wheel cars and produced more than any other maker over the years because the smaller Buicks, as well as the senior cars, were often sold with sidemounts. In advertising, as well as in catalog literature, Buicks were illustrated with 6-wheel equipment as early as 1927, and rather consistently through 1935. Marquette, Buick's junior partner for 1929-30, also featured sidemounts both years. The 1932 Buick sales catalog showed all "90" series cars and several cars in both the "80" and "60" series with sidemounts. There was no comment except with the illustrations of the phaetons which stated, "Six wire

1. There was certainly enough fender space to carry a sidemount on a V-12 '38 Packard, and it was deeply inset.

2. There is argument over whether Chevrolet offered factory-installed sidemounts for '38, but this example turned up in Holland and careful inspection by experts seems to verify its authenticity.

3. The year 1938 was one of recession and few Hudsons were sold, especially with the extra-cost sidemount. This fine 6-wheeler is estimated to be one of only two or three left.

or demountable wood wheels, fenderwells and trunk rack are standard equipment." Sidemounts, then, were optional on all others. Several varities of tire covers were listed as extra. The 1934 sales catalog showed seven models with sidemounts and noted, "Fenderwells . . . at extra cost." In 1936 the catalog included illustrations of sidemounts in all series and an additional sketch of the sidemount feature. Convertible coupes and rumble seat coupes were available only with sidemounts since there was no tire compartment, although on other GM lines, 5-wheel coupes had the spare in a compartment behind the front seat.

In 1937 through 1940 all series 80 and 90 cars were shown with six wheels, and many of the other models were also shown that way. The 1937 Salesman's Fact Book made the point that now buyers did not have to take sidemounts on convertible coupes since a tire compartment beneath the rumble seat was provided (as on other GM cars). The Roadmaster convertible sedans were, it was stated, available only with six wheels. There is no evidence to suggest that single mounts were offered at any time, as happened on Cadillac.

In both the 1938 and 1939 catalogs the majority of cars were shown with sidemounts but in neither was any mention made as to optional or standard equipment. Two illustrations of open trunks in the 1939 edition failed to mention added capacity when the spare was sidemounted. In 1939, for the first time (and again in 1940) two styles of sidemounts were offered; the one on the big cars was essentially similar although not identical to the previous year, and the mount on the Special and Century was entirely different. This latter mounting was at best very awkward and clung to the side of the car rather than fitting into a well. Covers were different, too; senior Buick covers closely resembled 1938 covers, but covers on the small Buicks, while slightly contoured had chrome trim. Apparently buyers resisted this clumsy design and Buick redesigned the front fenders for the 1940 small cars. Front doors simply could not be opened as far on 6-wheel small Buicks as on those same models without sidemounts. In order to prevent doors from hitting the sidemounts, front door check links were shorter on 6-wheel cars. The 1940 catalog of the small Buicks showed several cars with sidemounts and included a sketch under the illustration of the Century convertible sedan that showed a covered wheel mounted in a fender. The caption stated, "The smart lines of this spacious convertible are enhanced by the use of sidemounts, available at added cost." This is perhaps one of the most direct promotions of sidemounted wheel equipment by any maker in the last years of its availability. The 1940 Buick Deluxe Limited brochure showed all cars with sidemounts but does not mention that they were optional at extra cost. By 1941 slab-sided styling precluded sidemounts even on the senior cars.

Costs remained fairly constant in the last 4 years of the 6-wheel option. In 1937 6-wheel equipment included bumpers and guards, two tires and tubes, dual windshield wipers, two metal covers, two tire locks, two fenderwells, spring covers, dual taillights, dual signal horns, two extra wheels and two side tire carriers, all for a cost of $95 on the Special, $100 on the Century, $105 on the Roadmaster and $140 on the Limited. The same extras and 5-wheel equipment cost $40 less, resulting in an actual price for sidemounts of $55, $60, $65 and $100. In 1938 and 1939 six wheels were standard on the Limited (they could be removed optionally if desired) and cost $45 on Specials and Centurys and $60 on the Roadmaster. The prices in 1940 were $47 on small cars and $62 on senior cars. Tire covers from 1931 through 1935 were two-piece metal units that exposed the wheel. In 1936 through 1939 full contour covers were used. For 1940 smooth-sided covers were seen, and used restrained trim on the senior cars but a bit more on the small series. Wheels were higher on the small cars than on the senior mod-

2

3

A history of the sidemount spare

els and fenders also reflected the difference in size. An educated guess on production (figures are not available) suggests that about 75-95% of senior Buicks were equipped with sidemounts. Small Buicks with six wheels varied in number between 20-30% in 1936; in 1937-38, the big years for sidemounts, 30-35% probably had sidemounts; 10-20% of the 1939-40 cars may have had this option.

LUXURY CARS

Among the luxury cars all had sidemounts either as optional or as standard equipment. Virtually all Duesenbergs came equipped with six wheels with very few exceptions. Auburns and Cords most often had them. The 1936 Auburn sales catalog featured sidemounts. Half of the illustrations show cars with sidemounts, both 6- and 8-cylinder cars. Magazine ads consistently showed 6-wheel cars, in both Cord L29 and Auburn ads. The Auburn speedster could not be had with sidemounts, and there is no evidence that this assembly was ever attempted. (No Auburns with the flashy chromed exhaust pipes offered six wheels, only a single right-hand sidemount, leaving the left side clear for viewing the pipes.) However, the coffin-nose Cord surprisingly enough offered sidemounts in 1937. Two such cars exist today, a convertible phaeton and a Custom Beverly in Canada. Glenn Pray estimates that perhaps six cars were built with sidemounts. The factory complete parts list for the "812" lists the welled fenders, indicating clearly that the equipment was definitely a factory option although some historians feel only one prototype was built and failed to win approval. One can only guess at the proportion of Auburns and L29 Cords made with six wheels, but it might be well over half. Franklin featured sidemounted cars from 1928 until the end in both ads and sales literature, with one exception: the V-12 never seemed to be shown with six wheels. All Franklin models were very handsome with sidemounts with one exception, the Pirate phaeton in 1930-31 on which the wheels are very high, well above the belt line. Sidemounts were available on the last cars in 1934.

Both Marmon and Stutz featured sidemounts. Marmon began to favor sidemounted spares in 1927 and many ads showed cars that way. This was true for the next few years. The 1930 sales folder showed almost all cars with six wheels; the top-of-the-line Big Eight illustrations included the notation that, "Spares are carried forward on all Big Eight models." On the other two lines they were optional. Apparently all V-16 models included sidemounts as standard equipment. Marmon offered sidemounts until the end in 1934. Stutz also went all out for sidemounts by 1927; almost all cars seemed to have had them and a Stutz with a rear-mounted spare was the rare one. This practice continued until the last model in 1934.

Lincoln featured this accessory prominently in both ads and catalogs, and, excluding the Zephyr, offered 6-wheel equipment through 1940. Very few senior Lincolns were seen after the mid-'30's, and a 6-wheel car after that time is rare. There is no information available on the actual production of sidemounted cars nor the cost of the equipment when it was optional.

Pierce-Arrow, one of the great practitioners of the art of the side-mounted spare, probably had as high a proportion of 6-wheel cars in the late '20's through 1938 as almost any other single make. Ads and sales literature featured sidemounts. In the 1932 sales brochure 17 of 20 cars illustrated had sidemounts; some were canvas covered, on sport models, and the rest two-piece metal with wheel and hubcap exposed. Standard equipment, however, was stated to be five wheels. Sidemounts continued until the last models in 1938; in the last few years almost no cars appeared with rear-mounted spares. Almost all of the many custom models from the late '20's until the end had included sidemounts. No information is presently at hand as to the cost of this equipment when optional.

One of the most unusual Pierce-Arrow design attempts occurred with the 1933 Silver Arrow, a highly streamlined, slab-sided model. Rather than

1

abandoning sidemounted spares, wheels were mounted behind body panels in the usual position, and the panels were hinged. The sidemounts were there but not visible.

CADILLAC AND LASALLE

Cadillac, like the other great classics, came equipped with six wheels a high proportion of the time and promoted this feature, though not as actively as Buick or Packard. From the '20's through 1933 Cadillac and LaSalle were more often than not seen with sidemounts. Tires were covered by fabric, or with two-piece metal covers exposing the wheel, or were bare. Mirrors often adorned the spares. Ads and literature showed 6-wheel equipment. About the mid-'30's Cadillac seemed to have lost interest in promoting sidemounts although they continued to offer them through 1940. The radically new and stunning 1934 LaSalle was not shown with six wheels and it is not certain if they were available until the 1935 model. Catalogs of the late '30's seldom showed sidemounted cars and almost never mentioned this option. The 1937 LaSalle catalog made no mention nor did it illustrate sidemounts other than noting that one sidemounted spare tire was provided as standard equipment on the convertible sedan at no extra cost—tire in trunk on special order only. The same was true for the 1937 Cadillac which shared the same body on the small series. The 1938 Cadillac and LaSalle catalogs made no mention of sidemounts, but several cars were shown so equipped. In 1939-40 no ads showed 6-wheel cars whereas many ads had done so in previous years. Sales brochures ignored this option in both illustrations and information. On the other hand, almost all senior Cadillacs were seen on the boulevards complete with sidemounts until the end in 1940. Probably sidemounts were always standard equipment on the V-16 models in the beginning but later became optional at extra cost. All Cadillac and LaSalle models (except series 52) were offered with six wheels; even the Cadillac 62 Torpedo (GM "C" shell) could be had with sidemounts which were rather awkward since the wheels were high and pointed toward the hood due to the lack of room by the cowl. These sidemounted cars and the LaSalle, which did not try sidemounts on their Torpedo series (52) are among the very rare 6-wheelers; the 1939 LaSalle is even more rare. The last year of real interest and promotion of the 6-wheel option by Cadillac seems to have been 1938. Prices for this optional equipment were about $100. The 1939 Cadillac-LaSalle price list included side-mount costs as follows: LaSalle, $95 for six wheels, fenderwells and covers, and $40 for a right-hand fenderwell; Cadillac 61 and 60 Special, $100 for six wheels, etc., and $42 for a right-hand fenderwell; Cadillac 75, $120 for six wheels, etc., and $50 for a right-hand fenderwell; Cadillac 90 (V-16), $130 for six wheels, etc., and $55 for a right-hand fenderwell. The implication seemed to be that you did not get a tire cover with the right-hand sidemount. It is not clear when Cadillac began offering a single sidemount; in any event it seems ludicrous to consider a majestic V-16, for example, with one right-hand sidemount without cover! Although no precise information is available on the production of sidemounted Cadillacs and LaSalles, it is certain that toward the end the proportion dropped considerably from the high point of about 1930. It also seems clear that LaSalle never resulted in as many sidemounted cars

1. Widening bodies, narrowing runningboards of late '30's period made use of sidemounts awkward. Spare is barely hanging on to this '39 Buick.

2. Considered very rare today is this '40 Cadillac Series 62 convertible sedan. Styling incorporates the spares handily.

3. Another scarce item today is a '40 LaSalle, an elegant car indeed.

SPECIAL INTEREST AMERICAN CARS/37

A history of the sidemount spare

proportionally as did Cadillac.

PACKARD

Packard, the King of the Classics, was, after Buick, perhaps the chief advocate of 6-wheel cars beginning in the early 1920's, and the last to abandon this accessory offering with the 1942 senior cars. Mirrors often topped the spares and covers ranged from canvas on early cars to metal two-piece units which exposed the wheel and finally to one-piece smooth-sided covers. Even the last 2 years mirrors were often seen on dual sidemounts. Sales brochures of senior cars nearly always showed 6-wheel cars, and after Packard entered the medium-priced field with the 120 in 1935, these cars occasionally were shown with sidemounts.

By 1928, as with most other luxury marques, the sidemounted spare was a prominent feature of Packard design, perhaps even characteristic of Packard. Sales literature and ads for all models almost never showed a 5-wheel car; only occasionally did the famous Packard ads circa 1930 deviate from illustrating 6-wheel cars. The sumptuous portfolios of that time showed almost all models with sidemounts. When Packard was reduced to conventional sales catalogs, the art work was also merely conventional. The 1932 Deluxe 8 catalog showed 10 of 12 cars with sidemounts although it was stated that five wheels were standard. When the junior Packard 120 appeared in 1935, early ads did not show sidemounts; the company did not seem to be promoting them on their inexpensive car although they were offered so that the buyer of modest means could savor the true flavor of a Packard. Few cars were produced however. The 1936 folder on the 120 illustrated no cars with six wheels although an incidental photo showed one. The new Packard 6 introduced that year as a companion to the 120 was not available with sidemounts; this remained true through 1942. The 1936 senior literature showed almost all cars with sidemounts; some standard 8 models were shown without sidemounts. The 1937 junior sales catalog stated that on the 120, "The graceful length of the car permits the sidemounting of spare tire as extra equipment". This was just barely true; there was just barely room in the short fender. An open trunk was pictured minus spare noting, "With sidemounted spare tires, the Packard 120 adds even more space to an already roomy built-in trunk." It was further stated that one spare was standard under Specifications. Sidemounts could have also been fitted to the 6, since all body components were the same; the rationale may have been that any buyer of an inexpensive car would not be interested in expensive optional equipment.

The 1938 sales literature continued the previous approach. The Super 8 and 12 brochures showed 8 of 10 models with sidemounts while noting that one spare was standard. The junior catalog illustrated only the 120 Club Coupe with sidemounts; this was a somewhat high mount in an unusually shaped fenderwell and was redesigned for 1939. A trunk picture noted more room, "... when sidemounted wheel equipment is specified as extra to carry the spares forward." The 1939 Super 8 sales brochure showed several cars with six wheels and a photo of an open trunk minus the spare and noted that ,"... no less than 21 cu. ft. with sidemounted spare tires." The junior sales catalog showed two 120 models with six wheels. Again, a trunk illustration was included with the notation that, "The Packard 120 with fenderwells has more than 21 cu. ft. of usable space." In the plush 1940 senior brochure all cars except the three Darrin models were shown with sidemounts. Darrins for 1940-42 were never offered with sidemounts and there is no evidence than anyone ever attempted such a conversion. The junior sales catalog showed the 120 convertible sedan with six wheels. Two incidental sketches, a sidemount and an open trunk, were accompanied by the notation that, "The 120 with fenderwells has 21 ft.," and that, "Greater length permits sidemounting of spare wheels if this extra equipment is specified thus reserving the entire spacious trunk for luggage.

In 1941, perhaps Packard's final year of greatness, senior cars with three exceptions were sidemounted in the illustrations in the senior sales brochure; in

1. Buick's last gasp was in 1940. The spares ride well on this Series 80 convertible sedan, but appeared awkward on the smaller models.

2. A fine example of out-with-the-old, in-with-the-new; Packard emblazoned their air conditioning emblem across their sidemount cover.

3. Author Mehl currently owns this fine example of the 1941 Packard 160. Alas, the sidemount was nearly dead.

the junior catalog the 120 convertible sedan was so shown. No mention was made other than to note that five wheels were standard except on two LeBaron models which came with six wheels.

Packard ads for the last several years of sidemounts through the 1940 models most often showed 6-wheel cars on the senior models; junior models very seldom were shown that way. After 1940 the senior Packards were ignored in most ads as the company began to put all its efforts behind the promotion of the new streamlined Clipper models, introduced in mid-year 1941. The Clipper design appeared in all series for 1942, both junior and senior models. Many conventional models, which were carryover models with minimal changes, were offered with sidemounts. Several 160 and 180 sedans and limousines among the senior cars and the convertible coupe on the 110 and 120 chassis were offered. A senior 160 convertible coupe was also offered. All had the sidemount option except the 110 convertible. As in 1940, two LeBaron limousines included six wheels as standard. There is no evidence that Packard ever offered a single sidemount; although 1941 station wagons and hearses sometimes had only a righthand mount, no cars seemed to have been produced that way.

In 1929 6-wheel equipment, including trunk rack, was $45 extra, but by 1931, for some unexplained reason, that same equipment was $148. Accessories over and above the sidemounts in 1933 included metal tire covers at $18 a pair and mirrors at $16. Prices in 1934 for six wheels were $144, and then dropped in 1935 to $65 for six wheels and trunk rack, but the two tires were not included in that price. Senior cars for 1937 offered six wheels and rack at $240. Senior cars in 1940-42 could be equipped with sidemounts for $77, which was the price for the same equipment on the 120 also. A trunk rack on the senior cars in 1940 was an additional extra.

As all good things come to an end, what could be more fitting and expected than that Packard, the conservative aristocrat, should end the era of the sidemounted spare in 1942? Sidemounts were and still are undoubtedly the single most popular accessory among automobile collectors who eagerly seek out 6-wheel models in preference to 5-wheelers. Sidemounted cars are clearly more valuable. In today's hobby, and 6-wheel car of any make is worth collecting. Almost all manufacturers offered this option, but as the automobile diminished as a work of art and became as utilitarian as a refrigerator, sidemounts had to go. Love those sidemounts—gone but never forgotten!

2

COURTESY HARRAH'S AUTOMOBILE COLLECTION

3

Ford Motor Company

Edsel
The magnificent mistake

In August of 1957, a brand new car set its rubber soles upon the American consumer stage with no small amount of bravado. It was an entrance that was ultimately to lose the Ford Motor Company a whopping $250 million.

In the first place, had Edsel lived, he probably would not have approved of the new car. It was the wrong design, in the wrong market, in the wrong year, with the wrong name to announce its coming. As a matter of fact, it was reported that Edsel's widow and heirs *vetoed* his name for the new car, but were overridden in an eleventh hour skull session by Board Chairman Ernie Breech, Henry Ford II finally "squaring it" with his mother.

Yet all of these things might not have spelled disaster if the Edsel's fundamental body shape had found that illusive magic—something that starts a tradition of shrine worshipers. It did not. It meant little, and it went nowhere. Somehow, the computer had missed its target.

People bought Fords because they were cheaper; they moved up to Mercury because they were heavier and looked more solidly built. What appeared to be a market became a nightmare. In 1956, Ford Motor Company had scored heavily with introduction of the Continental Mark II, by moving into a price class that had no domestic competitors. Cadillac's Eldorado Brougham later upstaged the Mark II, but by that time most of the FoMoCo Mark II offerings had been sold out. It had been a commercial success. More importantly to a connoisseur, however, was its resource for design copying. Thunderbird, to some extent Cadillac, and all future Continentals freely borrowed aristocratic line and shape hints from the Mark II.

To over-simplify what became a disconcerting and confusing problem to FoMoCo executives, it is accurate to say that two years earlier or later might have made the Edsel click. In 1960, prior to Edsel's early death, Chrysler's 30-year medium-priced entry, DeSoto, was quietly killed. A trend had been developing within new car bastions, a thing of danger to industry bean-counters, as total car movement was slipping from less than 8 million sales in 1955 to less than 4.5 million sales in 1958. Medium market penetration fell nearly 10%, down from some 25%. In the lower end of the upper-medium price range, Buick, as an example, was feeling a drop in consumer interest, slipping from 10% to nearly 5% of the total market.

Into this vortex of medium-priced muddy water came the Edsel, flags flying, corporate trumpets blaring, advertising men advertising, the shrill voices of hail-fellow-well-met everywhere. One brochure said of the 1958 Edsel's now well-known vertical grille: "An innovation in front bumper arrangements is featured on the Edsel. Two separate wrap-around bumpers, combined with a center impact ring, provide protection for the front of the car as well as providing the new 'Vertical Theme' to every Edsel car." It was nice to know such sacrosanct information. People flocked to Edsel showrooms to see if, indeed, what they had been seeking was really there.

Once confronted with the new '58 Edsel for the first time, the feeling among many—the writer no less than anyone else at the time—was one of being cheated. The marvelous vertical grille was indeed a vertical theme, but it was too small, cramped by intereference with lines moving at all angles. It was styling degeneration in its clearest form. If there was a vertical theme to "every Edsel car," then the FoMoCo Product Engineering Office did not make it clear in its big brochure, with the vertical grille on the cover. With words describing the taillights, emphasis suddenly shifted elsewhere: "The long horizontal tail lights provide a distinctive motif for the Edsel." And so on, ad infinitum.

Standing at the rear of the new Edsel at the time, gazing with swimming senses at the mass of empty sheetmetal under the high-flying taillights, one could sense the similarity to a drowning man, looking up from the last plunge to see the high transom of a fast-moving motor boat, just out of arm's reach.

Recently, an executive in the Edsel program during its lifetime uttered some interesting comments which may reflect a look at the state of mind among that FoMoCo division at the time. The individual in question purchased, several years ago, a mint-condition '58 Pacer Convertible. The executive, who by the way, is still a Ford Motor Company decision-maker, is reported to have put it this way: "When I first got the car home, I walked around it and tried to be objective. I told some of the people at the design office that, on the '58, trying to find a bad line on the car was a difficult job.

1. Top-of-the-line!, and a new face in Detroit. The 1958 Edsel Citation 4-door hardtop, with a high-torque V-8, and body sculpturing, nevertheless was a sales failure—an irony that makes this model now desirable.

2. Perhaps the most beautiful design feature of the '58 Edsel station wagons was the taillight assembly—a much sought-after unit to customizers of 2-seat Thunderbirds and Rancheros. The Bermuda 4-door wagon in the Edsel, however, had light-colored wood inserts (imitation) which detracted from normal wagon appearance.

3. Refined look of stylish radiator-grille was marred by lines of various thickness converging at all angles. What could have been a great design was caught up in fuzzy economics.

4. The '59 Corsair became the top-of-the-line, in a major re-shuffling within the marque.

5. Stylists, smarting from the below-par sales performance of the entire Edsel experience, fitted circular taillight housings, but the '59 Edsel still suffered from a high beltline.

6. If a contest were held for the "best looking station wagon rear ends of all time," the Edsel would be in the running for both '58 and '59.

It has real nice lines. All the detailing is good, and so forth. So I was just as pleased today, after 14 years, as I was when we first did it." And so forth.

Others have recently lauded the faint hint of the narrow hood that the Edsel re-introduced, now somewhat of an industry standard, as Detroit, like suit styles, returns to what is so far out of date that it becomes "new."

But in 1955, when the Edsel was being planned, a record 7.9 million cars were finding a hallmark sales niche. It was presumed that Americans would buy cars as fast as they could be welded or bolted together. Further, it was assumed that the public wanted chrome, tailfins, horsepower, exciting paint jobs, size, big windshields. Size, sex, and excitement were the watchwords. The Edsel looked like an automatic winner—in 1955. By 1958, things were sufficiently different to change it into a loser. A business recession of that year did nothing to help.

But the bomb was dropped, and became a portent of missed targets as far as the public was concerned. Ergo: today, American buyers are not so easily swayed by glowing promises and increased prices as they once were. For years, worshipping at Detroit's shrine had nearly begun to establish a myth of invincibility. But the Edsel helped in no small measure to change the blissful ignorance of the American mass market.

Today, well into the second decade from the Edsel's burial, the fickle fortunes of time and a hungry definition of what constitutes a "special interest car" have caused a radical shift in the worth of all Edsels left standing. Just to have the Edsel name is worth a few more dollars, even to the most jaundiced of ho-hum owners.

While the '58 Edsel seemed a bit strange in the design department, a backward glance gives it strong resurgence possibilities on at least three points. The first is, of course, having suffered an economic death. Modern orphan cars are highly prized, more so if in short supply. That rule is basic. Secondly, modern communication machines invariably assure that a loser's name will be known far and wide. The result: Edsels were literally abandoned on the marketplace and could be scarfed up at next to nothing. Third, the very cancerous appearance of its design, has begun to indicate *prima fa-*

Ford Motor Company
Edsel

cie evidence of a special interest car. While few people may have been interested in "telling what car it is from a mile's distance" (a decade ago), the situation in today's shoe-box auto scene has been reversed. The vertical grille is "in." The hint of the long, slim, late 30's radiator and hood, resurrected by the Edsel, is "in." The concave rear fender with its anodized insert is also "in." And for those collectors who like to swoon over the Lord's Prayer on the head of a pin, a bit of trivia: The '58 Edsel's horizontal grille portion culminated with a delicate wraparound under the headlight moldings. It was long and narrow and comprised of nine thin chrome bars, similarly wrapped around a 90° parking light, with the entire grille package ending just forward of the front wheel wells. Take a look at AMC's phenomenal Pacer. Similarly, its parking lights wrap around front fenders, in a long and narrow grille, comprised of 10 thin chrome bars. Parking lights are 90° not unlike the recent Porsches. A note here: the name "Pacer" was in the running for Ford's new Mercury in 1938, and also lost out to Edsel, only to find a home among Edsel's models—Ranger, Pacer, Corsair, and Citation.

In 1968, Edsel as a collectable item hit high gear with an article in *The Wall Street Journal* about Edsel buffs. Books, articles, and word of mouth picked up the slack. The subject was briefly discussed on Johnny Carson's "Tonight Show." Carson, always a shrewd listener to the public's words and moods had uncovered a unique bit of Americana—something very nearly a social law: The public always has a way of fighting back when finally aware it's been cheated. Edsel collecting and restoration became a rage across the country, highlighted by the formation of the Edsel Owners Club of America, now well more than 650 people and 900 cars.

There is a frenzied car-hunt in junkyards and other nooks and crannies that have driven prices to at least $3300 for a mint example, $1700 for an Edsel of good condition, and $600 for an Edsel barely able to get out of its own way.

With less than 27,000 Edsels coming off the production line in 1958, and nearly 30,000 following in 1959, the supply was large enough to attract collectors but small enough to lately vanish in alarming fashion, primarily due to its relatively low cost. But in 1960, it was a different story. By mid-year, the Edsel was gone, leaving very roughly some 2800 4-doors, and around 275 station wagons as a swan song for the final year. The real collectibles, however, are the 1960 convertibles. Only some 76 were built. Of those, at first it was very hard to find any. Then someone found one. Another painful search. For a long time, it was presumed that 13 could be located. Gradually, more 1960 Edsel Ranger convertibles turned up. Today, about 50 of the 76 have been accounted for. Paul Karnes of Indiana found a white, '60 Ranger convertible in Georgia, to go along with his mint condition blue '59 Corsair convertible, and bring his Edsel collection at that time to 21. Karnes is the same man who later stretched his Edsel total to 31.

The problem now is, of course, one of running into *fake* 1960 Edsels. Total Ford production in 1960 was 1,511,504. With the Edsel situation in 1960, plus the fact that body dies were identical with Ford, it didn't take long for a lot of fake Edsels to start showing up. Grilles, rear and side panels were the only difference. Dashes were the same, too, outside of a few Edsel markings. Gone was the well-known Edsel "Teletouch" Electric Push Button Transmission Selector, mounted in the center of the steering wheel hub. Even though the push-button affair lasted only for the first year, neither the '58's or '59's are today subject to much acetylene finagling. They were saved by their blatantly individual looks. It would do well for the collector to be wary, however, before seeking out an Edsel in earnest. Even though $3300 is a good mint example figure, and $600 for one decidedly rough, averages can swing even wider. One could deal at $150 for an absolute bucket of bolts example, and yet have to shell out more than $5000 for a top concours Edsel. Best guesses have said that Edsel's rate of appreciation will be slow, due obviously to the large number that have been resurrected. One must not forget for a moment that the basic design of the Edsel never has been, and never will be a world beater.

It's amazing how proficient some of the more enterprising violators have become in torching up '60 Fords into Edsels. An expert has been known to find confusing answers until he really uses his noodle. It's not surprising that others in the restoration/special interest scene have charged up to $25 an hour to diagnose the problem for dubi-

1. Here it comes, for 1960. But look again—it's not an Edsel! That's right, it's a Ford.

2. The 1960 Edsel used the Ford body shell. Edsel models were now down to a pair of offerings: the Ranger and the Villager, the latter in a wagon only.

3. 1960 Ford—looks like an Edsel, basic body shell for '60 is same. Few available Edsels but many Fords have led to "fake" Edsels.

4. 1960 Edsel—looks like a Ford. Acetylene "creativity" to a Ford can produce hundreds of dollars profit. The prudent shopper is careful. This Edsel is the real McCoy, however.

5. Next time you see a '60-'61 Ford dash, take this book along. Dashes are nearly identical. Will the real Edsel please stand up!

6. Last of a dream—1960 Edsel. Grille is not unlike Pontiacs of same era. License is prophetic.

ous Edsel owners—not always with happy results. The only solution is to become familiar with a '60 Ford—preferably in a junkyard so you can check welds, tolerances and overall appearance. Never mind that many among us holler with a cynical laugh: "Why in blazes would anyone in his right mind want to counterfeit an Edsel—now I've heard everything!" Just do what Alexander Graham Bell did—*Observe, Remember,* and *Compare.*

Engineering-wise the Edsel was a good car, quite unlike its styling weakness. The 1958 Edsel appeared in four models and three station wagons. Moving upward from the cheapest, there was the Ranger, Pacer, Corsair, and Citation. Wagons were the Roundup, Villager, and Bermuda. Base price for the 1958 Citation convertible, f.o.b. Dearborn was $3801. The 1958 Ranger could be had in a 4-door hardtop, 4-door sedan, 2-door hardtop, and 2-door sedan. The Pacer came in a 4-door hardtop, 4-door sedan, 2-door hardtop, and 2-door convertible. Corsair could be purchased in a 4-door hardtop and a 2-door hardtop. Citation (the top of the line) came in a 4-door hardtop, 2-door hardtop, and 2-door convertible. The Roundup station wagon was a 2-door 6-passenger model. The Villager came in two 4-door models, either a 6- or 9-passenger. The Bermuda was the plushest of the wagons, either 6- or 9-passenger, and used the outside wood applique. It was on the station wagons that the "flying Vee" taillights appeared, so well-known to '57 Ranchero and Thunderbird customizers. It was one of the few actually beautiful styling creations to come out of the entire Edsel program, and is a highly sought-after item.

Engines were basically the same in 1959 as the year before, and especially engineered for torque in the 4000-lb. car. A 410-cu.-in. V-8 pumped out 345 gross horses at 4600 rpm, and a whopping 475-ft.-lbs. of torque at 2900 rpm. A stock '58 Edsel Citation convertible would normally have a 2.91:1 rear axle ratio, running through FoMoCo's well-proved 3-speed torque converter transmission. A convertible would stand at about 4480 lbs. curb weight, and would average some 15 to 16 mpg in a perfect stage of tune. Acceleration of a 1958 Edsel Corsair, performed in October 1957 by *Motor Trend* magazine gave 3.4 secs from 0 to 30 mph; 6.3 secs. from 0 to 40, and 9.7 secs. from 0 to 60 mph. They were swift times for what it was, and the Edsel did not have to hang its head in shame. In 1959, an economy push gripped concerned executives in Edsel's less than ecstatic program, resulting in a 50-lb. lighter 2-speed automatic trans, and a bold statement that "an Edsel, comparably equipped item for item, will sell within $50 or less of the top series of Chevrolets, Plymouths and Fords." There were three V-8's, and a 223-cu.-in. six. There was the 292-cu.-in. *Ranger* V-8, well-proved in Ford products since 1956. A 332-cu.-in *Express* V-8, and a 361-cu.-in *Super Express* V-8 completed the offering.

The '59 Edsel was a trifle lighter than its predecessor and was cleaned up all around, although its basic body shape suffered, as many products that year, from a high belt line. Gone were the Bermuda and Roundup station wagons, as well as the entire Pacer line. The convertible could only be bought in the Corsair series—now the top of the line, since the Citation, too, was gone.

In late 1959, fanfare for the 1960 was nakedly low-key. The enthusiasm was drained, and the car itself looked like a Ford. Indeed it was, on a Ford shell, with only a grille and trim the difference. People wondered if it was a Canadian Ford. Few people bought. The new Edsel was lower and wider than ever before; cornering ability was apparently better. There was the small V-8, the six, and a 352-cu.-in. V-8, rated at 300 hp. Almost ashamedly, the first press releases said: "The new Edsel styling is characterized by simplicity and good taste in ornamentation." Almost before the new year hit stride, the Edsel production line began slowing to a halt. Mercury-Edsel-Lincoln dealers could only shrug. People began wondering who was giving up on whom? The public on Edsel, or the Ford Motor Company—after only a three-year life for its offspring that had been 10 years in coming to birth. But little did it matter now; not even remembrance of the ancient rolling-dome speedometer design of the '58's.

Edsels became the laughing stock of the highways, and the word synonymous with grave business debacles of all kinds. But collectors of special interest cars are a strange breed, not the least characteristic of which is a near-myopic regard for the value of a dollar. And as such, the dream of the Edsel car has been restored; not to what it was, but to what it might have been, indeed what *should* have been.

Ford Motor Company

Ford

Truly the backbone of special interest cars

Within a month of incorporating in 1903, The Ford Motor Company sold its first car for $850, built in a wagon shop. From that day on, Ford worked to the end of his life to put a nation on wheels, and in three years became the top automobile producer. From 1903-1907, Ford produced the "letter series" of cars, and the financial success brought him the capital to expand rapidly and realize his dreams. Already on top of the new automobile industry, he worked night and day for over a year to finalize the designs for what would become the "Universal Car," the Ford Model T. From its introduction in 1908, the T was a cheap, lightweight, durable, go-anywhere car, which Ford produced in such great numbers that it kept him the leading manufacturer of automobiles for *19* years.

As good as the fifteen million Model T's had been to a country starved for practical transportation, the design had become stodgy by the late '20's, and under increasing competition from other manufacturers, notably Chevrolet (which passed Ford in 1927), Ford introduced the entirely new Model A in December, 1927. A project shrouded in secrecy during its development, this first new car from Ford in twenty years stirred such public interest that total crowds estimated at ten million people saw the car in its first two days. Wrapped in a completely new and handsome body, the features of the new Ford included such improvements over the T as a three-speed transmission, four-wheel brakes, a water pump and oil pump, more instrumentation, softer seats, more plating, and a locking ignition switch. Insurance companies were quite impressed with this latter improvement, and lowered theft rates about one third, which was partially offset though by an increase of 20% in the *fire* insurance rates, due to the fuel tank being now mounted in the cowl, rather than under the seat as on the T. Performance of the all-new Ford also contributed to its great popularity, with economy between 20 and 30 mpg and quick acceleration leading to a top speed of around 60 mph. Production was down in '28 (633,594) due to the many delays in getting the new line started and the bugs worked out, but the next year was a full one that saw Ford back on top with production over 1.5 million. The A had been accepted as the finest Ford ever made.

We now come to the period that is within the 30-year scope of this book of special interest American cars, and before we delve into the year-to-year specifics, we should spend a little time discussing Ford's place in the overall special interest "market" of which Fords are the most popular and their desirability as potential projects for the readers of this book.

There have been many Fords of special interest built in the period 1930-1960, as well as some outside of those parameters, and all of them occupy somewhat unique positions when put into the SIAC hopper along with such little-known and interesting marques as Darrin, Muntz, Playboy, and others that come quickly to mind when car enthusiasts talk of special cars. Ford? The Universal Car, the car that "put America on wheels," the car built in the millions and driven by everyone from GI's to geriatric cases, doughboys to Dillinger, how could the most common of cars become "of special interest?"

The answer is that, even more so than the other marques which have survived through more than seventy years in the auto business, the Ford name is inextricably woven into socio-economic fabric of this country. There isn't a family in middle America who hasn't owned at least one, and there are few special interest car enthusiasts reading this book who can't recall fond memories of the Model A their father (substitute uncle or grandfather, if appropriate) used to have, or the '37 sedan, '47 convertible or '57 hardtop they drove in high school or college. Common and mundane as it may be alongside such impressive marques as Lincoln, Cadillac, Duesenberg, Pierce-Arrow and Packard, nothing tugs on the nostalgic heart-strings of Americans like an old Ford. As beautiful and impressive as the true classic cars are, we doubt there are many restored Auburn speedsters that can evoke curbside responses of familiarity like a Ford. "Gosh, I remember the one my grandmother drove...just like this one... had it for *years,*" or what Ford owner hasn't encountered the elderly gentleman who wistfully recalls his experiences on his "first double-date in the rumbleseat of one of those Fords."

Nostalgic emotions are only a part of

44/SPECIAL INTEREST AMERICAN CARS

the reasons Fords are of special interest. A large part is pure economics. Of the many cars built before WW II, Fords are today among the most affordable cars, both in unrestored and restored conditions. There is a ready market crowded with enthusiasts waiting to buy your restored early Ford when you finish it. While an advertisement in the newspaper for your '34 Hudson sedan may bring a number of responses, the same ad for a '34 Ford sedan will bring four or five times the number of interested buyers. If the resale value of your special interest car is going to be of importance to you in your selection of a car to restore or collect, then you'd do well to consider a Ford. No one can tell you positively that you "can't go wrong" on restoring a particular car (there are those who have blindly spent $10,000 restoring a car whose market value is only half that), but chances are excellent for recovering your investment with a Ford, given certain conditions.

One of those conditions would be the price you have to pay for an unrestored example of the car you've selected. Naturally, if you spent too much for a car to begin with, you would have to cut corners somewhere during the restoration in order to just break even. The Ford enthusiast has the advantage over, say, a Packard collector, in that millions more Fords have been built over the years than some other makes, and thus there are many more examples of Fords to be found in America's fields, barns and garages, waiting patiently there for you to take home and restore to their former glory. It would seem that the mass-production level of Ford output would make them less collectable, but the demand for these cars is also in large numbers, and the once prodigious supply (of *all* old cars) has been whittled down considerably, especially in recent years. When you do find "an old Ford" in a barn somewhere, chances are you can purchase it for a reasonable sum, which may not be the case with some of the cars more widely considered under the loose classification of "classic."

Finding the "raw material" for a special interest restoration is of course only half the battle; now you have to restore it. With some of the more obscure makes, this can become a real challenge to your researching and scrounging abilities. Finding that replacement headlight rim for your Rockne might take you many months of searching the antique car publications and correspondence with collectors all over the country. Generally, restoration of a Ford will be a great deal easier. Not only are there more unrestorable-but-parted-out cars around to get parts from, but there are countless sources for new reproduction parts and NOS parts ("new old stock," which means that the part is an original part that has never been put on a car). Because of the widespread interest in restoring old Fords, numerous companies have seen the capitalistic writing on the wall and have available reproductions of many of the parts needed in a restoration. "Repro" is a bad word to many restorers, because in the past many parts have been so unfaithfully reproduced that having a worn *original* part on your car would be better. This situation is changing now that the enthusiasts are more discerning and demanding better quality parts. There are now American companies (many of the poor repro parts, particularly rubber, come from the Far East or South America) making first-class parts that are virtually impossible to tell from the originals, and thus don't detract from your restoration job. In many large cities, there are stores which deal in nothing but parts for early Fords, both repro and collected used and NOS originals, plus there are dozens of mail order companies specializing in Ford parts. It's been said by some that you could just about fab-

1. Of all the attractive Model A's, one of the rarest body styles is that of the '30-'31 Deluxe phaeton, with sporty 2-door configuration. It was the only 2-door Ford phaeton ever.

2. In late 1931, several slant-windshield body styles were introduced as forerunners to the new '32 to come. All of these were built in limited amounts, and are very desirable today. This is the Victoria, the first of that special body in the Ford line.

3. The wholly-new '32 has become one of the most desirable of all Fords, especially the open cars like this accessory-bedecked Deluxe roadster.

4. The cast-iron V-8 introduced in '32 was a milestone achievement for Ford, or any manufacturer in the low-price field, and was largely responsible for Ford's reputation as a durable, snappy-performing car.

Ford Motor Company
Ford

ricate an entire Model A Ford from modern reproduction parts. This is testimony to the extent that parts are available for Fords, and one of the advantages if you select one of Henry's products for restoration.

Something else to consider is the availability of good technical information on the restoration of the car you choose. Again, Ford owners are in luck. With the great numbers of enthusiasts who have been working on Fords for many years, the answers to such specific technical questions as: "Should the firewall bolts on my '39 convertible sedan be cad-plated or painted black?" are available and doesn't call for any Sherlock Holmes researching techniques.

The first consideration of the new owner of a restorable special interest car should be to join a club which is devoted to that marque. Even if you're not the club "type," this move will prove to be the smartest, and perhaps most enjoyable part of your restoration. Most members of auto clubs are enthusiasts just like yourself, who are happy to share technical knowledge, parts sources, factory literature and shop manuals with other club members. Even if you don't presently have a car, joining a club and receiving their newsletter may be one of your best leads in finding the car you desire. Being a member can probably get you a better price, too, since most clubs are more willing to make a good deal to a fellow member than to an outsider.

Most of the recognizable collectable cars have established national and regional clubs, but the Ford owner has many to choose from. Ford car clubs are probably the largest auto clubs in terms of membership, and there are clubs for the T, the A, the V-8's, and even several clubs for the postwar cars. The bigger clubs have regional groups and local chapters all over the country, with national and regional meets, seminars, and club publications loaded with valuable restoration information. With the advantages of good clubs, good parts availability, reasonably-priced cars, great resale value, and nostalgic interest, almost any Ford built in 1955 or earlier is interesting enough to collect or hang onto, but naturally some are more valuable than others. Let's get back to 1930 and look at just which Fords are the most desirable.

After producing cars for two decades with only minor annual changes, Ford (and the other auto companies, too) finally got into the swing of producing cars to suit the increasingly fickle and discerning American car buyer. The original Model A was produced for only two years before the "improved Model A" was introduced for 1930. It featured wider fenders, more interior room, new hubcaps, and stainless steel on the grill shell and cowl molding. It also had smaller wheels (19 ins. as opposed to 21 ins.) with slightly fatter tires. As this "new" car continued in production, various new bodies were introduced to keep public interest high. Many of these cars were enough out-of-the-ordinary to have become low in production figures, and thus assured of status in present-day collecting circles as special interest.

The first of these, and perhaps foremost among special interest Model A's, would be the Deluxe Phaeton introduced in June, 1930. Of course, prewar open cars of any make are generally much more valuable than their steel-topped brethren, but this one particularly so, as it was the only 2-*door* phaeton built by Ford. None had ever been built before that time, none have been built since, and during the '30-'31 period only 7281 were produced. While there are some manufacturers whose total production for a year may have been less than this figure, when compared to the two million other Fords built in those two years, the Deluxe represents quite a relative rarity. In addition, the car was extremely attractive, with the two-door aspect and extra detailing making for a sporty package.

Other Model A's definitely worth consideration, if you're looking for something out of the ordinary, would be the rarer of the commercial models, such as the roadster-pickup and the sedan-delivery, and of course the wooden-bodied station wagons. Not every car enthusiast will want a commercial model, even if it is a rare one, but rest assured there is a guaranteed market for them. If you really want a rare commercial one, try to find one of the "drop-floor" deliveries—like a regular sedan delivery except that the floor was lower to carry more cargo. Below the single back door (if there are *two* rear doors then you have the truckier *panel* delivery, which had a higher roofline and is less appealing to many collectors) was a panel that could be dropped down to allow straight access to the floor for easier loading. Slanted windshields were becoming the styling idea of '31, and Ford introduced several new bodies with this approach in the Model A's last year, anticipating the new "mystery Ford" to come out in 1932. There was the standard four-door sedan with slanted windshield, the town-car delivery, and the late '31 slant-windshield convertible-sedan. The town-car delivery, with the driver's compartment open and the cargo compartment closed, is extremely rare, and you won't likely see one even at a

large Model A meet. The convertible-sedan is also quite desirable.

Despite the claim made by Edsel Ford (then president of the company) in late 1930 that no new car was planned for production and that more Model A's would be built than Model T's, a new car *was* in the works, and 1932 became a landmark year for Ford. Feeling increasing pressure from other manufacturers who offered six-cylinder engines, Henry decided to try mass producing a cast iron, inexpensive, and reliable V-8 engine, and wrap it in a totally new body for 1932. No manufacturer had ever mass produced a cast iron V-8 engine, but Mr. Ford didn't like six-cylinder engines, and if the public thought they had outgrown his reliable four-banger, then he was bound and determined to produce a "twin-four" and rattle his competition despite the immense production and foundry problems that might arise. Although his son Edsel was the titular head of the organization, the senior Ford still called most of the shots.

Because of the numerous problems in successfully casting the new V-8 block, production was delayed such that the first V-8 didn't roll off the line until March of '32, and the total production was the lowest (except for 1942) of any year except 1913. This comparative rarity only helps increase the popularity of these cars today. If you're interested in restoring an early Ford, be advised that the earlier the car, the more expensive it will be (both in parts and original price), and 1932 heads the list in price. The new V-8 Ford was one of the fastest cars of its day, and certainly the fastest car for the money. In addition, it was one of the cleanest designs to ever come out of Dearborn, with a chassis that allowed a lower profile, smaller wheels and larger tires, and Ford's first front end that didn't expose the radiator.

It's hard to pick out special interest cars among the '32 Fords, not because there aren't any, but because there are so many. It was such a milestone year for Ford, in both styling and engineering, plus their relatively low production, that today they are among the most expensive Fords. *Any* '32 Ford is worth collecting, whatever the body style, but we'll try to give you a "pecking order" of relative values. If you go strictly by rarity, then the top-of-the-line is the '32 roadster pickup. Probably less than a hundred were ever built, all of which had the improved B 4-cyl. engine, and we've seen less than half a dozen restored examples in all the car meets we've ever been to.

In the passenger car line, the open '32's are the most desirable today, as is true of most of the Ford V-8 years. Long considered the most collectable early Ford, the '32 phaeton is tops on anyone's list. Beautifully restored examples have sold for over $20,000, which is a lot of money for an old Ford. The '32 roadster is not far behind the phaeton in either price or popularity, although there were almost three times as many made (8996 roadsters—standard and deluxe—compared to only 2706 phaetons). Even rarer than the phaeton is the convertible sedan, Model B-400, of which only 1142 were built, but being a semi-closed car it's slightly less desirable to most Ford nuts than the roadster or phaeton. Ranking right along with the roadster pickup in terms of rarity, but considerably more popular would be the '32 woodie station wagon. A total of 334 were produced at Ford's Iron Mountain, Michigan facility, but they are of course rare today out of proportion to production figures because of the low survival rate of wooden-bodied cars. The sedan delivery, while at least as rare as the roadster pickup (only 58 built), would not be considered as desirable as a phaeton to most collectors, simply because it is a commercial body and a closed one at that. These two commercial bodies would nevertheless still bring an extremely high price today due to their scarcity.

To fill out our discussion of the '32, the rest of the passenger car line, the coupes and sedans, is where readers might find an affordable car. Of the sedans, the 2-door Victoria, with its bustled lines at the rear, is the most desirable. Only 8870 were built, and most Ford enthusiasts consider them more attractive than the other sedans, as well. The bulk of '32 production was in the coupes and 2-door and 4-door sedans, as these were the most practical cars, then and now. In the coupe lineup, the most desirable would be the Sport Coupe (2409 made), which is a convertible model different from a roadster only in that there were solid, stationary windshield posts, the doors had rollup windows, and the top, although it folded down, could not come off the car. Next would be the Deluxe Coupe, 3-window, a really attractive car when restored, and then the Standard (5-window) coupe. Many beginning enthusiasts get confused as to what is a 3-window and what is a 5-window coupe, but just remember not to count the windshield and it'll be easy. The sedans are probably last in popularity today, although being '32 Fords they are certainly still very desirable. About 60% of all '32 production was in sedans, and of these, almost three times as many 2-door sedans were built as were four-doors, the four-doors having been one of the most expensive cars in the Ford line at that time. Even so, many restorers and enthusiasts would probably prefer to

1. Due to their relative scarcity and high popularity, any body style of '32 is highly collectable today, but one of the really rare and attractive models is this B-400 convertible-sedan.

2. Rarest of the '32 body styles is this roadster-pickup. Right behind it in rarity, and more appealing to most collectors, is the sedan-delivery.

3. Most rare of the 1933 Fords are the very early production cars with the unskirted fenders, which resemble the '32 fenders. Only about a half dozen are known to exist today. All sedans!

4. Generally the most expensive Fords to purchase or restore are phaetons, like this fine '34. A few '32-'36 phaetons have sold for $20,000., a lot of money for "an old Ford." With classic styling and an improved V-8, the '34 has everything going for it.

Ford Motor Company
Ford

have the slightly sportier 2-door sedan.

Ford lost over $70 million in 1932 (due in large part to the late introduction of the car), despite the engineering breakthrough of the V-8, and started into the annual model change syndrome that became characteristic of American manufacturers. The '32 was the first Ford whose body lasted only one year. A totally new car was designed for 1933, based on the successful lines of the smaller Model Y built in the Dagenham, England, Ford plant in 1932. The wheelbase was longer, the fenders dropping down to meet below the laid-back grille like a streamlined snowplow, the bodies were bigger, the bumpers lost the heavy ribbing of '32 and had drop centers, and for the first time Ford had skirted fenders. The successful V-8 engine was further improved with aluminum heads of higher compression, raising the advertised horsepower from 65 to 75, and this was mounted in an all-new frame. The familiar Ford suspension was still there, but the frame was beefier and had a sturdy X-type center crossmember. The design was beautiful, the engine about the healthiest you could buy (Fords won most of the important stock car road races in '33-'34), and despite another bad delay in introduction time (Feb. '33), sales were up 44% over the disaster of the year before.

Many running production changes were made during the '33 model year, sometimes making it a difficult choice to restore authentically. Ford thankfully retained the styling of the Model 40 for another year, with slight improvements that have made the '34 Ford as sought after today as the '32. Basically, the changes were small but significant. The grille didn't have the slight concavity of the '33, so the grille bars were straight, and this made the front end perfect. Other changes included straight louvers in the hood side panels, two painted hood handles on each side instead of one plated handle, and some dash and hubcap changes. An improved intake manifold and carburetor boosted the engine's horsepower again, up to 85, insuring the Ford V-8's continuing rave reviews among young people, race drivers, law enforcement officers, and even law breakers.

Most of the body styles covered under 1932, and their relative collectability, apply equally to the Model 40 ('33-'34), with a few notable exceptions. The 4-cylinder cars were gone by '34, and there were no '33 or '34 convertible sedans. The other models run in about the same order of popu-

1. A banner year for Ford sales, and a good year for a first restoration, is 1935. This Cabriolet differs from a true roadster in that it has fixed windshield posts and roll-up windows. Still a very desirable model.

2. One of the all-time favorite Ford years is the '36, represented here by the classic phaeton, with accessory Spyder hubcaps. Parts are expensive for the '36, and in some ways (such as alignment of the front sheetmetal) tougher to restore than the '32-'34.

3. The first Fords without a canvas roof insert were introduced in 1937. Other features included Zephyr-styled grille and headlights in the fender rather than on. This was also the first year for the two-piece windshield and the little 60 hp V-8 engine.

4. Low production in most models makes the '38 a rare one, though most collector's don't like the front end looks. A convertible like this would make a good restoration investment.

larity as '32. The '33's are generally rarer than an equivalent model of '34, due to the late introduction and consequently lower production, but the subtle improvements in styling for '34 have made them more desirable to most collectors. Personally, this author finds the '34 roadster the most beautiful Ford *ever* built (despite owning a '32), but the debate will probably rage between the '32, '34 and '36 enthusiasts as long as people collect Fords. Like the '32's, the Model 40's are expensive to restore, not only because most any body style is highly sought after today, but also because most of your fellow collectors will sell you parts only when paid for with the equivalent weight of platinum, gold, or other precious metal. Parts for '33's aren't any easier to come by. One interesting final note on a truly special interest Model '40, the so-called skirtless '33's. These had no lower skirt to the front or rear fenders, plus some unusual deviations in the rear bumper brackets and the rear of the body. This was originally assumed to be strictly a one-off prototype, but at least four such cars, all sedans, have turned up in the past several years, to the amazement of most Ford "experts." It's not known how many may have been built like this in early '33, but if you find one in a barn somewhere, don't hesitate on the purchase, it's one of the rarest Fords we can think of. Another milestone year for Ford was 1935. The bodies were restyled again, and the chassis had some major improvements this time. Mr. Ford had restricted his engineers to the transverse-leaf-spring concept, but they managed to soften the ride by lengthening the spring base, mounting the front spring out ahead of the front axle and allowing them to move the engine forward in the chassis for more interior room. New cross-arm steering had less bump-steer, too. This time the doors were hinged in front, as were most of the competition, since the front-opening Model 40 doors had taken on the nickname of "suicide doors," alluding to the comical, if not downright dangerous possibilities of the door opening while driving at anything over 30 mph. Ford finally beat back the competition (Chevrolet) in 1935, a feat that the company would fail to duplicate for another 24 years! Almost every manufacturer had a good sales year in '35, and it was obvious that America was pulling itself out of the depression by its bootstraps—or whatever.

While the changes in the new 1935 (Model 48) Ford evidently appealed greatly to the public at the time, it hasn't been favored with similar affection by most collectors today. Perhaps it is the grille that they don't like, or that the next year's offerings just appealed so much better. Whatever the reason for their relative lack of popularity to some, the Model 48 is definitely worth going after, and because so many were made, they make a good choice for your first Ford restoration because parts cars and parts aren't in great demand yet. As far as the special interest models are concerned, the body styles we've talked about so far for the other years of the V-8 are still in the same order of priority. Two exceptions in '35 are the convertible sedan and the Victoria. The convertible sedan was back among the Ford offerings after a two-year absence, only 4234 were built, and it is one of the best-looking '35's to be found. The Victoria is somewhat of a question mark. One knowledgeable Ford historian claims 235 were built, another historian claims none were built due to the sloping back of the tudor sedan not lending itself to a restyling into a distinctive Victoria body style. In any case, if you come across one, rest assured that it is truly a rare bird, since no Victoria's were offered after 1935.

Although not quite the sales year for Ford that '35 had been, 1936 has become another landmark year for Ford enthusiasts. The 16 body styles offered by Ford was more than the competitors could boast of, and despite some of the antiquated brake and suspension problems Ford forced his engineers to retain, the Model 68's were some of the most beautiful Fords ever. Although the basic body wasn't changed greatly from '35, the front end had been streamlined with a beautiful new grille and front fenders. The horns were mounted underneath the sheetmetal for the first time instead of exposed, and the welded-spoke wire wheel was gone forever. From then on, all Fords would be equipped with steel disc wheels, in an effort to shave some unsprung weight so that the buggy-sprung Fords could even stay in contention with Chevrolet and Plymouth in the smoothness department. While the new wheels don't seem today to have the *dash* or nostalgia of the earlier Kelsey-Hayes wires, Ford offered as an accessory the Spyder hubcaps, which along with the trim ring covered the whole wheel with brightwork. Such hubcaps are popular accessories today.

Cars and parts for the Model 68 are expensive and hard to come by today. The roadsters, phaetons, sedan deliveries, convertible sedans and station wagons are still the most desirable body styles, with a few additions. The new Club Cabriolet introduced that year was produced in low numbers (4616) and would only be produced for one year more. Only half as many of the three-window coupes were built in '36 (21,446) as the year before, and although still built in some substantial numbers, this was to be the last year for this attractive Ford body style. As is the case for the '32's and '34's, restoration of the '36 Ford is usually a high-dollar proposition, due to the scarcity of parts created by their overwhelming popularity.

The introduction in 1936 of the Lincoln-Zephyr, designed to fill the price gap between the low-price Fords and the high-dollar regular Lincolns, caused quite a stir with its revolutionary streamlined styling and frameless, unitized construction. Some of the influence of the new car was seen also in the new Ford line for '37, the Model 78. Basically the same car mechanically, it had an all-new body whose most striking features were the new Zephyr-inspired grille and "alligator" hood (no side panels). The Model 78 was the first of the many Fords to come with the headlights designed *into* the fenders, rather than mounted *on* the fenders in round buckets. Gone also in '37 was the upholstered insert in the roof; the new Ford had a new all-steel roof. Another feature not to be seen on Fords for many years to come was the familiar flat, one-piece windshield; from '37 right up until the Fifties, there was a new two-piece, V'd windshield. There were mechanical im-

Ford Motor Company
Ford

provements, such as the easier cable operated brakes (still mechanical), better steering, and even a new engine was introduced. The "baby flathead" or V-8 60, was the regular 85-hp V-8 scaled down from 221 cu. ins. to 136 cu. ins. Designed as an economy engine, the 60-hp engine had a willingness to rev up and go, but never had the torque for comfortable highway cruising. Unique though the engine was, it was offered only in the lesser of the standard body styles (the trusty 85 hp being optional in those cars); you won't find this engine in the more collectable Fords of '37. The perennially favorite body style of enthusiasts, the roadster, took a last painful breath in '37 and finally died. Less than 1250 Model 78 roadsters were built. They weren't *real* open cars in the traditional Ford sense, they had fixed windshields, and were in fact just convertible bodies, but with steel caps welded on over standard doors. Underneath the cap, they had all the provisions for roll-up window mechanisms just like the rest of the line. Though not perhaps as pretty as the previous Ford open cars, the Model 78's are nevertheless quite rare today. Don't be searching for any '37 3-window coupes, though, there weren't any, alas. A new body style introduced in that year which is interesting is the Club Coupe, with a little more room behind the front seat. Overall, the Model 78 is a good one for the modern collector. In the past, when the earlier Fords were more available to the average collector, the '37 had always been passed up for some reason, maybe they didn't like the front end. In any case, they are still around in good numbers although they have become more sought after since the earlier cars have gotten so scarce now.

Ford and the other manufacturers had a poor year in 1938, with most companies down 50% or more from their previous years' sales. The additional bad news for the Ford enthusiast is that the Model 81-A was to be the one year that goes against the axiom that, of the early Ford V-8's, "the even-yeared cars are the best-looking and most desirable." To most enthusiasts, besides being the worst sales year since the disaster of 1932, '38 was the biggest ugly duckling Ford ever produced. The new bodies of the Model 81-A marked the first time that Ford would have different bodies for the standard and deluxe versions. The standard '38 had basically '37 sheetmetal, but with a new, painted grille with long horizontal slats that blended right into the hood side louvers, in effect creating a longer front end look that was designed to alleviate the "short" look of the '37. On the deluxe models, the grille stopped about midfender, the front fenders were slightly different, and a stylized V-8 emblem fit into the plain sheetmetal section between the grille and hood louvers.

The heart-shaped grille of the Model 81-A has never endeared it to collectors, although we must add that there are those who do favor them. The lack of popularity of this model has certain advantages today, in that parts are relatively inexpensive for the '38's, as well as complete cars. They could be a good bet for a first restoration, since they will undoubtedly increase in value through the years as unrestored early Fords get harder to find. Also remember that the recession year meant that all of the '38 body styles were made in less numbers than in any other year. The Model 81-A phaeton is truly scarce today, since only 1169 were built, and of course, no roadsters at all were made. The convertible sedan and other folding-top cars were all made in low numbers that will make them desirable in the future.

The Model 91-A introduced in November 1938, has always been a Ford fan's sweetheart. The '39 continued the '38's lead in making distinct differences between the standard and deluxe versions. In fact, the '39 standard models had the general front end and grille design of the '38 *deluxe* models, while the '39 deluxe cars had an all-new front end. The new front end was similar to the newly-introduced line of Mercury cars, except that the Ford Deluxes had vertical grille bars while the Mercury's were horizontal. Like the Mercury, the new deluxe hood was larger than ever before, with the side panels part of the hood (the '39 Standards still retained the alligator-type hood). The headlights on the deluxe were now mounted further apart, so that they were pleasantly centered in the crown of the very-rounded fenders.

The 91-A marked many important changes for Ford. After the dismal

1. While the '39 Standard models are similar to the '38's, the Deluxe '39 had a tasteful new front end. Alas, this was to be the last year for the rumbleseat convertible like this one.

2. Many of the '38-'40 model changes are confusing due to overlapping use of grilles, such as this '40 Standard, which has a grille that in the year before was the Deluxe version!

3. The 1940 Ford, here in its Deluxe form, is a perennial favorite of the Ford collector. Don't overlook the commercial models of early Fords, like this sedan-delivery. They were low in production every year, and much-sought after by Ford enthusiasts today.

4. The '41's were a whole new body with little of the roundness of the previous cars. The running board was gradually receding, and the fat Ford era was beginning. These are a good choice for a first Ford restoration.

50/SPECIAL INTEREST AMERICAN CARS

sales of the year before, Edsel finally convinced his father to let the engineers work up a hydraulic brake system so their cars would not remain so technologically backward compared to the GM and Chrysler cars, which had featured hydraulic brakes for years and used this to great sales advantage over Ford during the Thirties. The new Ford hydraulics worked great, and make the '39 the first of the truly practical Fords for restoration today. If you plan to use your restored early Ford in everyday driving among modern cars, you're advised to seek out one of the '39 (or later) variety, for their excellent braking without the constant and fussy adjustments of the mechanicals. The transmission was also improved in the '39 for easier shifting with a shorter throw. The engine is easier to work on (in the deluxe models) because the side panels raise with the hood.

Deluxe versions of the Model 91-A, especially the open cars, are the most collectable today. This was to be the last year for both the rumbleseat (in the Convertible Coupe) and the Convertible Sedan. The phaeton was gone, as were the Club Coupe and Convertible Club Coupe.

The 1940 Model 01-A was another winner seemingly designed to foster daydreams in high school classrooms during the Fifties, and satisfy collectors today. Long a favorite model for hot rodders and restorers alike, the '40 Ford had a new front end, sealed-beam headlights, softer front spring with a sway bar, improved ventilation, and a column shift. Although Chevrolet and Plymouth sales gained a proportionately higher share of the '40 market than in '39, Ford was also up in sales, despite the styling and ride/handling advances these other companies (with unrestricted engineering departments) had over the Ford.

The Standard models for '40 retained basically the same grille as the '39 Deluxes, with the '40 Deluxes having the new narrower, die-cast and plated grille flanked by body-color louvered panels on either side. Most desirable of the Model 01-A's are the Convertible Coupe, the "opera" coupe with its single-passenger auxiliary rear seat (fold-out), and of course the perennially collectable sedan deliveries and station wagons. The convertible, we might add, had a vacuum-operated "automatic" top mechanism, the first of its kind for Ford cars.

The 1940 Ford marked the end of the era when all Fords looked as fast, sturdy and dependable as they were; a new era began with the totally restyled '41's. This was to be the beginning of the "Fat Ford" period, in which Ford attempted to catch up for many lost years in the styling race. The Ford chassis, kept at a 112-in. wheelbase since 1933, was finally stretched another two inches for the new, larger bodies. The lineup now included Super Deluxe models in addition to the Standard and Deluxe models, and for the first time in Ford history, a 6-cyl. model was offered. The Convertible Club Coupe was offered only in the Super Deluxe line, and now was equipped with an *electric* automatic top mechanism. The new bodies featured more nearly square, flat fenders, a narrow grille flanked by grille panels set into the fenders, new bumpers and trim, and parking lights set on top of the front fenders. The familiar running boards were almost gone, being covered by an extension on the bottom of the doors and quarter panels that made their usefulness apparent only when the door was opened.

The fat, un-traditional looking '41 Ford has not been very popular among collectors, until recent years when the earlier cars became expensive to obtain and restore. The Ford was beginning to look like the other cars on the market, and in the rush for new styling, production assembly methods came along that make restoring these "later" cars more difficult than any before. The front fenders, for instance, are not one-piece but bolted together from three separate sheetmetal sections. Parts are not expensive for them, but you rarely see 'em at swap meets.

The '42 Ford, although not substantially different from the '41 except for a more unitized and attractive grille, is truly a special interest year. All car manufacturers were down to very low production levels, because the beginning of concerted involvement in producing war materials displaced car production early in the '42 model year. The attack on Pearl Harbor came less than three months after most new models had been introduced, and Ford's entire '42 production numbered only 43,407 units, with Chevrolet only slightly higher.

Because of this low production, any '42 Ford can be rightly considered as of special interest due to their rarity alone, however there are specialties *within* the year, too. Some 1800 Army staff officers of WW II received a "sedan, four-door, one each, color OD," which was a '42 Ford equipped with blackout lights front and rear. These are especially rare today, and the perfect collector car for the military history buff. Just three days before Pearl, the OPA (Office of Price Administration) gave the automobile industry 15 days to use up all existing stock of

3

4

Ford Motor Company
Ford

plated trim, so after this period all the cars produced were delivered without chrome; all the trim was painted body color, including the bumpers. These cars are also highly sought-after today. Chances are if you do find a '42 model today, it will be quite complete, but needed parts will be hard to find.

After turning over the nationwide facilities of the many Ford plants to wartime production of tanks, trucks, gliders, engines, Jeeps, and building B-24 bombers at the incredible final rate of one an hour at Willow Run, Ford Motor Company was ready in mid-1945 to resume production of civilian automobiles. The first of the "new" 1946 Fords rolled off the assembly line July 3, 1945, ready to be snapped up by a car-starved public denied new automobiles for the period of the war. Even though basically just a warmed-over '42 with a new grille and trim changes, the '46's sold well, aided by the fact that Ford was the first manufacturer to get back into postwar production of civilian cars. The '46 was still available with the 100-hp flathead V-8 or the 90-hp six, and in nine body styles. The six Super Deluxe models were the wagon, convertible coupe, coupe, sedan-coupe, and 2-and 4-door sedans, while Deluxe styles included just the sedans and the basic coupe. Late in 1946, the famous Ford Sportsman convertible was introduced. A limited production version, it was a cross between the body of a convertible coupe and a wood station wagon, with leather upholstery, power top, and even power windows. Only 3392 of the beauties were sold, and very few of the wood-bodied open cars have survived today, making it one of the hardest Fords to restore, but also one of the most desirable.

With the public buying cars as fast as they could be produced by the manufacturers, Ford and the other auto makers weren't about to jump into production of a whole new car, so the '47 was basically just a facelifted '46. The changes included different medallions and bumper guards, wider trim, lower moldings, and the rub strip along the bottom of the front fenders now ran the full length from behind the wheel opening to the "running board" molding. Upholstery, interior trim, and paint color changes were also made on a running basis.

Although rumors had persisted around Dearborn that a totally new Ford with independent front suspension would be introduced for 1948, many production problems delayed the project to the point that very minor changes were made to the '47 models and with title changes they were sold as '48's. Despite the many minor differences, both running and yearly changes, the '46-'48 Fords are much the same, and as representatives of the end of an era of Ford history they will always be remembered. Good convertible models are starting to bring higher prices now, and parts for these postwar cars are still not too hard to find. Also the NOS (New Old Stock) parts are certainly a lot more plentiful than for any of the pre-war cars.

When the new Ford car that had been so talked about was finally introduced as the '49 model in mid-1948, it marked the definite end of the "traditional" Ford and the beginning of a whole new chapter in the company's history. Most of the leading makes introduced new body styles in '49 that were totally different from what had come before, but none so overwhelmingly new as the '49 Ford. When the

1. Any of the '42 Fords are quite collectable today, due to the very low production. Especially rare, and desirable to military buffs, are the chromeless military "blackout" models.

2. Only a little over 3000 of these late '46 Sportsman convertibles were made. Like the highly-desirable woodie station wagons, these cars are hard to restore, but truly special-interest. The rest of the '46 Ford line were minor modifications of the '42 body, and the '47 and '48 are 98% the same.

3. The 1949 Ford was probably the most "new" car since the Model A, with independent suspension, Hotchkiss rear end, and styling ahead of the competition. These cars are going up in value now, and practical enough to drive everyday in modern traffic.

public invaded the Waldorf in New York on June 10, 1948, to view the '49's, they saw the first Ford passenger car in the company's history that didn't have the "buggy spring" transverse springs front and rear. With new and aggressive leadership under young Henry Ford II, the company was finally ready to match their engineering strides and annual improvements with those of any other company. The all-new, slab-sided Ford body was one of the first Fords to be truly contemporary in styling with it's competitors, and in fact ahead of many. About the only characteristic of earlier Fords still continued was the venerable flathead V-8, unchanged in basic design since introduced in 1932. Under the new '49 body was a totally new chassis, up front the good ol' beam front axle and transverse spring were replaced by modern independent front suspension with coil springs and upper and lower A-arms. The traditional torque tube was also relegated to history with the '49's introduction. Now Ford had a regular driveshaft (with U-joints and all) hooked to a sturdy Hotchkiss-drive rear end with two semi-elliptic springs. The difference in ride at that time to experienced Ford owners must have seemed like night and day, and the car handled, too.

These milestone improvements in the car made for a 53% improvement in sales for '49, which shows the public's response to the first "new" Ford in a long time. Its place in collectors' circles is only slightly different. Since it was such a radical change in body and chassis, many traditional Ford enthusiasts still don't consider the '49-'51 Fords as "classic." In fact the Early Ford Club of America has only recently (within the past two years) accepted the '46-'48 variety. Nevertheless, the car still has the same flathead engine, and represents such a dramatic departure in Ford history that it should grow in value over the years. Already, some of these cars (especially the convertibles) are bringing good prices.

The '50 and '51 Fords were not much altered from the '49, having basically just different grilles and trim, but that didn't stop Ford from advertising "50 improvements in the '50 Ford." Among these changes were a quieter engine, improved steering with better "touch," a sway bar for better cornering, and optional Borg-Warner overdrive. The '51 still wasn't enough of a change to ruin a good thing (Ford sales for 1950, with basically the same cars as '49 were up to 1,187,122), but it did have a lower hood, a two-spinner grille, larger headlight rims, new park lights, and a large chrome bezel-fin around the taillights. Although some interior areas were skimped on due to the shortage of materials created by the Korean War, the interior was one of the nicest ever in a Ford.

Introduced in '51, for you collectors out there, was the no-post Victoria, which was in keeping with the then-current Detroit fad of the "hardtop with a convertible look." It had some 3000 sq. ins. of glass, and like the other Fords of '51, it could be ordered with a choice of five solid colors or five two-tone combinations. Also introduced in '51, if you're the lazy-type restorer, was the Ford-O-Matic; Ford Division's first automatic transmission. It was about time they met this consumer demand, because by late 1951, some 44% of Detroit passenger cars were being fitted with the "slush-box." The convertibles, Victorias and station wagons are the cars of '49-'51 to be looking for, and most of the raw materials for your restoration are still dirt cheap. They make an eminently practical car to drive in everyday use. We might add that the '49 station wagon was the first Ford wagon to have a steel top, and steel doors and quarter panels with the wood being bolted onto the steel from outside.

It was time for a new car again in '52, although the '51 had still been a good seller. The new car was described by *Motor Trend* Magazine as the "most radically-changed car of 1952." The new body was the first of the "finny" Fords, having the basic embryo of a developing tailfin in the round "tube" that ran along the top of the rear quarters and ended in the round taillights. The body also wasn't as slab-sided as the earlier cars, with a bubble on the lower part of the rear quarter that suggested a long fender skirt was molded on. These were the first Fords to have curved, one-piece windshields and rear glass, and the gas filler was now discreetly hidden behind the rear license plate. The "triple-spinner" grille and choice of 22 colors on the new Ford must have pleased car-buyers, because the public reaction was good enough that Chevrolet scrapped their "backroom" design for '53 to go back to the drawing board for a new one. Among Ford's mechanical changes were a stiffer ride and better handling, 10 more horsepower in the V-8 (increased compression), overhead "swinging" clutch and brake pedals (as introduced on the Lincoln-Mercury line first), and the biggest change of all, an all-new, overhead-valve six-cylinder engine. The new six was rugged, quiet, and actually faster than the V-8 in road tests. Automotive writers were impressed with Ford's first overhead engine, even if it was a six. It's interesting to note that even as early as this (1952), there was quite a list of options and dealer-installed accessories. Among the Ford accessories for '52 were: overdrive, Ford-O-Matic, a govenor, fender skirts, ornaments, electric clock, light-

2

3

Ford Motor Company
Ford

ed inside mirror, engine compartment light, and a choice of two radios.

The '53's don't leave us a great deal to talk about that's especially new, since the body was virtually unchanged, but the public ate them up to the tune of 1,184,187 cars. The ride was improved over the year before, and rubber snubbers added to the front suspension made "bottoming out" a lot easier to take. A new grille, taillights, and some chrome changes took care of the cosmetics. In late '53, Master-Guide power steering became available for $125 (only when ordered with the V-8); the first time this modern amenity had been offered on a Ford. Though '53 is not distinguished by its appearance or sweeping mechanical innovations, it will nevertheless occupy a special place for Ford collectors of the present and future. It was after all, the 50th anniversary model of the Ford Motor Company (as the steering wheel's horn button reminds you), and it was to be the *last* of the flathead V-8-powered Fords.

We include '54 with the two previous years here, only because it shares the same body basic, but in terms of collecting, it represents the end of a long era of V-8 Fords, and begins an entirely new period, that of the overheads. The new overhead V-8 engine (expected two years before but delayed several times due to war shortages, steel strikes and labor problems) and other changes made the '54 a new car despite the same body. *Motor Trend* Magazine described it as being "as much better than the '53 as the '49 had been compared to the '48," which is pretty strong stuff. The new engine had 130 hp (with only 7.2:1 compression), and proved to be both quieter and more powerful than any of the flatheads had been. It also had valve rotators, something we now think of as strictly a recent development for low-lead engines. The Thriftmaster Six was still continued, and proved to be an excellent seller, due in part to its having won the Mobilgas Economy Run the year before. The lineup was now composed of three levels, Mainline, Customline, and the more expensive Crestline, all with the new five-cross-member frame and ball-joint front suspension adapted from the '52 Lincoln. The new dash design of the '54 Ford featured what *Motor Trend* Magazine described as "54's most legible speedometer," which was the Astra-Dial. Built up in a half-shell pod above the regular dash, it had a transparent panel that let light in from the front to help make it more readable. Ford was definitely into the option routine in full swing, usually adapting luxuries from the Lincoln-Mercury line to the Fords a year later. The '54 list offered the new Midland power brake booster, and power windows were optional in the Crestline series.

By far the most collectable special interest Ford of 1954 was the brand-new Skyliner with the plexiglass roof insert. The front half of the Victoria roof was fitted with a tinted plexiglass panel for moongazing or whatever, and a special headliner, carried in a pouch near the glove box, could be unrolled and snapped into place (inside the car) to screen out the sun on hot days when the greenhouse effect was too great. The Skyliner was part of what Ford's ad agency (J. Walter Thompson), had called "motivation engineering," which is Madison Avenue talk for a sales gimmick. It was intended that each dealer have a Skyliner to get people into the showrooms, where they would realize that they either couldn't afford or didn't want the Skyliner, and could then of course be talked into buying a more practical Ford. It's not known exactly how many were built in '54, but it was a neat car, ahead of its time perhaps, and considered quite rare today. Supposedly, you could also order some kind of transparent roof insert for a convertible, but we don't see how that could work, and have never seen a car to substantiate it.

A period of rapid change for Ford and the automobile industry as a whole started in 1955. The horsepower race was in full swing, *six* brand new V-8 engines were introduced by Detroit in '55, and most companies came out with major restyling. Ford's introduction of their overhead V-8 the year before had evidently had its effect on the other manufacturers. Ford's offerings had many changes, including the new body with a Thunderbird-inspired grille. The fins grew a little, along

1. Although improved in details, the '50 Ford continued the winning form of the '49. The wagons like this one were the first Ford woodies with a steel roof and wood-over-steel sides.

2. The cosmetic, model-year changes made for 1951 aren't appreciated by every Ford buff, but Victoria hardtops and convertibles are still collectable.

3. The '54's shared the same body as the two previous years, but it was the first Ford offered with an ohv V-8 engine, and the first year for the very-collectable, limited-production Skyliner hardtop with the plexiglass roof insert. Through the windshield here you can see the Astra-Dial speedo.

4. Our personal vote for the most attractive post-war Ford goes to the new-for-'55 Crown Victoria, with the brightwork over the roof. The 1955 Skyliner is a twin, but for plexiglass.

COURTESY AUTOMOTIVE CLASSICS, SANTA MONICA

with the taillights, and there were now 13 solid colors offered and 36 (count 'em!) possible two-tone combos. This was also the first Ford with a true wraparound windshield.

Mechanically, the '55 chassis was all-new, including revalved shocks and tubeless tires, a revamped automatic, new front end engineering, rear springs mounted *outboard* of the frame and fitted with rubber snubbers, and beefed up engines. The six was now 120 hp, and the "regular V-8" was up to 162 hp, while the Fairlane models offered the "Thunderbird V-8" with 8.5:1 compression, 4-bbl. carb, dual exhausts, and 182 hp. The new V-8 had grown to 272 cu. ins. and featured redesigned heads, pistons, manifolds, and had been increased in both bore and stroke. If you were the lazy type, but still liked to keep your car well-maintained, you could have opted for the new Multi-Luber (dealer-installed), which at the touch of a button would lubricate the whole chassis except for the driveshaft.

New to the Fairlane Victoria line, and of definite special interest, was the top-of-the-line Crown Victoria, which had a stylish crome band that went from the door-post area up and over the top, making the top kind of like the semi-landau tops we see today on customized luxury cars. These are really good looking cars, and you could still buy a Skyliner Fairlane, too.

A very minor facelift for '56 saw different park lights, and slightly different trim and deck treatment on the '55 body. Incongruous as it may seem today, Ford became very safety-conscious in '56, while still in the midst of the Detroit horsepower race. On the one hand, the Fairlane engine was now up to 202 hp with 8.4:1 compression (with Ford-O-Matic), yet such features as padded dash, padded visors, dished steering wheel, seat belts, and improved brakes were introduced that same year and Ford advertising made much of the safety aspects. The convertible, Victoria, Crown Victoria, and the plastic-topped Skyliner are still the collectable '56's. This was to be the last year for the Skyliners, due to a lack of public response, and only 608 were made. Find one today if you can, and hang onto it!

It may seem unlikely to group the '57 through '59 Fords when you consider their three different body styles, but we have a reason for this under the coverage of this book. There's only one truly special interest Ford left to talk about, the retractable hardtop, and it was made for these three years only. The new line of Fords for '57 featured a completely new body and chassis, a 245-hp, 312-cu.-in. Thunderbird Special engine was added to the option list, and the car was really into the mid-Fifties styling with long, sweeping fins, sculptured sides, and 14-in. tires. The car was now nine inches longer than the previous year, and four inches lower. Though many Ford fans still find the '57 styling attractive, we would consider the retractable as the only one *of special interest*.

Hinted at in a show car many years before, the idea of a hardtop convertible had intrigued Detroit for some time, and Ford reportedly worked on their design for five years before bringing it out in '57. It was three inches longer overall than the regular Fairlane (the retractable was not offered in the less expensive lines), the new top was over three inches shorter, and the trunk opened the opposite of normal. Within 60 seconds from the time the owner pushed the dash button, the complicated *melange* of motors, servos, relays, switches, and circuit breakers went into scheduled action and raised the trunk lid, tucked under the front edge of the roof, and neatly stowed it in the trunk, which then closed. This neat hat trick had cost Ford some 20 million dollars to produce, and it was five months after the December 1956 preview of the prototype that the first Skyliner retractable was delivered, to the White House. Despite the Skyliner being the most expensive Ford (only $400 less than a Thunderbird), over 20,000 of them were built in the short first year. Another interesting vehicle introduced in '57, while we hesitate to classify it as a true special interest car, is the Ranchero. Basically a 2-door station wagon with the rear two-thirds of the roof removed, the crossing of a utilitarian pickup truck with passenger car comfort and styling was the first really nice blending of good looks and high practicality. Over 20,000 of these un-trucky trucks were built the first year, and they have been selling like gangbusters ever since.

The year 1958 brought out new bodies for the Ford line, along with new and larger engines (the 332 and 352 that stood as the basis for many larger engines to come), and finally a *3-speed* automatic transmission, the Cruise-O-Matic we know and love today. The next year was both a high point and a low point for Ford enthusiasts. While Ford did finally beat arch-rival Chevrolet in sales, 1959 has to go down as the *worst* year for Ford styling. The best things about '58 and '59, as we mentioned about '57, are the Rancheros and Skyliners. Skyliner retract-

SPECIAL INTEREST AMERICAN CARS/55

Ford Motor Company
Ford

able production was down to 14,713 in '58, and the Rancheros down to only 9950, making the '58 the rarest of that breed. The Skyliner was finally down to 12,915 in 1959, as public response to a car with such limited luggage space was dying, and no convertible hardtop would again be built by Ford or any other company. The Ranchero, on the other hand, had found a small but enthusiastic market, and production had crept up to 14,169. This was enough to keep the project alive at Ford. Unlike Chevrolet (who had to tool up many special body panels for their first El Camino, which didn't go over), Ford had been able to share so many parts with its 2-door wagon that they could afford to produce the Ranchero even in the limited numbers we've discussed here. It's unfortunate that we must close our discussion of special interest Fords with two such uninspired styling years as '58 and '59, but we Ford fans can always point with pride to the Ranchero, the first "civilized truck," and the Skyliner retractable, the first (and last) convertible-hardtop.

After reviewing the pros and cons of various special interest Fords, you would do well to sit down and plan your total budget for the restoration on paper before ever selecting a car. How much you have to spend may very well determine which cars you can afford to acquire and restore. One of the general rules to guide you would be the earlier the year, the more costly the car. Most of the pre-1935 Fords are going to be expensive to acquire original parts for, and the '32 especially so. Your best bet if you pick one of the most popular early Fords, such as '32, '34, '36 or '40, is to bide your time until you can find a very *complete* example at a price you can afford. The open cars are particularly expensive today because of the high mortality rate, and high popularity among modern restorers. If you still *must* have a '32 roadster for example, then your best bet would be in locating one yourself from a private party. Normally the best place to hunt for a car is through the pages of the several antique car monthly publications that feature classified advertisements, but if it's truly a special interest Ford you're after, the high prices published for good examples may frustrate your search. Better to find one yourself in a farmer's barn somewhere, so that you can get it cheaply enough that you still have a budget for restoration. Depending on how much of the restoration work you plan to do yourself, completing the car can be twice as expensive as buying the basic car to start with. Even if you're highly skilled, such things as chrome plating and upholstery usually have to be done by well-paid professionals. Take all of these factors into your budgetary consideration before picking a car. It may be, especially if this is to be your first restoration, that one of the less popular '37's or '38's is a more practical first choice.

The year of the car also has a lot to do with how complicated it's going to be to work on. The pre-1935 Fords are the easiest to work on, with simple front sheetmetal and readily-accessible engine compartments, but like anything else, the question is relative to your skills. Most early Ford restorers would shudder at the thought of restoring as "late" a car as a '49 convertible, and yet if you've had any experience working on *present*-day cars, with their extra plumbing and all, then restoring even a '59 would seem relatively easy.

The accessories on your present or potential Ford can have a bearing on its future value, as certain ones add special interest. Even if you showed up at a V-8 meet with a rare '32 roadster, only to find that there were a dozen others there too, the fact that yours was the only one there with an origi-

1. Introduced in 1957, the Skyliner retractable hardtop (the see-through top died the year before) had taken five years of development. Remarkable cars, the retractables of '57-'59 are definitely of special interest.

2. Surprisingly, all the switches, relays, motors and over 600 feet of extra wire that make the retractable top work are usually trouble-free. As happened to the plexi-Skyliners, the retractables died in '59 due to a lack of public interest, making them that much more desirable to collectors now.

3. The only other special-interest Ford of the late Fifties is the first of the Rancheros, from '57-'59 (this is a '58). Another Ford better idea that caught Chevy with their lineup lacking, the Rancheros were sturdy, good-looking and wholly practical.

nal dealer-installed radio (extremely rare today) would still make yours a standout. There are some restorers who would rather restore a car equipped just as they found it; there are many others who like to improve the value and fun of theirs by adding those accessories which were available in that year. Since the accessories seem so desirable today, many are high-priced when you can find them, and there's been more than one restoration started because the owner found a rare accessory and then set out to find the car to restore around it! Some of the more popular accessories for Fords include: spotlights, fog lamps, and radios (all years from '32 up); accessory gauges ('32-'34); inside rear-view mirrors with windup clocks ('32-'36); trunk racks ('32-'37); accessory trunks, fitted to sedan bodies, ('33-'34); stainless steel Spyder hubcaps, ('36-'39); fender skirts ('37-'42); backup lamps ('41-'48); bumper wing-tips ('40-'48); and Columbia two-speed rear axles (up to '48). If you find any of these on your car when you purchase it, great, if not, you can always hunt them down and add them to your car during the restoration.

Unfortunately, the most collectible early Fords to restorers have over the years found the same popularity with the hot rod set. Hot rodding has its place, too, and there have always been enough good Fords around for both the hot rod and the restoration set, but there are some things you should watch out for, since you plan to restore your Ford. A lot of good Fords were horribly butchered up in the backyards during the '40's, '50's and '60's, and evidence of any work done with an oxy-acetylene torch or "smoke wrench" can mean that the Ford you found is going to be harder to restore than you thought. When the rash of overhead V-8's came into prominence in the '50's, many of them found new homes in the engine compartments of early Fords, and some cutting of the chassis or firewall or alterations to the steering gear were usually made. Even if the Ford you're considering appears to have the correct flathead engine in place now, you might check around to be sure that some early Olds, Chevy, or Buick didn't reside there at one time, too. Look for cut-and-welded firewalls (these can be replaced with a stocker from a parts car, but it's a lot of work), cut up flooring, non-stock steering gear, non-stock rear ends adapted to the original springs, and holes cut in crossmembers for dual exhaust pipes. It often takes some real skill to correct some of these faults so that the completed restoration looks original in all respects. Such is the price we pay for Ford popularity.

In light of all we've discussed, you should now be convinced to rush out in search of a '39 convertible sedan or a '59 Skyliner. If you hesitate because you don't know where to start, don't worry. There are more clubs for Fords than for any other make, and there are more people in these clubs than in other-make clubs. Your first move should be to join the club that covers the Ford you're looking for, and the other members can be of invaluable help to you with technical information, parts, and even cars. Fords have the advantage in their numbers when it comes to restoration, too, in that there are more cars and used and reproduction parts available, plus the technical knowledge required for restoration is well researched and available.

Lest you are still in doubt, we might add that not only is the hard work of restoration rewarded instantly on that first day you drive out of the garage in your special interest Ford, the whole process between searching and driving is also more fun than being lifeguard in a Japanese bath house.

2

3

Ford Motor Company

Lincoln/Continental

Pinnacle of FoMoCo achievement

The year, 1930, marked the beginning of the era of the "big classics." From Ford's takeover of the Lincoln in 1922, much was done with the Lincoln and with automobile manufacture in general. It was during this time that 4-wheel brakes and laminated safety glass came on the scene. During the Twenties and Thirties body builders and designers in excess of 23 companies vied for the business of building Lincoln bodies.

Lincoln was still in its infancy, and by 1930, with the Depression coming on, the luxury car buyers would be more demanding and limited. Lincoln would have to meet these demands. Bodies would have to be lower, longer, and more streamlined. This was the first year that one color would be used on the entire body, taking in the fenders that had always been black. A significant change in wheel size was made also, from 32x6.75 to 20x7. This allowed for the lower designs that would take place in the Thirties.

The highly successful L series was dropped at the end of the model year in 1930, to be replaced by the K series that was introduced in 1929. It was this body that lent itself to the designers at the drawing board to "sweep" the designs. Again, the wheel size was reduced to 19 ins., and an 18-in. size was made optional. Lincoln introduced an improved V-8 with this series K and, while the V-8 would be dropped in 1929, the K series would stay with Lincoln through 1940.

The KB and the KA series were introduced in 1932. The KB, considered by many to be the "most classic" of all Lincolns, would sport a new V-12 engine of 150 hp on a wheelbase of 145 ins., and would be the more expensive model. The new KA would be less expensive with a V-8 engine of 125 hp on a 136-in. wheelbase. It is interesting to note that prices in 1932 ran from $4600 to $7400 and weights were 5315 to 5950 lbs. The more weight, the higher the price.

After June 1933, all Lincolns would have skirted fenders and the classic lines of the earlier Lincolns would take on a streamlined look. Rounded, slanted radiator shells and flowing fender lines would be the design of the day. The KB series that had come out only a year earlier was dropped at the end of the model year. The KA was dropped the following year in 1934 and only the K would remain as the basic big Lincoln until its end in 1939. The "new" model received another new engine, of V-12 design, that developed 150 hp. From 1933 through 1948, Lincolns were powered only by V-12's and the V-8 would not return until the 1949 models.

In 1934 Edsel Ford commissioned a

Tjaarda-designed, Briggs-built "small" Lincoln, with unitized body on a wheelbase of 125 ins. This design would lead to the Zephyr that was introduced in November of 1935 as a 1936 year model. The era of the "big classics" was rapidly coming to a close. The K series was available in two wheelbases, a 145 in. that was designated the series 321 K model and the 136 in. that was the 541 K model for 1935. It was in this year that the "big" line received major restyling.

Including Zephyr, there were 18 body styles offered by Lincoln in 1936 and sales were now up to 15,449 for the calendar year. The Museum of Modern Art, in 1951, awarded the original Zephyr the distinction of being the "First Successfully Designed Streamlined Car in America." It was the Zephyr that was the forerunner of Edsel's dream car, the Continental that would make an appearance in 1939. The K series for 1937 received a major restyling that was to be its basic design until its demise in 1939. The K remained virtually the same in 1938, too, with the exception of a new rear body treatment. Beginning in 1937, the headlights were molded into the fender, rather than being a separate unit.

The last 4-door convertible was built in 1939 and would not appear again until 1961. It was in this year, 1939, that the first Continental appeared. It was a prototype built expressly for Edsel Ford. It is believed that Edsel was so pleased with the design of the car that he had two more built, for his sons. It is also believed, that one of these cars has been found by a Lincoln Continental Owners Club member and will be undergoing restoration. Edsel drove the first prototype to Florida, on vacation, where he was besieged with orders. On returning to the Ford fac-

1. Depression-era Lincolns were highly favored by law enforcement agencies and can drive today's collectors to a frenzy. Professional restoration work is expensive though and anything less is unthinkable.

2. 1932 Lincoln V-8 with Murray body displays dual sidemounts and modern (oh, shame) mirrors. This Model KA is not as sought-after as the classic KB's, so it's apt to be more reasonable in cost.

3. This superb '33 Lincoln dual-cowl phaeton is owned by A.T. Heinsbergen and is beautifully prepared for show.

4. Available to the enthusiast of more than moderate means, but quite reasonable compared to the true classics, this '36 K Series Judkins Berline Lincoln can still turn a few heads at the yacht club.

5. This very special Lincoln V-12 convertible of 1939 vintage weighs 9300 lbs. after addition of armor plate and bullet-proof glass in 1942. President Franklin D. Roosevelt, for whom it was built, nicknamed it "Sunshine Special."

Ford Motor Company
Lincoln/Continental

tory, management was convinced to put the car into production and toward the end of the year, production convertibles began leaving the plant.

The series K sales were lagging and only 120 of the "big" Lincolns were produced for the year. They were identical to the 1938 models and the 120 cars were sold throughout 1939 and 1940. The 1940 differed only in the black on the emblems and the car was available only on special order. This also was the first year for hydraulic brakes.

From the first Presidential Limousine ordered in 1923 by Calvin Coolidge, the White House has always used Lincolns. Another Limousine was ordered in 1939 and in 1942 it got updated trim and was used until 1950.

The Continental in 1940 was still a part of the Zephyr line. It was this car that was destined to be called the "World's Most Perfectly Styled Auto" and would make all Continentals recognized by the Classic Car Club as classics. The car cost $2783 and weighed in at 3850 lbs. There were 54 cabriolets and 350 coupes built this year. And, sadly, this was the last year for the "big" Lincolns.

No significant changes were made to the Lincoln line in 1941, with the exception of the Continental gaining its own name identification, separate from the Zephyr.

The very beautiful lines of the Continental were changed in 1942 to a more massive and bulky body. The grille was now slanted and wide use of stainless steel was apparent. An increasing amount of plastic was used on the interior trim and dash as the impending war caused a shortage of steel.

No cars were produced for the public during 1943, 1944, and 1945. During these years the black market would raise the prices considerably on a Lincoln, many times twice its original cost.

The 1946, 1947, and 1948 Continentals were all identical to the 1942 with only minor changes such as hood ornaments and hubcaps. The grille treatment was different on the 1942. The Lincoln line, too, was very similar. Only the rear was modified slightly and the bottom of the body had a flare whereas the Continental had flat sides.

In 1948 the Continental was dropped, due to high production costs. The great Continental died, not to be resumed again until 1956-57 and 1969-70-71 with a "classic" body design that was recognized as such almost instantly. The name "Continental" would appear again on all the luxury versions and then still later on all Lincolns, confusing the entire Continental name.

An all-new styling change took place with all auto manufacturers (as well as Lincoln) in 1949. Lincoln produced two wheelbases: the Lincoln at 121 ins., and the Cosmopolitan at 125 ins. Lincoln was now back to the V-8, not used since 1932. The Cosmopolitan was available in a fastback version for its only time. The 1950 models were essentially the same as the 1949. A new Presidential limousine was also produced to replace an aging 1939 model.

Relatively unchanged were the 1951 models. The rear fenders received minor sheet metal change. The deep-set headlamps, part of the 1949 styling,

1

would be eliminated at the end of the model year.

In 1952, the Capri succeeded the Cosmopolitan in being the top-of-the-line Lincoln.

The now famous Pan-American (Mexican) Road Race Lincolns of 1953 and 1954 swept the field in being the first four to finish in both 1952 and 1953. The 1952 race was actually won with 1953 model cars since they had been released early for the race. In 1954 the first two cars across the line were Lincolns and this was the last year of the Carrera Panamericana. Perhaps as an indirect result of these races Lincoln sales in 1952 jumped to 31,992 units for the calendar year production.

In 1953, production again jumped, this time to 41,962. However, 1954 production dropped to a disappointing low of 35,733. The 1952 body style was completely new and was used basically unchanged throughout 1955.

October 1955 saw the introduction of the very beautiful and classic Continental Mark II, the most talked about auto in 1955. At $10,000 and 5190 lbs.,

1. Unusual view reveals much about this 1939 Continental convertible.

2. 1940 Continental coupe exhibited minor trim changes over previous year. Push-button doors caused quite a stir among youngsters.

3. The 1942 Continental is a rare one today and reveals altered styling that would last (but not improve) through 1948, Continental's final year.

4. Only more massive chrome pieces separate the 1948 from the prewar 1942 model. This was last of production for Continentals due to high production costs, low sales.

5. The 1950 Lincoln 6-passenger coupe had the same styling as the Cosmopolitan series. Was carried over from 1949 and lasted through 1951.

SPECIAL INTEREST AMERICAN CARS/61

Lincoln/Continental

it was the most expensive and heaviest car in the industry. From the outset it was destined to become a classic and today prices commanded for the Mark II in restored or original condition are reaching up to $30,000! There were only 3012 of these beauties built before their demise in early 1957. There was only one sanctioned cabriolet built by FoMoCo and this was done by Derham. In 1965, the Classic Car Club of America bestowed upon the Mark II the distinction of being a classic. Death came to the Mark II for several reasons, high production costs not the least of them.

The Cosmopolitan series was dropped from the line with the 1956 models, and now the Premiere took over, above the Capri. Quad headlamps were used this year for the first time and the line received a complete facelift. So beautiful were the Lincolns that, again, the Industrial Designers Institute gave an award to the Premiere Hardtop Sport Coupe for "Excellence in Automotive Design."

A totally new body change was made in 1958 with the use of unit body construction (no frames, just like the first Zephyrs). The new car had a length of 229 ins., the longest 6-passenger production car in the world. Its engine was also the largest in any production car, being 430 cu. ins. Sadly, the name Continental Mark III was attached to the top-of-the-line Lincolns. The original Continentals of 1939 through 1948 were tagged "Mark I" and there were the Mark II's of 1956 and 1957, and now the Mark III of 1958. While it may be an impressive auto, it was not a Continental Mark by design features. The following year the Continental Mark IV appeared with little change. If this were not enough to bastardize the name, all Lincolns from 1961 on would be known as Lincoln Continentals. Then to throughly confuse the issue in later years, the once again "classic" lines would appear as a Mark III in the 1969 through 1971 models.

The 1958 had three models, the Pre-

1. The 1952 Lincoln styling continued through 1955 with virtually no sheetmetal alterations of any consequence. Powerful V-8 made quite a name for itself in racing circles.

2. 1955 Lincoln Capri hardtop coupe merits special attention by enthusiasts of special interest cars.

3. Premiere convertible was the second most beautiful (and collectable) Lincoln in 1956.

4. The most beautiful Lincoln in 1956 was the Continental Mark II. Current prices seem to favor oil well owners, but restorable examples can still be found at fairly decent prices if you're patient.

5. The 1957 Premiere convertible showed off the latest styling rage in a pair of swoopy tail fins. Quad headlights were another style gimmick.

6. The Continental Mark III debuted in 1958, but it was not the equal of the Mark II which was phased out in early '57. And, things got worse!

miere, Capri and the Mark III. Very few differences were apparent among the three series, the Mark III having an operable rear-slanted window and the lack of chrome trim on the sides. This was the last year for the Capri. Sales were drastically low this year with a production run of 25,871 units, while the previous year's run was 41,123, and the 1956 total had been 50,323. Lincoln was in trouble but corrections were not forthcoming until 1961 when the very graceful 4-door convertible would return to bail Lincoln out.

Little changes were seen in the styling department in 1959 and 1960 and sales were getting lower. By 1960 the production run bottomed out at 20,683 units. Sales had not been so low since 1938 when it was 19,751, and in contrast, 1940 sales had been 79,040. And so ends the struggling years of Lincoln and its great classics of the Thirties and Forties.

With the exception of the "classic" Continentals, which are generally too costly for the enthusiast of average means, Lincoln produced nothing of really special interest during the Fifties. But any Fifties Lincoln fanatic willing to ignore the time, effort, and money required to restore one of this vintage, would probably do better to lavish the investment on a convertible or limousine. Remember, though, that regardless of the year or body style selected, a Lincoln is a Lincoln!

Ford Motor Company

Lincoln-Zephyr

Status at a reasonable price

A gentle, mild breeze is a thing of transitory beauty. It is the west wind personified. It passes quickly over the land. It is simple. It is smooth in bearing. But it is gone without warning; passing out of sight as easily as it came. A Lincoln-Zephyr was true to its name, for it was all of those things. Perhaps it—and not the Edsel—should have been reintroduced in 1958. The country needed a smooth wind then. There was too much chrome; American buyers found their incentive nearly choked-off, for lack of things new.

In 1936, there was a similar situation: revolt at the Chrysler Airflow, yet fatigue at Detroit's array of blunt designs. It was time for a cleansing breeze of design change. The Lincoln-Zephyr provided that option.

By 1935, Ford Motor Company reports showed an increasing awareness that there were marketing gaps between the low-priced Ford and the expensive "K" Lincoln. And the concern was that there was literally no concerted arm of the manufacturing giant capable of filling the marketing gap. This may have been a blessing in disguise, of course, as witnessed the $250 million FoMoCo debacle on the 1958-60 Edsel.

Nevertheless, the inspiration of John Tjaarda, who worked for the Briggs Manufacturing Co., resulted in a far-out, neatly streamlined, unit-bodied 4-door sedan. A rear-engined prototype, with a front end design of great similarity to the present Volkswagen Beetle, appeared at the 1934 Chicago World's Fair.

Actually, the Zephyr may never have been born if somewhat strained feelings hadn't erupted between Ford and the Briggs Body Company. Ford's production chief, Charles Sorenson, felt that Briggs was concentrating on its Chrysler business, and not enough on Ford's. The big Lincolns were not selling well, and Ford had been counting on Briggs to finish up many more Lincoln bodies. Briggs, not to lose Ford's business, hired two men: John Tjaarda, and Howard Bonbright, the latter a personal friend of Edsel Ford's. The idea was simple: Tjaarda would design a new car to fill Ford's marketing void, and Bonbright would sell it, so Briggs, of course, could do all the bodywork. As Tjaarda was to write later: "I was to work on designs for Briggs customers, and for Ford in particular... The assignment was just what the doctor had prescribed for both Briggs and myself." Edsel, who quickly saw the designs, was able to convince his father in a relatively short time.

A built-up Ford V-8 was to go in the rear of the new car, but problems were too sticky for those involved, and Frank Johnson, Lincoln's chief engineer, produced a small V-12, based on the Ford V-8 block. With public opinion on the side of a front-engine location, it remained for Ford's styling head, E.T. Gregorie, to design the 1936 Zephyr's prow-like hood and cowl.

There were similarities in design, particularly in the slope of the rear deck between the Zephyr and the Chrysler Airflow. This can be partly explained, since Tjaarda, at Briggs, was working on both designs. But the Zephyr, with its smaller, cleaner lines, had represented the beautifully timed introduction of a V-12, then at its zenith in popularity, and until then unaffordable to most people. Finally, the Lincoln-Zephyr made money; the Airflow did not. The V-12 of the Zephyr became the best selling V-12 of all time. In only its second year of production (1937), the Lincoln-Zephyr was selling some 25,186 cars. It was an excellent start, since by 1939, a Model 96-C Convertible Coupe would cost $1748 f.o.b. Dearborn—for that time not exactly a cheap figure.

The V-12 was essentially a stretched L-head V-8, with a little more torque to put against more than 900 lbs. of extra body weight. Whereas the 1939 Ford Deluxe Convertible Coupe cost $765 from the factory and weighed some 2840 lbs., the Lincoln-Zephyr for the same year and model, cost $1748 and weighed 3790 lbs. The 85-hp Ford V-8 came from 221 cu. ins., while the Zephyr's 110 hp needed 267.3 cu. ins., not the ultimate efficiency from the 46 extra cubes. Worse, the Ford V-8 was getting its max reading at some 3600 rpm, but the Lincoln-Zephyr needed *3900* rpm to do the same job. In 1936, even though the V-12 had the '39's same 110 hp, this was to mean that the Zephyr's engine had a higher rpm for peak horsepower than any engine in America, except the blown Lycoming GH, as used in the Auburn and the similarly supercharged Graham 110. That the Lincoln-Zephyr could reach 90 mph, was more a tribute to its body design than to its engine.

The anemic performance, over what it might well have been, was to plague the Zephyr for its entire 7-year life; and even into 1948, as the '46 to '48

Lincolns were but warmed-over Zephyrs, with only the Zephyr name dropped.

In 1940 the Zephyr V-12 was bored out by an-eighth, keeping the same stroke. Factory figures show a drastic climb in remaining specs, the end result being a gain by 10 hp at 300 less rpm. One must remember that four stock versions of the V-12 were eventually produced, and both the '40 and '41 engines wound up in '40 through '48 bodies, as well as the more powerful 1942 offering. The differences didn't amount to much. All the Zephyr V-12's but the first one, had improved manifolding, and could produce peak horsepower at 3600 rpm.

The 1936 V-12 had a 2.75-in. bore and a 3.75-in. stroke. With 267.3 ins. of displacement, the engine put out 110 hp. At a taxable horsepower rating of 36.3, the same engine was kept through 1939. In 1940, the specs were: Bore—2.875 ins; Stroke—3.750 ins, and 292 cu. ins., with a taxable horsepower rating of 39.6. The 1941 engine was the same, but in 1942, the V-12 was bored out another 1/16-in. to 2.9375

1. Lincoln production zoomed from some 5500 to more than 22,000 in the new Zephyr's first year—1936.

2. By 1938, the Lincoln-Zephyr's teardrop styling became well-known on the Nation's highways.

3. The 1939 4-door Convertible Sedan is one of the most desirable of all special interest cars.

4. In 1940, Zephyr reached its zenith of sensitive styling, becoming a precursor to the classic Continental.

5. "Like a silent leaf," was a favored theme for the 1941 Zephyr. Big and graceful, there were 17,756 built.

6. A '42 Zephyr V-12—like all before and following—had shallow ribs on bearing caps, and thin casting around valve seats. Lugging, and slipshod re-boring, produced fatal results. Thin water jackets negated 30-qt. radiator.

ins. This, with the same stroke, produced 130 hp at 3600 rpm from 306 cu. ins. It would last in the marque until the big flathead V-8 rolled off the lines with the 1949 models. By then, of course, it was a different ballgame.

It must be said, that the Lincoln-Zephyr V-12 has suffered from almost universal bad publicity regarding anemia and lack of durability. As the former owner of a '46 Lincoln V-12, and a confidant in the lives and fortunes of three earlier Zephyrs, the writer can say that such a tag was not necessarily true.

All H-series Lincoln V-12 engines (built from 1936 to '47) suffered from inadequate crankcase ventilation. The oil pump was too small for the mass that it was asked to cool. If you own one, or have recently bought, it must be known that a V-12 cannot be lugged, ever. Keep the revs up. Use second gear or second overdrive in the city. You must take the same care with oil as a VW owner must take: frequent changes, the highest quality money can buy. Install an electric fuel pump. Hot temperatures caused chronic vapor lock problems. Keep your piston rings within prescribed tolerances. The four main bearings on the long Zephyr crank were good, but not good enough. Crankshaft inserts should be replaced, along with rings, or the long crank is liable to get eggshaped. Rings and inserts are inexpensive, compared to engine rebuilding. It's not fair for an "egg-headed owner" to blame reliability problems on the "damn V-12 engine." Some V-12's have now passed the 300,000 mile mark, but by far the largest percentage died before they reached 10% of that figure, and were long ago relegated to the ash heap.

Like the V-12, the trademark Ford-built "buggy springs," or long transverse leafs, were nearly without peer if they were treated right. In the heavier Zephyr, the suspension meant more up and down oscillations, more sensitivity to crosswinds, more high-speed uncontrollability than should have been the case.

On the plus side, the cooling system was enormous—averaging some 27 quarts—the 3-speed manual transmission may have been the most durable ever built.

The Zephyr's handsome bodies are desirable as a special interest car—every one. The 4-door convertible sedans of the late Thirties are the best, followed by the convertible coupes, the 2-door's next, with 4-door's bringing up the rear.

The Zephyr was comfortable to ride in, peaceful and flowing of design, yet nearly rattle-free, due to its channel-section and bridge-truss body. Its passing is not to be imbued with unnecessary drama, but rather was a shared fate to cars that were not so much machines, but dreams. ◆

Ford Motor Company
Mercury
But it might have been Cyclops or even Ford-Falcon.

Rome's god of commerce, symbol of dependability, eloquence, skill and speed—Mercury, winged messenger of the gods. It was the fourth of November, 1938, and Edsel Ford, Henry's son and then president of Ford Motor Co., introduced to the public a new medium-priced car which he called Mercury, for he felt that it possessed many of these same godly qualities. Edsel had chosen the name from a list of 104 suggestions that included such alternates as: the Groundflight, Pharaoh 8, the Gazelle, Ford-Falcon and the Cyclops.

The story of Mercury actually begins in the early '30's when Ford executives realized that they would have to enter the popular medium-price field in order to compete with the successful Pontiacs and Dodges. Their first effort came in 1933 when a Lincoln-Zephyr was displayed as a dream car at the Chicago World's Fair. Public reaction must have been good for just two years later, 1936 Zephyrs were rolling off the assembly line. Unfortunately, the Zephyr remained as just a dream car for too many Americans. The car *was* a medium-priced car but *high* medium-price and so, volume sales weren't very great. However, there were many Ford owners ready to move up to a bigger, higher quality car—but the V-12 Zephyr was a bit too expensive for them. Ford had nothing to fill their needs although GM and Chrysler did, so many defected to the low medium-priced Pontiacs and Dodges. Of course, this affected Ford's total sales and was a contributing factor in Ford again losing their first-place standing to the people over at Chevrolet.

To help increase sales, Ford introduced a new, more economical V-8 for 1937, a mini-flathead (134 cu. ins.) with just 60 hp and advertised as the "Thrifty Sixty." Production plans for two additional cars were initiated at this time, one smaller and one larger than the standard Deluxe Ford. The smaller car was never built for this country because its projected production costs were not much lower than those for the existing models. However, plans for the larger car were developed further and eventually materialized in 1938 as the Mercury prototype.

The Mercury's engine preceded the car by one year and had resulted from Edsel Ford's interest in racing supported by Ford's reputation as a fast car. In 1935, the standard Ford V-8 was powered by an 85-hp, 220-cu.-in. flathead. It had a reputation as being quite fast; in fact, the infamous John Dillinger once sent a letter to Henry Ford in which he said: "I can make any car take a Ford's dust." At the time, a good many police cars were big Buick Straight 8's, Packards or Lincolns, but Dillinger's stolen Fords usually managed to outrun them.

Edsel was proud of the Ford's performance but he wanted to see it improved. The engineering department accepted the challenge and came up with 10 more horsepower from the 85-hp. 220-cu.-in. engine. This was accomplished by removing the steel cylinder sleeves of the Ford 220-cu.-in. V-8, thereby automatically increasing the bore by 1/8 in. and the displacement to 239 cu. in. The larger bore necessitated a heavier cast alloy steel crankshaft and larger diameter crankpins.

Despite the close resemblance between the Mercury and the Ford, the Mercury enjoyed its own frame. The legs of the central X-member extended the full length of the side rails for added stiffness and the wheelbase was 116 ins., four more than Ford's.

Consumer demand for a low medium-priced Ford was high, plans for such a car had been initiated, and a bigger engine was now available. The time was right for an affordable Ford combining the styling and comfort of a Zephyr with the performance of a bigger V-8. America was definitely ready for Mercury.

America was ready, Ford dealers and executives were screaming for it and so was Edsel but, as expected, old obstinate Henry had to be convinced. Henry Ford had a reputation of being a very stubborn man and reluctant to try anything new. He believed that Ford Motor Co. should consist of only Ford, and any model diversification would be breaking a long company tradition. However, Henry finally gave in to Edsel's better judgment and gave the go-ahead for Mercury production. Winning Henry's confidence was nothing new to Edsel for he is also credited with persuading his father to replace the Model T with the A, and the A with the Ford V-8, and then introducing the Lincoln-Zephyr in '35 and the Continental in '39. Edsel Ford probably deserves to be called the father of the Mercury.

In 1937, Ford finally opened its own styling department and Edsel observed its work closely, for the stylists reported directly to him. Up until that time, styling had been handled by independent body builders such as Briggs and Murray. The Mercury, patterned after the Zephyr, was the department's first project and the first car to be built from a clay model exclusively by Ford stylists.

Edsel and his father also kept a close watch on Mercury engineering and, if Edsel had gotten his way, the '39 Merc would have come equipped with 4-wheel independent suspension. The engineers had already developed the suspension but, unfortunately, traditional Henry vetoed it in favor of the conventional transverse springs. Supervision by father and son resulted in a very thorough development of the new

1. First model year for Mercury was 1939, and the first production car came off the Richmond, Calif. assembly line on Sept. 21, '38. Mercury was a bold move to plug a marketing gap for Ford, and it obviously worked.

2. Though virtually any year or model Mercury built prior to 1948 is today of special interest, the '40 convertible sedan is definitely collectable and worth almost any investment cost to restore it to like-new condition. This was the only year the rare model was produced.

3,4. The '40 facelifting was on the subtle side. But for the unknowing the second year for Mercury (4) saw the addition of "Eight" to the hood emblem, the use of sealed-beam headlights, a more flowing grille which necessitated new hood design, non-fluted bumpers, and other minor differences.

Ford Motor Company

Mercury

Mercury. In the summer of '38, two prototypes were built, fully tested and improved upon before approval was given for assemblyline production. The tests included prolonged high-speed driving on Ford's new test track. The cars performed well and showed great endurance by covering 600 miles in just 8 hours. The future looked bright for Mercury.

Ford gave birth to its very first production Mercury on September 21, 1938. Birthplace was the Richmond, Calif., assembly plant. On October 8, regular Mercury production began at Ford factories in Chicago, Louisville, Kansas City and Edgewater. This same day, Edsel Ford announced that the company would have a new medium-priced car. On the 24th of October, the Mercury was revealed to the press at the Ford previews in Dearborn and on November 4, they were displayed and sold to the public at dealerships across the country. The Mercury had arrived and, with its introduction, Ford Motor Co. won representation in 95% of the 1939 price market.

The Mercury 8 was available in four body styles—a 2-door ($894), a 2-door Sport Convertible ($994) with automatic top and leather seats, a 4-door Town Sedan ($934), and the 2-door Sedan Coupe ($934) that featured stainless steel window frames and a thin center post suggestive of later-day hardtops.

Even with the relatively narrow range of body types, these gave the Ford buyer a chance to move up a notch in every configuration except the convertible sedan and station wagon.

Ford stylists designed the new Mercury to be unique from the rest of the Ford line; however, it takes more than a quick glance to distinguish its front end from that of the Ford Deluxe. Exterior differences were confined to rear fender treatment (Merc fenders were less bulbous and wheel cut-outs were semi-enclosed), the grille (horizontal bars instead of Ford's vertical), taillights (barrel-shaped instead of Ford teardrop), hubcaps, hood emblem and trim.

The big changes are to be found inside and underneath the car. Interior comfort and roominess were emphasized by the use of extra-deep seat cushions and wide, 3-person seats made possible by making the body wider than the Ford. Mercury was to be a notch above the Ford Deluxe, a bit more luxurious, and it was, with standard armrests on the sedans, and equipment that included an electric rather than a wind-up clock, front and rear ashtrays, a trip odometer, combination ignition switch and steering wheel lock, tools, locking glove compartment, rustless steel trim bands for the wheels, bumper guards, and cowl- rather than roof-mounted windshield wipers. Options included a heater and defroster, seat covers, a custom luggage set, whitewalls and a push-button radio with remote-control antenna. Beneath the hood was Merc's 95-hp V-8 which joined Cadillac and Ford as being one of only three V-8's in the industry.

The Motor magazine, a British publication, road-tested the '39 Mercury and in their March 21, 1939 issue, said: "Careful attention has been paid to the question of shock absorbing and its effect upon stability, with the result that it was found possible to take sweeping open curves at considerably higher speeds than one would quite reasonably expect to do so, except with a low-built model of the more sporting

68/SPECIAL INTEREST AMERICAN CARS

variety." Twenty-five years later, in 1963, *Motor Trend* compared a '39 4-door Town Sedan with a brand-new '64 Mercury and said: "In pure handling situations, the old transverse springing and solid front axle of the early Merc offered a bit more roll resistance, but that was all.... I always thought my old '39 was a real handler. Now I think I'm lucky I survived it." Yes, they sure don't build them like they used to.

Perfectly content with mechanical brakes, Henry could see no reason for changing to hydraulics but, after continuous prodding by Edsel and others, he finally gave his approval and all Fords for '39 received the new brakes.

Only one engine and transmission was available in '39—the 95-hp flathead coupled to a floor-mounted non-synchro-first 3-speed. The standard rear end ratio was 3.54:1 but several others were offered. *Motor Trend's* 1963 silver anniversary test of the '39 (with 30,000 original miles) produced a 0-to-60 time of 19.5 secs. and the ¼-mile in 21.7 secs. at 62 mph. Top speed was 85 mph at 3800 rpm although the speedometer read 90. Recommended redline for the Merc was 4800 rpm.

Within three months after its introduction, the Mercury ranked as the ninth best selling car in the automotive industry—at a time when nameplates were much more numerous. To meet the great demand, additional Ford plants had to be opened to Mercury assembly lines here and in other countries, including Canada, Mexico, Brazil, France, Holland and Denmark. There were 60,214 of the 1939 models built in the U.S. and 10,621 in foreign factories, and 75 of these were assembled in the Copenhagen plant (1941) while under Nazi occupation.

Despite the encouragement that Mercury showed by the end of the '39 model year, acceptance back in late '38 was slow. Only 6835 units had been delivered by calendar year's end, meaning a Mercury serialized lower than this constitutes a rare find.

Virtually any of the four body styles available for '39 today constitute a Special Interest car; in fact, the same can be said of any year or body style all the way through the '40's. The cars were built in large enough numbers—with a single exception in '46 that will be detailed later—that most are not in the "impossible to find" category right now. Trading at swap meets is brisk in Mercurys, and individual parts—used or NOS—probably run a close second to Ford in availability.

It was October, 1939 and Ford announced its new '40 Mercury. The car was almost identical in appearance to the '39, the only differences being a slightly larger, more flared grille, wider, chrome headlight bezels, sealed beams, rectangular rather than barrel-shaped taillights, and slightly different trim including the addition of the word Eight to the Mercury nameplate. Mechanical changes were minor—the most obvious was repositioning the gearshift lever to the steering column. A new model, a 4-door Convertible sedan, was added to the 1940 line.

It is difficult to pinpoint today the reason why as expensive (to tool) a body style as the convertible sedan was offered for just one model year, but the fact remains that only 979 (out of a total '40 production run of some 80,000 Mercurys) units were built. Even though the average Mercury buyer was probably somewhat more affluent than his Ford counterpart, perhaps the stigma of having to replace the sizable convertible top about every three years discouraged otherwise potential buyers. The convertible sedan would place high as a Special Interest prewar Mercury.

True running boards were not evident on the all-new '41 Mercurys, a sign that the industry was leaning toward wider, all-enveloping bodies.

1,2. Changes were also effected 'round back, too. First-year '39's used an odd barrel-shaped taillight (1), but the '40 adopted a design more in keeping with the car's styling (2).

3. First major overhaul in styling came with the '41's. Gone was the bulbous-looking appearance and the car was more Ford-like.

4. Rear end design for '41 was more in keeping with contemporary cars of the period. Rear fenders flowed aft to fair into the body instead of the earlier, down-flowing rear fender line.

5. High on list of Mercury rarities is the '42 club convertible. The short production run of '42's, which ended Feb. 10th, found only 22,816 cars built. The approaching war period saw sedans built in large quantity, while luxury models like this were at an ebb.

Ford Motor Company
Mercury

However, the opened door revealed a narrow footboard hidden by the sharp outward curve of the lower door panel. Replacing the convertible sedan in the '41 body style lineup was the first Mercury station wagon. Drastic restyling occured at Mercury for '41—perhaps another clue why the slow-selling convertible sedan was discontinued the previous year—and the wheelbase grew 2 ins. to 118 ins. A back-seatless business coupe was new this year, bringing total body offerings to six. Over 91,000 Mercurys went to buyers this year, up 12,000 from '40 and a third more than in the introductory year. An innovation for Mercury (and for Ford) was a unique front fender design to ease repair and replacement work. Instead of a single, large stamping, the front fender was designed as bolt-together segments. Thus, just a part of a fender would need replacement in the event of severe damage. This lucky development also eases the restorer's woes today for these segments are not hard to find at flea markets.

"The Aviation Idea in an Automobile, More Power per Pound!" This was the '42 Mercury with new "sky ride" and Liquamatic Drive. Introduced in October, 1941, the new Mercury continued with the same models and was lower, larger and restyled with a look that was to continue through 1948. The grille was massive and consisted of upper and lower sections. Parking lights were obvious with placement above the grille. Horsepower increased to 100 and wider tires, "slower-motion" springs and thicker body mounts resulted in a "sky ride"— for "the ease and smoothness of flight itself." Frame design was improved to permit a reduction in overall height without sacrificing head or leg room. Liquamatic Drive, Mercury's new automatic transmission, was introduced for '42. The United States entered World War II on December 7th and Mercury production stopped on February 10, 1942. Only 22,816 of the 42's had been built before that date and only 774 had Liquamatic Drive, which was not continued after the war. Larger front wheel cylinders were used for improved braking.

The father of the Mercury, Edsel Ford, died in May of 1943 and Henry Ford II, Edsel's 25-year-old son, took his place as president in September, 1945. Henry I had been getting rather senile and his empire was showing signs of crumbling. FDR was worried that this would jeopardize the production of war material at the Ford plants. Presidential orders were soon given in December of '43 to release Henry II from active duty and with his help, the Ford organization held together and production continued. The organization of the Lincoln-Mercury Division began in October, 1945, and Mercury production resumed November 1, with the '46 models.

The 1946 Mercury continued the '42 body with a slight grille change, different trim and the addition of a very rare wood-bodied convertible called the Sportsman. The business coupe of '41 and '42 had been dropped. At this time, Ford also had a Sportsman but 3473 ('46-'48) were built compared to only 198 Mercs. If you're lucky enough to stumble upon one of the survivors, chances are the wood has weathered beyond recognition. As a result, a '46 Mercury Sportsman in even poor shape will bring top dollar on today's market.

The '47 Mercury, not announced until February, was merely a continuation of the '46 with very minor changes. The Sportsman ran for just

1

one year and did not reappear in 1947. In April, at his Dearborn home, Henry Ford died; he was 83 and his death marked the end of an era. Benson Ford went with Lincoln-Mercury in October and one week later Ford and Lincoln-Mercury sales departments split.

The '46 to '48 Mercurys were basically the same car and, other than its steering wheel lock being eliminated, there were no basic changes for '48. In January of '48, Benson Ford was elected vice-president of Ford Motor Co. and general manager of Lincoln-Mercury.

Singling out a few select Mercurys from the pre-'49 models as being of Special Interest is a fruitless task, for as already noted, any prewar model—and the carried-over '42's which ran through the '48's—is a car worth having. If a parameter of Special Interest is low original production, then the '46 Sportsman (198 units) and the '40 convertible sedan (979) are the rarest. But because their worth today is beyond most enthusiast's purses, a worthwhile acquisition would be the next of the rarities, any club convertible or station wagon. The cost of restoring a basket-case woodie, though, is sky-high; both because of the high price for quality woods and the labor to shape them into the intricate forms required. Available, good-wood wagons, though, are seen so seldom, that a convertible would be the more logical car to seek out for ownership.

The totally new '49 was introduced very early—April, 1948. For the first time, Mercury styling was no longer a copy of Ford. Henry had kept them similar so that parts could be interchanged and money could be saved.

1. The rarest Mercury of them all, the one-year-only '46 Sportsman. Only 198 copies ever saw the light of day. Probable expense of resurrecting a basketcase would be astronomical, but worth every cent.

2. Somewhat more common but still a decided Special Interest car is the more conventional '46 club convertible. Any pre-'48 Mercury open car, for that matter, is certainly a collectable.

3. With the advanced '49's "in the works," design and engineering changes at Mercury were virtually nil in the immediate postwar period. The only immediately apparent difference between '46 (right) and '47 was the latter's abbreviated hood side trim. Further changes between '47 and '48, however, almost defy detection.

4. Styling of the totally new '49's was as bold as the license tag. Nothing was held over from the past except the famous flathead V-8 engine, but displacement was up to 255 ins. from 239 ins. and horsepower rose to a record high of 110. Only 4 models were produced this year and all are sought after, but the convertible and 2-door coupe (in that order) reign supreme as collectables.

SPECIAL INTEREST AMERICAN CARS/71

Ford Motor Company
Mercury

Pennypinching went out with Henry I and, in contrast, Henry II approved a Mercury styling departure from Ford which upgraded the Mercury considerably to the point where it more closely resembled the small Lincoln. In fact, it shared the same body. And, due to its similarity to the Lincoln, people felt they were getting a lot more car for the money and so sales climbed. Sales for all Ford products were good and Ford Motor Co. was back on its financial feet again. Merc topped 300,000 units while the '48 barely reached 47,000.

Model selection dropped from five choices in '48 to four in '49. Available were a 4-door sport sedan, a 6-passenger sport coupe, a 6-passenger convertible, and a steel-bodied, wood paneled 2-door station wagon. Engine size increased from 239 cu. ins. to 255, with a 10-hp raise to 110. Transverse springs were replaced by coils in the front and leaf springs in the rear. A smoother ride resulted. A 3-speed was standard with a 3.9:1 rear axle and, available as an option, was the Touch-O-Matic overdrive and 4.27:1 axle. The '49 Mercury—"longer, lower, wider... its broad-beamed sturdiness is artfully combined with fleetness of line."

Mercury for 1950 received an attractive new instrument panel to replace the rather ugly arrangement of the '49. Other changes were confined to only exterior trim. In January, a lower-price sport coupe was introduced and then in June, the Monterey, a 6-passenger coupe with padded vinyl top, was announced to compete with GM's successful new hardtops. Mercury hardtop production didn't begin until '51 so, with existing tooling facilities, the Monterey was the next best thing. Mercury received national recognition in 1950 by being chosen as the official pace car of the Indy 500.

The '51 Mercury got a slightly different grille, longer rear fenders and an automatic transmission—the Merc-O-Matic. This was the last year for the '49 body style and the last year for sharing bodies with the Lincoln. The Mercury of this era was not very quick; in fact, it wasn't much faster than the '39 model. Horsepower for the '51 engine was increased by two for 112; however, this rating was only 17 hp more than the '39, and overall vehicle weight had increased about 150 lbs. The models for '51 were the standard, deluxe and Monterey 6-passenger coupes, a convertible, a 4-door sport sedan and a station wagon.

The year 1952 brought a complete restyling of the Mercury with a body

1. Many Mercury advocates prefer the facelifted '50's over the preceding year. Chrome trim was beginning to appear in abundance and Mercury's grille had grown to incorporate the parking lights.

2. The grille grew even larger for '51, and extended rear fenders cause a bulbous look, probably why this last year of the particular bodyshell, while collectable, is not as high on the collector's list as the '49's and '50's.

3. Mercury's last use of the deservingly retired flathead V-8 was in '53, and the '54's bowed with an all-new ohv V-8 of 256 cu. ins; and any model of either of these could qualify as a milestone car. Highlight of the line-up for '54, though, is the Sun Valley see-through roof insert option.

4. Mercury sought to bring back the term phaeton with this '57 Montclair Phaeton, a 4-door hardtop. But it hardly embodies the folding top, glassless doors of the true configuration. This one has the Mercury-built and extremely rare long fender skirts. This is a good example of how an accessory or option can upgrade an otherwise barely collectable car.

5. For $192 over the cost of a standard '57 Montclair Phaeton, one could get the Turnpike Cruiser option; oval steering wheel, antenna-mounting pods above the windshield posts, a wrap-over windshield, interior air ducts above the windshield, power-retracting rear window, and a host of standard equipment goodies that were only options on the lower-level cars. The model was announced in mid-'57, but didn't sell well; is desirable now.

6. It is hardly appropriate to show a '64 model in this book—a Mercury Park Lane—but we couldn't resist the temptation to compare the 25th anniversary car to the first Mercury.

that was once again shared with Ford. A one-piece curved windshield, suspended instead of through-the-floor pedals, a compression increase from 6.8:1 to 7.2, a rise in horsepower to 125, and the addition of two models (Mercury's first hardtops) completed the big news for '52. The '52 was 5 ins. shorter (at 212 ins.) than its predecessor, and 3 ins. narrower (74 ins.) but continued at 63 ins. high with 118 ins. of wheelbase. Weight dropped about 100 lbs. (3450) but performance increased only slightly. An ohv V-8 was expected for '52 but material and tooling were not set up in time. However, a functional hood scoop was designed to improve cooling of the proposed engine and when it was found that the lower hood wouldn't close on the high air cleaner of the flathead, engineers went ahead and used the scoop but in a closed form.

Other than adding a one-piece rear window, Mercury for 1953 was basically unchanged from the '52 although power brakes, power steering and 4-way power seats were offered for the first time as options.

Though some Mercury diehards insist that the '52 and upward models are worth preservation, none seem to qualify for the Special Interest category. It was a period of boxiness and, unlike Ford which innovated during the '50's, there were no really unique Mercurys. If the collector is a flathead V-8 lover, though, he might seek out a '53 Merc as the last year that this tried-and-true powerplant was produced. The ohv 256-cu.-in. V-8 introduced for '54 is of no special significance, and though many were coaxed to run well in speed competition, the box-stock '54 - '59 Mercury is not particularly noteworthy in the performance department. Mercury didn't innovate as did the sister Ford Division, what with its Thunderbird 2-seater, the retractable hardtop and others, but a relatively rare '54 option in the Monterey series was a see-through roof insert officially tagged as a Sun Valley Coupe. Because the plastic used for the insert tended to discolor and craze after a few hot-sun years, it might be difficult today to find one with a clearly transparent panel, but by frequenting swap meets that specialize in FoMoCo parts, the restorer may be able to find a NOS unit. ■

3

4

5

6

Ford Motor Company

Thunderbird

A deathless design for personalized transportation

To auto lovers around the world, the word "Thunderbird" means only one thing: A racy high-styled model built by the Ford Motor Co. between the years of 1955 and 1957. And well it should.

In order to meet the demands of the American public, Ford launched plans to build a 2-seat sports model to compete with the Chevrolet Corvette for the sales dollar. The Thunderbird was the brainchild of Ford executive Lewis Crusoe.

Ideas for the Thunderbird were shaped in the mind of Crusoe during the 1951 Paris Auto Show where several European sports models were on display including the Jaguar XK-120, the newly introduced Spanish Pegaso and other exotic machines of the day. In 1951, Crusoe indicated that Ford should build a 2-seat "sports car."

It should be noted that, at this time, Ford was in a period of corporate reorganization, following World War II. Business was troublesome for the industrial giant and Crusoe was one of several key executives with experience with other auto makers to be lured over to the Ford team. Crusoe had retired in 1944, just 50 years old, from General Motors where he was assistant treasurer. Known within the industry as a tough, hard businessman with an eye for the future, Crusoe was exactly the type of man Ford wanted. In February of 1949, he was tapped to head the newly formed Ford Division of the Ford Motor Co.

Attending the Paris show in 1951 with Crusoe was automotive stylist George Walker. A consultant with Ford, it was Walker's firm that designed the 1949 Ford which put the company on the road to sales recovery. Walker, not known to think in small terms, was to be one of the guiding styling forces behind the original Thunderbird. Crusoe expressed his interest in a 2-seat model to Walker who indicated his firm had such a design in the works. In short, upon returning to his hotel, Walker called his Detroit colleagues, informed them of Crusoe's remarks and told them to get busy.

Following the Paris show, Crusoe returned to his Dearborn, Mich., office and quickly learned that George Walker was, indeed, a man of his word. A design for a 2-seat car was in the works. The seed was planted.

The winter of 1952 was the first time top Ford management had a chance to sit down and map out with Crusoe the future of the Ford Division. Ford management had several important decisions to make including what to do with various company divisions and especially, a determination of the future of Lincoln-Mercury. Crusoe, no one to sit idly by, had his own team run a market research project and expand on designs of a 2-seater. To further illustrate his business mettle, Crusoe embarked on a program to retain top stylists and engineers from other auto makers. It worked and many of the best of the motor city were retained, especially to work on the infant Thunderbird (at this time the project was unnamed) concept.

Crusoe instructed his styling team to make paper models of 2-seat cars, making sure they knew full well that the finished machine would have to incorporate many standard parts and be of a reasonable price. One of the first suggestions, quickly discarded, was to make a shortened model of a standard Ford.

Ford informed all of the professional staff in 1952 that a new model was wanted for 1955 introduction. It normally takes 3 or more years to get this accomplished. However, there was a snag in the line and it was Ford's number one rival, Chevrolet.

During the '50's, the General Motors Motorama, a traveling show of current cars along with experimental models traveled all over the U.S. and to some foreign nations. GM would always say the cars displayed were those of the future. Sometimes this was so, but sometimes not. The Ford camp learned that Chevrolet was to unveil the first Corvette at their 1953 Motorama. Crusoe surmised that this was not just another styling exercise, but that the Corvette would be for real. He was correct.

With the introduction of the Corvette, even though said to be an experimental model at the GM Motorama, the Ford project got underway in short order. Crusoe and his crew were ready to attack and in February 1953, the word was given by top management to start the 2-seat project with all possible speed.

At this point in time, one of the standard practices of auto makers was to build replica models from styling studio drawings. Because of the nature of the 2-seat project, this time-consuming process was eliminated. Instead, designers made full-size drawings, mounted them and made them look as close as possible to the actual finished product. This was accomplished through photos and scenic backdrops. This method, while not standard at the time, proved workable and saved Ford precious time which would be needed to overcome production problems.

Also, from the full-size drawings, clay models were taking shape displaying various design concepts. The clay models were of actual size and showed the proposed car as it would appear on the showroom floor. Paint and chrome were included in the clay mockup which featured two design ideas. One was on the driver's side and another was seen on the passenger side. This allowed a better comparison for decision making.

During the building and designing of Ford's two seater, top management laid down the law to the design staff. The car was to have the straight line style which was to mark Ford cars from 1949 to many years past '59. Ford upper management repeated that they didn't want anything remotely resembling any car turned out by General Motors. There was some disenchantment with this idea. However, it won out in the final decision.

Along with the clay models, stylists were dealt another low blow. It was decreed that standard '55 passenger car headlight and taillight bezels must be used along with the standard see-through speedometer rather than a custom unit. This was decided because of cost restrictions for tooling production for a new, limited model which might, or might not make it.

Incidentally, the hood scoop on the 2-seater was the result of an accident. During the clay model building, designers decided to drop the hood line a bit more than what was already on the model. Engineers working on chassis and drivetrain problems fought this change saying the engine was already installed as low as possible. However, Ford styling created the hood scoop to solve the problem and won.

With the body styling issue in full swing, designers turned their attention to the grille and rear bumper assembly. Many ideas for the car's front were tried. However, the final opinion of Ford was that the sheetmetal egg crate style was best. For the tail guard, a simple one piece bumper with two bullet-type guards was chosen over many of the exotic designs.

Styling, engineering and design work continued at a rapid pace, all under the watchful eye of Crusoe. Spring turned into summer and finally it was September and time for Crusoe's annual visit to the Paris Auto Show with his friend George Walker. Along with the duo was Robert Maguire, a member of the design staff working on the project. After entering the Paris show, and seeing what the top car builders on the continent were offering, including Ferrari, Porsche, Alfa Romeo and Jaguar, Crusoe instructed Maguire to call the Dearborn laboratory where the 2-seater was being held waiting for approval. Stylists were working on a sec-

1. Ford brothers, Henry II and William, inspect the prototype Thunderbird at a 1954 press preview. Differences between prototype and production units are virtually undetectable.

2. See-through speedometer on '55 Thunderbird was common to entire Ford lineup of that year. Designed as a sporty-looking personal car, early Thunderbird styling is ageless.

3. Soft-top was stowed behind seats and was positioned manually. The optional hardtop was a popular item in areas where winters were severe since soft-top wasn't weather proof.

4. The 292-cu.-in., engine was coupled to a 3-speed stick or an automatic. It pretty well filled the '55 Thunderbird engine room.

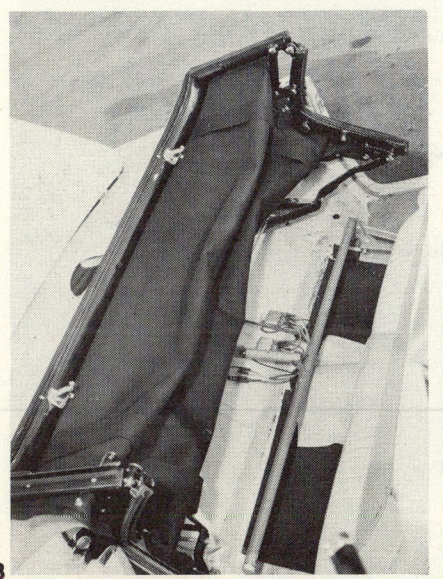

SPECIAL INTEREST AMERICAN CARS/75

Ford Motor Company

Thunderbird

ond model at the time Maguire told them to bring their first idea to reality.

In the meantime, the engineering team was not sitting idly by. They had built a mockup from Ford cars to resemble the chassis they wanted for the 2-seater. Tested and proved suitable, engineering was ready for the challenge of building the genuine article. Also during this time, Ford engineering got their hands on a Corvette and studied it closely. No stone was left unturned.

During the engineering and design stages, there had been no formal mention of Thunderbird as the name of the Ford 2-seater. It would be proper to explain here: Up until the Ford styling and engineering staffs had been given the official word to forge ahead with the car and make it a reality, the car had no name. Naturally, in the styling studio names were given; however, none of them hung on. Lists of potential names were requested and, according to Thunderbird experts, some of the suggestions tossed into the paper shredder included Roadrunner (Plymouth), Sportsman, Savile (anything like Cadillac's Seville?), Runabout, Arcturus, El Tigre and Coronado. Several lists also contained "Thunderbird." As a side note, model names are all properly registered with the office of the Automobile Manufacturers Assoc. Auto makers, as is their competitive nature, watch to see who records what and GM was dumbfounded when their pet name, yet to be logged for their experimental turbine engine car, was beaten to the punch. The car later became the Firebird which is of course, now, a Pontiac.

The first official Thunderbird was put on display at the Detroit Auto Show in February of 1954, the first following World War II. A few design changes were made following the show. First models sported the Fairlane "checkmark" design along the side. This was later changed as were various other subtle items on the car.

Now the problem ahead was the production of the Thunderbird. Crusoe, a master at looking at the market, perceived early in the game that there was a need for a 2-seat car. He also sensed there was interest in some of the refinements not offered in the current European sports models and the Corvette. He instructed his engineers to include as options power steering and brakes, wind-up windows, a power seat and a hardtop along with a convertible. Thunderbird design was intended for those who wanted both comfort *and* performance. For those who wanted to "rough it," a 3-speed transmission with overdrive was available along with the standard 3-speed Fordomatic. These features were to remain on all models built from 1955-57, except for changes in the engine size and hp rating.

Granted, it might seem like a lot of wasted space to cover the development of the car, however, many Thunderbird owners have no idea of how the car came into being and the shortness of time in which the development was achieved. Automotive historians will write much in the near future about the Thunderbird. We'll bet on it.

Prior to a discussion of each of the Thunderbird models from 1955 to 1959, a moment should be taken to expose some Thunderbird misinformation which has been carried around by light-headed quasi-enthusiasts.

Never . . . never was there any other

engine used in the Thunderbird than an 8-cylinder. And this goes for any Thunderbird.

There is also no substance to the rumor that the Thunderbird was a pirate design from an East Coast custom auto builder.

The dual seat models did not come with any form of retractable hardtop.

While these seem like incidental points, rumors persist and must be put to their final resting place.

Now, let's take a look at the models and features of this special interest car which has already been deemed a classic by some. Firstly, let us deal with the 1955 through 1957 models as a group since they are similar and offer many of the same extras.

Both the 1955 and 1956 models used the same basic body and sheetmetal. The '57 was similar but it had been redesigned. Body parts from the '55 and '56 cannot be used on the '57 and vice versa. We should note, however, that the '56 did have an air vent in the front fender but, other than that minor change, everything else is basically the same as the '55. The '57 is truly unique, including a special dashboard along with special body panels.

Concerning suspension, the '55-'57

1. Popularity of the '55 Thunderbird is reflected in the Junior Thunderbird built by Power Car Co., for small fry. Both sizes are worth seeking out and restoring.

2. The 1956 Thunderbird was virtually identical to '55 version except for trim. Big item in '56 was continental kit. It was featured in most of the ads for the '56 Thunderbird and is, today, an interesting accessory.

3. Installation of continental spare tire mount increased capacity of '56 Thunderbird trunk. It also increased vehicle weight in the rear due to need for stouter bumper and brackets.

4. Interesting option was the Paxton centrifugal supercharger on the 312-cu.-in., engine. Lucky is the collector who finds one of these.

Thunderbirds used the same unit that came on the 1954-56 passenger cars. As mentioned earlier, standard components were to be used when and wherever possible. The rear suspension was of the leaf spring type used on other Fords of the day but it did contain a different spring. Nothing fancy here, however.

In the engine compartment, some difference does occur from year to year. During the 1955 model season, standard equipment was a 292-cu.-in. engine, rated at 193 hp with stick shift or 198 hp with an automatic transmission. This was the only engine offered in 1955.

For the '56 edition, Ford installed its newly optioned 312-cu.-in., engine rated at 212 hp along with the 292-cu.-ins., the same as offered the previous year. Both used a 4-bbl. carburetor. Also featured were special Thunderbird air cleaner and valve covers.

The most engine options were offered in the '57 model. Along with the 312-cu.-in., the same as on the '56 car, Ford offered a dual 4-bbl. manifold option along with the seldom-seen Paxton supercharged engine which was designed for the Ford NASCAR racers. Both of these options are very rare and prices could be anything. If you are planning on acquiring a Thunderbird and have a chance to pick up either the supercharger or the dual manifold, do so. It will add to the value of your '57. Remember, these options only came on that model year. Putting them on a '55 would be cheating.

Interior design during these years ran along parallel lines. All interiors were of leatherette fabric. The seats are of the popular roll and pleat design and the dashboards featured partial padding in almost all cases.

Colors for the '55-'57 models ran through the standard Ford line color spectrum and all were of enamel paint. Some two-tone cars were offered by dealers, however, factory checks have

revealed that these were non-production. There is no information to the contrary stating whether wide, white sidewall tires were optional or standard items.

Fancied by some and hated by others are the continental kits which were available in '56. They required a special rear bumper and added 350 lbs. Another popular option was the hardtop. Easy to take on and off, the hardtop was especially desirable for those living in colder climates. It is designed to attach right to the standard mounts and could easily be changed.

Total production of the '55-'57 Thunderbirds was 53,166 cars. In 1955 alone, 16,155 were built. It should be noted that initial production runs called for only 10,000 cars. In 1956, 15,631 Thunderbirds reached the highways and in '57, the largest production year, 21,380 Thunderbirds were built.

A new 1955 Thunderbird sold for between $3200-4000. Standard items included tachometer, speedometer, clock and power seats. As mentioned earlier, transmission was either a 3-speed with overdrive or an automatic. The '56 and '57 were only slightly higher in price.

Should you be interested in a Thunderbird, we compared prices and found models in good shape selling for almost the same prices everywhere. The '57 is slightly more expensive. However, condition and care must be weighed in your decision. Major area newspapers list Thunderbirds on a regular basis and it's wise to check before going to the checkbook. If there is an owners' club in your area, check with them first. Many times, an excellent car might be for sale but the owner hasn't gotten around to putting an ad in the local paper. While experts say Thunderbirds of the 2-seat model will be classic, that status still remains to be seen a few years from today. It is still possible to obtain a nice car in good shape, although it might need some

Ford Motor Company
Thunderbird

work here and there, for not too much money. Do not be misled into thinking a '55-'57 Thunderbird can be obtained for the same price as a standard transportation car. This will not be the case. Seek out and look; these cars will be very much in demand in the years to come.

A special side note for the do-it-yourselfer: As wild as it seems, many vintage Thunderbird parts are still available from Ford. If you have a garage project in progress, two books will help you greatly. They are the official Ford parts and accessories catalogs. One contains the illustrations of the parts with the group numbers while the other gives you the exact part number to take with you to the dealer's parts counter. It is the experience of many that a dealer is the first place to check for parts. This is in lieu of the local auto dismantler who can stab you many times the new price for a part that could be on the verge of wearing out. Of course, Thunderbird parts are special order. For information write to the Ford Motor Co. and ask for forms FD 9462 and FD 9463. The price is moderate and you'll save a lot of time. Engine parts can be obtained through aftermarket channels without much difficulty at a better price than that of the dealer. Should you need something exotic, many specialty auto parts houses feature 2-seat equipment. Check your favorite specialty publication along with a local club, if any.

While it is the feeling of many that the 1958 and 1959 Thunderbirds, equipped with seating for four and a larger body, were not impressive cars, they will be covered here because of the years spanned.

Like the '55-'56 Thunderbirds, the '58 and '59 models shared a common body style. There was little difference except the '58-'59 models came in either hardtop or convertibles. No dual type cars were available.

These cars were designed by Ford to invade the luxury market of the day. Options included air suspension (troublesome and difficult to repair) air conditioning and larger engines. Power plants available in '58 included the 352 cu.in. which later became the 390 cu.in. This was standard in the '58 Thunderbird. In 1959, however, Ford made what some consider its largest blunder enginewise. The 430 cu.in. was the standard engine in '59 models. Owners of cars who still have this engine and haven't previously changed them are candidates for the Guiness records.

If the style of the '58 or '59 Thunderbird has your fancy, they are inexpensive and always will be. They are quite popular with family folks but experts cannot see them appreciating in value unless you have a mint condition specimen and park it in your garage and forget it.

If it seems that the opinion offered in reference to the '58-'59 Thunderbird is somewhat coarse, it is. These cars are very difficult to find in good condi-

tion and in checking with those that know, they are not bringing in nor seem to be worth any high dollars. In this area, a special interest model would be one perhaps owned by a famous personality but that is about all. Also, parts and pieces will be hard to find should you wish to embark on one of these as a home project.

The history of the early Thunderbird is most relevant to our times. It shows what men can do if they sit down and do it. Lewis Crusoe was a man of vision. How many auto makers today can say they sold every model they built?

1. 1957 saw the Thunderbird receive a rather extensive restyle. Even though the lines look similiar, the components are not interchangeable between '55/'56 and '57 Thunderbirds. Many enthusiasts feel that the '57 was the apex of Thunderbird design. Others consider the front and rear styling a bit too massive.

2. The beginning . . . or the end of Thunderbird? 1958 marked the introduction of the four-seater in coupe and convertible models and an attack by Ford on the prestige car market. The '58's may never become classics, but if you like 'em, they're of special interest.

3. Although overall height of '57 Thunderbird is slightly less than '55/'56 version, length increased to 182-ins., overall. And '57's used 14-in. tires. Dashboard layout was refined with dials grouped.

4. Interior of '58 Thunderbird has strong luxury car flavor that all but overpowers sporty car feeling. Extensive use of plastics makes '58's in poor condition hard to restore.

5. The 1959 Thunderbird was merely a 1958 with cosmetic upgrading and continued the trend farther and farther away from the original concept created by Lewis Crusoe.

The Wonderful Woodie

Wooden bodied station wagons are very collectable, but beware the basket case

The station wagon segment of body types available across the years is one in which almost any survivor may be deemed collectable. Almost without exception their production numbers were lower than most other models in their particular line-up, they are unique in appearance, and though most shared major front end sheet metal, engine, drivetrain and chassis components with their sister passenger cars, they are nonetheless singular in make-up and deserve the categorical title of Special Interest.

Ford, of course, was the pioneering manufacturer in massproducing all-wood bodies for installation on otherwise conventional chassis, but the woodie was around many years previously in the guise of custom-builts by a host of cabinet- and wood-working firms who found a ready market for what were termed depot hacks. The car manufacturers saw a market, although admittedly limited, in station wagons and most provided builders with bodyless chassis. But it was Ford who rightly predicted the rise in popularity of the style, and their Iron Mountain, Michigan, wood-working plant was opened for production in time for the '29 model year.

The station wagon was originally just that; a "wagon" useful for shuttling between railroad commuter depots and (mostly) eastern estates, but there were regular commercial users as well. Baggage and other cargo could be easily and casually tossed inside without fear of scuffing upholstered panels and seats. Windows were snap-on affairs left off during pleasant weather to simplify loading and unloading. The kids were free to fuss since spilled ice cream and taffy could be washed from interior wood panels more easily than from mohair. Mud tracked in from the great outdoors was just as easily disposed of. It wasn't long before the wagon became a "fun car" admired by many, hence Ford's gamble to produce his own bodies instead of letting a rising number of specialty manufacturers grab off this small but healthy segment of the automotive market.

As Ford was prone to do in gambles of this nature, he ordered the purchase of timber acreage in northern Michigan specifically for the custom growing of maple, birch, gum and basswood. Requirements for wood became hard-bound with the introduction of the first V-8-powered wagon in May of '32; framing and structure would be of hard maple with no knots permitted, paneling would be of cross-grained exterior birch or gum plywood, good on both sides, and quality basswood strips for roof slats.

While the Iron Mountain woodworking facility, the "box works," supplied the basic body components, the Chester, Pa. assembly plant was the first to be charged with uniting the crate to the chassis and front-end sheetmetal. Statistics were later to reveal that over two thirds of all wooden-bodied Ford wagons would be produced at east coast assembly plants due to their popularity in these areas.

Wherever Ford pioneered others were quick to follow, and by the early '30's virtually every major U.S. car was available in station wagon form except the biggest luxury cars. Ford led them all, however, in numbers produced. Here is a sampling of their production figures which reveals both manufacturing capability and style popularity:

```
1932 ............................334
1933-34 ......................4562
1935 ...........................4536
1936 ...........................7044
1937 ...........................9304
1938 ...........................6944
1939 ...........................9432
1940 .........................13,199
```

A similar breakdown of total U.S. station wagon production cannot be made since various manufacturers at various times do not single out the woodie from other body styles of a particular series, but it is fairly safe to

1. Unrestored woodies may be a little more dangerous to buy than a standard car, unless the would-be purchaser closely examines the wood for dry rot, mildew, missing pieces or, as in the case of this '29 Model A Ford, the non-stock sidemount spare which necessitated an odd cutout in the door. Familiarization with what's stock and what isn't is a prerequisite.

2. Ah, the glory of wood. This nicely restored '31 Model A is a pure delight. Countless hours of refinishing were obviously required to return this gem to Iron Mountain-like beauty.

3. Ford pioneered the factory-built station wagon in 1929. Design, engineering and production were down to an exact science by '31.

4. Chrysler Corp. was quick to follow Ford's lead. This handsome '36 Dodge is worthy of investment.

5. Ford kept up its wagon building momentum and always led the competition during the all-wood-body years. This is a nicely redone '36 model.

6. GM was a big wagon producer. This is their offering in the '40 Pontiac line—also the final year for the marque's use of the sidemount spare.

assume that while Ford lead in numbers, other builders had proportionate outputs.

At least one club is devoted to the preservation of the woodie; year and make are not important. The National Woodie Club, 5522 W. 140th Street, Hawthorne, Calif. 90250, approaching two years of age at this writing, numbers 431 station wagons among its membership (including a few foreign) and representing 18 makes. They have broken down their membership for us and the result probably comes as close as any yardstick can in determining not only the general availability of woodies, but their relative popularity among collectors:

(1)	Ford	267
(2)	Chevrolet	35
(3)	Mercury	32
(4)	Plymouth	22
(5)	Buick	16
(6)	Chrysler	15
(7)	Dodge	9
(8)	Packard	7
(9)	Oldsmobile	7
(10)	Pontiac	7
(11)	Nash	2

Further, American Bantam, DeSoto, Durant, GMC, International and Studebaker are represented by one version each.

The club goes on to detail for us the year models of each make, and a look at their Chevrolet membership as an example is revealing:

1930	1
1931	1
1933	1
1936	1
1939	3
1940	1
1941	1
1942	1
1946	1
1947	5
1948	16

A prerequisite in joining the club, incidentally, is not necessarily ownership of a woodie. Mere appreciation of the unique construction of an early all-wood or a later wood-over-steel version will suffice.

The Wonderful Woodie

Most of the Vintage Tin woodies unearthed today are in an incredible state of disrepair—just as those recently refreshened ones represent untold hours of sanding, filing, bleaching, panel and strut replacement, and varnishing (there's always need for one more coat of varnish).

Owners of original woodies, when they were common, knew that re-varnishing was necessary about every 3 years—more often in harsh climates or under hard driving conditions, less often where the wagon was kept garaged and used little. So, today's junkyard fugitive will be, at best, raw material for a toothpick factory. Weather does to wood what salt water submersion does to steel—and just as fast.

But, if the searcher finds a bedraggled old woodie with somehow salvageable chassis and metal parts, chances are the wood will need, if not total replacement, at least substantial substitution. The best bet here is to remove damaged or nonrepairable panels, one at a time, and use them as templates for new ones. A cabinet shop or wood working emporium can do the job if you give them the shape from either an original piece or a cardboard replica, and define the type of wood and graining to be used. Request that a panel be left "raw"—that is, unfinished—so you can do the re-varnish bit yourself once all the bits and pieces are united.

Of course, you could simply dismantle all the wood of a really bad hack, then cart all the panels, ribs and slats to a cabinetmaker for duplication. But be ready for a bill in the neighborhood of over $3000—and a pile of pieces that still have to be reassembled, then varnished.

The Seventy-One Society—a club devoted to the preservation of the '46 and '47 Ford, and '46 Mercury, Sportsmans (low-production Ford convertible station wagons similar to Chrysler's Town & Country counterparts)—report little success in having major wooden body pieces duplicated by either major custom furniture manufacturers or specialty cabinet shops. However, the truly dedicated woodie restorer, armed with perseverance and a full purse, should eventually find his way out of the dilemma of replacing a badly deteriorated or missing piece.

This section is not to be construed as a yearly make-by-make rundown of all U.S. station wagons, nor does it have a place in a book devoted exclusively to Special Interest cars as a wood-refinishing how-to-do-it. Never-

1. Ford was beginning to somewhat simplify its wooden construction by 1939. Note reduction in number of exterior door stringers as compared to the '36 version.

2. Careful selection of knot-free, straight-grain, honey-hued wood was always Ford's strong point in woodie construction.

3. The reason for the great number of individual wood pieces in pre-war wagons is partly due to the spaced roof slats and many crossribs. Though these pieces are among the easiest to duplicate during woodie restoration, their number makes total roof replacement on the tedious side.

4. Desirable with Ford wagon buffs is the fairly rare '42, though one with the immediate pre-war "black-out" trim is even scarcer hence more collectable.

1

2

3

4

theless, with the thought that the swap meet or auction attendee may find himself hopelessly enamored with a wagon in less than pristine condition, or a lucky searcher finds a relic behind that fabled barn, a word on the amount of self-applied elbow grease necessary to refinish the wagon's wood is in order. If nothing else, it may be helpful in steering the over-zealous toward something more mundane, like a regular passenger car.

Strip old varnish from wagon bodies with a quality paint and varnish remover, then scrub off the old material with coarse steel wool as it bubbles up. Lorin Sorenson, noted automotive historian and restorer, explains that in restoring his own '40 Ford woodie, after applying paint remover, he scraped the areas down with pieces of picture frame glass cut into 2-in. squares—just watch out for gouging. The glass quickly dulls from use; but after all, each piece has eight cutting edges, and it beats what you can buy in a hardware store. A typical old woodie panel may have varnish layers built up to 1/8-in. or better, so don't be afraid to bear down to reach bare wood.

The biggest problem that woodies present is that they're mostly a honey-hued color of pure wood—and Bondo, primer, paint, lead, or whatever, is of no help in concealing defects. Areas turned black by decay, wood rot or other fungus must either be replaced, bleached out, or left as is; they simply can't be disguised or covered up.

Sorenson reports trying several kinds of commercial bleaches, all with dismal results. The best luck he had was using TSP (Tri-Sodium-Phosphate), as used in laundries. He put a half cup into a glass container, then added enough Clorox bleach to turn the goop into a thick paste. He next applied it to a small patch on his wagon where rot had created darkening; he let it set for 3 mins., then sponged it away using clear water. Repeating the procedure several times, all the time being careful to not let the mixture run or drip down the panel, he noted progress and

SPECIAL INTEREST AMERICAN CARS/83

The Wonderful Woodie

eventually the affected area was almost its original color.

Once all old varnish has been stripped away and any discoloration played with, the restorer should next begin sanding all the wood—with the grain—using dry 1/0 paper first, followed by fine 00 paper. Sanding dust in crevices can be removed with a vacuum cleaner or air pressure, then the area wiped with a tack rag before finishing. Tackle just a panel at a time, rather than the whole car, and call it fun instead of work.

Modern-day plastic resin finishes are a no-no, and those who've played with them were sadly disappointed. The original manufacturers used good old varnish and the woodie freshener should use varnish—a good quality marine spar varnish is best. Rather than belabor you with a lengthy dissertation on wood varnishing, refer to instructions that accompany any quality spar varnish, arrange for a heart-to-heart with an expert cabinetmaker or, best, chat with someone who's been through a woodie himself.

Woodie restoration can be as hard and expensive, or as easy and low-buck, as you want to make it. Once the chassis and sheetmetal have been refurbished, a process identical with that on any older car, the vehicle should be pretty much driveable; missing, say, a door or two and maybe the tailgate. Tackle all the box structure in one fell swoop and the project might be given up somewhere mid-way. But by doing just a door one week, a quarter panel another, and so on, the ultimate result should be very rewarding. Once done, you can put all conventional-bodied restored cars to shame. After all, restoring a roadster or coupe is easy!

The true, all-wood wagon began its exit not long after postwar manufacturing began, although most '46's through '48's were, like their regular car counterparts, face-lifted '42's. But with the entrance of the '49's most manufacturers turned to using closed car inner metal door and quarter panel structures over which a veneered-and-ribbed outer wood panel was attached. All the major wagon builders, Ford, Mercury, Chevy, Plymouth and the others, "discovered" various types of wood-grained appliques very early in the '50's, and the era of wood was gone.

Survivors command a special price today, depending of course on actual age, relative rarity within the marque, condition, and so on. But Special Interest cars all woodies are, and will remain so until the world is overtaken by termites.

1. Prized as highly as any Ford could be is the scarce Sportsman, available only during the '46 and '47 model years and built in a low quantity of 3392. Mercury had a similar version, but for '46 only and with only 198 produced!

2. More common for '47 yet still high as a collectable item is Ford's regular woodie. At this point in time, wagon builders were only a year away from abandonment of all-wood construction.

3. This '47 Pontiac, though still with a primarily all-wood body shell, is an example of how sheet metal had begun to encroach upon exterior wooden surfaces even as the industry prepared to abandon this construction concept.

4. Some wagon restoration pitfalls are evident here. Through-bolts have been over-tightened allowing heads to pull into the wood. Restorers, and prospective purchasers of a car already refinished, should watch for this.

5. Discoloration of original wood will begin wherever finish deteriorates to allow moisture to seep into grain. Accompanying text describes how TSP, a laundry agent, can help whip this.

6. Last gasp for the wooden Pontiac was in '48. This yet-unrestored car would make a safe starting place for the first-time woodie resurrector, as its bits and pieces appear to be in salvageable condition.

7. The industry in general switched from the basic all-wood wagon body to wood-over-metal, as in this '51 Buick. Usually, the exterior wood was no longer stress-bearing; it was merely decorative paneling over a steel structure which in itself was often "borrowed" from the standard closed car. Nevertheless, refinishing these panels is as hard and time-consuming as with earlier models—there are just fewer of them!

8. Chrysler was one holdout for the all-wood concept. This is a stately '50 Royal woodie.

9. Living up to the dictionary's definition of a station wagon as "an automobile that has an interior longer than a sedan's . . .," the '50 Rambler Custom wagon, alas, has done away with wood altogether and gone to a grained applique on a limited scale. Far more expansive use of the glue-on material would come in the years ahead, but the true woodie was gone for good.

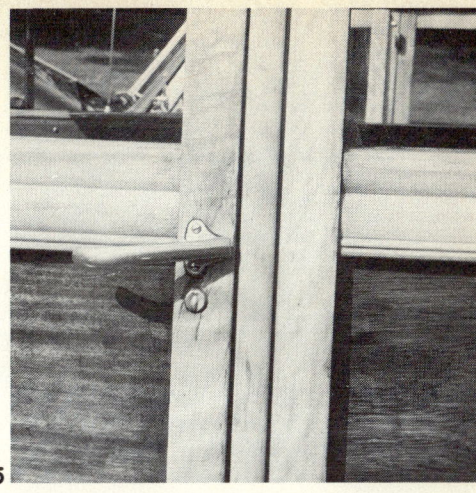

SPECIAL INTEREST AMERICAN CARS/85

General Motors Corporation

Buick

This interesting marque has many surprises in store for enthusiasts

"When Better Automobiles Are Built... Buick Will Build Them." There's a lot to that slogan, because no other automobile in American history has been able to threaten Ford and Chevrolet for sales supremacy, yet challenge Cadillac as America's top prestige automobile.

The first Buick was designed by an obscure Scotsman—David Dunbar Buick. He's so obscure, in fact, that many historical books credit William Crapo Durant as founder of Buick Motor Car Company.

David Buick was an inventor, a tinkerer. He couldn't be bothered beyond the inventing stage. You might be surprised to know that many of your bathroom fixtures were designed by Buick, particularly the bathtub. Buick patented a process for annealing porcelain to cast iron, which is still used today.

Buick's big fault was carelessness in management. This cost him a successful plumbing business and, after a few near misses, finally cost him Buick Motor Car Company. When the company was purchased for the last time, and moved from Detroit to nearby Flint, the new controlling group hired the brilliant W.C. Durant, who already had piled fortune upon fortune in the carriage business and in the stock market.

Taking complete charge of the Buick company, in just one year Durant increased annual production from 37 in 1904 to 750 in 1905, moving Buick into the ninth spot in automobile sales. Since then, Buick has never been lower than ninth in sales. And, though it never became number one, it was mighty close a couple of times. Durant eventually created the world's largest corporation, General Motors, of which Buick was the cornerstone and held GM together for two decades.

Buick's companion car, Marquette, is a rare special interest car that ushered in the Thirties. It was quite short-lived, being born in mid-1929 and died in 1930. Only 27,821 were sold in the United States. The remaining 7000 or so were shipped to Mexico, Canada and overseas.

Marquette came in six body styles, including 4- and 2-door sedans, two coupes, a roadster and a phaeton. The phaeton, of course, has to be the cream of the crop with a low production of 889 and a high price tag.

A serious consideration for special interest automobiles for the future should be styling. If they're not making certain features today, they become highly desirable to the special interest car owner. These include rumble seats, sidemounts, woodie wagons and convertibles.

Among the accessories offered on the Marquette were sidemounts and wire wheels. You're fortunate if you find both on any Marquette model.

The Marquette body was fitted over a 114-in. wheelbase chassis. And power was furnished by an L-head 6 producing 67.5 hp. In fact, the engine was often referred to as the "Oldsmobuick," because it was essentially a reworked Oldsmobile F-28.

Now comes 1931 and the Straight Eight, an engine Buick would continue to use for the next 22 years. Three distinct 8's were used in the four series that year. The Series 90 and 80 cars used the 344.8-cu.-in. version developing 104 hp. The Series 60 was 272.6 cu. ins., at 90 hp. And the Series 50 had the smallest, at 220.7 cu. ins and 77 hp.

The smooth, silent, powerful 8, for the first time coupled with a synchromesh transmission, made the 1931 Buick a desirable car... but not during the Depression.

Sales figures hit a low of 88,417 spread over 22 separate models, which makes the 1931 Buick of particular in-

PHOTOS COURTESY BUICK MOTOR DIVISION

terest. Especially since people of that day literally drove their cars into the ground.

Options included wood, disc, or wire wheels, dual rearmounted spares, dual sidemounts, trunk (or luggage) racks and trunks. The trunks were literally that—trunks. When extra carrying space was needed, the trunk rack was folded down at the rear of the automobile and a huge box (trunk) was set on it and strapped in place. Any car you locate with a trunk attached is certainly a real find.

Interiors on all these early '30's cars were mohair. Straps to assist entry and exit, window shades and footrests were commonplace. Some of the luxurious Series 90 cars even had velvet rear carpeting.

The limousine (Model 90-L), the Model 94 Roadster with rumble seat and the Model 95 Phaeton are the rarest Buicks in 1931.

With the Depression in top gear, Buick was again called on for rescue work. GM President Alfred Sloan approved a plan to form B.O.P.

1. Ushering in the Thirties was Buick's short-lived Marquette. Born: mid-1929, Died: 1930. This coupe is rare.

2. The 1931 Model 8-90L introduced an engine that would continue for 22 years. In the 90L 4-dr. sedan, the straight 8 pumped out 104 hp.

3. A five-passenger trunk-back Buick Series 68 was billed in 1936 as a "young man's car of exceptional performance." The desirable era for Buick began in 1936.

4. The 1937 Model 61 Century with sidemounts is considered by some to represent the epitome of Buick styling excellence. It's a good one.

5. A prime collectible—if not the most—is 1938's six-passenger Convertible Streamline Sport Phaeton, Model 80C Roadmaster. Fast, suave, comfortable.

6. Thundering out of 1939 was the giant beast. The Roadmaster 4-dr. Streamline Sport Phaeton was available on special order only; was only Buick Convertible without trunk back.

SPECIAL INTEREST AMERICAN CARS/87

General Motors Corporation

Buick

(Buick-Oldsmobile-Pontiac). Buick had a strong dealer network. So, to rescue the floundering Oldsmobile and Pontiac divisions, all Buick dealers were asked to take on one other make. B.O.P. was a manufacturing and sales organization having jurisdiction over all three divisions. The result was good for Oldsmobile and Pontiac, but because of this juggling, Buick lost over 25% of its dealers. This program was eventually shed in 1933.

The desirable Buick era began in 1936 and ended in 1942. Most Buick collectors concentrate on this period of time because of the many innovations the division came up with under their legendary boss, Harlow H. Curtice.

Curtice's aim was to have broad range of models in numerous price ranges, and to come out with a young man's car of exceptional performance. Thus, in 1936, Buick gave birth to the Century, the first lower-priced 100-mph car.

Buick was distinctive in 1936, even though most GM cars were similar in appearance. It had more than well-rounded styling; it had a well-rounded line of automobiles. The entire line had a definite purpose.

All Buick prices were lower, power was increased and the new hydraulic brakes were able to haul down the car more safely from high speed.

Another new engine was introduced, the 120-hp, 320-cu.-in. 8 with aluminum pistons. It was used in three of four Buick lines—Limited, Roadmaster and Century. The special used the 93-hp, 233-cu.-in. block.

The Limited series was the only luxury line now. It no longer had to compete with other Buicks. And to bring the price of luxury down, the Formal Sedan was announced, an interesting approach to middle-class luxury—a 6-passenger limousine. Its chief claim to fame was a sliding glass partition between driver and passengers.

Only one phaeton remained. It was on the 131-in. wheelbase Roadmaster chassis. Particularly interesting on this Model 80-C was the fact that both front and rear doors opened from the trailing edge rather than from the center as they did on all other 4-door Buicks. Only 1064 were built, making it a valuable special interest car.

Century was the hot line for car nuts. It was produced in sufficient numbers, 24,364 U.S. production, to make many models relatively easy to locate and parts are plentiful.

The real sparklers were the coupes, which came in two versions—the 66-SO opera coupe with a single fold-down rear seat and the 66-SR with rumble seat. These were the lightest and fastest of the Centurys. The SR came standard with a left sidemount. Dual sidemounts were optional. Model 66-C is also highly prized. It had a production run of only 717. This convertible coupe featured rumble seat and left sidemount, with dual sidemounts optional.

The two other Century models, 5-passenger victoria trunk coupe and 4-door sedan, accounted for 80% of Century sales.

For 1937, Buick produced one of its best cars ever. In the opinions of many aficionados, the 1937 and 1938 Buicks were the epitome of styling excellence and the best Buicks of all.

Not content to carry over 1936 styling, bigger and different-looking Buicks emerged. Styling highlights included a horizontal grille and fenders were squared off at the trailing end to make the cars look even larger.

Engineering changes were minimal because of the emphasis on styling. Those big changes would come in 1938.

Although all Buick models are sought-after, the real interest car remains the Century, which was enhanced by a new convertible phaeton, Model 60-C, which had a production run of only 410. Along with the phae-

1. Horsepower now reached 141 in the '39 Century. The Model 66C Convertible Coupe with two opera seats could be had with running or streamboards, a flush-mounted chrome strip.

2. In 1940, the Series 50 Super Phaeton was announced after original brochures had been printed. It is a rare and valuable find today.

3. Buick's first attempt at a station wagon resulted in the 1940 Model 59 Super. Straight 8 "Dynaflash" engine produced 107 hp in the Super, but best, the Buick wagon caught on.

4. Big 8 was now called "Fireball," with 165 hp in '41 Roadmaster Convertible Phaeton. Luxury personified.

5. 1941 Special Model 46S was a 6-passenger Sedanet with a full-width rear seat. Fender skirts were extra.

6. Postwar body style appeared in 1942. Roadmaster Model 76C Convertible Coupe was big favorite. Flowing front fender was only available on some Super and Roadmaster models.

General Motors Corporation

Buick

ton, the top special interest car is the convertible, Model 66-C. Only the convertibles retained rumble seats.

The 1938 Buick is considered the prime collectible of all post-1920 Buicks. Not that it looked any different from the 1937—only subtle styling alterations were made—but three major engineering changes took place.

The most important was 4-wheel coil springs—an industry first. Since the coils were much softer and more resilient than leaf springs, they had to be bolstered by shock absorbers roughly four times the size of any on the road. And the ride was superb. For years after, Buick's ride maintained the reputation of being the best in the world, even after many others went to coils all around. This was an important feature Buick challenged Cadillac with a few years later.

Again, Buick came out with an all-new Straight 8. It was called the Dynaflash. All dimensions remained the same in these new engines, but horsepower increased to 141 for Limited, Roadmaster and Century, and to 107 for Special. It was hard to believe that, since the Straight 8 was introduced, almost every year Buick was coming out with a new engine. Incidentally, Buick also became the first car maker to stick the battery under the hood in this year.

The third big engineering feat didn't really appear on Buick first, but was introduced in Oldsmobile in 1937. It was a 4-speed semi-automatic that Buick actually developed but didn't use until 1938. The Self-Shifter appeared in less than 7% of the cars sold.

The Self-Shifter still used a clutch when stopping, idling or shifting into reverse. Because it was column-mounted, it made room for one more passenger up front.

The interesting formal sedan appeared only on the Roadmaster line in 1938, and only 247 were built.

The 1939 was not important from a special interest standpoint, except when equipped with an optional sunroof. It's not known how many sunroof Buicks actually were produced, but according to one source: "Damn few."

It was available on Century and Special 2-door and 4-door sedans.

By 1941, Buick had a load of special interest cars. Mainly because of a dual carburetion system called "Compound Carburetion," a forerunner of the 4-bbl. carb.

Compound Carburetion didn't take full effect until the driver "tromped on it." Only one carburetor worked until

a demand was put on the engine. When the second carb kicked in, it was more of a smooth power than the sudden jar you might expect from today's high-power 4-barrels.

Compound Carburetion was standard on all Limiteds, Roadmasters and Centurys. It was optional for Supers and Specials, boosting horsepower from 115 to 125.

The real stylish bodies were the Brunn creations, which appeared in early Buick catalogs and were on Limited chassis. There were three: town car, landau, landau brougham and phaeton. At least one of each was built, although it's believed maybe two or three town cars and landaus were produced.

General Motors corporate chiefs killed the special-body program. Today, only one 1940 experimental version is known to exist.

The big Limited Limousine (Model 90-LO) could well be the best of any previous limousines. Curtice was really out to get Cadillac in 1941, and in doing so, easily created the best luxury car for the dollar this year. Making a return was the limited formal sedan.

Only two phaetons appeared in 1941—the Model 71-C Roadmaster and Model 51-C Super. These were the last phaetons built by Buick.

Buick also came out with fastback styling for the first time.

Compound Carburetion saw its final days in 1942, but horsepower was dropped to 118 because of material

1. The first big-production hardtop coupe came—along with the portholes—on the 1949 Roadmaster chassis, was named "Riviera."

2. Receiving plenty of debate on proper credentials for special interest is the 1950 Buick. Disproportionate design was noted for its blatant dental work.

3. A more conservative grille prevailed in '51, and refinement was once again noticeable in the senior lines.

4. The 1951 Special Model 56S slope-back coupe was an interesting design.

5. Recent diminishing sales reversed with introduction of the expensive Skylark convertible. The '52 Buicks still had the straight 8, but the '53's had the Skylark and a beautiful V-8.

6. The new Buick V-8 swiftly gained a reputation as having the strongest bottom end of any engine in America. And the '53 Estate Wagon became among the classiest of its breed ever built.

SPECIAL INTEREST AMERICAN CARS/91

General Motors Corporation
Buick

shortages created by World War II.

Buick styling for 1942 was once again all new, and would continue through 1948.

This was also the last year for the limousine. Never again would a production Buick have jump seats or a glass partition.

The next special interest car didn't appear until 1948, when Roadmasters were offered with Dynaflow. This was the first real torque converter used in automobiles.

But it wasn't until 1949 that Buick combined styling with Dynaflow when the first production hardtop was introduced—the Roadmaster Riviera. And the portholes first appeared in this year, too.

However, with most manufacturers turning to the V-8, Buick sales began to diminish until its historic 50th anniversary year—1953.

The anniversary year brought not only an unusual V-8, but the highly prized, limited-production Skylark convertible, which lasted only two years.

The V-8 engine was a real gem. Buick had worked on V-8's as long as anyone, but never put one into production until the public began crying for them en masse.

The Special continued to use the 263-cu.-in., 130-hp inline 8, but the over-square V-8 carried the biggest bore (4.0-ins.) in 25 years, and the highest compression ratio in the industry (8.5:1).

Three versions of the 322-cu.-in. engine were available. The Super had 2-bbl. carbureted models of 164 and 170 (for Dynaflow). The Roadmaster and Skylark handled the 188-hp version with 4-bbl. carb.

Only 1690 Skylarks were built on Roadmaster chassis, much to the chagrin of Buick executives, who expected sales to skyrocket. This $5000 car—Buick's most expensive to that date—marked the first time a GM division had taken an existing car, the Roadmaster convertible, and reworked it into a different model. The windshield was lowered four inches, the beltline was cut down and notched at the rear fender line, rear wheel cutouts were rounded and raised to match the height of the front ones, and Italian Borrani wire wheels with knock-off hubs touched it off.

Only two chassis were used in 1953—121.5-in. wheelbase for all models, including Roadmaster, and a 125.5-in. for Super and Roadmaster Rivieras.

It had to be irresistible to Buick management when they saw the performance of their new V-8 to bring back the Century. Well, it was! When 1954 rolled in with a totally new Buick, the Century rolled—or should we say raced—right in with it.

It wasn't just a matter of putting last year's Roadmaster engine into the new 122-in. wheelbase Special chassis, either. Buick hyped Century's horsepower to 195 with stick and 200 with Dynaflow, making it the most powerful engine in the line to make sure it would go. Roadmaster used the same powerplant, while Super developed 177 or 182 hp, depending on transmission.

This was the last year for Skylark. It used the Century body and 200-hp V-8. The decklid sloped, and heavy chrome extensions housed the taillights. Since other Buick models adopt-

ed open-wheel cutouts, Skylark went a step farther and elongated them, painting some of the fender-wells in red.

For the first time a true, pillarless 4-door hardtop appeared in the 1955 Buick line. It was available only in the Century and Special series.

The next special interest Buick appeared in 1957—a 4-door hardtop station wagon named "Century Caballero." It was a real pillarless hardtop. Over 10,000 of these fancy wagons were produced.

The last special interest Buick in our time period appeared in 1959. It was the 4-door hardtop with wraparound rear window. All GM lines of 1959 produced a similar model, which lasted only two years. It was a most unusual body style, and one that's not expected to be repeated again.

Among car manufacturers, Buick ranks near the top in special interest cars available. Unfortunately, our limited space here doesn't allow getting into the subject in depth. But look for a new *Automobile Quarterly* Library series book about Buick's complete history. It's written by Bob Kovacik and Terry Dunham—two contributors to this book.

1. Buick management found it irresistible to bring back the Century concept of big engine into little body. With 200 hp, the V-8 "got it on right well," even in the Century wagon.

2. Then there were these: Final Skylark luxury convertible in 1954.

3. The 1957 Century Caballero. About 10,000 of the fancy wagons were built.

4. The 1955 Century convertible was solid, massive, powerful.

5. As was the 1956. A little more windswept in ornamentation, yet still a "goin' machine."

6. But times were changing, even though gargantuan size was resurrected with the 1958 Limited. If size is your ticket, this is it.

SPECIAL INTEREST AMERICAN CARS/93

General Motors Corporation

Cadillac

Deserving of the title of: "Standard of the World!"

As the roaring '20's drew to a close, America's love affair with the automobile was at its zenith. The new Model A Ford was selling like hotcakes, eagerly snapped up by thousands who had waited impatiently for a successor to the legendary Model T; Chevrolet had just introduced a new overhead-valve six that brought new standards of silence and smoothness to the low-price field; and a new low-price entry, the Plymouth, was an immediate success since it was a good-looking car with hydraulic brakes, and backed by the integrity of the Chrysler name. At the opposite end of the price scale, the patrician Packard reigned supreme as the best-selling luxury car in the world, prestigious Pierce-Arrow had a new straight eight, while at the pinnacle the almighty Model J Duesenberg, the most powerful automobile in the world, was already assuming the mantle of legend. (It is an historical accident, but an appropriate one, that the fastest, largest, and most expensive racing yachts ever built were called J-boats; they were exact contemporaries of the Model J Duesenberg.) But as the decade of the '30's began, Cadillac was already well under way in an intensive campaign to displace these other famous marques and establish itself as the premier luxury car in the land.

GM's flagship was well equipped for this extraordinary challenge. It had a heritage of quality dating back to its founding in 1902, when the uncompromising Lelands, Henry and his son Wilfred, agreed to supply engines and transmissions from their Leland and Faulconer company to the Detroit Automobile Company. This company, facing bankruptcy after three years in operation with a chief engineer named Henry Ford, reorganized after Ford's departure as the Cadillac Automobile Company, and never looked back. Aside from its quality, Cadillac was remembered chiefly for two things. It won Britain's prestigious Dewar Trophy in 1908 for a spectacular demonstration of precision and reliability when three complete cars were assembled from a jumble of mixed parts, and each went on to complete 500 miles at full throttle around Brooklands racetrack; and since 1915 it continually espoused the V-8 engine configuration. Though not the first, Cadillac's V-8 was certainly the best and most famous; but even in 1930 it was not a common design. Low-price cars had fours, medium-price cars had sixes, while the straight eight was the darling of the country club set. Cadillac was about to change all that.

The first act in this industrial drama occurred in 1928, when Cadillac introduced its Syncro-Mesh transmission for the 1929 model year. The syncronization operated on 2nd and 3rd gears, and was the first appearance of this principle in America. It was based on a patent issued in 1922 to Earl A. Thompson, who later became a Cadillac engineer specializing in transmission development. Clashless shifting was a revelation and took the country by storm, and Cadillac derived great prestige from being the first to offer it.

At the New York Automobile Show in January 1930, Cadillac unveiled their monumental V-16. It was a masterpiece, the crowning achievement of GM's famous Vice-President of Engineering, C.F. Kettering. Although it had plenty of power for its time—165 hp from 452-cu.-ins.—the prime reason for the V-16 was abundant low-speed torque and incredible smoothness. This was the world's first series-produced automotive V-16, and its total refinement has never been surpassed. It was an instant sales hit with the moneyed set, and over 2500 were sold the first year before the deepening Depression rapidly slowed sales to a trickle.

The introduction of an all-new V-16 would have been considered quite a good year's work by any other manufacturer, but in September Cadillac loosed another heavy salvo at its rival luxury makes. This was a V-12, and with it Cadillac had an unmatched range of cars to offer the wealthy and discriminating.

A lot of stuff and nonsense has been written about GM's money being the only reason Cadillac survived the dark years of the Great Depression which killed off most of its competitors. Certainly GM's money was no hindrance, but the real reason was that Cadillac rather adtroitly outmaneuvered its rivals in the early '30's. By the end of 1930 Cadillac had a V-16, a V-12, a V-8 and the LaSalle V-8, while not one of its rivals had anything more glamorous or advanced than a straight eight. Marmon came out with a V-16 the following year, and in 1932 Lincoln, Packard, and Pierce responded with V-12's, but they were too little, too late. In the words of Confederate General Nathan Bedford Forrest, Cadillac

94/SPECIAL INTEREST AMERICAN CARS

1. Okay, so this is a '29 Cadillac, not a '30, but we still had to show you rising young MGM star Walter Pidgeon posing proudly beside his lush Model 341B convertible sedan in 1930. That center light is really the cat's pajamas. Look closely at the hood. Does the whole thing look engine-turned? It is. Hot cha, and twenty-three skidoo.

2. Here's a real 1930 Series 353 roadster, and a sweet thing it is. The artillery wheels make it look a bit older than its true age, but it's still just the ticket for takin' your sweetie to a picnic 'neath the orange groves or a business prospect to lunch at Ciro's.

3. In 1931 the Series 355 Cadillac used the same 134-in. wheelbase as LaSalle and the same 95-hp V-8. Snap-open doors replaced the hood louvers, and wire wheels added a dashing touch.

4. A smooth enveloping shape with bullet headlights was given to Cadillac for 1934, the same year all models received independent front suspension. This 1935 sedan shows the similar styling for that year, but is distinguished immediately by its flat bumper, instead of the peculiar biplane bumper of '34.

5. Despite the exclusive use of Vee engines, 1936-37 Cadillacs had a very narrow hood line, as this '37 V-8 Series 60 sedan displays. With its high headlights and tall grille full of tiny rectangles, this Cadillac could almost be mistaken for a '37 LaSalle; the Cadillac crest on the bumper quickly reveals its identity.

had been there "firstest with the mostest," and skimmed the cream off the remaining demand for ultraprestigious luxury cars. By 1932 this demand had all but evaporated, and the other marques were forced to launch their most expensive models right in the blackest depths of the Depression. They all lost shocking amounts of money, while Cadillac had already amortized its tooling.

Nor was Cadillac's wide range an example of profligate spending. Their four engines were actually variations of only two. The V-12 and V-16 were very closely related, sharing the same narrow 45 degree angle between the cylinder banks, the same type of overhead valve gear, the same carburetion, the same stroke, and almost identical bores—the V-16's was 3 ins., the V-12's 3.125 ins. The V-12 was, in reality, a shortened V-16. Similarly, the LaSalle flathead V-8 had much in common with the Cadillac V-8, and in fact by 1931 the two cars were using exactly the same engine.

The V-12 and early narrow-angle V-16 Cadillacs belong to the elite legions of recognized classic cars, while the LaSalle has its own chapter in this book. The prewar Cadillacs which concern us, therefore, are the V-8 and that strange engine usually considered the black sheep of the family, the wide-angle V-16.

While the big overhead-valve dual-carburetor engines were garnering all the publicity and dazzling the country club set, the more prosaic V-8 was doing its job of holding Cadillac's position in a shrinking market. The bottom was reached in 1933, when only 3173 Cadillacs were produced; of these, two-thirds were V-8's, the rest V-12's and V-16's. Thereafter production rose gradually until by 1937 combined Cadillac/LaSalle production finally exceeded the previous record of 1928.

By 1930 Cadillac's "second generation" V-8 had been in production for three years, although available in Cadillacs for only two. It was introduced in the 1927 LaSalle, which was the first year for Cadillac's little brother—a new engine in a new car. It had several major advances over the earlier V-8, which dated back to Cadillac's 1915 model year (except for an important change to a 2-plane crankshaft in 1924). One was its use of side-by-side connecting rods with offset cylinder banks, rather than the previous fork-and-blade rods with symmetrical cylinder banks; another was replaceable main bearings. In the LaSalle it had the same 3⅛-in. bore as the 1927 Cadillac "first generation" engine but

COURTESY AUTOMOTIVE CLASSICS, SANTA MONICA

General Motors Corporation
Cadillac

a shorter stroke, 4 15/16 ins. compared to 5⅛ ins. This gave a displacement of 303 cu.-ins., and it was rated at 75 hp. The following year Cadillac received this new engine, bored out to 3 5/16 ins. for 341-cu.-ins. and 90 hp. This was the Series 341 Cadillac, the series number nicely designating the engine displacement. It was to be Cadillac's principal powerplant for the next eight years. In 1930 the bore was again increased to 3⅜ ins., forming the 95-hp Series 353. Thereafter the engine remained the same in displacement up through 1935, although the power was boosted to 115 in 1932 and 130 for 1934.

Cadillac series designations follow a set pattern through the first half of the '30's, with one slight exception. The 1928 Series 341 logically became the Series 341B the following year, since the displacement was unchanged. Then came 1930's Series 353, which somehow became the 1931 Series 355 although the engine did not change. Thereafter the Series 355 acquired a letter suffix each year, forming the 355B for '32, the 355C for '33, and the 355D for '34. Then in 1935 came a redesignation for the entire Cadillac line, possibly because management felt that the previous designations emphasized the engines too much. The V-8 became the Series 10, the V-12 the Series 40, and the V-16 the Series 60. The following year, which saw the introduction of a new V-8, had an even more confusing nomenclature shakeup. The V-8 cars were divided among Series 60, 70, and 75, the V-12 became the Series 80 and 85, and the V-16 the Series 90. From then on, however, things became simpler. Although certain lines were dropped and added at periodic intervals, V-8 powered cars were always in series numbered in the 60's or 70's until 1965, when series names replaced the numbers.

In 1934 Cadillac made an across-the-board change to independent front suspension, using the modern concept of unequal-length A-arms with coil springs. Again Cadillac was the first of the major luxury cars to have this important feature, beating the Packard 120 by one year.

The 1936 model year was a milestone one for Cadillac, as several important changes were made. One was hydraulic brakes, which Cadillac had been slow to adopt. Unlike engines, braking was one area where Cadillac was not superior to its rivals. Another change was the new short-wheelbase (121 ins.) Series 60, which shared its body with the small Buick; GM was starting to flex its interchangeability muscles. This car was Cadillac's response to medium-price competition from the Packard 120 (introduced the preceding year) and the Lincoln Zephyr (new for 1936). But the biggest change was a new engine, Cadillac's "third generation" V-8.

This engine was a "monobloc" casting, the blocks and crankcase all one iron casting; the previous engine had two separate iron blocks bolted to an aluminum crankcase. Though slightly heavier, the new engine was much stiffer and far cheaper to manufacture. The valve design was still a flathead, and the exhaust flow was still directed up between the cylinder banks rather than down away from them, but the carburetor was now downdraft rather than updraft. The stroke, at 4½ ins., was shorter than the older engine's, and there were two different bore sizes giving two displacements. The new Series 60 received the 322-cu.-in., 125-hp version with its 3⅜-in. bore, while the larger Series 70 and 75 models had the 346-cu.-in., 135-hp version with a 3½-in. bore.

For 1937, Cadillac juggled their V-8 line again. The 322 engine was relegated to the LaSalle, and all Cadillacs

1

2

COURTESY AUTOMOTIVE CLASSICS, SANTA MONICA

3

4

had the 346 version. Unchanged except for a boost to 150 hp in 1941, this would remain the basic Cadillac engine up to the 1949 model year. The Series 60 had proved to be a big hit in the marketplace, so for '37 it not only got the bigger engine but a longer 124-in. wheelbase. The wheelbase of the Series 70 remained at 131 ins. and that of the Series 75 at 138 ins., but a new line was added—the Series 65, mechanically identical to the Series 70.

The appeal of the expanded Cadillac V-8 line, not to mention the success of the LaSalle and the still-tight effects of the Depression, had caused the sales of the V-12 and V-16 models to dwindle away to uneconomic levels. Only 207 V-16's, for example, were produced in the four years 1934-37, which was ridiculous. And the 346 V-8 engine was almost as large in displacement and produced almost as much power as the heavier, bulkier, and much more expensive V-12. Both of these complex engines were dropped at the end of the '37 model year.

It came as a great surprise, then, when for 1938 Cadillac announced a brand new V-16. This unexpected engine had absolutely nothing in common with the previous V-16 except the power rating: 185 bhp at 3600 rpm, the same power at 200 less rpm than its predecessor (which was uprated from 165 bhp in 1933).

Its design blended simplicity with sophistication and sturdiness. The block and crankcase were one iron casting, with the cylinder banks spread apart at a wide 135-degree angle. It had nine main bearings, yet was six inches shorter than the old 5-bearing V-16. The cylinder banks were treated like two separate 8-cyl. engines; each had its own downdraft carburetor, water pump, exhaust manifold, and 8-plug distributor. The flathead valve arrangement was simple and cheap to produce. The cylinder dimensions were square, at 3¼ x 3¼ ins., making this the first Cadillac with a stroke as short as the bore. With its 6.75:1 compression ratio and 431-cu.-ins., this engine produced the same power as the previous 452-cu.-in. narrow-angle V-16, yet used many fewer parts, was smaller, cheaper, and no less than 250 lbs. lighter.

As installed in a car, this remarkable engine showed further advantages. Its much lower center of gravity aided handling, and since it was so flat, the firewall could actually be moved over the rear part of the block. This enabled it to fit in the same 141-in.-wheelbase chassis as the V-8-powered Series 75 Fleetwood, a great reduction over the special 154-in. wheelbase used by the narrow-angle V-16 in its later years. For the three years of its production ('38 through '40) the new V-16 carried the same Series 90 designation used by the old one, but was additionally known as the "Sixteen Fleetwood" to distinguish it from the same-sized Series 75, which was called just plain "Fleetwood."

Any Sixteen Fleetwood is a magnificent special interest car. It has never really been welcomed by the classic car set, for two reasons. The first is that despite the fact that the wide-angle 16 is a far better engine as a piece of engineering than its narrow-angle predecessor, it is admittedly far less satisfying as a work of art. By the great Harry, that early 16 really *does* look like the proper motor to find under the long narrow hood of a real classic. The second reason is that the Sixteen Fleetwood bodies are practically identical to those of the lesser Fleetwood series, which look like Buicks, which frankly didn't look like very much. Nobody could say that about the earlier 16's, which were magnificent-looking giants that couldn't be mistaken for anything else on the road. And because of its clever engineering and shared bodies, the Sixteen Fleetwood also cost a lot less than its predecessor, a black mark against it in the eyes of the monied collector. But it is a satisfying and rare automobile. Exactly 508 were produced in 12 different body styles, of which two were for President Roosevelt and had special 161-in. wheelbases.

For the latter part of the '30's, Cadillac juggled its lower-priced series in a rather confusing manner, but special mention must be made of the important 60 Special, introduced in 1938. Basically a lowered and stretched Series 60 sedan, it was a new car which had its own unique frame and body, shared with no other Cadillac or GM car. The frame had a high kick-up at both ends, which enabled the 60S to be 3-ins. lower than the other '38 Cads without sacrificing headroom. It also had a massive central X-member, making it the stiffest frame in American production cars.

The lower 60S body used the same

1. The 1938 Sixty Special was an epic design which increased glass area and dispensed with running boards. It was an immediate success, and remained basically unchanged for three years. The owner of this car has added several non-standard trim pieces on the fenders and roof, as well as the ever-popular windshield visor.

2. This big 1939 Series 75 7-passenger sedan is one of the largest cars powered by a V-8 engine that Cadillac has ever made. It used the same 141-in. wheelbase as the Sixteen Fleetwood of the same vintage. All '39 models except the Sixteen can be identified by the very thin grille bars and the headlights, which have elongated housings, a horizontal ridge, and painted rims.

3. Cadillacs for 1940 were a lot flashier up front than their predecessors. The grille bars were larger, the headlight rims and ridges were chromed, and parking light bezels perched on top of the fenders. This is a Series 62 sedan, and shows influences from the 60 Special in its clean sides without a trim spear.

4. Thought fabric-covered roofs were a recent development, did you? This big Sixteen Fleetwood formal sedan shows its massive size in a field that was a trifle muddy. All of the 508 Sixteens made in 1938-40 had the same big egg-crate grille. This is revealed as a '40 because the headlight rims are chromed and it has the same parking lights as the '40 V-8 cars.

5. This Sixty Special shows the new styling introduced for 1941, with a bold horizontal grille and headlights mounted in the fenders. The 60S was the only '41 Cadillac with the front fenders continued back into the doors, a styling theme picked up the following year on all models in the Cadillac range.

6. New rounded styling made its appearance in 1942, and was continued in the postwar '46 and '47 models. The quickest way to tell them apart is by the nose ornament above the grille. The '42 model has a raised-wing emblem identical to the '41, while postwar cars have the Cadillac crest in a large V. The '46 cars have five layers of grille rectangles, while the '47 has only four; this is a '47.

General Motors Corporation
Cadillac

new squared-off pontoon fenders as other series, but was lower between the fenders. This made its lowness very evident to a customer on the showroom floor, as the proportions of fender line to hood line and roofline were noticeably different. This lowness was further emphasized by the 60S wheelbase, 3-ins. longer (127 to 124 ins.) than that of the 60.

Nor was this all. There were some subtle but remarkable changes above the beltline of the 60S. The windows were taller, crisply angled at the corners instead of gently rounded, delicately edged in chrome, and set almost flush with the outside edge of the body rather than indented. The wide rear window was in three pieces with two thin dividers, rather than two pieces with a thick central divider. Combined with thin central pillars, thin windshield pillars, and a thin flat roof, the total effect was to give the living quarters of the 60S a lighter, cleaner, and airier appearance than any contemporary sedan.

But perhaps most remarkable about the 60S body were two things *not* there: the running boards. Considered together with its other changes, the 1938 60S can therefore be pinpointed as the exact model when Cadillac made its first giant break with the styling of the past. All this was the work of William L. Mitchell, the new and youthful head of the Cadillac styling studio. In this, the first car he created for GM, Mitchell showed the great talent that eventually made him the successor to Harley Earl as a GM vice-president and head of the corporate Styling Staff.

The 60S (or Sixty Special—the name looks more impressive spelled out) wowed its public. Despite the fact that it was offered only in 4-dr. sedan form in 1938, it outsold every other Cadillac model that year—3703 were produced. For '39 and '40 it received a facelift, was offered in additional body styles, and sold very well both years. It is a special interest car of the first order, a handsome machine that set the pattern for future GM styling.

For 1940 there appeared a new line, the Series 62, which replaced 1939's Series 61. On this Series 62 only was a new body notably smoother and more integrated than the holdover body on other Cadillacs. It was called the "torpedo body," a name greatly used and misused by so many manufacturers that it is practically meaningless today. The torpedo showed many influences from the 60S, notably the absence of side chrome trim, the bulgeless coupe-like trunk flush with the rear deck, and headlights lowered till they were sitting right on top of the fenders. Any of the four 1940 Series 62 models—sedan, coupe, the rare convertible coupe (200 built), and even rarer convertible sedan (only 75 built)—is a special interest car today because of this body. Mechanical improvements for 1940 were turn signals standard on all models, and recirculating-ball steering only on the Series 72 (another new line for 1940 which lasted only that year).

The last full model year before U.S. entry into the war, 1941, saw sweeping styling changes and a major expansion of Cadillac's line. The reason for this was the discontinuance of the LaSalle after the 1940 model year. In order not to lose all those customers, Cadillac had to have something to offer them. This turned out to be a revival of the Series 61, a low-priced line introduced in '39 but replaced in '40 by the Series 62. Cadillac also retained the 62 for '41, and cleverly cut costs by reducing its wheelbase to 126 ins. and making it share the same chassis as the 61. Also sharing this same chassis was a new model, the Series 63, available only as a 4-dr. sedan. Another new line was the Series 67, a big car with a 138-in. wheelbase. This vied for top-of-the-line honors with the established Series 75, as the turbine-like Series 90 Sixteen Fleetwood was no more. Noteworthy again was the 60 Special, which still retained its low-slung frame and tall glass areas. It shared the same basic styling as the rest of the '41 line, with V-shaped grille and headlights integrated into the fenders but had a different hood line, longer rear fender skirts, and longer front fenders which swept back into the front doors. It was one of Mitchell's famous "stalking horses," as this fender line was used on all '42 Cadillacs and other GM cars as well.

With the formidable revised '41 line-up, Cadillac had more models and body styles to choose from than ever before in its history, though all used the same 346-cu.-in., V-8 now rated at 150 bhp. It was a tempting array for the luxury buyer, especially so since Hydra-Matic and air conditioning became options the same year. This marketing strategy worked, as the Series 61 sales alone were greater than 1940 LaSalle sales. Altogether Cadillac sold 66,130 cars in the '41 model year, a new record that stood until 1949. The fastback 2-dr. sedan body shape (which Cadillac called a coupe) was introduced in the '41 Series 61 and 62 lines, and along with the 60S is the most special interest model of that year.

Seeming almost like a reward for

such a spectacular year, for 1942 Cadillacs went through another major styling revision. The frontal shape of the '41 models was retained, but the grille rectangles were considerably larger and the headlight rims painted instead of chromed. However, the rest of the body was more softly rounded and the front fenders extended well back into the doors, as on the '41 60 Special. Alas, that once distinctive model was now just a tiny variation of the standard sedans, distinguished only by a slightly different side window treatment and rows of useless chromed louvers along the fender bottoms.

As did almost everyone else, Cadillac pressed their prewar design into service as soon as possible after the war, to take advantage of pent-up buying demand until the true postwar designs were ready. Except for minor rearranging of grille bits and pieces, the 1946 and '47 models were identical to the '42 models. In the interests of product simplicity, however, two lines were dropped: the Series 63, mechanically identical to the more popular Series 61; and the low-production long-wheelbase Series 67, which had never sold very well and competed with the top-line Series 75. Hydra-Matic was made available for all models, and rapidly became an almost universal choice among buyers. It took a little while for material shortages and labor problems to be sorted out, but by 1947, production volume was right back up to that record 1941 level.

Cadillac had been working on a new engine since before the war, but it was still not ready for the '48 model year. A new body was, however, so it was introduced with the same mechanicals as the '47 model. It was a stunner, and American automotive styling would never be the same.

It was those fins. Obviously aircraft-inspired, they captured that elusive connective spirit between ground and air transportation, for which the automotive stylists had been striving for two decades, better than anything before. In later years these tailfins would become tasteless monstrosities, but in their early form they were delightfully distinctive features which instantly identified a Cadillac and added to its already immense prestige. An especially masterful touch was the concealment of the fuel tank cap under the swing-up left taillight at the fin's tip.

The highly successful '48 styling was a tribute to Harley Earl, who demonstrated once again the accuracy of his interpretation of automotive forms which were both tasteful and highly salable.

The following year came Cadillac's new ohv V-8, a milestone in the history of the American automobile. Along with the 303-cu.-in. Oldsmobile V-8 introduced shortly afterwards, the 1949 Cadillac V-8 established the general pattern followed by all large American engines down to the present day.

There were four main features of this engine which made it a technological landmark. The first was its combination of overhead valve gear with crossflow porting. Neither of these ideas was new, of course; Cadillac itself used overhead valves on its V-12 and narrow-angle V-16 engines. What was new for Cadillac as well as other American makers of V-type engines was the combination of these features,

1. Cadillac's overhead-valve V-8 came out in 1949, which also happened to be the year for some of the handsomest Cadillacs ever. This splendid example is a fastback Series 62 coupe, which everyone calls a sedanette since it has a rear seat and is not a true coupe. The '49 models can be distinguished from the similar '48 cars by their use of only two layers of rectangles in the grille, instead of three. The clue that this is a Series 62 and not the lower-priced Series 61 is the trim panel behind the front wheel. Though a desirable model, the '49 sedanette is not rare; there were 6409 of them made in Series 61, and 7515 more in Series 62.

2. This is the '49 Coupe de Ville, one of the most desired postwar Cadillacs. Introduced late in the model year into the Series 62 line, only 2150 were made. Its distinctive roof shape and large rear window made it look like a convertible with the top up, and was widely copied styling idea—not only on GM cars, but others—right into the '60's.

3. The Eldorado made its debut in 1953. Sporting a daring new wraparound windshield, all-leather interior, disappearing top, and chrome wire wheels, it had a hefty $7750 price tag; only 532 were made. Like all Cadillacs that year, the Eldorado had a 210-hp engine and a new 12-volt electrical system as standard.

4. The Eldorado for 1954 shared the restyled body and lengthened wheelbase of the standard '54 Cadillacs. Power steering, power brakes, power seats and wire wheels were standard, while the cover for the top was now made of fiberglass instead of metal.

5. In 1955 the Eldorado acquired a distinctive rear end, which was to appear in modified form on the '57 standard line of Cadillacs. All power accessories and leather interior were still standard, while new that year were the intricate Sabre Spoke wheels and a 270-hp engine with two 4-bbl carburetors.

General Motors Corporation
Cadillac

which allowed much better breathing. However, the switch was done not so much to improve breathing as to increase compression ratio. Antiknock lead-additive gasolines were now widely available, which allowed the compression ratio of engines to be substantially raised. However, it was found that the flathead engine design ran into combustion roughness, regardless of its gasoline, at compression ratios much above 7.5:1. An overhead-valve design, on the other hand, was free from this problem until it reached much higher compression ratios.

The second great improvement was the 5-bearing crankshaft. All previous Cadillac V-8's, as well as the Ford V-8, used only three main bearings. The improvement in crankshaft stiffness and the reduction in vibration afforded by the 5-bearing design more than compensated for its increased manufacturing cost.

Third was the oversquare cylinder design. This was a clean break with the long-stroke engines of the past, and allowed higher rpm. It also made the engine lighter, since it reduced block height.

Last but far from least was a development uniquely Cadillac's. It was an idea which had simmered in the mind of piston specialist Byron Ellis, as he—like all engine designers before the war—pondered the path down which the increasing use of shorter strokes was leading. The theoretical limit would be reached, he reasoned, when the crankshaft counterweights interfered with the piston skirt at the bottom of the stroke. But was that a limit which could be skirted? Ellis thought so. His experiments culminated in the "slipper" piston, which had its sides cut away so that it could partially nestle down between the counterweights. This considerably reduced the length of the connecting rods, and therefore the block height.

The result of all this was a new engine that was more powerful, yet smaller, more economical, and enormously lighter than its predecessor. With its cylinder dimensions of 3 13/16 x 3⅝ ins., the displacement was 331 cu. ins., 15 less than the '48 346-cu.-in., flathead engine; but it had ten more hp., (160 to 150) and weighed 188 lbs. less. With the exception of the two V-16 models, this was the most powerful Cadillac engine ever built. With it the handsome '49 Cadillac became a genuine 100-mph car, the fastest car in America except for the lighter Oldsmobile.

Once again Cadillac had caught its competitors flat-footed. There were now only three—Lincoln, Chrysler, and Packard. Of these, the first two had quite uninspired styling, while once-mighty Packard had a melted-marshmallow shape which looked like one of its earlier (and very handsome) Clippers set out in the sun too long. Worse, all were making do with prewar engine designs. Chrysler's magnificent hemi V-8 was still two years in the future, Lincoln had a "new" flathead V-8 that was much like the prewar Ford and was three years away from an ohv design, while Packard was stumbling around with their old flathead sixes and straight eights. Packard, in fact, would not get around to introducing a modern V-8 until 1955, a delay that was to prove fatal.

GM's prestige division was rewarded for its diligence by a surge of customer enthusiasm, and established a soaring new sales record of almost 93,000 cars in the 1949 model year. This was a tremendous jump of nearly 50% over its previous record (1941), and clearly fixed Cadillac as the hands-down top U.S. luxury car. The drive to the top, begun 20 years earlier, was now complete.

All '48 and especially '49 Cadillacs are special interest cars because of the trend-setting styling and that milestone '49 engine. But there are nuances of desirability. The topline Series 75 cars, for example, did not receive the new styling in 1948, nor even in '49. They were therefore the last Cadillacs to hold on to the pleasantly rounded styling introduced in 1942. Combined with the quality of Cadillac's most exclusive and expensive line, this makes a '48 Series 75 a sought-after model.

Cadillac made only four series in these two years: the 61, 62, 60 Special, and 75. The 61 and 62 shared an identical chassis with a 126-in. wheelbase, and differed only in trim. The plusher Series 62, which carried a slightly higher price tag than the 61 ($3050 compared to $2895 for the base model 4-dr. sedan in 1949) was by far the most popular line, and can be distinguished from a 61 by ribbed trim panels behind the front wheel opening and at the forward edge of the rear fender. The Series 61 was available only in 4-dr. sedan and 2-dr. fastback sedan ("sedanette") forms both years, while the Series 62 had those two and a convertible, as well as a special model for '49 discussed more fully in the following paragraph. Interestingly, the convertible outsold the sedanette both years. The 60S had a 133-in. wheelbase and came only in 4-dr. sedan form, while for the big-buck Series 75, a variety of large bodies seating from five to nine people were available on a 136-in. wheelbase.

Undoubtedly the single most coveted model of the '48-'49 years is the Coupe de Ville. This was a brand new model introduced into the Series 62 line only a few months before the end of the 1949 model year. Below the beltline, the Coupe de Ville was identical to a Series 62 sedanette. But its roof was a notchback rather than a fastback shape, there was no central pillar, and the large 3-section wraparound rear window had more glass area than that of the sedan's. The windshield was also subtly different, with squared-off edges and chromed coverings for the corner posts. It looked like a convertible with the top up, which was the whole idea. This was Cadillac's first "hardtop convertible." It was introduced on Buick and Oldsmobile models at the same time, and was another of Harley Earl's styling bellringers. The Coupe de Ville, of course, went on to become a famous staple in the Cadillac lineup; that it was introduced in the milestone year of 1949 only makes one more desirable. It is also rare. Because of its late introduction, only 2150 were made. By comparison, there were 8000 convertibles and 7515 Series 62 sedanettes made in 1949.

Unfortunately for purists of line, the 1950 Cadillac and its successors for the next few years had revised styling which was gross and dumpy compared to the lithe and fleet-looking '48-'49 models. In fact, for the rest of the decade the standard Cadillac line was not outstanding esthetically, and in the late '50's became positively ugly. There were major styling revisions in 1954, '57, and '59, but by 1959 a Series 62 sedan was 225 ins. long and weighed 4460 lbs., compared to 215 ins. and 3840 lbs. for the same model in 1949. It was 7.2-ins. lower, however, at 56.2 ins.

Technical development continued throughout the decade. The 1952 line was outstanding, and one almost suspects the division management of holding off on some of its goodies so that they could be introduced in that year, which happened to be Cadillac's golden anniversary. In that year came power steering (one year after Chrysler), power brakes, Dual-Range Hydra-Matic which could be held indefinitely in third gear, and a 4-bbl. Rochester carburetor with progressive linkage on its two secondary throats. This last item, another first for Cadillac, rapidly became the standard type of carburetor for all big V-8's.

With these 1952 innovations, the modern luxury Cadillac was basically complete. Almost all technical advances since then may be considered gadgetry, or improvement of existing devices, not major breakthroughs in automotive development. Power seats, electric windows, Autronic-Eye, Cruise Control, Climate Control air conditioning, electric seat warmer—all such things are nice (as long as they work), but none are really essential.

So the sedans of the '50's are nice cars but not really collectable, and even the Coupe de Ville was made in ever-increasing numbers after 1949. But there remain the Eldorados.

The first Eldorado appeared in 1953. It was a convertible, mechanically and bodily identical to the standard Series 62 convertible except for three things: it had cut-down doors, a top that stowed neatly under a flush-fitting metal cover, and a wraparound windshield. This was the first such windshield on a GM production car (or any other car), and it caused great comment; it appeared a little later on the '53 Corvette, and the following year it was made standard on all Cadillacs, Buicks and Oldsmobiles.

The '53 Eldorado's $7750 price tag was a bit staggering, even if it did include the chrome wire wheels and power steering that were options on other models. It was easily the most expensive Cadillac of its time. For comparison, the standard Series 62 convertible cost only $4144, and even the luxurious long-wheelbase Series 75 limousine was $5818. The extra money was lavished on the interior, in which various combinations of leather and broadcloth were available. The Eldorado was and remains a limited-production item, but it was especially so in 1953; only 532 were made. Since this was its introductory year and it was completely restyled the following year, a '53 Eldorado is one of the rarest and most valuable postwar Cadillacs ever made.

For 1954 the whole Cadillac line was restyled, and the wheelbase on all models was increased by three inches. This meant the big Series 75 had 147 ins., the Sixty Special 130 ins., and the Series 62 129 ins. (the lower priced Series 61 was discontinued after 1951). On the 62 chassis, the '54 Eldorado continued the theme of its predecessor. Again a convertible, it had a distinctive bright ribbed trim panel on the lower rear fender. The interior was not quite so lavish, and the price a more reasonable $5738. This low price at-

1. By 1956 the Eldorado was offered in two body styles. The traditional convertible became known as the Biarritz. All Cadillacs had a bored-out 365-cu.-in. engine for '56, and the Eldorado's exclusive version put out 305 bhp. The double-fin hood ornament was used only on Eldorados in '56, made its appearance on standard Cadillacs the following year.

2. This is the coupe version of the Eldorado that was new for '56, the Seville. The rear styling was quite similar to '55, except that the exhaust ports were oval instead of round, the license plate bracket was integrated into the bumper, and there were no vertical trim strips above the bumper. As an option, the grille and wheels could be gold anodized on '56 Eldorados. The Seville's top was covered with a synthetic cloth called Vicodec.

3. The '57 Sixty Special retained its 20-year history of being a unique car in the Cadillac line. It retained its exclusive 133-in. wheelbase, a bright trim panel adorned the rear flank, and the double-fin hood ornament of the standard line was removed but duplicated in miniature atop each front fender. Production of the 60S set a record in '57 which remains unbroken to the present day, with 24,000 made.

4. The rear styling of the '57 Eldorado was completely different from the standard Cadillacs, as this Biarritz shows. The fenders were much cleaner, the fins were smaller and set inboard, the taillights were single instead of paired, and the split bumper wrapped completely around the corner of the car and blended with the fenderwell trim. Lots of chrome here. The Biarritz continued the Eldorado tradition of hiding the convertible top under a hard cover.

General Motors Corporation

Cadillac

tracted more buyers, and 2150 Eldorados found a home that year.

In 1955 the Eldorado shared the minor facelift all Cadillacs had that year, but began acquiring an even more distinctive personality. Rakish chrome-edged tailfins sat atop jet-pod twin taillights, "Sabre Spoke" (that's Cadillac's name, folks) disc wheels replaced the chrome wires, the fender skirts disappeared along with the ribbed fender panel, which reappeared in smaller form at the tops of the doors. For the first time, Eldorado power was greater than the standard line, 270 bhp to 250. Production was up again, to 3950 cars.

This successful exclusive line expanded to two models the following year. The convertible was now called the Biarritz, after the famous French resort city on the Atlantic coast near the Spanish border, while a new coupe with a textured roof was named for the romantic Spanish city of Seville. Both had 305 bhp (standard:285) from the bored-out engine all Cadillacs shared, 4x3⅝ ins. and 365-cu.-ins. There were only detail body changes from '56, notably a larger rear bumper with bigger exhaust pipes and the no-cost option of gold anodize on the grille mesh and the Sabre Spoke wheels. Those wheels, incidentally, were not just fancy hubcaps. The centers really were cast aluminum, riveted to steel rims. The new Seville proved to be a faster seller than the Biarritz, 3900 to 2150; their combined total of 6050 cars set a new Eldorado production record.

In 1957, all Cadillacs received new styling and a new frame, which allowed the bodies to be lower. The frontal styling was very massive, with big rubber-tipped bumpers and heavily hooded headlights. The Biarritz and Seville shared this styling, as well as the new frame with its 129½-in. wheelbase. Again they had a higher-than-normal power rating, 325 bhp to 300, thanks to dual 4-bbl. carburetion. The Eldorado rear end treatment was quite different from the Series 62, however, with a gently rounded huge deck on which perched two jaunty fins. Eldorado production went down, for the first time however, with only 2100 coupes and 1800 convertibles coming off the line. The big news for 1957 in Eldoradoland, however, was something quite new, yet a third Eldorado variant: The Brougham.

The 1957-58 Fleetwood Eldorado Brougham was a strange car. It was a hyper-expensive and hyper-exclusive version of the Eldorado, which was an exclusive version of the Cadillac, which was itself considered a pretty exclusive machine by nearly everybody. It was brought out specifically to counter the Continental Mark II, Ford's bid to build the best and most exclusive automobile in the country.

The specifications of the Brougham were mid-'50's gadgetry carried to an extreme. Its wheelbase was 126 ins., the once-standard dimension of the Series 62, but which by 1957 was unique to the Brougham. It had an air suspension system that was of dubious advantage but enormous complexity compared to the standard steel springs. Dozens of electric motors adjusted everything, and merely to list them all would take about a solid page of this book. The Brougham undoubtedly had more of these than any automobile before or since. The striking roof was of brushed stainless steel that was horrendous to refinish if it got scratched. There was a special tray in the glovebox lid for six stainless steel tumblers, the rear armrest was equipped with goodies for him (notepad, pencil) and her (mirror, perfume bottle), Karakul carpeting was only one of 45 available interior coverings, and . . . well, you get the idea. Cadillac had gone into overkill mode, trying to build a modern version of their fabulous Fleetwood classics of a quarter-century earlier.

Externally, a Brougham can be dis-

1. Cadillac's great year of 1957 also saw the introduction of the Eldorado Brougham, and it was a stunner. It had its own 126-in. wheelbase, the 325-hp engine was standard, and everything under the sun was standard in and on the Fleetwood body. The price was a royal $13,075, and for this princely sum the lucky buyer received the most exclusive car in America.

2. The Brougham's striking low build is evident in this comparison with a standard '57 Series 62 sedan. Only 55½ ins. high, the Brougham was 3½ ins. lower than the sedan, which itself was 3 ins. lower than the previous year's. This was the last year for single headlights on the standard Cadillac.

3. Fleetwood Brougham interiors were posh little boudoirs full of mouton carpeting, expensive brocade, and fine leather. A total of 45 different material choices were available.

4. The '58 Eldorado had the same new 4-headlight styling as standard Cadillacs, but single fins on top of fenders. Louvers appeared on the rear quarter behind door. Fins and rear deck remained same as '57, but rear bumper was changed. Standard engine had 310 bhp, optional 3-carb version 335 bhp.

5. The Eldorado Brougham for 1959-60 was this elegant machine with body by Pinin Farina of Turin, Italy. Wheelbase was now 130 ins., and horsepower was up to 345 from the new 390-cu.-in. engine. They were made only upon firm order with substantial deposit, and cost the same as the previous Fleetwood Brougham. Very rare—only 200 built.

1

102/SPECIAL INTEREST AMERICAN CARS

tinguished immediately from other Eldorados because it is a 4-dr. pillarless hardtop. The two doors on each side open from the center, and latch to a very inconspicuous central post which extends up only as high as the midpoint of the doors. These doors lock automatically upon closing, a good safety feature that the rest of the industry would have done well to copy. The Brougham also had four headlights, which the rest of the Cadillac line acquired in 1958.

The Fleetwood Eldorado Brougham was in production only two years. All specifications remained the same for 1958, except for a change from two 4-bbl. to three 2-bbl. carburetion and 335 bhp for '58. The list price was an astronomical $13,075, and the principal reason only a total of 704 were made those two years. Despite the inflation since 1957, this list price has not been exceeded by any American car until the 1975 Seville, Cadillac's compact anti-Mercedes. (Actually, the new Seville's base price of $12,471 is lower, but it has so many extra-cost options that the price can go over $15,000. There were no extra-cost options on the Brougham.)

Whether the Fleetwood Brougham succeeded in checkmating the Continental Mark II is a matter for conjecture. It certainly exceeded its Ford rival in cost and rarity, but it sold far less and is generally considered to have been more flamboyant and less elegant of line.

The "standard" Eldorados underwent minor trim changes and a 4-headlight facelift for 1958. The price had been creeping upward with each year, and now stood at $7500 for both the Biarritz and Seville. There was an economic recession at the time, and this was reflected in Eldorado sales reaching an all-time low. Only 855 coupes and 815 convertibles reached the market that year.

For 1959 there were substantial changes throughout the Cadillac range. The Sedan de Ville and Coupe de Ville, which had formerly been considered as part of the Series 62 line, now received their own designation, the Series 63. The Eldorado Biarritz and Seville were now the Series 64, a new Brougham was the Series 69, and in a thoroughly puzzling move, the prestigious Series 75, which had an unbroken history dating back to 1936, became known as the Series 67 Fleetwood Seventy-five. This was just so much paper shuffling, for the Series 62, 63, and 64 all shared a common chassis, now stretched incrementally to a wheelbase of 130 ins. The engine stroke was lengthened by ¼-in. to 3⅞ ins., enlarging the smooth V-8 to 390-cu.-ins. Together with a slight increase in compression ratio, this boosted the standard engine to 325 bhp, and the Eldorado's triple-carb version to 345 bhp.

Cadillac was having a puppy love affair with that air suspension from the Brougham. It was optional on all models from 1958 to '60, and standard on the Eldorados in '59 and '60. The '59 Eldorados, like the rest of the restyled line, had monstrous fins, a fake rear grille, and rear fender skirts for the first time since '54. The nation was slowly recovering from the recession, and this time the Biarritz outsold the Seville, 1320 to 975.

In that same year a restyled Brougham appeared. This shared the 130-in.-wheelbase chassis of the normal Eldorados, and its 4-dr. pillarless body was built in Italy by Farina, Ferrari's favorite body builder. The super-steep price tag remained unchanged, but this new version did not have all the gadgetry that its Fleetwood predecessor had. It was a very striking and clean-lined car, much "purer" in shape than either the Fleetwood Brougham, the standard '59 Cadillac, or the '59 Eldorados. It had a formal roofline with lots of glass, no phoney rear grille, and its subdued fins foreshadowed the shape of those on the standard 1961-63 cars. It remained in production for two years, and production was very low: 99 in 1959, 101 in 1960, which makes it the rarest of all series-produced postwar Cadillacs. Aficionados do not value this '59-'60 Brougham nearly so much as its Fleetwood predecessor, but it remains an excellent example of a very rare and desirable custom-built automobile.

By the end of the decade Cadillac had consolidated its positon as America's best car and by far the world's largest-selling luxury car. Packard was gone, the Continental Mark II ceased production after two years, and Lincolns and Chryslers simply did not sell in anything like the quantities that Cadillacs did. The ultra-expensive Brougham was discontinued after 1960, but the Eldorado has remained right down to the present day. And through the Depression, World War II, and the postwar era which witnessed a general but inevitable cheapening of cars from the days of the grand classics, Cadillac has continued to build cars that live up to its proud slogan, "Standard of the World."

General Motors Corporation

Chevrolet

From stovebolts to fuel injection

The year was 1929 and the machine was Chevrolet's famous "six for the price of a four" which was set against the Model A Ford introduced the previous year.

Known as the Stovebolt Six from its liberal use of quarter-twenty "stovebolts" and as the Cast Iron Wonder for its durable cast iron pistons, it became synomous with the sort of practical durability Americans needed to carry the nation through the Depression, and breed the loyalty which would put Chevrolet ahead of Ford for all but four of the next 30 years.

After all the excitement of '29, Chevrolet kept things pretty much unchanged in its Universal Series AD for 1930. The valve-in-head six produced 50 hp at 2600 rpm with a displacement of 194 cu. ins., the lowering trend of the past few years continued with tires reduced an inch in diameter to 19x4.75-ins., hydraulic shocks were added, along with a slanted rather than vertical windshield, but otherwise styles were similar to the International Series of '29 and mounted on the same 107-in. wheelbase.

Though all cars made prior to World War II are of increasing interest to the collector, special interest must be paid to those models of limited production. Once the enthusiast departs from the big three for this year—the coach, sedan and coupe—and dips below the 100,000 unit mark, the hunt is on.

Though the Sport Coupe ranked fourth in popularity its sales were half those of the regular coupe—just over 45,300 to be exact. This model featured rumble seat, wire wheels, and a rear window that lowered as standard equipment.

Following the Sport Coupe in sales was the prestige model, the new Special Sedan, a 4-door offering that earned a comfortable 35,000 sales.

Its volume was paced by that of the Sport Roadster, a rumble seat-equipped, 4-passenger car that featured wire wheels, and a jaunty air with the top lowered.

The seventh most popular model was a new one, the 4-door Club Sedan. A blank rear quarter differentiates this from the other sedans and its production figures (fewer than 24,900) make it the rarest of the style.

There was an extremely limited production of the last two models that year—the 2-passenger Roadster, of which fewer than 5700 were built, and that elegant throwback to an already vanishing age, the Phaeton, whose production was just a hair over 1700. The whole rationale of these great touring cars was declining along with the economy and in a few years the Phaetons would disappear altogether.

Among the more interesting accessories this year were black cloth tire covers, wood spoke wheels, detachable trunks, trunk racks, spotlights, bumpers, and single or dual sidemounts—though in the Depression the price of $15 apiece for outside spares proved more than many drivers could afford, and the currently desirable fixtures are rare.

For 1931 Chevrolet introduced the Independence AE Series with three new models for an even dozen in the line. A curved, chromed headlamp tie bar replaced the straight black enamel one of the year before, headlamps had the whole surface chromed rather than just the rims, taillamps went oval and a three-spoke, hard rubber steering wheel was introduced. The cars lengthened to a wheelbase of 109 ins., and the year's most distinguishing feature, a chromed-mesh radiator screen, covered the vertical-bar grille of the previous year.

Another new for 1931 model, a 5-passenger, 2-door coupe enjoyed a good first season and earned almost 20,300 orders, though when you consider that that's about one for every ten thousand Americans you know what your chances are of finding one today. The remaining three in Chevrolet's dozen are rarer still. The Roadster dipped to fewer than 3000 sales, the new Landau Phaeton—which had foldaway center posts but no landau irons—had under 5650 units produced, and the regular Phaeton accounted for a scant 850 sales. It is a highly prized collector's item today.

For 1932, the Confederate Series BA was divided into two sub-series, Standard and DeLuxe. Both were mounted on the same 109-in. wheelbase and used the reliable six, now attached to Chevrolet's synchromesh transmission. Rear axles were heavier, and rubber engine mountings were used for the first time.

Most noticeable styling difference this year was the use of four hood ports, small doors which replaced the series of louvers used in '30 and '31; also new were horns in the shape of

1. The sportiest model in Chevrolet's '31 line was the Sport Roadster, which had folding windshield and rumble seat. Wheelbase was up two in. from '30 to 109 in., but 50-hp six was same introduced two years before in '29.

2. The Landau Phaeton was a new model for '31, one of 12 Chevrolet offered that year. Rather like a 2-door. version of a convertible sedan, this desirable car had a heavy folding top, folding center posts, and leather upholstery.

3. Rarest '31 Chevrolet is the Phaeton. Only 850 were made, so if your aunt Matilda has one tucked away in her garage, pounce on it. All '31 models had a mesh grille screen and chromed headlights joined with a chromed bar.

4. The public turned away from Chevrolet phaetons in the '30's, which makes them sought after today. Only 420 of this car were made in '32.

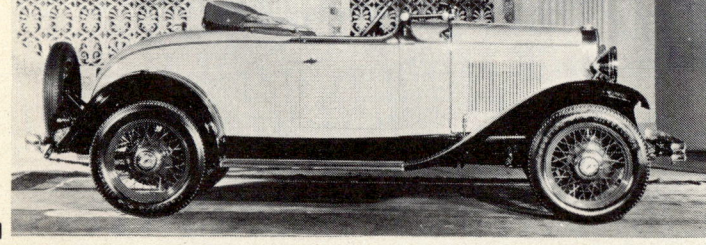

trumpets (these were mounted under the left headlamp, but right-hand horns were available this year along with right-hand taillamps) and the tie bar for front headlamps was double rather than single.

The chief difference between Standard and DeLuxe models was in the latter's use of brightwork, most noticeable on the distinctive chromed hood ports of a DeLuxe model. It's too bad Chevrolet had such a bad year: thanks to the Depression and the introduction of Ford's new V-8, production slid to fewer than 324,000 for the model year. Thus, any '32 is of special interest.

In order of rarity, the Phaeton is tops for the lover of 1932 Chevrolets since only 420 were supposed to have been made, and only in Standard form, but like many cars of this year it could be dressed up by fitting it with the DeLuxe brightwork—a fairly simple task since most goodies were of the bolt-on variety.

Also somewhat of a status symbol among enthusiasts is the '32 Landau Phaeton (1600 units), followed at a distance by the Sports Roadster (8550 produced), the 5-passenger coupe, the Sport Coupe with rumble seat and on into the DeLuxe 2-door and so on, through both DeLuxe and Standard sedans.

In 1933, a hard-pressed Chevrolet leadership came out with the Eagle Series CA, sometimes called the Master. Its wheelbase had grown an inch to 110 ins., and engine improvements nearly doubled the gas mileage from 206 cu. ins. The grille was no V-shaped, and surmounted by a jaunty Eagle; the radiator shell was painted rather than chromed, and the same was true for the hood ports, now reduced to three. Cars dropped the headlamp bar and got a more streamlined look, augmented with fender skirts, and although rear-mounted spares were standard, buyers could still purchase sidemounts.

Despite the dressed-down look of these cars compared to the '32's, Chevy management came out at midyear with an even smaller and cheaper car, the Mercury Series CC (also known as the Standard); it had a wheelbase of 107 ins., louvers instead of hood ports, headlamps with black rather than chrome bodies, a horn tucked demurely under the hood, and a displacement of 182 cu. ins.

Lucky is the special interest car buff who locates a restorable '33 Phaeton—there were only 540 produced. You'd do better by searching out an Eagle Series Sports Roadster or Mercury Series Sports Coupe. The rumble seat-equipped Cabriolet (available only in the Eagle Series for 1933) is, likewise, a superb investment. If you're interested in the odds, there were 4300 Cabriolets built, 2900 Sports Roadsters, and less than 2000 Sports Coupes. Compare these figures to 162,000 units for the best-selling 2-door sedan and just 200 less for the 4-door sedan.

A number of major changes were made for the 1934 model year. Two distinctly different series were developed from the '33 offerings; '33's Eagle Series becoming '34's Master Series (DA) and the Mercury giving way to the Standard Series DC. Although the Standard Series was virtually unchanged mechanically from the year before, there were two major engineering developments to boast about in the Master Series.

One was the introduction of "Knee-Action," the type of independent front suspension which replaced the rigid I-beam axle of previous years. The other change was in power, the new "Blue Flame version of the fabulous Six delivering, as the ads put it, 80 mph from 80 hp, thanks to a higher compression ratio and a new head design.

By far the most popular model was the 2-door Coach, which had a production of almost 164,000 in the Master Series with an additional 69,000 in the Standard Series.

The Master Town Sedan, while a distant third, continued strong with sales in excess of 49,400, quickly followed by a new entry in the Master Series, a 4-door Sports Sedan with better than 37,600 sales.

Model sales dropped off quickly after that—the rumble seat-equipped Master Sport Coupe turned in sales in excess of 18,300, the Standard 2-passenger coupe had a production under 16,800, and the Standard 4-door sedan completed the above 10,000 production range with sales just under 11,850. This last-mentioned car—consisting of a '35 body mounted on a '34 chassis—did phenomenally well considering that it wasn't introduced until October.

Among the really rare ones, the Master Cabriolet continued to decline in popularity with production under 3300, while the Master Sport Roadster posted fewer than 2000, and the Standard version of the Sport Roadster showed fewer than 1050 units as the rumble seat craze rumbled lower in public esteem.

The Phaeton, as usual, proved the least popular of Chevy's models, which of course makes it highly popular with collectors today; available in the Standard Series only, fewer than 240 were built this year.

The Standard Series for 1935 saw the last of the Phaetons (fewer than 220 were produced) and the last of the Sport Roadsters, though these snappy little cars bettered last year's production figures, turning out almost 1200.

In the other Standard models, Chevy manufactured more the 42,000 sedans and 32,000 3-window coupes. For those customers still reluctant to accept Knee-Action, there was the Master Series ED, which without this option was still exactly like the Master DeLuxe Series EA except for being $20 cheaper and 30 pounds lighter.

Significantly, the oiling system for rod bearings was changed from the old splash-type to the Pressure Stream system. The Cabriolet was dropped, too, this year, but it would be back. Fender skirts remained, and they were straight across the bottom.

The styling changes of the 1935 Masters featured the new Turret Top, a one-piece all-steel top made possible through development of new presses and dies. In addition there was a V'd windshield rather than a one-piece, a return to doors hinged at the trailing edge, a slightly taller and narrower V'd grille, and an optional headlamp beam indicator.

Sidemounts could be had only with the Town and Sport Sedans, which carried regular spares in their trunks; these models as well as the ordinary 4-door sedan were outfitted with steel spoke wheels whereas all others used wire.

Both the Sport Sedan and Town Sedan made good showings this year—with production runs in excess of 67,000 and 66,000 respectively—no doubt due to the convenience of their

3

4

General Motors Corporation
Chevrolet

built-in trunks, though that might have been boosted by a taste for steel spoke wheels: the trunkless 4-door sedan posted sales of almost 58,000.

The 2-passenger, 5-window coupe had a respectable showing with sales in excess of 40,000, but the new Master DeLuxe Sport Coupe couldn't buck the declining interest in rumble seats and enjoyed a production of just over 11,900. Also new for the year was an 8-passenger Suburban Carryall; and though the all-steel vehicle was classed as a truck it might prove of special interest to the collector who can't get hold of one of the last Phaetons.

The last year for sidemounts was 1936, apparently offered only in the 3-window coupe and the Sport Sedan. Headlamps were now attached to the radiator shell and the grille was taking on more of an oval shape; the center grille molding carried up into the center hood molding, for a nice effect, and the front door was once again hinged at the leading edge.

In mid-season steel spoke wheels became standard on all body types—Master DeLuxe Series FA, Master Series FB, and Standard Series FC, the latter now increased to a wheelbase of 109 ins.—though wire wheels continued as optional equipment.

As mentioned previously, the Cabriolet made a reappearance this year, in the Standard Series, though it was by far the lowest production model of the line with barely 3600 units. This put Chevy's only open car miles behind the Town Sedan which sold almost 221,000 units in the Standard Series and an additional 244,000 in the Master DeLuxe Series to become the nation's most popular car this year.

The Master DeLuxe Coach turned in a respectable run of 40,800, but the bottom dropped out the market after that and the remaining models, the good old 4-door sedans, sold just 14,500 in the Master DeLuxe Series and fewer than 11,150 in Standard Series, while the public bought fewer than 11,000 Master DeLuxe Sport Coupes. Apparently the public was less and less interested in trunkless sedans and inconvenient rumble seats, though in today's market not a few probably wish they'd salted a couple away.

The dozen models fielded for 1937 were broken into just two series; you either wanted Knee-Action, in which case you chose something from the Master DeLuxe Series GA, or you chose the knee-less Master Series GB which evolved from the old Standard Series. In either case you got a new exterior skin and a new engine.

Even though the new Six had a larger bore, it was shorter by 2 ins., and with a displacement of 216.5 it gave 85 hp at 3200 rpm. Both camshaft and crankshaft were supported by four main bearings rather than the three which had been used from '29 on; there was also a new shorter and lighter transmission, and wheelbase for both series was standardized at 112¼ ins.

Other than front suspension the two series differed mainly in items of trim such as a lack of right taillight on the low-priced models. A streamlining effect was achieved from the groove which creased the side, slanting downward from the front fender to a fade-out point near the rear end of the front door; the hood sported a series of short louvers set at an angle, and the radiator shell now extended past the rear of the headlamps, which were painted to match the body color.

The Master DeLuxe Sport Coupe, with rumble seat, had a production of fewer than 9000, the 2-door Master DeLuxe Coach fewer than 7300, and the increasingly unpopular 4-door Master DeLuxe Sedan barely squeaked out 2200.

The 4-door sedan fared only slightly better in the less expensive Master Series, with just over 2750 being manufactured. This would've put it at the bottom of the popularity polls were it not for the sales figures on the Master Cabriolet; though these were Chevy's only open cars now, and a convertible with rumble seat is highly desirable today, demand in 1937 was so low that just over 1700 were produced.

The most popular model for 1938 was the Master DeLuxe Town Sedan, with a production of more than 186,000 units—double that of the next most popular model, the Master version of the Town Sedan which saw a production of just over 95,000.

The Master DeLuxe Sport Sedan posted sales of better than 76,300, twice as many as the series' next most popular model, the Master DeLuxe business coupe, of which just over 36,100 were made.

Not one of the remaining three models in the Master DeLuxe line could post figures even 10% of that, however, and are naturally the most sought-after by the special interest collector. The Sport Coupe, Chevrolet's last closed rumble seat model, showed a production of under 2800, but that was a good deal better than the Master DeLuxe Coach of which just over 1000 were made. Sales of the 4-door sedan were so poor that production was halted before it reached even 240, which makes this one about as rare as the last Phaetons, though not as collectible.

The sedan fared only a little better than that in the Master Series where just over 520 were turned out—which meant the public was for once buying less of some model than the Master Cabriolet, the open rumble seat-graced car that had a production of just under 2800, thus giving the convertible fancier about a thousand more to choose from this year than last.

Of the three remaining models in this series the Master business coupe sold the most—just under 40,000. Half as many Sport Sedans were made, just under 20,600, but the much rarer Master Coach—of which fewer than 3330 were made—should really be of interest to the collector who comes across one.

In 1939 the Master Series became

the Master 85, pointing up its horsepower rating though the Six remained virtually unchanged mechanically from the engines of last year. The chief changes this year were in exterior styling. The slanting crease was dropped in favor of plain sides; the new grille treatment, with bars of all the same width, extended back along the fender line; it disappeared behind the headlamps, now mounted on the front fenders above louvers which balanced the grille's narrow bottom. Right-hand taillamps were standard on the low-priced line for the first time, and were placed much higher up on the body.

A whole new style was introduced in 1939, the station wagon. Although Chevrolet continued to offer the Suburban Carryall designed for optional passenger use, this year's new car was mounted on a passenger car rather than a truck chassis. Lovers of woodie wagons may have some difficulty locating these gems, however, since there were fewer than 990 made in the Master DeLuxe Series JA and fewer than 440 in the Master 85 Series JB—in this latter series about half were built with rear doors and a half with folding end gates. Early production models had but one horizontal brace strip in the side panels, though later year models would add one more. They were the only models to retain sidemounts.

Having added this new style, management decided to drop the Cabriolet

1. Like all GM cars in 1934, Chevrolet offered new independent front suspension, which it called "Knee-Action." This was also the first year the name "Blue Flame" was applied to the smooth 6-cyl. engine, which now boasted 80 hp. This is a Standard Coach body.

2. This smooth Master DeLuxe Sport Coupe shows the new split windshield for 1935 and the surprising return to rear-hinged doors on some models. A new model this year, the Sport Coupe with its rumble seat didn't sell well.

3. Another new model for '35, the Suburban Carryall was the forerunner of Chevrolet's station wagon. Check one of these out if you're the old car buff who always gets stuck taking the Little League team to play.

4. This is a very rare model, a 1938 Master DeLuxe Coach. Only a little over 1000 were made, and it is a good example of a car which is rare without necessarily being a collector's item.

this year, and before the year was very far along they also decided to drop some other models—the trunkless 4-door sedans and 2-door coaches. Fewer than 70 Master DeLuxe Sedans were turned out, and fewer than 190 Master DeLuxe Coaches; things were only slightly better in the Master 85 Series which saw just over 330 sedans and 1400 coaches produced.

This year again the first choice of Chevrolet customers was the Town Sedan, some 220,000 being produced in the Master DeLuxe Series and an additional 124,000 put into service in the Master 85 Series.

The Sport Sedan sold about half that many in the Master DeLuxe Series, which was far better than its companion in the Master 85 Series, of which fewer than 23,000 were built.

The Business Coupe did about the same amount of business this year as last—41,700 were made in the Master 85 line and an additional 33,800 were turned out in the Master DeLuxe Series. The Master DeLuxe Sport Coupe lost its rumble seat this year, though it was still a 4-passenger car and had a production of just over 20,900. Some early versions of the Sport and Business Coupes had the gas fillers mounted in front of the right fender, but by mid-year they were being mounted on the rear fender proper.

For 1940 Chevy again fielded three lines, the Special DeLuxe Series, KA, with all the fancy equipment, the Master DeLuxe Series KH, a middle-priced line, and the Master 85 Series KB which lacked the trimmings and the Knee-Action of the other two.

Among the coupes the Special DeLuxe Sport Coupe did the best, with 46,600 units produced, followed at a fair distance by the Business Coupe with over 28,000 manufactured in the Master DeLuxe Series and more than 25,500 turned out in the Special DeLuxe range. In addition, Chevrolet made over 17,230 Master DeLuxe Sport Coupes.

The really rare ones for this year are the Special DeLuxe convertible coupe, now a full 6-passenger car without rumble seat, of which just over 11,820 were made, and the station wagon. This year the wagon had its spare mounted outside on the tailgate, and was available in two series, though in

extremely limited numbers: in the Special DeLuxe line Chevrolet built just over 2100 with conventional tailgates, plus an additional 360 with double rear doors; fewer than 415 were made available in the Master 85 Series.

Elsewhere in this low-priced line you'll find a few more to choose from. Chevrolet made 66,000 Town Sedans in the Master 85 line, and added almost 26,000 Business Coupes and nearly 11,500 Sport Sedans.

Chevrolet's designers went to all-steel welded construction for 1941, put the cars on a 116-in. wheelbase, hinged both front and rear doors at the leading edge, added rubber gravel deflectors to the rear fenders and kept the lovely teardrop skirts of the previous year, set headlamps into the front fenders and made Knee-Action standard on what were now just two models—Master DeLuxe Series BG and Special DeLuxe Series BH.

Under the hood Chevrolet made changes in the valve spacing, water pumps, points, rocker arms and pistons, resulting in the "Victory Six;" it had the same 216.5 displacement but now delivered 90 hp at 3300 rpm.

As usual, the Town Sedan sold well; almost 228,500 were produced in the Special DeLuxe Series, plus an additional 219,400 in the Master DeLuxe line. Chevy made nearly 156,000 Special DeLuxe Coupes, and almost 80,000 Master DeLuxe Coupes. The 3-passenger Business Coupes, which had their gas fillers in the side rather than on the fender, came in both lines, too—almost 49,000 in Master DeLuxe but fewer than 18,000 in the Special DeLuxe version.

This pattern was reversed in the Sport Sedan offerings—they had a run of more than 148,000 in the Special DeLuxe line and fewer than 60,000 in the Master DeLuxe Series.

The rarest models again this year were the Special DeLuxe Convertible, with a production of just under 16,000, and the Special DeLuxe Station Wagon. These woodies sported ash framing over mahogany panels and were Chevrolet's heaviest and most expensive models—which may be why fewer than 2050 were built.

As a prelude to coming things Chevrolet at mid-year introduced the Special DeLuxe Fleetline Sedan, a 4-door

General Motors Corporation
Chevrolet

model with blind rear quarter in its new upper body; it had a run of just over 34,000.

For 1942 the company extended the front fenders back almost to the midpoint of the front doors, installed a gravel shield between the front bumper and grille, and the cars lost their side hood louvers. Pretty soon the cars were lost, too. By government order civilian automobile production was suspended in early February of 1942. Consequently, models in the Master DeLuxe Series BG and the Special DeLuxe Series BH are a little harder to find than their immediate predecessors.

The star of the year was, surprisingly, a brand new model—the Special DeLuxe Fleetline Aerosedan, which featured a roofline that swept down in an unbroken line to the taillights plus a distinctive trim of triple chrome strips on the fenders; it had a production of almost 62,000 units. Its companion, the Fleetline Sportmaster Sedan, likewise sported the triple chrome striping, but had a more conventional roofline derived from last year's Fleetmaster Sedan; just over 14,500 were produced.

The Town Sedan continued strong, turning out almost 42,000 in the Master DeLuxe Series, and better than 39,000 in the Special DeLuxe Series. The 5-passenger coupe saw a production of 22,000 in the Special DeLuxe Series and an additional 17,400 in the Master DeLuxe Series—however the little Special DeLuxe Business Coupe saw a production of barely 8000 and of the Special DeLuxe version only 1700 were made.

You'll have a better chance of finding a Master DeLuxe Sport Sedan, since Chevrolet put more than 14,000 into production, and an even better hope of picking up one of the 31,400 Special DeLuxe 4-door Sedans made before the ban. But they're not really of special interest.

Once again, convertibles and station wagons are hard to come by; Chevrolet produced fewer than 1800 ragtops and barely 1050 woodies.

In 1946, the former DeLuxe Series was now called the Stylemaster Series DJ and the Master Series became the Fleetmaster Series DK.

In the Fleetmaster Series Chevrolet turned out 73,700 Sport Sedans, nearly 58,000 Fleetline Aerosedans, 56,500 Town Sedans, and 27,000 Sport Coupes. In the Stylemaster Series it produced 75,000 Sport Sedans and 61,000 Town Sedans.

Among those models with production figures under 20,000—or one for every 10,000 persons in the country today—you'll probably have the greatest chance of finding the reliable 5-passenger Stylemaster Sport Coupe; Chevy made more than 19,200 of these, and in addition turned out more than 14,200 3-passenger Stylemaster Business Coupes.

The Fleetline Sportmaster Sedan again fell far short of the Aerosedan in popularity and barely 7500 were manufactured. The Fleetmaster Convertible was down to a production of just over 4500, but woodies were even scarcer: Chevrolet didn't begin making them until quite late in the year and only some 800 Fleetmaster Station Wagons made it to the streets.

For 1947 Chevrolet eliminated the strip of brightwork that had run from the hood to the rear of the body; it also made the obligatory grille change—to one of three thick horizontal bars attached to the fenders. Except for interiors and finish there was little difference between the Fleetmaster Series EK and the Stylemaster Series EJ.

The collector interested in late Forties ragtops is in luck since this year saw a record production of more than 28,400 Fleetmaster Convertibles. Those with a yen for woodies, however, will have a bit harder time since fewer than 5000 were made.

A wide vertical strip divided the three horizontal grille bars in the 1948 cars and they got new rods and precision bearings, but otherwise there was virtually no change; it would be another year before the first dramatic changes in postwar styling. Reflecting this, vehicles still came in Stylemaster (Series FJ) and Fleetmaster (Series FK) versions, though the customer could opt for 15 in. rather than 16-in. standard wheels.

The Fleetmaster Convertible, with its automatic top, leather upholstery and brightmetal window trim, sold not quite 20,500 units. The Stylemaster

1. The Fleetline Sportmaster sedan was a new model in the Special DeLuxe line for '42. Like the fastback Fleetline Aerosedan, it had triple trim stripes on the fenders, the only '42 Chevrolets with such trim; 14,500 were made.

2. The postwar styling revolution which integrated the fenders into the body caught up with Chevrolet in 1949. With modifications to the grille, this body would serve for the next four years. This is the sport sedan version of the notchback Styleline series; the Fleetline series all had the fastback shape.

3. A new body for 1950 was the stylish Bel Air hardtop coupe, with its wraparound rear window and lack of a central pillar. An instant hit, the Bel Air eventually gave its name to a whole line of Chevrolets. Powerglide, and a bigger engine for it, were mechanical news.

4. A new body with three vertical grille bars marked the 1953 cars; styling the following year was similar except for five bars, different headlight rims and taillights. Bel Air was now top Chevrolet line.

5. Spectacular news for 1955 was the new lightweight V-8, which went on to become a legend in its own time. Ultra-short stroke, stud-mounted rocker arms, and a weight 41 lbs. less than the Blue Flame six made this the engineering marvel of its day.

6. The Bel Air Nomad, introduced in '55, is probably the only non-woody station wagon that has attracted hordes of collectors. Never wildly popular during its day, it was made for two more years and remains perhaps the handsomest wagon ever.

Business Coupe, still showing a gas filler in front rather than on the rear fender, saw a manufacture of fewer than 18,400 units. As for the one model priced over $2000, the ash and mahogany, leatherette-topped Fleetmaster Station Wagon—which still sported a rear-mounted spare—it saw a production of just under 10,200 units.

When the new styles came out for 1949 they were a complete departure from all that had gone before, and Chevrolet never looked back.

The most noticeable difference was in a section of the design that had previously seemed almost as much a part of the car as the wheels. The protruding front fender was dropped completely in favor of a slab-side look; the body moved in one plane from headlamp to rear fender. The look was augmented by designing skirts as panels that fit flush with the rear fenders. The grille had a series of seven short vertical bars set between the two lower horizontal bars, the wheelbase was shortened to 115 ins., there'd been some improvements in the front suspension, and pushbutton door handles were in use for the first time.

Those interested in the fastback look should consider the Special Fleetline Sedans; 36,000 of the 4-door versions and 58,000 of the 2-door versions were produced.

Other special models, with Styleline bodies, include the town sedan, with a production of 69,000, the sport sedan with 46,000, the sport coupe with 27,000, and the years' lowest-priced model, the business coupe with 20,000 units manufactured. Those interested in a sport coupe with a fancier look are in a bit better position—more than 78,000 were made in the DeLuxe Styleline version.

There are considerably fewer ragtops and wagons around, however, Chevrolet did turn out more than 32,000 DeLuxe Styleline Convertibles, but it made fewer than 3400 woodies before going to all-steel construction for the DeLuxe Station Wagon—and it barely made 6000 of those.

So the woodies went the way of the Phaetons, but the wagon line itself gained tremendously in sales as the division roared into the Fifties with a record-breaking production year.

The biggest news for 1950 was the introduction of Powerglide, the first automatic transmission in the low-priced field. The engine which powered it, adapted from a truck engine introduced in 1941, displaced 235 cu. ins. and delivered 105 hp at 3600 rpm.

Both Styleline and Fleetline versions were available in the Special Series HJ and DeLuxe Series HK, just like last year. There were only minor differences in trim between the two lines—such as chrome gravel guards on the DeLuxe, in addition to the brightmetal stripe running from headlamp through the front door. The number of vertical grille bars was reduced to two, surmounted by the parking lights.

There was, though, a new car for a new decade. This was the DeLuxe Styleline Bel Air, which may be of special interest not so much because of limited production, since better than 76,000 were made, but by virtue of being the first of an illustrious line. By removing the center posts between side windows and bringing the rear glass around to the side of the roof a

3

4

5

6

SPECIAL INTEREST AMERICAN CARS/109

General Motors Corporation
Chevrolet

tremendous feeling of space was achieved.

The new all-steel DeLuxe Styleline Station Wagon with painted wood trim was manufactured in too large a quantity—almost 167,000—to qualify for special interest status; but the DeLuxe Styleline Convertible remained almost static in its sales—under 33,000—and the increasing rarity of this type recommends it.

Out of the eight different sedan models, one shows promise: it is the Special Fleetline 4-door Sedan with a production of 23,000 units.

Among the three coupe models the Special Styleline Business Coupe is of interest since its sales continued low, numbering fewer than 21,000 this year.

The cars got longer in 1951, expanding to 197.8 ins. overall, wagons included, though the wheelbase remained 115. Though the standard engine remained the 216.5 cu. in. developing 92 hp at 3400 rpm, nearly 40% of buyers this year elected Powerglide and its larger engine.

The Fleetline 4-door Sedan is of interest since it was discontinued—after a production of 57,000 in the DeLuxe line, but only some 3300 in the Special Series, the lowest of any model for this year.

The Special Fleetline 2-door Sedan was likewise terminated after a production of fewer than 6500 units. Thus the only fastback model carried over into the next year was the DeLuxe Fleetline 2-door Sedan, which had a run more than double that of the other three combined.

Sales of the Special Styleline Sport Coupe slackened off, with fewer than 19,000 made; the same is true of the Special Styleline Business Coupe, of which just 17,000 were manufactured.

Sales of the DeLuxe Convertible took a one-third decline this year, and fewer than 21,000 were turned out. But that was minor compared to what happened to the station wagon market, with a production of under 24,000, which was about a seventh of what it'd been only the year before.

For 1952 the cars added five small vertical moldings on the center horizontal grille bar, and added—in the DeLuxe line only—a trailing strip of trim from the stone-guards on the rear fenders. Otherwise, the DeLuxe Series KK and the Special Series KJ looked just about like the previous year's styles.

Production was down across the board. Management decided to drop the DeLuxe Fleetline 2-door Sedan after a run of just over 37,000, though it kept the Special Styleline 4-door Sedan with a run of fewer than 36,000 units.

There are four models this year of particular interest to the collector. The DeLuxe Convertible, with a run of under 12,000 is definitely on the list, as is the DeLuxe Station Wagon, now down to a production of under 12,800. Both the Special Styleline Business Coupe and the Special Styleline Sport Coupe had limited productions, the former seeing a manufacture of under 10,500 and the latter one of just over 8900.

Three lines were offered for 1953—the 150 Special Series A, the 210 DeLuxe Series B and the Bel Air Series C. The grille now had three teeth instead of five and all models utilized wraparound windshields. Except in the lower-priced 150 line all models featured a similar wraparound rear window; the 150 models were the only ones where Powerglide was not an option.

Those who didn't elect Powerglide got a brand new version of the Blue Flame Six with a bore and stroke of 3-9/16x3-5/16, displacing 235.5 cu. ins. and delivering 108 hp at 3600 rpm.

Cars with Powerglide developed 115 hp at 3600 rpm; since these engines used aluminum pistons they marked the beginning of the end for the famed Cast Iron Wonder. However, Chevrolet this year came out with the Corvette, a car destined to be as much a legend as its famous Six.

Among other cars of limited production and special interest for 1953 are the 210 DeLuxe Convertible, of which just over 5600 were built, the 150 Spe-

1. You'll get a lot of arguments that this is the best-looking car Chevrolet ever bolted together, period. The '57 has legions of the faithful, and this Bel Air Sport Coupe is their Holy Grail. Equally sought are the Sport Sedan, a 4-dr. pillarless hardtop, and the Bel Air Sport convertible.

2. There were a lot of Chevrolet engines available in '57, but this one was undeniably the star. The Rochester injection system on top of the new 283-cu.-in. size developed 283 bhp at 6200 rpm. Optional in any series or body style, the injected engine was an automotive milestone.

3. A new and massive body with a longer wheelbase made the scene in 1958. In addition to the "little" V-8 was a new optional engine of 348 cu. ins., the first year for the "big-block" V-8. Impala was the new top line, and this is its Sport Coupe.

4. Wait a minute there, Zora Arkus-Duntov, Father of the Corvette and Wizard of Automotive Alchemy; that doesn't look like any 2-seat fiberglass sports car you're getting into. In fact, it doesn't even look like a car, let alone a Chevrolet. You say it's the new '59 Biscayne coupe with batwing fins? And you're about to take it out on the GM Proving Grounds to show everyone that it's really safe? Hmm. Well, if it's good enough for you, Zora, it's good enough for this book.

cial Club Coupe, which saw a run of just under 7000, and the 210 DeLuxe Townsman Wagon, which enjoyed a manufacture of fewer than 8000.

You might also take a look at the 150 Special Business Coupe, since it had a fairly low run of under 13,600.

There were mechanical changes in the Blue Flame Six for 1954 which raised its horsepower rating to 115 at 3700 rpm for the standard block and to 125 hp at 4000 rpm for those engines equipped with Powerglide; the Corvettes used the same engine but with a rating of 150 hp at 4200 rpm.

In future years there might be a scarcity of the Bel Air Convertible, of which fewer than 19,500 were made.

Not content with reworking the venerable Six, Chevrolet in 1955 came out with an overhead valve V-8. The 265-cu.-in. engine used a bore and stroke of 3.75 by 3 ins. and developed 162 hp at 4400 rpm in standard form; when accompanied by Powerglide it delivered 170 hp at 4400 rpm.

In addition to a new engine Chevrolet also had a new style for buyers this year. Graced with a distinctive rear end treatment of curved glass windows and a series of seven vertical bright-metal strips on the tailgate, the Bel Air Nomad wagon has gone on to collect the same sort of special interest fans as the old woodies and Corvettes.

Only 8400 Nomads were made this year, making it a particularly intriguing piece for the collector. It would've been Chevrolet's lowest-production model for the year were it not for the disastrous showing of the Corvette which had about 675 sales in 1955.

General Motors turned out its 50-millionth car this year, a Chevrolet, and as if to underscore the zesty new image of the line's changed styling a pre-production '56 Chevrolet broke the Pike's Peak record which had been held by Ford for 20 years.

When the 1956 line came out there were few changes from the previous year, at least in the regular lines. The Six had a new horsepower rating of 140 at 4200 rpm, but the V-8 remained the same, except for more compression. Though the new grille now enclosed the parking lights to give the cars a wider look, and last year's side molding was accentuated so the cars had more of a forward-swept look.

The Bel Air Nomad, which saw a slight drop in sales this year to fewer than 7900 units, is a choice item to seek out.

One other limited production model, a wagon, bears watching. The 9-passenger, 4-door Bel Air Beauville, had a production of under 13,300.

Twin aerodynamic ornaments marked the hood of the 1957 Chevrolets, a horizontal bar of brightwork cut through the middle of the grille, and the rear fenders were now showing what could definitely be called fins.

The wheelbase remained 115 ins. but the cars were now lower thanks to a switch from 15-in. to 14-in. wheels; they were also lengthened to 200 ins. overall. But the important news was under the hood.

There were eight different engine options, from the 235.5-cu.-in. Six delivering 140 hp at 4200 rpm to the new fuel-injected V-8 which developed one horsepower for each of its 283 cu. ins. at 6200 rpm. V-8 production exceeded that of Powerglide for the first time.

This year the lowest production figures were those for the Bel Air Nomad. Its run of 6100 was less than that of the unchanged Corvette which turned out almost 6250 units.

Chevrolet put out a wholly new automobile for 1958. It had a new shape, a new X-member frame, new interiors, new 117.5-in. wheelbase, new engines and new series names. There were new dual rather than single headlights, new fin treatments that ran from the middle of the rear door to curl around the taillight, a new mesh grille enclosing dual parking lights.

The Impala was now a major sub-series of the Bel Air line, the Biscayne took over from the 210 Series, and the Delray replaced the 150 Series.

The V-8 was now capable of developing 230 hp at 4800 rpm when using a 4-barrel carburetor; fuel injection pushed it to 250 hp at 5000 rpm. But there was an optional 348-cu. in. engine with a bore and stroke of 3.875 ins. by 3 ins. and a compression ratio of 8.5:1 that delivered 250 hp at 4400 rpm or 280 hp at 4800 rpm when equipped with three 2-barrel carburetors. The good old Six was rated at 145 hp at 4800 rpm.

One additional candidate for the collector, in spite of its volume of almost 60,000 units, is the Bel Air Impala Convertible, particularly for those who have a penchant for fancy trim.

For 1959 Chevrolet designed a car that produced only 16,000—the pickup-like El Camino; and a car that detonated more controversy than anything since the introduction of Knee-Action. It was the height of the tailfin hysteria at GM and Chevrolet's version of the fad stands comparison with any, including the Batmobile Cadillac turned out. With its gull-wing fins cantilevered over the cat's-eyes of its taillights, Chevrolet had indeed come a long way from the dowdy styles of yesteryear.

Too far, according to some special interest car enthusiasts. But they said the same thing about Picasso and he did fairly well. Beauty, it seems, is in the eye of the collector.

3

4

General Motors Corporation

Corvette

Americas most popular sports car.

PHOTOS COURTESY OF GM PHOTOGRAPHIC

It was a select group of men which met in the Styling Auditorium of General Motors. Together, Harlow "Red" Curtice, then President of GM, Chevrolet General Manager Thomas H. Keating, and the Division's young chief engineer Edward N. Cole were among the most influencial people of the American automobile industry.

They were meeting this day in May 1952 to preview a new car which, as history would prove, was destined to be one of the finest mass-produced sports cars ever made. A certain amount of drama accompanied the occasion as a curtain was swept aside to reveal a 2-seat, low-slung vehicle looking for all the world as if it had just arrived from the winding mountain roads of Europe with its gleaming white paint and bright red leather interior. The reaction within the auditorium was electric as Curtice, perhaps the last man to single-handedly rule GM, decided the car should be built for display in the company's roving Motorama show. With that decision, Curtice, Keating and Cole created the Corvette.

In actuality, though, the genesis of the Corvette can be traced back to early 1951 when General Motors styling chief Harley Earl began considering the practicality of building a small sporty car for the youth market. The idea so intrigued Earl that he established a private styling studio where he and a personal crew began work on the project.

Earl's initial associates on the Corvette-to-be were body engineer Vincent Kaplan, draftsman Carl Peebles and stylists Bill Bloch and Tony Balthasar. The original concept was to design a simple car that would sell for only $1850, and to meet these parameters the small staff borrowed heavily from the Willys Jeepster with a few touches added from the classic British sports cars. Earl rejected this first attempt but his enthusiasm for the project continued unabated so he brought in design engineer Robert F. McLean, a Caltech alumnus who was also a sports car enthusiast.

Defying traditional Detroit practice, McLean drew a basic construction layout starting at the rear of the car and worked toward the front. He located the rear axle center and then placed the two passenger seats as close to the wheel housing as was practicable. The occupants were drawn in a straight-legged sitting position. From here McLean sketched in the dashboard line and brought the rear of the Chevrolet 6-cylinder engine as near to it as possible. To complete the layout, the front axle was located slightly in front of the motor resulting in the vehicle's 102-in. wheelbase.

Earl viewed the unusual design with much interest and noted the radical differences from stock Chevrolet models. After hearing McLean's explanation that this was how the English MGs and Jaguars were constructed, Earl decided that this, too, was how the Corvette would be built. In retrospect, this perhaps was the most important decision made in connection with the Corvette since it meant the new car would be a real sports car rather than a sporty-type car, that a special frame was needed therefore ruling out the possibility of a low price, and that the Jaguar and MG influence would saddle the automobile with many problems for many years.

While the exterior shape was being refined, Joe Schemansky was assigned the task of designing the interior. Following the European example, Schemansky used individual bucket seats and dash-mounted gauges for monitoring engine functions. Unfortunately, these gauges were arrayed in a single row across the bottom of the dashboard and, as numerous customers complained later, were almost impossible to find and read. A plaster and wood mockup was now made, trimmed, painted and readied for that fateful May preview before Curtice, Keating and Cole.

Immediately following Curtice's approval to build the car for the Motorama show, a cloak of secrecy descended on the project and the fledgling automobile was code-named "Opel" so competing car makers would confuse it with GM's German subsidiary should the existence of the little sportster become known.

On June 2, 1952, Maurice Olley of the GM Research and Development department was shown a plaster model of the Corvette and instructed to de-

1. Conceived, designed and built in less than a year, the original Corvette made its debut in January 1953 at the New York Motorama show. The car created such a sensation that GM rushed it into production within months of the showing.

2. The production '53 Corvette was an exact replica of the Motorama car except for the full-length chrome piece along the side. Only 300 were built and a mere 183 were sold due to an erroneous marketing scheme and some poor design features.

3. Starting with the old Chevy 6-cylinder motor rated at 115 hp, Cole increased the compression, installed a high-lift cam and used mechanical lifters. Three side-draft Carter carburetors were fitted to clear the Corvette's low profile hood. These modifications netted the "Blue Flame Six" a healthy 150 hp.

sign a chassis for the car. Eighteen months later, at a meeting of the Society of Automotive Engineers, Olley described the assignment like this: "The need was to produce a sports car using components of known reliability, with adequate performance, a comfortable ride, and stable handling qualities, in something less than seven months before showing, and 12 months before production. There was not much time."

Olley, though, was nonplussed by this prodigious order and within 10 days of being handed the assignment he had sketched a virtually finalized design of the Corvette's chassis. Earl's original idea of using existing components was by now long forgotten due to McLean's radical approach, so Olley began with an entirely new frame for the car composed of boxed side members and a central X-member for extra rigidity. The normal Chevrolet torque tube rear axle was discarded in favor of a Hotchkiss drive which relied on leaf springs as locating members. Since the driveshaft was very short, a mere 36 ins., straps attached to the rear axle were needed to prevent undue suspension travel that could cause excessive universal joint angularity.

At the same time Olley and his engineers were fitting a chassis beneath the automobile, Ed Cole was busy modifying Chevrolet's venerable 235-cu.-in. 6-cylinder motor so that it would produce the amount of horsepower needed by a sports car. His job was made somewhat easier since the Powerglide engine was due to receive aluminum pistons in 1953 along with full-pressure bottom end lubrication and steel-backed rod bearings. Even these changes, though, netted only 115 hp at 3600 rpm—by no means enough to satisfy a sports car enthusiast.

Cole's first act was to increase the compression ratio from 7.5:1 to 8:1. Then the major changes centered around induction, timing and exhausts. Mechanical lifters were fitted to the engine to match a special camshaft which had a .405-in. lift for the intakes and .414-in. on the exhausts—both unheard-of specifications for a stock cam in 1952. With a 240° duration, this new camshaft afforded the engine with high rpm potential and to support this newly found capability each valve was equipped with dual springs.

Because of the car's low profile hood, it had been predetermined that some sort of horizontal induction system would be needed. At the time, multiple carburetion was considered a must for any sort of performance car, so Cole went all the way and installed triple side-draft single-barrel Carter carbs mounted on a special aluminum intake manifold. When Cole had finished with all the engine modifications, the sedate little 6-cylinder had been upgraded to 150 hp at 4200 rpm with 223 lbs.-ft. of torque at 2400 rpm. It would eventually be the "Blue Flame Six." The Corvette-to-be now had the power to match its image.

Two pivotal decisions were now made that set the course for the new sports car. One almost killed the automobile and did, in fact, haunt the vehicle for years afterward. The other would eventually become the Corvette's hallmark.

The first decision involved the choice of the Powerglide as the car's only available transmission. On the surface this seemed logical, at least for the Motorama car, since the engine was designed for the 2-speed Powerglide and a floor-mounted shifter was easily adaptable. When the transmission was used on the production Corvette, however, the resultant criticism was deafening. Maurice Olley replied that he foresaw a time when sports cars would appeal to wide segments of the population and automatic transmissions would be the vogue. In the end Olley was right, but it took 20 years for his prediction to come true—much to the detriment of the early Corvette.

The Corvette's early development period is the story of one rush order after another. It was a series of tight deadlines which resulted in the ultimate decision to use glass reinforced plastic (GRP), later known as fiberglass, for the vehicle's body. Initially, GRP was used, as in most General Motors prototypes of the time, merely as an expedient to get the car built in time for the rapidly approaching Motorama show while Chevrolet concentrated its efforts on a steel body for the 10,000 Corvettes scheduled to be produced in 1954. Public reaction to the car was so favorable, however, that GM decided to rush the automobile into production a year early. To build a steel body on such short notice was impossible, so the decision to use a fiberglass shell, which became the Corvette's hallmark, was largely forced on the engineering group as the simplest means to beat another deadline.

In January 1953 the Corvette, named for the fast naval ships which fought in World War II, made its debut at the Motorama show in New York City. A press release issued at the debut stated that the vehicle was an experimental sports car which might be produced in a year. However, production was much nearer than that since, while the gleaming white and red show car was attracting thousands to its viewing stand, an exact twin was already being tested at the GM Proving Grounds in Milford, Mich.

Clearly, people were interested in Chevrolet's little sports car and GM planners felt production should not lag too far behind or else the demand might slacken. Thus the order was issued to build 300 Corvettes for mid-year introduction in 1953. Chevrolet engineers immediately began boning up on plastics since a GRP body was the only way to meet stringent production schedules and, besides, marketing

CORVETTE PRODUCTION BY YEAR	
1953	300
1954	3640
1955	700
1956	3467
1957	6339
1958	9168
1959	9670

General Motors Corporation

Corvette

analysts thought the public would be intrigued by a fiberglass car. Bids were accepted on the body panels and the Molded Fiber Glass Company of Ashtabula, Ohio, was selected to produce the units. A small assembly line, large enough to build three cars a day, was set up on one floor of Chevrolet's Flint, Mich., plant. There, on June 30, 1953, barely 6 months following the Motorama debut and 18 months after Harley Earl's original sketch, the first Corvette rolled off the line.

The 1953 production Corvette was an exact replica of the Motorama car except for the full length chrome strip along both sides which replaced the prototype's dartlike design on the front fenders. Because of the tremendous expense incurred in rushing the vehicle through development and production, plus the need to fabricate many new components, the Corvette's initial advertised price was $3490. Harley Earl's concept of a low-priced sports car had obviously been forgotten.

Earl had also conceived of the Corvette as being a "youth cult" car, but corporate marketeers had other ideas. They decided the best way to showcase the car was to sell it to only a select few "prestige owners"—celebrities, the socially prominent and national political and military figures. Invitations were extended to such people to buy a Corvette but by the end of 1953 only 183 cars of the 300 that were built had been sold. Chevrolet was not overly concerned since many of the Corvettes were on display at dealerships to draw attention to other models and it was thought winter might not be the best time for sports car sales.

Plans went ahead to produce 1000 Corvettes per month in 1954. These were to be completely unchanged from the original 300. And therein lay the problem which almost meant death for the automobile. Chevrolet soon learned that not every VIP wanted a Corvette. Besides the high price, the car's inherently leaky side curtains, complicated convertible top and relatively poor performance when compared to European sports cars did not appeal to these "prestige" people. Sales lagged more and more until, finally, in June of 1954, the division abandoned the "prestige owner" marketing philosophy and allowed anyone to purchase a Corvette. Still, sales were slow, forcing a halt to production after job number 3939 was built. Only 2863 models had been sold.

The Corvette project was a serious trouble, but Ed Cole was determined to save the car. A styling facelift, including a new grille, taillights and hood, was proposed and then rejected as Chevrolet struggled to find a direction for the Corvette. Into this confused atmosphere stepped a Belgian-born engineer who had extensive experience in designing, testing and racing sports cars. Hired by Cole in 1953 to assist in the Research and Development department, Zora Arkus-Duntov naturally gravitated to the Corvette and would be the one person most responsible for the automobile's survival then and for its direction over the next 20 years.

Strangely enough, Ford Motor Company figured prominently in GM's decision to continue the Corvette when it introduced the sporty 2-seat Thunderbird in 1955. The T-Bird's success was also destined to be the turning point for the Corvette.

By late 1954 Duntov had become involved with the Corvette program. He knew from his European experience that a sports car should out-perform other cars in a straight line and around corners. The Corvette could do neither and Duntov was determined that it should. He tested the automobile's handling and found that there was 15% roll-understeer in the rear and 10% oversteer in front. To solve this unstable situation, Duntov limited the rear spring travel and also installed a larger front stabilizer bar. "Before long," he later said, "I produced a car which I could put into drift and have it respond as the car should."

The improved handling characteristics succeeded in getting the Corvette around corners more quickly, but the car's straight line performance remained poor. The only answer, though, seemed to be a new engine and this became even more apparent with the introduction of Ford's V-8 Thunderbird.

Actually, GM had been experimenting with a V-8 in the Corvette since early 1954 and had even installed one such engine in the Motorama car. The project had worked well and under Cole's supervision the 231-cu.-in. engine was eventually enlarged to 265-cu. ins. before being offered in the Corvette. Further engineering work resulted in updated cylinder heads and combustion chamber design, the light stamped steel rocker arms and a 195 hp rating.

The car's performance was dazzling, 0-to-60 mph in less than 9 secs., and the limited availability of a manual transmission held the transmission held the promise of even more acceleration—although fewer than two dozen V-8 3-speeds were built in 1955.

Despite these improvements, the

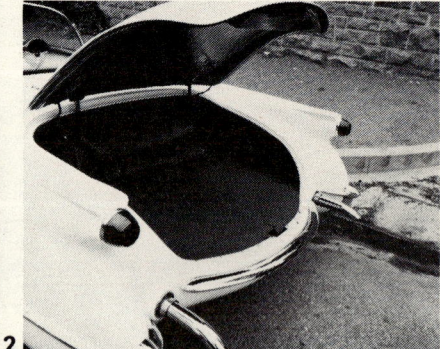

114/SPECIAL INTEREST AMERICAN CARS

Corvette's existence remained tenuous at best thanks to the sporty Thunderbird's design which clearly outclassed Chevrolet's 2-seater. Corvette sales continued to tailspin, amounting to only 700 during 1955, and the corporate red pencils were now fully poised for the kill.

Ed Cole, by now on the verge of becoming general manager of Chevrolet, did not intend to let the car die so easily. Backed into a corner by Ford's success with the boulevard cruiser appeal of the T-Bird, Cole realized the Corvette could not survive in the same market. The die was cast, he decided; the Corvette would become a fullblooded sports car.

To do this would involve many modifications and so massive were the changes to the 1956 Corvette that its introduction was delayed until Jan. 11, 1956—months after the other Chevrolet models had debuted. In styling, every aspect of the car's body was refined, with careful attention paid to the classic design of the Mercedes 300SL. This Mercedes influence accounted for the forward thrusting fender lines and the twin bulges in the gently sloping hood. From the LaSalle show car of 1955 was borrowed the scooped-out side panel that swept back from the front wheel. And finally, the "rocket pod" taillights were discarded in favor of less obtrusive inset lamps. More comfort was provided by wind-up windows (with optional power assist) and a power-operated convertible top.

Arkus-Duntov, who had become ex-officio chief engineer on the Corvette, developed the mechanical trappings to match the vehicle's new-found sports car image. His goals in chassis preparation were to reduce rear wheel lift during cornering, increase high speed stability, and provide constant steering response during all types of driving. All this was done by placing shims between the frame and front crossmember to increase the caster angle by 2°. Roll oversteer tendencies in the front end were also negated by the use of shims while roll understeer at the back was cured by sloping the leaf springs less steeply than before. After testing his new chassis design Duntov stated, "The car goes where it is pointed."

Nevertheless, the Corvette's heart was the engine and Duntov's suspension would have been worthless without a suitably matched motor. Realizing this, the old "Blue Flame Six" was phased out and left for the historians. In its place the 265 V-8 became the only available engine but was now offered with two power ratings: 210 and 225 hp. The added performance was gained by raising the compression ratio to 9.25:1, developing cast iron exhaust manifolds that had central outlets plus larger internal passages, and valves made from very durable 21-4N alloy steel. To insure against ignition breakup at high rpm, a dual-point distributor was included in the electrical system. Carburetion on the 210-hp motor was a single 4-bbl. Carter while the 225 hp version sported dual 4-bbl. carbs. Of more importance to the enthusiasts, though, was the fact that a 3-speed manual transmission was now standard equipment on the Corvette.

1. Full instrumentation was a must for a sports car but the '53 Corvette's gauges were practically illegible due to their placement across the bottom of the dashboard. Further inconvenience came from a poor driver's position and leaky side curtains.

2. Unlike modern-day Corvettes, the '53 version lived up to its touring car image by having a large trunk. Chrome tailpipe extensions are not stock, having been added to avoid the car's common problem of blackening the white paint with exhaust smoke.

3. For '54 the car remained unchanged and production was increased to almost 4000 units. However, the car's many faults, when compared to European models, resulted in sales of only 2800 and managment considered abandoning the Corvette project.

4. The '55 Corvette proved to be a major turning point for the car. Although only 700 were sold and styling was unchanged, the car received a V-8 engine and an updated chassis design.

5. The new V-8 for '55 had a displacement of 265 cu. ins. and was rated at 195 hp. When installed, the Corvette could accelerate from 0 to 60 mph in less than 9 secs. Combined with a newly offered 3-speed manual trans, this engine provided the performance dictated by the sports car image.

6. Due to Ford's introduction of the semi-sporty Thunderbird in 1955, GM decided to retain the Corvette for 1956 and make it an actual sports car. To meet this order, Duntov redesigned the car's suspension to remove the troublesome understeering tendencies while the V-8 engine was improved to produce 210 and 235 hp and the old "Blue Flame Six" was phased out.

CORVETTE SERIAL NUMBER INFORMATION			
Year	Serial Prefix	Beginning	Ending
1953	E53F	-001001	-001300
1954	E54S	-001001	-004640
1955	E55S or VE55S*	-001001	-001700
1956	E56S	-001001	-004467
1957	E57S	-100001	-106339
1958	J58S	-100001	-109168
1959	J59S	-100001	-109437

*A "VE" prefix in 1955 meant the car came with the optional V-8 engine.

General Motors Corporation
Corvette

Chevrolet was, without a doubt, serious about making the automobile into a sports car.

Public acceptance of the 1956 model was still slow in coming, due in part to the car's delayed introduction and its past reputation. Then came the starling news that Zora Arkus-Duntov, driving a specially prepared 1956 Corvette, had set a speed record at Daytona Beach, Fla., of 150.583 mph. This unbelievable performance was backed up by acceleration times of only 7.5 secs. to 60 mph from a stock Corvette. Suddenly, sports car enthusiasts began to take the car seriously.

Duntov was openly pleased about his transformation of the Corvette, and the corporate accountants were more than happy with the car's rapidly accelerating sales figures. Still, Zora felt something was missing. The Corvette had the potential of the Mercedes and Porsche and Jaguar, he thought. If only it had a little more power.

Duntov had long harbored the idea of beating the exotic European grand touring cars with a Corvette. Attempts at road racing had been made but met with singularly unsuccessful results. What the car needed was more power and, in this belief, Duntov had one very important ally: Ed Cole. Cole, however, was probably not as interested in defeating the European cars at their own game as he was intent on cementing his recent promotion to general manager of Chevrolet. He needed some major breakthrough to properly establish his regime. New model introduction dates were only months away, too near to allow time for rushing an all-new car through development, so Cole chose to advance the state-of-the-art as it pertained to the Corvette. With this in mind, he decreed that the Corvette would get fuel injection for 1957.

Fuel injection in 1957 was not a new idea. The automotive industry had been experimenting with it for many years and Mercedes' awesome injected 300SL of 1954 proved the system's superior performance. General Motors' Research and Development department had done some investigation into injection, primarily directed by John Dolza with a lot of help from Zora Duntov. Dolza's main thrust was along the lines of aircraft systems which metered fuel depending on engine speed and air density. This worked extremely well but was very expensive, so Duntov suggested that they should measure the mass of air directly as it entered the engine and then meter the fuel to match the amount of air. This system worked splendidly and tests on complete engines were begun in 1955 using normal intake manifolds.

Power output with this system was disappointing at first, although no attempts had yet been made to increase compression or use ram-air intakes. A new manifold was devised which incorporated long ram pipes to pass air connected by a plenum chamber that was fed by the metering unit. This manifold also served as the valley cover on the V-8 engine. Before final production, the new manifold was slightly redesigned into a dual-plane structure to inhibit heat reaching the injection nozzles.

By now, time was dangerously short for introducing the new induction system in the 1957 model Corvette. Work on the injection unit had virtually ceased when Duntov was seriously injured in a proving grounds accident. Cole, desperate to have something new to show the stockholders, persuaded the ailing engineer to work as much as was physically possible in order to complete the injection system in time for final approval. Duntov completed the assignment just as the '57 Corvette went into production and the first few factory injection units were actually assembled under laboratory conditions at Rochester.

The effort, however, was worth it since the Corvette's engine, now enlarged to 283 cu. ins., developed 250 hp with fuel injection. A high-performance option, including the famous Duntov camshaft and a 10.5:1 compression ratio, had a rating of 283 hp—a milestone in engineering since it marked the first time a production motor boasted power equal or superior to its displacement. The price for this performance was high—$481 for the injection unit alone—and only 240 Corvettes were equipped with it in 1957.

With the availability of fuel injection and the additional performance provided by the larger 283-in. engine displacement, the 1957 Corvette had at last become a true sports car. As if to proclaim this fact, Chevrolet finally acquiesced to the enthusiasts and offered an honest-to-gosh 4-speed manual transmission in the car.

1. The 1956 model's styling was modified with careful attention paid to the Mercedes 300SL. Front fenders were raised and did away with headlamp screens while the rounded rear body discarded the useless "rocket pod" taillights.

2. Of all the early Corvettes, perhaps no year is as desired as the 1957. Its clean design is considered a classic and the performance characteristics clearly moved it to the fore-front of sports car engineering.

3. Both Cole and Duntov wanted something special for the Corvette in '57, so they pushed into production Chevrolet's fuel injection system. As installed in the Corvette, the FI motor displaced 283 ins. and developed 250 hp. Fewer than 250 cars were equipped with the unit, though.

4. Following the technical achievements of 1957, the '58 Corvette was a disappointment. Stylists muddied the car's clean design. Only the new interior with the gauges finally placed in front of the driver showed any advancement.

5. Only minor alterations marked the '59 model although the appearance was improved by removing the phony air vents in the hood and much of the excess chrome trim. Ride comfort was increased as was power of all engine versions. With sales of 9670 units, the '59 Corvette was the last to sell less than 10,000 models a year.

Performance, power and handling—the 1957 Corvette had it all and sports car enthusiasts loved it. Despite the lack of the normal annual styling facelift, the car attracted thousands to dealer showrooms forcing production to nearly double to 6339 units. The '57 Corvette became an instant success and soon afterwards a late-model classic that is still highly sought after.

While the 1957 Corvette had been an engineer's delight, the 1958 model became a styling exercise. All Chevrolet models were undergoing massive facelifts that year, and it was decided that the Corvette needed more gloss and glitter in order to increase sales. This line of thought indicated that many corporate decision-makers still had no idea what a sports car was.

Dual headlights were the rage in 1958 and GM decided the Corvette had to have them. They were fitted into the fenders and surrounded by chrome bezels while another chrome strip adorned the fender ridge to accentuate the headlamps. The familiar oval grille with its vertical tooth design was retained but now two smaller, and nonfunctional, nostrils were placed on either side of it. All three openings were outlined with bright chrome moldings. In the rear the trunk kept its rounded form and the taillights were still recessed, but more chrome was added to "highlight" the shape.

For awhile these were the only alterations. Then, as the car was being readied for final approval, the styling department suddenly added to the list of unnecessary trim items. Dummy air outlets were positioned in the previously smooth body side cove behind the front wheels and more phony scoops were incorporated into the grille. To top off the entire melange, the hood received 18 raised ridges which were supposed to be hot air louvers. Like the rest of the styling changes, these louvers were also completely nonfunctional. This new body added 8 ins. to the Corvette's length, 2 ins. to the width, and pushed the total curb weight of the car over 3000 lbs. for the first time. As one GM employee remarked at the time, the stylists had managed to take the Corvette and turn it into a Cadillac.

Perhaps the only meaningful change the stylists executed on the 1958 Corvette was the vehicle's interior. And this was accomplished primarily because Duntov demanded the dashboard gauges be placed so the driver could read them. They were all located within round dials and positioned directly in front of the driver while a 160 mph speedometer sat atop the instrument cluster housed in its own semi-spherical pod. The seats received some slight alterations to make them narrower in order to accommodate the center console which held the radio, heater controls and shift lever. The use of a console in the 1958 Corvette, long a feature of American show cars, marked the beginning of an industry-wide switch to this form of interior layout.

Technical improvements on the 1958 model were few. The fuel injection engine received a small boost in horsepower to 290 while a new motor, RPO 469C, combined the Duntov cam with two 4-bbl. carburetors to produce 270 hp. Sintered iron brake linings became available and were capable of stopping the car almost as quickly as the engines could accelerate it.

The 1959 Corvette, although almost identical with its predecessor, faired somewhat better thanks to the simple decision to discard the phony hood louvers and rear deck chrome work. The '59 also showed signs of Duntov's emerging philosophy which stated that it was not practical to mix a racing car with a touring car. If you wanted a Corvette with on-track performance, you ordered RPO 684 and got higher rate springs, finned brake drums and ceramic-metallic lining, in addition to the more powerful engine. Should pleasure driving, albeit fast pleasure driving, be your desire, you settled for the stock 283 motor with its softer springs and less harsh ride. It was an engineering philosophy which was to become a marketing plan for all future Corvettes.

The continuing development and growing luxury was not being accomplished without cost. By 1959 the price of a basic Corvette was $3875. After judiciously checking the option list, it was all too common to pay well over $5000 for the pleasure of owning a Corvette. Sales, though, continued to climb and totaled 9670 at the end of the 1959 model year. And that was the last year the Corvette would sell less than 10,000 cars.

Guided by the aspirations, and, at times, the egos, of many people, the Corvette in only six years had matured from the crude, rough-riding, ill-performing Americanized sportster of 1953 into an honestly designed (forgetting the temporary styling setback of 1958) sports car. Clearly, the Corvette, as it entered the 1960s, had come of age and was poised to burst into prominence.

CORVETTE ENGINES				
Displ.	Cyl.	C.R.	HP	Yr. Offered
235	6	8.0	150/4200	1953, '54
235	6	8.0	155/4200	1955
265	8	8.0	190/5000	1955
265	8	9.25	210/5200	1956
265	8	9.25	225/5200	1956
283	8	9.5	220/4800	1957
283	8	9.5	245/5000	1957, '57, '59
283	8	9.5	250/5000*	1957, '58, '59
283	8	9.5	270/6000	1957, '58, '59
283	8	10.5	283/6200*	1957
283	8	9.5	230/4800	1958, '59
283	8	10.5	290/6200*	1958, '59

*Fuel injected models

General Motors Corporation

La Salle

A fitting companion to the Cadillac

The LaSalle was the longest lived, and undoubtedly the most famous, of GM's "companion" marques. Just as the Viking was a lower-price Oldsmobile, the Marquette a Buick stablemate, and the Oakland associated with Pontiac (actually the other way around), so the LaSalle was conceived from its beginning as a junior-grade Cadillac. Today there is considerable overlap among all GM cars, but this was not true in the mid-'20's. There was then a definite gap between Buick and Cadillac, and GM management determined that the most satisfactory way to fill it would be to issue a new car which brought much of Cadillac's V-8 power and exclusivity to a lower price range. It was only logical, then, to have this car actually built by Cadillac and share many of its parts and pieces, which would not only assure the ruboff of prestige but also keep costs down.

Even the name was heavy with Cadillac associations. Le Sieur Antoine de la Mothe Cadillac was a noble-born French explorer who founded the city of Detroit; Rene Robert Cavelieur, Sieur de la Salle, was another French nobleman who explored much of the Mississippi and claimed the Louisiana territory for France. Note that "la Salle" was really part of the gentleman's title, not his name; but in typical fashion among European nobility of the time he was invariably addressed and referred to by his title, which was contracted to LaSalle.

The marque was introduced with a great flourish in 1927. It was the first volume-produced automobile ever designed anywhere by a stylist, and the first job done for GM by Harley Earl, a custom body designer from Los Angeles. Earl, of course, went on to become head of GM's Art and Color Section (later named Styling Staff, now its Design Staff) when it was formed shortly afterwards, and was in charge of all GM styling for 30 years. As automotive historians never tire of pointing out, the 1927 LaSalle looked much more like a smaller Hispano-Suiza than a smaller Cadillac. Even its winged emblem and (a little later) the radiator mascot showed strong similarities. Until 1934, the LaSalle mascot was a heron with its wings raised, while the famous Hispano ornament was a stork with its wings downward. All this was no accident. Earl was an admirer of the best European coachwork, and deliberately tried to bring the Hispano's elegance to a volume-produced car.

Technically, the new car also had a lot to offer. It had a brand new Cadillac V-8; so new, in fact, that Cadillac itself didn't even get it until the following year. This was Cadillac's "second generation" V-8 (see Cadillac chapter), and in the LaSalle it had a bore and stroke of 3⅛ x 4 15/16 in. for 303 cid and 75 bhp. The line of cars was therefore conveniently known as the Series 303 LaSalle, and was considered internally by GM as one of the Cadillac range, which carried similar Series numbers.

There were originally two wheelbase lengths. The bulk of LaSalles were on the short 125-in. wheelbase, a healthy 15 in. shorter than Cadillac's. There were eight different standard Fisher bodies for this short chassis, and three more for a longer 134-in. wheelbase. At base prices from $2495 to $2695, the LaSalle fell exactly where GM management wanted it to: right between the dearest Buick ($1995) and the cheapest Cadillac ($2995). For those with more money who still preferred LaSalle's handy size instead of a larger car, there were custom Fleetwood bodies.

In the halcyon days of the late '20's with money on the land, the LaSalle was a great success. Over 10,000 were sold in 1927, helping to boost Cadillac Division sales to a record 47,136. This was promptly broken the following year, when more than 16,000 LaSalles and the tremendous number of 40,000 Cadillacs set a new division record of 56,038 cars, which stood until 1941.

During its first three years LaSalle's star was ascendant. It sold more cars each year than the one preceding, and in 1929 outsold Cadillac for the first time. By 1930, however, things were not so rosy. The steepening decline of the Depression, which had made its first chill effects felt at big brother Cadillac the previous year, now struck at LaSalle. Sales tumbled to below 1928's level, despite the many improvements. In 1929 the longer 134-in. wheelbase was made standard for all body styles except the 2-seat coupes and roadsters, and chrome plating, synchromesh transmission, and safety glass were all introduced. That same year the engine was bored out to 3¼ in. for 328 cid, forming the Series 328.

With minor restyling each year, by 1930 the LaSalle was drawing away from its delicate Hispano detailing and acquiring the more massive appearance of a Cadillac. The 134-in. wheelbase was now standard for all models, and the engine bore went up by another 1/16-in. to form the Series 340. This was the same 90-hp engine used in the 1928-29 Cadillacs (see comparison chart), which Cad called their Series 341; the exact displacement was 340.41 cubic inches.

By 1931 the retreat for all luxury cars was being sounded. In an effort to entice more buyers to the LaSalle it again received the previous year's Cadillac engine, which was simply their common V-8 bored yet again to 3⅜ in. for 353 cid and 95 bhp. And to cut

118/SPECIAL INTEREST AMERICAN CARS

costs, the Cadillac V-8 was now made to share the LaSalle's 134-in. wheelbase. This situation of an identical chassis and engine remained through the 1933 model year, so for 1931-33 a LaSalle Series 345 buyer really was getting a Cadillac Series 355 for less money.

Despite more horsepower and two more wheelbase lengths (130 and 136 in.) in 1932, and a major facelift in '33 which really made it look like a Cadillac, LaSalle sales continued to plummet. Cadillac and all other luxury makes were in the same boat, of course. By 1933, the absolute bottom of the Depression, only 3482 LaSalles and 3173 Cadillacs were made, and it just didn't seem to make sense to GM management to keep two separate lines of cars going that used so many common parts. LaSalle would have to go, replaced by a cheaper line of Cadillacs.

As future events would prove, this may well have been the proper decision to make from a corporate standpoint. But it was made before management knew what the 1934 LaSalle would look like. As one story has it, Harley Earl personally saved LaSalle's bacon by calling a management meeting and dramatically unveiling sketches of the new styling he had planned. The directors were so impressed that they changed their minds. Whatever the truth of that tale, it is undeniably true that the 1934 LaSalle did indeed go into production, and it was brand spanking new from the wheels up.

At one stroke was abolished the old "classic" styling, with its clamshell fenders, large stanchion-mounted headlights, wire wheels, large grille, and fenderwell spare wheels. In its place was a streamlined and "tight" body dominated by a very thin and aristocratic grille. Flanking this tall grille were the slim teardrop headlights, mounted very high, while hot underhood air was exhausted by five circular ports on each side that were the purest Art Deco. Especially masterful were the fenders, pontoon-shaped with a sharp cutoff at the rear. This fender shape proved to be a prophetic one for future GM cars, and in fact the '36 Cadillac quite resembles the '34 LaSalle.

Sweeping mechanical changes matched the body change for 1934. All LaSalles had independent front suspension, introduced throughout the GM cars that year. There were hydraulic brakes, two years before Cadillac. And the wheelbase was chopped to 119 in., making the shortest LaSalle ever. But the biggest change was under the narrow hood, where the Cad V-8 was replaced by an Olds straight eight. With a bore and stroke of 3 x 4¼ in. this engine had 240 cid and 95 bhp. Since this was down 20 hp and a whopping 113 cid from the '33 engine, it would seem that LaSalle was moving in a retrograde direction. But this was a much less expensive engine.

In another cost-cutting move, the former wide variety of body styles was reduced to just four: 4-dr. sedan, 2-dr. sedan (club sedan), coupe, and convertible coupe. All this allowed the price of a LaSalle to drop well below $2000 for the first time. No longer a junior Cadillac, LaSalle was now poaching in previous Buick territory, but Buick had also lowered its prices. This was the Series 350 LaSalle. That series number just sounded like a nice one to follow the previous Series 345, as it now bore no relationship at all to engine displacement.

Although the dollar-starved public did not overwhelm LaSalle dealers

1. It's 1930, deep in the classic period of coachbuilt bodies, and this convertible coupe of that year shows the formal yet sporty lines that made LaSalle so popular in its early years.

2. The Hispano influence lingered with LaSalle for several years, and is still in evidence in this front view of a 1930 convertible coupe, the fourth model year after LaSalle was introduced.

3. By 1931, as this delightful period advertisement shows, the LaSalle had acquired the more massive look of a Cadillac. The headlights were lowered, the hood louvers were replaced by vent doors, the bumpers were simpler, the hood line straighter, and the taillight right out of a Cadillac parts bin. This was the first year LaSalle used exactly the same engine and wheelbase as the Cadillac V-8.

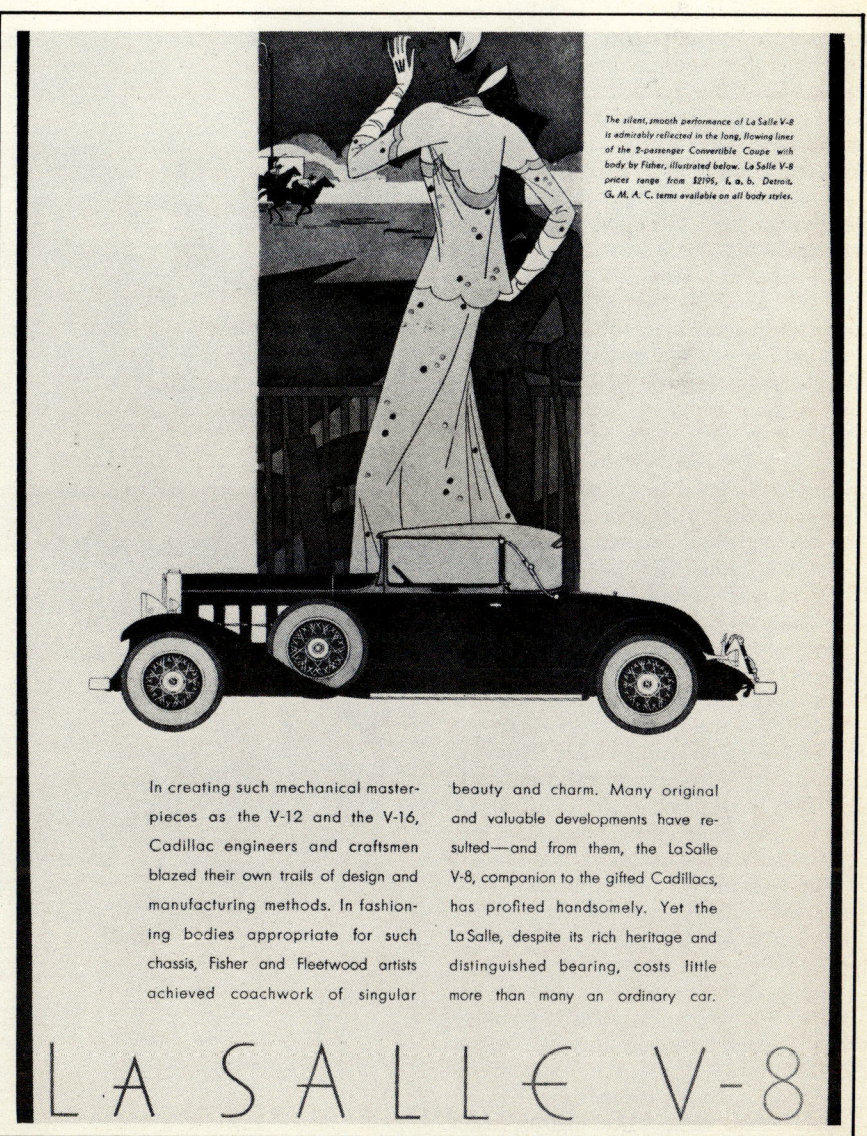

General Motors Corporation
La Salle

with orders, sales increased 100% to 7128 cars. For 1935 the engine's stroke was increased 1/8-in. to give 8 more cid and 10 more hp, the wheelbase went up by one inch to 120 in., and Fisher Body's new all-steel construction method, named "Turret Top," was used. The new body was stronger, but looked the same to a customer since the styling was unchanged. It was cheaper to manufacture, however, and this enabled LaSalle to dramatically cut prices again, the coupe selling for only $1255. Production went up again, this time to 8653 cars.

The gradual recovery of LaSalle would normally have been viewed with satisfaction by GM management, especially since it was comfortably outselling Cadillac. But they had their eyes somewhere else, watching with mounting alarm as a formidable new competitor moved right in on LaSalle's and Buick's territory. Mighty Packard was invading the medium price field, and its model 120 was a triumph of Packard prestige, impressive styling, contemporary engineering, and moderate cost. New for 1935, it promptly outsold LaSalle by a 3:1 margin. GM responded by cutting costs again on the unchanged '36 LaSalle, which took a big sales jump to a record 13,004 cars. Yet the Packard 120 now outsold LaSalle by a 5:1 margin, and another new competitor with a prestigious name, the Lincoln Zephyr, also outsold LaSalle.

What to do? Sales were good and getting better, but those of LaSalle's new competitors were getting better faster. To GM this looked like a rising market, and they decided to meet it by upgrading LaSalle's image. So out went the Olds engine and in again came the Cadillac engine. In the intervening three years Cadillac had introduced a new V-8 (see Cadillac chapter), and what the '37 LaSalle received was the 322-cid V-8 used in the '36 Series 60, Cadillac's lowest-priced line. This was a good engine, very smooth, and with 125 bhp it resulted in the most powerful LaSalle ever. The frame was lowered, stiffened, and lengthened to a 124-in. wheelbase. An additional body style made its appearance, the convertible sedan, which remained for the rest of LaSalle's few years and is eagerly sought today because of its beauty and rarity. Though only slightly changed, the '37 styling made the car appear more purposeful, since it was lowered and had skilfully repositioned headlights. Prices went down slightly again,

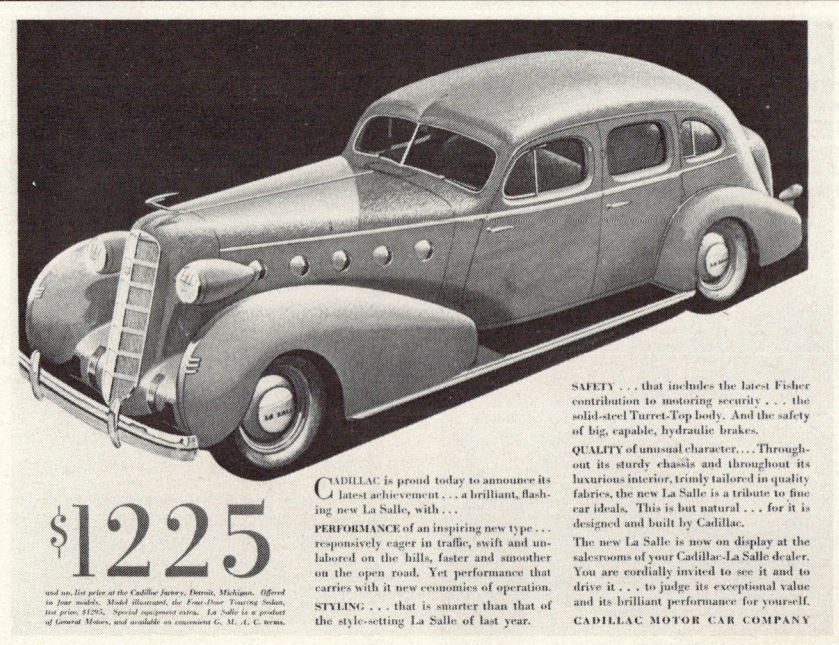

the club sedan selling for a base price of $995. Whether it was the lower prices, the return of the V-8, the improving economy, or a combination of all three, can never be determined, but production rose spectacularly to a new record of 32,005 cars, which would remain the best in LaSalle's history. The marketing people at GM must have despaired of ever catching Packard, however, as even in this record year the 120 easily outsold LaSalle.

Holding fast to a winner, LaSalle entered the '38 recession with a car basically unchanged from the '37, and watched sales plummet to only 15,501 cars. The '38 line had column shift and a one-piece hood which opened from the front (rather than a split hood hinged in the center), but these were not enough to counteract the economic climate. GM's consolation was that everyone else was hurting too.

For 1939 came a revised grille, more glass area, and running boards made optional instead of standard. Without the boards the '39 model was quite handsome, the sedan greatly resembling the trendsetting '38 Cadillac Sixty Special. The wheelbase was changed again, this time shortened to 120 in. Sales picked up as the nation climbed out of the Depression, going up to 23,028 for the model year.

The year 1940 was to be LaSalle's last, but you'd never have guessed that from the product. In common with several other 1940 GM cars the LaSalle's headlights were faired into the front fenders, resulting in the handsomest year ever. The wheelbase was juggled again to 123 in. and the horsepower increased to 130 by increasing the venturi size of the twin-throat carburetor, but these technical niceties were lost in the news of a marketing decision. For the first time, LaSalle would be available in two separate series, instead of itself being simply a series of Cadillac. Retained was the standard Series 50, which had been around since 1935, but new was the Series 52 Special.

Mechanically identical to the Series 50, the Special cars had subtly different "torpedo" styling also seen that year on the Cadillac Series 62. They can be distinguished from the standard models at a glance by the absence of the beltline trim spear and the use of only two strips of bright trim on the rocker panel instead of three. Less obvious, but more important, is the fact that the torpedo body was lower. This was only evident around the hood area. On the Special the hood parting line was right down on top of the vent castings, which themselves were so low they were practically touching the catwalk area of the fenders; on the standard models, there were several inches of space above and below these vents. Initially offered only in coupe and 4-dr. sedan form, after several months these two were joined by a convertible coupe and convertible sedan. Including the five bodies available on the Series 50, this meant that in 1940 LaSalle offered nine bodies altogether, a return to the good old days of 1928.

Public response to the 1940 line, and

1. This 1932 Model 345B sedan was a Cadillac in all but name and price. Power was upped to 115 bhp.

2. A real Cadillac look-alike is this 1933 Model 345C 2-dr. sedan. That year LaSalle—like Cadillac—received a Vee radiator and enclosed fenders.

3. The radical 1934 model ushered in streamlined styling, independent front suspension, hydraulic brakes, and a straight-eight engine borrowed from Oldsmobile. This '35 sedan was identical to the '34 except for its flat bumpers. New for '35 was stronger all-steel Turret-Top construction.

4. It's the spring of 1935, and two young ladies in their snappy new LaSalle convertible coupe try to entice a third away from her contemplation of John Milton to explore a country lane. Away, Dull Care!

CADILLAC—LASALLE ENGINES

	LASALLE					CADILLAC				
Year	Series	Type	B x S	Disp.	BHP	Series	Type	B x S	Disp.	BHP
1927	303	V-8	3 1/8 x 4 15/16	302.96	75	314A	V-8	3 1/8 x 5 1/8	314.47	86*
1928	303	V-8	3 1/8 x 4 15/16	302.96	75	341	V-8	3 5/16 x 4 15/16	340.41	90
1929	328	V-8	3 1/4 x 4 15/16	327.68	85	341B	V-8	3 5/16 x 4 15/16	340.41	90
1930	340	V-8	3 5/16 x 4 15/16	340.41	90	353	V-8	3 3/8 x 4 15/16	353.38	95
1931	345	V-8	3 3/8 x 4 15/16	353.38	95	355	V-8	3 3/8 x 4 15/16	353.38	95
1932	345B	V-8	3 3/8 x 4 15/16	353.38	115	355B	V-8	3 3/8 x 4 15/16	353.38	115
1933	345C	V-8	3 3/8 x 4 15/16	353.38	115	355C	V-8	3 3/8 x 4 15/16	353.38	115
1934	350	ST-8	3 x 4 1/4	240.33	95	355D	V-8	3 3/8 x 4 15/16	353.38	130
1935	50	ST-8	3 x 4 3/8	247.40	105	10	V-8	3 3/8 x 4 15/16	353.38	130
1936	50	ST-8	3 x 4 3/8	247.40	105	60	V-8	3 3/8 x 4 1/2	322.07	125
						70,75	V-8	3 1/2 x 4 1/2	346.36	135
1937	50	V-8	3 3/8 x 4 1/2	322.07	125	60,65,	V-8	3 1/2 x 4 1/2	346.36	135
						70,75	V-8	3 1/2 x 4 1/2	346.36	135
1938	50	V-8	3 3/8 x 4 1/2	322.07	125	60,60S,70	V-8	3 1/2 x 4 1/2	346.36	135
						75	V-8	3 1/2 x 4 1/2	346.36	140
1939	50	V-8	3 3/8 x 4 1/2	322.07	125	60S,61	V-8	3 1/2 x 4 1/2	346.36	135
						75	V-8	3 1/2 x 4 1/2	346.36	140
1940	50,52	V-8	3 3/8 x 4 1/2	322.07	130	60S,62,72	V-8	3 1/2 x 4 1/2	346.36	135
						75	V-8	3 1/2 x 4 1/2	346.36	140
1941						60S,61,62,	V-8	3 1/2 x 4 1/2	346.36	150
						63,67,75	V-8	3 1/2 x 4 1/2	346.36	150
1942						60S,61,62,	V-8	3 1/2 x 4 1/2	346.36	150
						63,67,75	V-8	3 1/2 x 4 1/2	346.36	150

*Last year for older design never used in LaSalle

General Motors Corporation
La Salle

especially the Series 52, was very good. The Special, in fact, outsold the standard model by more than 3000 cars, despite its higher price. Together the two series accounted for 24,330 cars, making it the second best year in LaSalle history.

All of this does not sound like a marque thrashing around in its final agonies. But 1940 turned out to be the last for LaSalle. In a controversial move, GM killed LaSalle and replaced it with a low-priced Cadillac line, the Series 61. The apparent reason for this was the continued great success of the medium-priced Packard 120, which outsold LaSalle by wide margins every year in spite of every thing that GM could do. GM management believed that the reason for this was psychological. The buyer of a 120 could bask in the comforting illusion that he had bought a "real" Packard, not a second-rate Cadillac, despite the fact that La-Salle's base price was higher. GM felt the only way to counter this was to replace LaSalle with an equivalent car carrying the Cadillac name, and so it was done.

A superficial examination of subsequent sales figures would seem to validate GM's decision. In 1941 the Cadillac Series 61 sold 29,250 cars, over 5000 more than the '40 LaSalle. But '41 was a good year for all auto manufacturers. Cadillac itself made almost 25,000 of its Series 62, an enormous jump from the 5900 of the same model made in '40. And it sold over twice as many high-priced Series 75 cars. So it is not really clear that replacing La-Salle with more Cadillacs sold more cars.

Next to Packard, LaSalle was the most successful of the unsuccessful marques in American automobile history. All LaSalles were relatively expensive cars, and all were handsome. For these reasons all of them are special interest cars; the interest is a matter of degree. For those with an interest in "classic" styling, the '27-'33 cars offer plenty of scope for activity. There were a great number of different bodies made in this period, and the Fleetwood custom ones are especially desirable. Approximately 82,000 LaSalles were made in this '27-'33 "classic" period.

The 1934 model ushered in the "modern" LaSalle, with its hydraulic brakes, independent front suspension, and streamlined styling. Over 122,000 were made in the next seven years.

Since LaSalle retained the same general styling from 1934 through 1940, the inveterate LaSalle spotter has memorized the subtle differences that distinguish each year from the others. From '34 to '36 the grilles were very similar, a narrow shallow-angle vee with many thin vertical bars, a thicker center bar, and short horizontal bars. There were six of these horizontal bars in '34 and '35, but nine in '36. All three years there was a circular "LaS" emblem in the upper right-hand portion of the grille. The '34 models had most unusual bumpers, the tipoff to that year. Nicknamed the "biplane" bumpers, these had two bullets sandwiched between two flat blades, and were shared with the '34 Cadillacs. They were spring mounted and would retract when pushed, but were rather fragile and costly and were replaced with plain flat bumpers for the '35 model, which otherwise is almost identical to a '34. The clue for '36 is those hood air vents, now enclosed in a long pod shape which ran the length of the hood. For '37 and '38 there was a new grille, more rounded, more upright, and composed of hundreds of tiny rectangles. The circular "LaS" emblem was replaced by a gold "V-8", also mounted in the upper right section of the grille. The '37 model still retained the triple chrome chevrons on the leading edges of the front fenders that all previous LaSalles since '34 had, but the headlights were mounted noticeably lower. The underhood venting was quite different, with six thin chrome strips trailing rearward from a tall ductwork casting mounted right beside the headlights. For '38 the fender chevrons were gone, the headlights were lowered still further (almost to the midpoint of the grille) and had three vertical chrome strips under them, and the venting was now a massive casting with four horizontal bars running the length of the hood. For '39 and '40 came another grille change,

1. For '36, LaSalle doors were hinged at the front and opened from the rear. This was the last year for the straight eight, unchanged from the '35's 105 hp.

2. This pristine '38 club coupe shows the bold egg-crate grille of the '37-'38 models, although this one is missing its V-8 emblem. Vertical strips below headlights, lack of front fender chevrons, and long hood vent casting mark this as a '38 model.

3. In '39 LaSalle was given a very narrow and delicate grille, a vent casting of similar delicacy, and large supplementary grilles in the fenders. There was a lot more glass area for '39, improving visibility and lightening the overall appearance.

4. LaSalle advertising heavily promoted its close relationship with Cadillac, as this 1939 ad shows. By keeping the price down and beating the drum about that V-8, LaSalle hoped to draw customers away from Packard.

5. LaSalle's last year, 1940, brought smooth new styling with the headlights mounted in the fenders. This is a rare model, a Series 52 convertible coupe with its torpedo body—only 425 were made, and it is a handsome beast.

6. Here's another one of the rare 1940 Series 52 convertible coupes. In complete but unrestored condition, it was offered for sale at a recent car auction in southern California.

122/SPECIAL INTEREST AMERICAN CARS

this one with exquisitely thin horizontal bars only and mounting a script "LaSalle" in place of the previous emblem. The '39 version had a very large supplementary grille in each front fender apron, and the teardrop housings for the headlights were much longer than in previous years and had a prominent horizontal ridge running around them. The hood vent casting was now a more modest affair and echoed the grille with its delicate horizontal ribbing. The final '40 models are easy to spot; the hood vents were three separate small castings, the supplementary grilles in the fenders are much smaller than in '39, and—instant giveaway—the headlights were integrated into the fenders.

Of the cars from this period, the '34-'36 Olds-powered cars are considered less desirable than the later Cad-powered ones, but they are rarer, so take your pick. The rarest and most attractive single body style of the later years is the convertible sedan, made from '37-'40, followed by the convertible coupe, which was offered every year. If it is rarity you seek, the 4-dr. sedan production greatly exceeded the combined production of all other body styles, so don't pick a sedan. In order of rarity, the five body styles of '37-'40 rank convertible sedan, club sedan, convertible coupe, coupe, and sedan. In terms of sheer beauty, most LaSalle lovers agree that the '40 Series 52 cars with their sleek torpedo bodies are the tops. This would indicate that the most valuable of all LaSalles are the two open body styles in this series, but you won't find them on every street corner. Only 425 convertible coupes and a miniscule 75 convertible sedans were made in that series, compared to 3000 coupes and more than 10,000 sedans. But keep looking.

Any LaSalle is worth restoring. If you drive one, you can rest assured that at least once a day, and twice on Sunday, some delightful older person will come up to you and say "That sure is a right pretty LaSalle. My daddy (uncle, aunt, old drinking buddy) used to have one just like it. Nossir, they don't make them like that no more." And they don't.

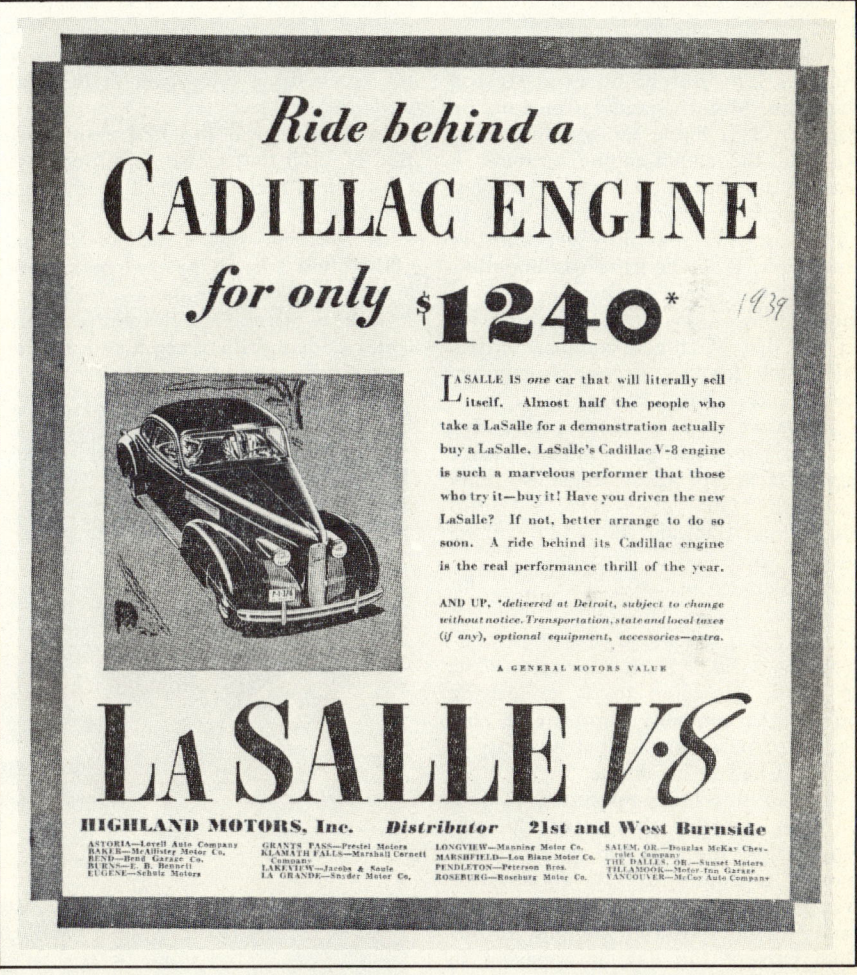

General Motors Corporation

Oldsmobile

The "guinea pig" of GM has a string of "firsts" to its credit

Oldsmobile has long been known as the engineering division of General Motors. And because of this, they've been the guinea pig a number of times for inventions by other divisions. Oldsmobile founder, Ransom Eli Olds, probably would not have minded this role, because he, too, was a bit venturesome for his day.

Young Olds was tinkering with automobiles long before he even started the Olds Motor Vehicle Company in August 1897. Since he and his father were in the steam-engine business, it was no surprise that his first horseless carriage was steam-powered back in 1887. In 1891, he built yet another steam car. But when the gasoline-powered engine began to show promise as motive power, his 1896 prototype led to the first Michigan company organized solely for the purpose of manufacturing and selling automobiles.

It wasn't easy in those early days, though, because the public wasn't ready to accept those ungainly, noisy creations. Olds even tried to build electrics in 1899 and 1900, but nothing seemed to appeal to the public.

A calamity in 1901 gave Olds his first real boost. The Olds factory in Lansing burned down, destroying almost everything. With numerous orders in hand, Olds had to do something quickly, so company efforts were concentrated on a vehicle that was easy to build. It had to be simple.

Out of this hurry-up return to production emerged the famed Curved-Dash Olds, the first car to carry the name "Oldsmobile." Its acceptance was phenomenal. Because of its similarity to horse-drawn buggies rather than cars of the day, it appealed to consumers. For three years—1903 to 1905—Oldsmobile was the best-selling car in America, before relinquishing the leadership to Ford.

During those banner years, Ransom E. Olds left to form another company—Reo, which built automobiles from 1904 to 1936.

With the inventive Olds out of the way, the company dropped its low-priced line and concentrated on the medium-price market. When William Crapo Durant bought Olds and merged it with Buick to form General Motors in 1908, he soon discovered he paid twice as much for the floundering enterprise as he should have.

Using Buick's highly successful Model 10 as a base for Oldsmobile, the company reentered the low-priced market and was once again successful.

One of Olds' early contributions to the auto industry was the introduction of nickel plating, and later chromium plating. They even offered a V-8 from 1915 to 1922, and produced an economy truck for a few years in the early Twenties.

It wasn't until the GM reorganization of 1920 that Oldsmobile finally established a niche for itself in the marketplace.

By the time the "Crash of '29" hit, Oldsmobile was in pretty good shape, just having set a company sales record. And like other GM divisions of the time, Oldsmobile introduced a companion car called Viking, a name which was meant to epitomize the rugged, adventuresome Norsemen of old. Unfortunately, its timing was wrong. The car was killed after the 1930 model run because it was a top-of-the-line model. And in those early years of the depression, expensive automobiles were left largely unsold.

The Viking of 1930 was a startling car in many respects. In 1929 it sold 6612, and only 1390 left the production line a year later.

Compared with the austere F-30 six-cylinder, the Viking must have been the pride of Oldsmobile engineering. It carried the first American production L-head V-8 cast en bloc. Before then, all V-8's had detachable cylinder barrels and separate casting for the crankcase. It was also the first 90° V-8 in

the medium-priced field.

There was nothing unusual about the chassis and bodies of the Viking-... they were quite conventional, although all-new from those used on the smaller F-30.

Unusual features of this new powerplant included a chain-drive camshaft in the crotch of the Vee and horizontal valves. And it performed on a par with the powerful cars of its day. Later, Oakland borrowed the same configuration for use in its cars.

Although Oldsmobile created a highly prized, special-interest car for us early in the Thirties, there weren't that many outstanding automobiles before World War II. This means that there should still be quite a few good

1. Unrestored 1930 Oldsmobile Deluxe Sedan sports wood spoke wheels (in good shape, too) and fender-mounted spare. Less desirable than open or coupe models, it might be rewarding project for family man.

2. Extremely rare Viking-series Oldsmobiles of '29 and '30 featured V-8 engines of 90-degree configuration.

3. Viking series deluxe convertible coupe of same era is built on shorter wheelbase also displays sidemounts.

4. 1932 Oldsmobile Model F-32 had 6-cyl. engine. This Fisher-bodied car has compartment behind door for golf clubs and running lights on the chrome embellished front fenders.

5. Any 1939 Oldsmobile (including this 4-door) with the optional Hydra-Matic transmission is a special interest car worthy of whatever it takes to restore it.

prewar Oldsmobiles for those who aren't particular as to model.

One thing to remember though, was that the Olds 6 was the weak link in an otherwise good automobile. Not until 1937 was the engine completely redone, offering reliability and durability.

Any open-top car—roadster, phaeton or convertible—should be considered for special-interest.

After introducing synchromesh in its lone 1931 model (the F-31 six-cylinder), Oldsmobile came out with a straight 8 in 1932, the model L-32 priced in the $1000 class. The eight, of course, was smoother and more reliable than the F-32 six, and now gave Olds two lines instead of one. Also, Oldsmobile introduced the industry to the automatic choke on both the 74-hp Six and the 90-hp Eight.

In 1933, Oldsmobile doubled its production and jumped from 12th to 9th in the industry. From that point on, Olds has never been out of the top ten sales leaders.

Why the big jump, when everyone else was floundering badly? It was the beautiful styling.

Oldsmobile Division had gotten the jump on most of the industry with a conservative, streamlined look. It was soundly acclaimed as the style leader, with sloping Vee grille, skirted fenders and steel-spoked wheels. Others wouldn't follow until a year later.

The F-33 six accounted for almost three-fourths of the more than 36,000 automobiles produced. The L-33 eight continued to make Oldsmobile a two-

model line, as it would remain until 1939. By now, the price on Oldsmobiles dropped to a $745.

The price was dropped even further in 1934, to $645, sales bounced sky high, and the company claimed the highest owner loyalty in America. An expansion program was begun, as Olds climbed to 6th in sales.

The F-34 six was hiked to 84 hp, only six less than the large L-34 eight.

Engineering features were numerous, including Knee-Action Wheels, giving Oldsmobile independent front suspension. "Super-Hydraulic Brakes" were announced to supply equal pressure on four wheels. Center-control steering, ride stabilizers and reinforced steel bodies were greatly extolled.

It's no doubt the B.O.P. (Buick-Oldsmobile-Pontiac) sales program helped Oldsmobile in those early Thirties. The B.O.P. organization meant that Oldsmobile and Pontiac were using Buick's extensive and stable dealership network to sell their products. And Oldsmobile's own concept in those early Thirties didn't hurt, either.

Oldsmobile advertising aimed at the low-priced market with the F-34, claimed: "Only a little more than low-price cars with high-price features and greater economy." The L-34 eight, on the other hand, aimed at higher-price buyers. "A bigger, finer 8 at last year's price ... comfort and power."

The following years—1935, 1936 and 1937—were each record sales years for Oldsmobile, even though the company dropped to 7th in production. The new styling on all GM models was an immediate hit with the public.

But it isn't until 1937 that we come up with another really special-interest Oldsmobile. It's in the form of the Automatic Safety Transmission—a semi-automatic that was later used on Buick Specials, and which led to the development of the Hydra-Matic.

The Automatic Safety Transmission was available only on the L-37 eight-cylinder models, and was an $80 extra. It was available, in 1938, on both the F-38 and L-38. In all, 28,000 cars equipped with these transmissions were sold.

The semi-automatic used a conven-

General Motors Corporation

Oldsmobile

tional clutch to engage any gear from the steering-column lever. Oldsmobile, then, was one of the first automakers to move the gearshift off the floor. The positions on the selector were "N" (neutral), "L" (first and second gears), "H" (third and fourth gears) and "R" (reverse).

When moving, the transmission could be up- and down-shifted automatically between "L" and "H." However, the clutch was needed when stopping and starting, and when using reverse.

Economy was also increased for 1937 by the use of higher rear-end ratios. But a lot of those niceties we regard as special were leaving the scene. Rumble seats were losing favor to folding rear seats in coupes and roadsters, while the sidemount tire had become a dealer option. One thing that remained was the lustrous and durable five-coat lacquer finish, which is one reason so many older Oldsmobiles still have original paint even today.

Body styles remained much as they had in previous years for the 6- and 8-cyl., models: Business coupe, club coupe, 2-door coach and touring coach, 4-door sedan and touring sedan, and convertibles.

By 1939, Oldsmobile began to break away from the GM look that prevailed throughout the corporation's product lineup. And 1939 was the year of the Hydra-Matic Drive, a $77 option, and the first publicly accepted automatic transmission in history.

This time the clutch pedal was completely eliminated. Borrowing experience from the Safety Transmission, this step-ratio automatic made driving considerably easier. Any 1939 Hydra-Matic-equipped car has to fall in the category of special-interest, especially if it's linked to a convertible or one of Oldsmobile's first woodie station wagons.

A new model was added, too, to bring Oldsmobile back into the low-priced market following a sales slump in 1938.

The new model was the Series 60, identified as the F-39. It was powered by a 90-hp six and sold for $777. The old F model was Series 70 (G-39) with a 95-hp six. While the Series 80 8-cyl., pumped out 110 hp.

A number of other improvements included four-wheel coil springs, which didn't prove as successful on Olds as they had on Buick a year earlier. They would later be dropped.

The most unusual-looking Olds-

1. The 1948 Oldsmobile Futuramic 98 represents a landmark in styling. The 66, 68, 76 and 78 models had holdover shapes from before WW II. Only the 98 Futuramic convertible and sedan are special interest.

2. New ohv V-8 and fastback styling made the 1949 Oldsmobile Series 88 a terror on the highway and a hit in the dealers' showrooms.

3. 1953 marked the introduction of the Oldsmobile Series 98 Fiesta convertible and Fiesta hubcaps became the symbol of a real "kool kemp." Fiesta owners were nearly driven to paranoia by "hot-rodders" looking for a set of Fiestas to embellish their wheels. Fad lasted for years, too!

4. Another special interest possibility is the 1954 Oldsmobile Starfire 98 convertible.

5. The first 4-door hardtop was introduced by Oldsmobile in 1955. The Super 88 Holiday sedan had wraparound windshield and rear window, but no center pillar support for the doors—an innovation which swept the automotive industry.

6. 1956 saw Oldsmobile escalate the horsepower war by giving the "98" Deluxe Holiday coupe a 240-hp Rocket T-350 engine and Jetaway Hydra-Matic. Two-tone paint jobs, which Oldsmobile re-introduced to the industry in '54, continued in popularity.

1

mobile, at least to my mind, was the 1941. You don't see many around today—probably because they were driven into the ground with the scarcity of automobiles for the next several years.

In this year, Oldsmobile actually had six different models. The Special 66-6, Special 66-8, Dynamic Cruiser 76-6, Dynamic Cruiser 76-8, Custom Cruiser 96-6 and Custom Cruiser 98-8. This meant that each series was available with either a 6- or 8-cyl., engine. The 66-8 is the most desirable of these, since its power-to-weight ratio and low-sales (10,356) bring it close to the special-interest category. The underhood difference in length, between the six and eight, was made up by using a larger fan shroud.

By 1942, the wider, roomier, lower and, perhaps, uglier Oldsmobile took advantage of World War II lingo, with Fuselage Fenders, Dreadnaught Frames and engines of greater "fire power." This body style lasted until 1949.

Meanwhile, there was a war. Car production stopped, and Oldsmobile concentrated on artillery ammunition, aircraft machine guns, tank cannon, high-precision parts for aircraft engines, and forgings for military trucks, tanks, aircraft and guns.

Much overlooked in the special-interest cars field is the postwar car equipped with special-controls for the paraplegic war veteran. Oldsmobile was a leader in this field, building more than 26,000 automobiles with Hydra-Matic and Valiant equipment. Since many second owners often ripped out these controls, chances of finding one of these cars are slim.

Harley Earl, GM's mastermind stylist, had designs on Oldsmobile for 1948. Not all 1948's, though—just the 98. While the 66, 68, 76 and 78 models continued with the same old body, the 98 was given "Futuramic" styling. It was made available in convertible and sedan form.

The Futuramic styling was so modern and pleasing that the high-priced 98 had the greatest sales volume of any Olds model, including 50% greater than the low-priced 66-6.

But the best of Oldsmobile still lay ahead. And it was to begin in 1949, when the first modern, high-compression, overhead-valve V-8 was introduced.

Model lines were reduced from five to three—the 76, 88 and 98—all with Futuramic styling. It was a record sales year for Olds, with all three models within a few thousand sales of each other.

Originally, the V-8 was only to be available in the 98, but someone's foresight along the way made it available in the smaller, lighter 88, which soon became the terror of the highways, with unmatched performance.

Though most of the thunder had been taken away by Cadillac's introduction of a similar V-8 earlier, the oversquare Olds V-8 soon rectified that with the 88. The Rocket V-8 remains

2

3

4

5

6

General Motors Corporation

Oldsmobile

to this day, legendary for its smoothness and tractability. With a stiff crank and five main bearings, it produced 135 hp.

The big-engine, small-car trend promoted by Buick in the mid-Thirties, was now being brought to its peak by Oldsmobile, as another sales record fell in 1950. This time, the 88 far outstripped the sales of the 76 and 98—in fact, double the total of the other two models combined.

Far and away the most popular among speed addicts of the day was the light, two-door 88 sedan. Yet, as with other manufacturers of the day, the four-door sedan was the bread-and-butter car.

This would be the last year for all-coil suspension. In 1951, Olds would go to front coils and rear leafs. For now though, they retained lever shocks and two massive stabilizer bars.

The Rocket emblem, with 88 emblazoned over it, soon became the status symbol of every Oldsmobile owner of the day. Acceleration was a phenomenal 12 seconds from 0-60 and a top speed of 92 mph for the Chevy-bodied 88. With Hydra-Matic and its higher rear-end ratio, top speeds would nearly reach 100 mph.

Oldsmobile obviously seemed satisfied with the 303-cu.-in., 135-hp Rocket V-8, because it remained relatively unchanged since it was first introduced through 1951.

For 1951, the model lineup was now 88, Super 88 and 98. And emphasis was now on the Holiday Coupe, a two-door hardtop first introduced a year earlier. In succeeding years, the Holiday models would account for the biggest portion of Oldsmobile sales.

Olds continued to push performance and put a lot of emphasis on the use of premium fuels, as compression ratios would soon reach the highest in automotive history.

Although displacement remained the same, horsepower was increased to 160 in 1952 with the use of the industry's first four-barrel production carburetor for V-8's—the Quadri-Jet—available on Super 88 and 98 models only.

Oldsmobile also punched up the Hydra-Matic with a new option on the selector quadrant. The transmission now had a Super (S) range along with the Drive (Dr) range. Super held the transmission locked in third gear to speeds of 75 mph, improving acceleration. Coupled with 25 extra horsepower, the Super 88 and 98 were truly 100-mph cars.

Another industry exclusive was also introduced this year—Autronic Eye, the automatic light dimmer. They were a headache in their day, because they were ill-adjusted and drivers often refused to override the switch, much to the disgust of blinded night drivers.

A prime special-interest car popped up in 1953—the 98 Fiesta convertible. This limited-sale car featured a unique wraparound windshield, hand-buffed leather upholstery and two-tone body colors of alpine white and either raven red or turquoise. Almost every accessory was standard on the Fiesta, including power steering and power brakes. It was powered by a 170-hp V-8 with 8.5:1 compression ratio.

Oldsmobile also introduced the first air conditioning since 1941. The blower was mounted in the trunk, with clear plastic ducts running along each side of the rear window and into the roof. Cold air exited from four louvers, two on each side, just above the doors.

In 1954, Oldsmobiles were completely restyled, bringing the fender lines even with hood and trunk lines. The styling was an instant success as Oldsmobile pushed into fourth place in the industry, the highest position it had attained since 1905. But now the Super 88 was being challenged for road supremacy by its cousin, the light and powerful Buick Century.

Oldsmobile punched up the horsepower to 185 and added lower rear-axle ratios for higher speed and better economy.

The 98 came out with yet another special-interest possibility with its posh Starfire convertible.

One of the prettiest Oldsmobiles of all came along in 1955. Headlights were recessed and a fiberglass boot was optional for all convertibles to

give the appearance of a built-in look.

But the biggest special-interest catch of this year is the Holiday Sedan, the industry's first four-door hardtop. With this new model, Oldsmobile's hardtop production was two-thirds of its total for the year.

The 98 Starfire convertible continued, now standard with electric windows, two-way power seat, padded instrument panel, electric clock and windshield washers.

By 1956, the horsepower race was really on a tear. The 88 engine was up to 230 hp with two-barrel carburetor and 9.25:1 compression ratio, while the Rocket T350 was now running 240 hp on a four-barrel. A new high-lift cam and the increased compression ratio made the biggest improvement. Displacement was now 324.3 cu. ins.

The automatic transmission, now called Jetaway Hydra-Matic, also got a performance boost. A new second fluid coupling replaced the former front friction clutch and pan which helped smooth out gear-ratio changes.

But it took the wild J-2 Rocket engine, introduced in January 1957 for the '57 models, to really get Oldsmobile back on top in the performance race. It was an $83 option, and well worth it—as far as special-interest car buffs are concerned. The J-2 pumped out 300 hp from 371 cu. ins. and three dual carburetors. The Super 88 and 98 were boosted to 277, with 400 lbs.-ft. of torque. The four-barrel Quadri-Jet was now standard on all three models. The 88 now was called the Golden Rocket 88.

The prize body style this year was the Fiesta wagon, which looked like a four-door hardtop with a rear station wagon section added. These are really special-interest cars, since their production lasted only two years and there has been nothing like them before or since.

Printed electrical instrument panel and two-piece driveshaft were two of the new engineering feats of the year.

A not-so-attractive 1958 Oldsmobile again drew the division into fourth place on the sales list. And gimmicks were becoming more prominent on the automotive scene, including on Oldsmobile.

One was the Trans-Portable Radio, which was removable from the instrument panel. It ran off the car's electrical and speaker system when plugged in, and off its own dry-cell batteries when removed.

Then, there was the infamous Safety Sentinel Speedometer. When a predetermined speed was reached the speedometer face would be lit by an amber light and a buzzer would sound.

But the gimmick of the year was New-Matic Ride—a true air-suspension system. All the GM divisions had a form of air suspension, but it turned out to be a dismal failure, purportedly a whim of the sales department.

The big drawbacks were that air suspension really didn't seem to differ that much from the conventional system... and it leaked.

In all, 100,000 GM cars were sold with air suspension.

New-Matic Drive used four air chambers located just inboard of each wheel. Air was stored in a high-pressure tank (250-300 psi) behind the right rear wheel, while a low-pressure tank was located behind the left rear wheel. The rear frame was altered slightly on New-Matic Ride cars. The compressor was on the left side of the engine and ran off a dual pulley on the crankshaft. Air and oil filters were used to keep dirt and moisture from entering the system.

Should you find a 1958 Olds with New-Matic, hang onto it—'cause it's special-interest.

In the meantime, the J-2 was rated at 312 hp, the Super 88 and 98 were up to 305, while the Dynamic 88 carried 265.

In 1959, the gimmicks kept coming: adjustable dome light, power antenna and Safety-Spectrum speedometer where speed was indicated by a moving band of color—green from 0-30; orange from 35-65; and red above 65.

Everyone was going for greater glass area, too—over one-third more on many new Olds models. This brought about two models to consider for special-interest—especially the SceniCruiser, a four-door hardtop with wraparound rear window. The two-door hardtop, named SceniCoupe, had a rear window that stretched well into the roof; so far, in fact, that a rear-seat passenger could look straight up and see the sky, with its big red sun giving him a nice burn.

By now the Rocket engine was up to 395 cu. ins., in the Super 88 and 98, producing 315 hp and 435 lbs.-ft. of torque.

The horsepower race continued for a decade after that, with Oldsmobile always in the middle for the right to be fastest on the street. And it's only right they should be... because they pioneered the over-square, modern V-8.

The nice thing about Oldsmobile special-interest cars is that most of them are somewhat easily obtainable today, since their big years came in the Fifties. And the price is generally right... after all, that's half the battle when looking for a special-interest car.

1. The 300-hp J-2 Rocket engine with three 2-bbl. carburetors (operated by progressive linkage) made its debut on '57 Oldsmobiles.

2. 1958 Oldsmobiles could be ordered with New-Matic Ride air suspension systems. The pressure tanks can be seen behind the rear wheels. The four air chambers were located just inboard of the wheels above each axle. Four-link suspension system replaced the rear leaf springs.

3. Oldsmobile's Super 88 Fiesta station wagon exhibited unusual styling (some say bizarre), but may be of special interest because of it.

4. Extreme wraparound of rear window and acute overhang of roof mark Oldsmobile's 1959 models.

General Motors Corporation

Pontiac

The "happy hunting grounds" for special interest car fans

In the early 1920's, General Motors encouraged its divisions to build "companion cars," so the corporation could saturate the market. The first of these emerged in 1926—Pontiac. Although it was developed by Chevrolet, and shared many of that division's components, it was refined and sold by Oakland.

That first companion car became so successful, that six years later it would survive its sire. In fact, it was the only GM companion car to remain today. Marquette (Buick) and Viking (Oldsmobile) lasted only two years, while La Salle (Cadillac) continued into the early 1940's.

The name "Pontiac," however, wasn't new to the Oakland line. Because Oakland—named after a street in Pontiac, Michigan—was a direct outgrowth of the Pontiac Buggy Company in 1907. Two years later it was merged with the fast-growing General Motors Company.

Although the Oakland was a good seller in the Teens, it never achieved the sales status Pontiac would attain soon after its introduction. Since that announcement of the 1926 model, Pontiac has never been out of the top-ten selling cars in America, reaching as high as third place numerous times.

Many industry firsts are credited to Oakland-Pontiac. Among these were oil and fuel filters, air cleaner, crankcase ventilation, automatic spark control, interchangeable bronze-backed main bearings, harmonic balancer, oil-tight U-joints, honed cylinders, full-pressure lubrication, and rubber spring shackle bushings. Also, Oakland-Pontiac was the first GM division to use Duco finish in quantity.

Pontiac was named after the great Ottawa Indian Chief, rather than the city in which it was built. Later Pontiacs would capitalize on this, with such model names as Chieftain and Star Chief.

The Pontiac was to be a "step-up car," designed to entice second buyers to move up from an inexpensive Four to the slightly higher-priced Pontiac Six. This philosophy proved to be successful. During the Twenties and Thirties, Pontiac was soon recognized for its durability and dependability. But along with this, it also gained a reputation as being an old man's car; this, in itself, did not begin to be a detriment until the Fifties.

Two men play an important role in the history of Pontiac: William S. Knudsen (father) and Semon E. Knudsen (son). The elder Knudsen was to give Pontiac its "old man image." The son, nicknamed Bunkie, would make it a "young man's car."

Oakland and Pontiac were quite similar in appearance (and mechanically) which no doubt led to the demise of the higher-priced Oakland by 1932. In fact, Pontiac too was fated for the chopping block, until GM incorporated the B.O.P. (Buick-Oldsmobile-Pontiac) program, in which dealers were required to take on two models of either of these three makes.

Any early Pontiac is a dependable, solid automobile for anyone who wants an older automobile. Unfortunately, very few qualify for the special-interest category. But of those that do, you can expect fewer problems with them than with many other makes of the same era—this is particularly true of the Thirties.

Pontiac entered the Thirties with a V-8 it shared with Oakland. Similar to Oldsmobile's Viking V-8, the engine had horizontal valves, with camshaft mounted in the valley of the V. Unlike Viking, however, it used a 180° crankshaft. Although the 180° crank usually offers more power, its dependability and roughness of operation make it unpopular for passenger-car use. It was one of the few V-8's not to use a 90° crank after 1924.

This L-head V-8 was used through 1932 in both Pontiac and Oakland on 117- and 118-in. wheelbases. Both qualify as special interest automobiles, especially in open-top form. A V-8 wasn't offered again on Pontiacs for more than 20 years.

Pontiac continued to use its inde-

1. First of a long line of cars to bear the famous Indian chief's name, Chevrolet's companion line started with this 1926 Pontiac, marketed and sold in Oakland dealerships.

2. A stylistic theme that was carried for a number of years on Pontiacs, the Silver Streak was introduced in 1935, when this 4-door touring sedan, still with wire wheels, was built.

3. Like the other GM cars of the late '30's, the identical '37 and '38 Pontiacs with sidemounts look great today. Wouldn't you like to have this 1937 convertible sedan in your garage?

4. Not many true special-interest Pontiacs were built in the '40's, but a nice '40 woodie like this should be fairly rare and desirable today.

COURTESY MOTOR TREND MAGAZINE

structible six during those years and later, until it was dropped after 1954.

In 1933, Pontiac produced a milestone car. Under the leadership of William S. Knudsen, the struggling division overcame a depression slump. While other GM divisions were down in sales, Pontiac almost doubled its output.

The V-8 was gone, and in its place was an L-head straight 8 of 223.4-cu.-in. displacement and 77 hp. Somewhat contrary to today's thinking, the inline 8 was a better performer than the 85-hp V-8 of the previous year.

Although the 1933 Pontiac shared many components with Chevrolet, you'd never know it by looking. It was one of the first automobiles to offer streamlined styling. That, along with its low price—the 601-8 Roadster, at $585, was cheaper than the Six of 1932—established Pontiac firmly in the "step-up" class GM hoped it would fill. From 1933 on, Pontiac had a successful line of automobiles that would become virtually unchallenged in its price line.

Body styles for 1933, all on 115-in. wheelbases, included 2- and 4-door sedans, sport and convertible coupes.

The following year, 1934, produced one of the cleanest-looking Pontiacs of the decade. Though special interest is limited to the convertible coupes and sedans, it's worth talking about Knee-Action front suspension, which it shared with Chevrolet. Actually a Dubonnet suspension, Knee-Action has been much maligned, only because it was misunderstood.

I'd like to quote here from a fine automotive magazine, *Special Interest Autos*, concerning the 1934 Pontiac 8 and Knee-Action:

"This system has a long-standing, largely unmerited reputation for quick deterioration, lousy handling, and even total collapse.

"You have to remember that all early IFS systems, including the SLA variety, wore out and deteriorated fairly quickly....With proper care, Dubonnets enjoyed long, useful lives. Very few owners or mechanics ever bothered to service them, though. The Dubonnet kingpins, for instance, had needle bearings and needed lubing with a low-pressure grease gun every 1000 miles or so. High pressure lubes burst the grease seals and soon ruined the needles. The lower link on the threaded pivot bushings needed similar periodic lubing. Then, too, the cylinders themselves needed topping up about once a year, which again no one ever got around to. Sooner or later, the units got so dry that the shocks wouldn't work, and this put an undue strain on the primary and secondary coil springs. All of which led to the Dubonnet's reputations for poor ride, poor handling, and total failure."

The famed Silver Streak styling made its first appearance in 1935. It simply consisted of chrome trim, which instantly made a Pontiac recognizable in a crowd.

After eliminating Knee-Action sus-

2 COURTESY MOTOR TREND MAGAZINE

3 COURTESY ROBERT F. MEHL, JR., COLLECTION

4 COURTESY MOTOR TREND MAGAZINE

SPECIAL INTEREST AMERICAN CARS/131

General Motors Corporation
Pontiac

pension after 1936, Pontiac also quit using wood in its bodies with the 1937 model year and began sharing bodies with Oldsmobile and Buick instead of Chevrolet. The Silver Streak Six came with 117-in. wheelbase, while the Eight was up to 122. An interesting gadget also appeared this year. It was called Gaselector.

It consisted of a knob under the distributor to change timing from 10 advance to 10° retard. Because of the uncertainty of fuels in those days, it was designed to eliminate pinging.

Pontiac models were pretty austere until 1940, when fastback styling made its first appearance on these cars. They came in 2- and 4-door versions only. In 1940, this styling was available only with the 8-cyl. engine. But from 1941 through 1950, you could get them with either the six or eight.

One other interesting, pre-World War II Pontiac was the woodie station wagon, first introduced in 1937. It was the second GM division to offer a wagon—Chevrolet was first.

Pontiac was a "nice" car through the Forties and early Fifties. But not much on special interest. In 1948, Hydra-Matic was offered for the first time as an option. In 1949, the Chieftain series was inaugurated. And in 1950, the Catalina 2-door hardtop made its appearance.

Although not special interest cars, I happen to be partial to the 1949 through 1952 Pontiacs. The styling is neat and clean, and the automobiles were simple and most dependable in either 6- or 8-cyl. form. However, progress was catching up with Pontiac. Everyone else had a V-8, and the absence of one began eating into Pontiac sales. Consequently, 1954 proved to be a big disappointment to dealers, who expected the startlingly new Pontiac to have a V-8. However, that "startlingly new" car turned out to be the Star Chief—up to then, the largest Pontiac ever built. It had a 124-in. wheelbase and was almost the size of Cadillac and Lincoln, because of its elongated trunk. The Straight 8 performed admirably when compared with many V-8's of the day, but the public was clamoring for V's, not inlines.

The "old man's car" image was about to change, though. Bunkie Knudsen was then Pontiac's chief, and he claimed he was going to undo what his father started. "You can sell a young man's car to an old man," he said, "but you can't sell an old man's car to a young man."

So when 1955 rolled in, so did the Strato Streak V-8. And with it, some highly desired special interest cars.

The V-8 of 1955 came in two forms—a 287.2 cu. ins. of 180 hp and 8.1:1 compression ratio (premium fuel) and 173 hp, 7.41:1 compression ratio (regular fuel). For the first time, too, Pontiac was using overhead-valves. All previous engines had been L-heads. And the famed Pontiac Six disappeared.

Two series were offered: the 124-in.-wheelbase Star Chief and 122-in. Chieftain. A 2-door, all-metal station wagon was offered for the first time in the 12-model lineup.

A year later, Pontiac was really on the move. The Strato Streak V-8 now boasted 316.6 cu. ins. With 4-bbl carburetor, it put out 227 hp, and with 2-bbl carb it was 205 hp.

Two new models appeared—the Catalina 4-door sedan, Pontiac's first 4-door hardtop, and the highly sought-after Safari station wagon.

The Safari is a Nomad-like wagon,

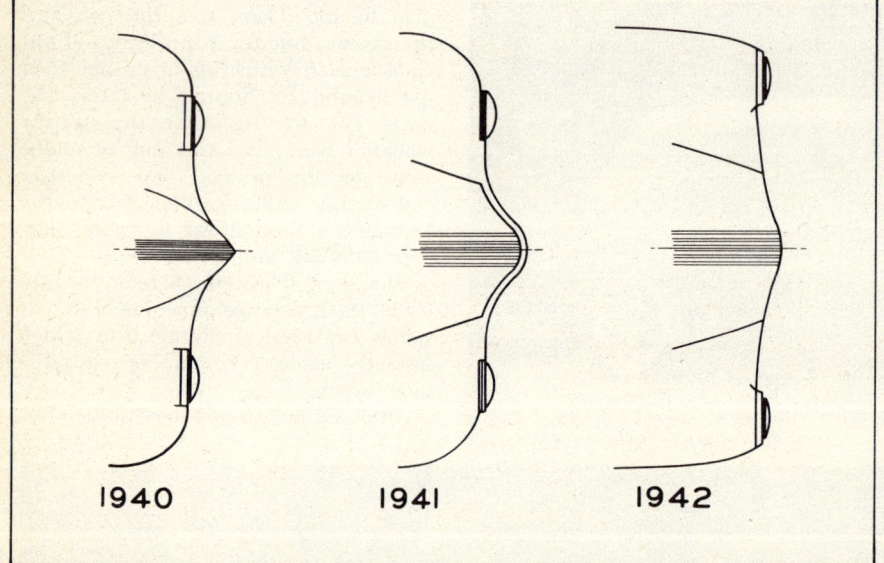
1

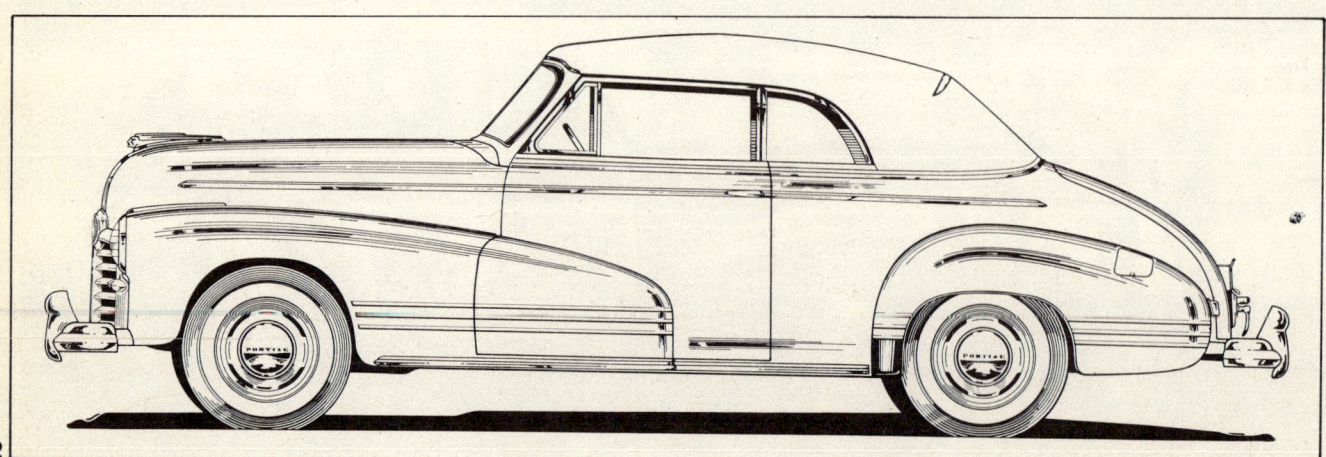
2

1. Along with the fastback styling introduced in 1940, Pontiac also began modernizing their designs with more flattened front ends. The "prow" in front was shrinking every year.

2. The '42's are especially rare now. The fastback styling of the closed cars was almost post war-looking, and the open cars like this are definitely worth collecting and restoring.

3. All of the '49-'52 Pontiacs look similar, which is to say retrimmed versions of the clean-looking Chevys.

4. New line for '54, still without the V-8 dealers had hoped for, was the Star Chief series. Note the optional stainless wire-wheel hubcaps on this convertible, with infant tailfins.

5. All-new styling and the 180 hp V-8, the Strato Streak, made this two-tone Star Chief convertible a big hit in '55.

General Motors Corporation

Pontiac

with wraparound rear, side windows. Production was low on these models, mainly because of price and the presence of standard station wagons in the Pontiac line.

By 1957, Knudsen had built Pontiac into a superstar on the nation's racetracks. Displacement was up to 347.04 cu. ins. and compression ratio up to 9.2:1. The cars were smaller, too, with 122-in. wheelbases. And Pontiac was right in the midst of the horsepower race. But by 1958, it would be king of the road.

The famed Bonneville debuted in 1958, along with fuel injection, three 2-bbl carburetors and Air Ride.

To handle the new power from the Tempest 395 V-8, Pontiac offered Safe-T-Track, a non-slip differential. The engine was now up to 370 cu. ins., 10.5:1 compression ratio and 310 hp in fuel-injected form.

The special interest cars can't really be pinned down, because of the variety of options available on each of the 16 models. One thing for sure, though, if you can locate a fuel-injected Bonneville with Air Ride suspension, you've really got a winner.

Body styles in four series—Bonneville, Star Chief, Chieftain and Super Chief—covered the gamut from convertible to sedans, hardtops and station wagons.

The engines make the real difference between special interest and run-of-the-mill Pontiacs for 1958. Here's what was offered for the year: Fuel injection and triple carb engines (300 hp) were options on all Hydra-Matic equipped Pontiacs. The stick shift cars used either the 2- or 4-bbl versions which produced 240- and 255-hp, respectively. So, if it's got a Hydra-Matic, look under the hood. If you see three carbs or no carbs, grab it.

The Air Ride suspension was similar to Chevrolet's, producing 250 psi from a 5-cu.-in. compressor engine mounted on the left side of the engine block. As with other GM air suspensions of the time, any car so-equipped is rare, and the system tends to leak.

In 1959, Pontiac probably has more special interest cars than any other GM division, even though it shared body styles with most of the others. Many of the names were changed, although Bonneville, Star Chief and Safari (no longer the Nomad-type) remained. Like many GM divisions of the time, the names were ludicrous—Parisienne and Laurentian.

Unlike other GM divisions, however, Pontiac wasn't satisfied with a narrow track with the new, wider Fisher bodies. As *Motor Trend* magazine put it: "Other GM divisions decided to bite the bullet and produce their cars with the previous year's track dimensions, 5-in. wider body or no. But not Pontiac. It put the '59 models' front and rear wheels out almost as much as the new body was wide and created the widest track and best handling full-sized cars in the industry."

The most interesting body style for all GM cars that year was the 4-door hardtop with wraparound rear window. In Pontiac's case, it was called the Catalina Vista, available in Bonneville, Star Chief, and Parisienne series.

Also of interest was that Pontiac offered Powerglide and Turboglide...but only for 1959. The Hydra-Matic factory had burned down, so a quick changeover was necessary.

The six also returned this year in 261-cu.-in. form, with 8.5:1 compression ratio, 150 hp and single-barrel carburetion.

Three separate V-8's were offered for the first time. The hot one was the Super Strato Flash V-8 with three 2-bbl at 348 cu. ins., 9.5:1 compression, and 280 hp. The 340-cu.-in. version with a single 4-bbl put out 250 hp. Two Strato Flash V-8's also were offered in 283-cu.-in. form: the 4-bbl version produced 230 hp, while the 2-bbl had 185 hp.

The nice thing about Pontiac special interest cars, as it is with Oldsmobile, is that most of them are readily available. If you can latch on to the older Pontiacs, they make nice cars. But for special interest, you can't beat the late Fifties. 🐞

1. Also new to '55 were the Safari wagons, Pontiac versions of the Chevy Nomads. Not as expensive to find now as the Nomads, these are certainly good special interest investments.

2. Rear view of the '55 Safari wagon shows the chrome strips and interior detailing that gave these wagons the "luxury and distinctiveness of a passenger car," as well as utility.

3. Pontiac, which had built a line based as "Chief of the sixes," became strictly a V-8 company after 1955. This is Pontiac's first 4-door hard-top sedan, introduced in '56, with Strato Flight transmission and 227-hp engine, now up to 317 cu.ins.

4. Calling it "the boldest advance in 50 years," Pontiac brought out the first of the sporty Bonnevilles in '58 with a host of options. The rare options like fuel injection and air suspension are quite desirable today.

5. Although by no means collector's items today, the '59 Pontiacs did introduce all-new bodies coupled with a new frame incorporating the famous "wide-track" suspension.

Pictorial of minor marques

Some of the lesser-known or short-lived American cars.

AMERICAN BANTAM

The American Austin Car Co., was formed in 1930 to manufacture under license, the English Austin Seven, though with U.S.-style bodywork. Its 4-cyl. engine displaced 45.6 cu. ins. and produced 13 hp. It sold for $445 out the door of the Butler, Pa., plant, and had a 75-in. wheelbase and a track of 40 ins. Advance orders for the sub-compact supposedly totalled 180,000 cars, but first-year production was only a dismally low 8500 units, the best year the company would have.

Diving to less than 1300 cars built in '31, sales rose to 3850 for '32, the year American Austin went into receivership. The firm's assets were sold for a pitiful $5000 in 1935 to one of Austin's board members, Roy Evans, who recapitalized the company and titled it American Bantam Car Co. The first Bantams weren't ready until early in 1938, and when they appeared, they were similar to the preceding Austins in size, but enjoyed new bodies. The engine was the same as used before, but had been upgraded to 20 hp. Despite loud press acclaims, only 1500 '38's were built, and the picture remained the same for '39 at about 1220 cars. New coachwork appeared for '40, and a new engine; 4-cyl., 22 hp. from 50 cu. ins. But Bantam was by now the recipient of a military contract and its passenger car efforts dwindled to zero by early in 1941.

1930 American Austin 2-door sedan

1939 American Bantam roadster

CHECKER

Checker Motors Corp., has been a quiet mainstay in the automobile industry since 1922, though only in the private passenger car business since 1959. Relatively little known or appreciated by car buffs, Checker is the world's largest builder of taxicabs. To this end, Checkers have always been maneuverable marvels; even with a wheelbase of 120 ins., it can swing a small 37-ft. circle. Doors are wide, and swing open wide. Trunk space swallows as much as any two Chevrolets. The floor is high to virtually eliminate the driveshaft tunnel—all these considerations and more take taxi-use into account. For years Checker has offered two basic models; a 4-door sedan and a station wagon, with two standard trim levels of each but which are often modified for large fleet buyers. Checker used the Continental L-head 6 for years, not switching to a modern V-8 until the mid-'60's, and then using the Chevrolet engine. Taxi sales only were concentrated upon, as was noted, until 1959, but in '48 Checker began hinting in rare advertisements that private car use could be made of their products as long as the buyer made concessions to accepting taxi amenities. The '59 (and later) pure passenger cars differed not one whit from the sedan and wagon taxis, except in creature comforts through interior appointments. The distant history of Checker is vague, but apparently it evolved from the Commonwealth car which itself was an outgrowth of the Partin-Palmer and, before that, the Cartercar.

1959 Checker Superba Sedan

1959 Checker Superba Station Wagon

According to official requirements of certain racing associations, a car cannot compete in a "stock" or "production" category unless a specified minimum of at least superficially identical cars have been manufactured. During the height of the recent TransAm sedan racing series, for example, the sanctioning organization required no less than 500 cars be made available to the public. That is basically why millionaire yachtsman Briggs S. Cunningham arranged to build a batch of 25 Cunningham C4R's for 1952, and another 50 for 1953. Cunningham ar-

CUNNINGHAM

rived on the world automotive scene in spectacular fashion when he fielded two Cadillacs in the 1950 Le Mans 24-hour race; one a regular-looking sedan, but the other custom-fitted with an unbecoming but effective 2-seater body. To incredulous race fans, the cars finished 10th and 11th in their division, bringing Cunningham heaps of praise and the determination to return with cars bearing his own name.

He did, and returned for the '51 event with three race cars, heaps of spare parts, back-up cars, and a crew that would do justice to the German racing teams of old. Only one completed the distance, but Cunningham returned to the United States vowing he would race *and win* on our own shores, which he eventually did in races at Elkhart Lake, Wisconsin, and Watkins Glen, New York. This is briefly how and why the now-rare street-driven versions appeared, in roadster and coupe form.

1952 Cunningham C4R Coupe   **1952 Cunningham C4R Roadster**

The immediate postwar period saw a car-hungry public clamoring for automobiles, and it also saw the hard-pressed major builders short of steel and with supplier strikes that kept production to a trickle. These basic factors combined to create a rash of folks eager to get on the receiving end of—to be blunt—money. If a new car—any kind of car, with any number of wheels—could be made available in these trying times, the world would beat a path to the factory door, wherever it may be, and Detroit could go to blazes. Some of the catch-as-catch-can companies that set out to capitalize on the shortage of cars and the availability of money were purely and simply stock manipulations, where for example a single prototype would be

DAVIS

exhibited and franchises sold with promises of vehicle delivery in a specified length of time. Millions were dumped into coffers as a result. Others were serious attempts to produce and sell automobiles, but the Securities and Exchange Commission was often able to find something unorthodox going on and slammed the door. The 3-wheel Davis falls somewhere in between, since though developer Gary Davis was serious in his plans for production, he was nonetheless indicted, then put on probation with the stipulation he would never again build a car. Davis was headquartered in Van Nuys, Calif., where he could draw engineers and de-

signers from the aircraft industry. Once the unique machine was sorted out, Davis ordered parts for 100 cars, and although only 17 were produced in his plant, he told Michael Lamm in 1970, when the latter was editor of *Special Interest Autos,* that it is likely all the parts were eventually built into Davis's. Lamm traced four of them, including Harrah's example, before he met Gary Davis personally where he found two more and a complete chassis. Oddly, none were ever sold since the Davis trial came up before signed-up dealers received any. Kinmont disc brakes were used on some of the prototypes, all were powered by a 60-hp Hercules 4-cyl. Alas, the Davis Motor Co. was disbanded in 1949, the unfortunate victim of bureaucratic intervention.

1948 Davis 3-wheeler

Pictorial of minor marques

Many great automotive names are absent from this book simply because their products do not properly qualify for inclusion within our parameters. Among them are Auburn, Cord and Duesenberg—high-priced, low-production cars of their times, they are far, far beyond the purse of today's average restorer or collector. Franklin would be included in this elite list, except for a particular series produced from '32 through '34; the singular air-cooled Franklin that has not yet been established as a Classic by the august body of the Classic Car Club of America (CCCA). Lacking space here to detail Franklin's long and colorful history, suffice it to say that the U.S. car-buying public was not big on air-cooling by the '30's, despite the reputation for reliability and cool-running these magnificent machines achieved. Sales waned, and when founder H. H. Franklin was pushed

FRANKLIN

aside by his fund-loaning banks to stave off total bankruptcy, they installed one Edwin McEwen in his place. One of his suggestions was to produce a lower-priced car than anything then in the Franklin line, and produce it in massive quantities. Another move was to order the Franklin's senior bodies made in the firm's own plants instead of buying from an outside supplier. This meant the big Franklins would be produced by men unaccustomed to sheetmetal work and quality would obviously suffer. On the other hand, the subject of this treatise, the Olympic, did have its bodies farmed out; to Reo who agreed to supply their Flying Cloud bodies at the rate of four per day. The Olympic engine was a 6-cyl., ohv inline engine of 274 cu. ins. and air-cooled in Franklin

tradition. Output was 100 hp at 3100 and mated via an adaptor to Reo's 3-speed transmission which incorporated freewheeling. At 3500 lbs., the Olympic was the smallest (and least expensive—$1500) of contemporary Franklins, yet it would out-accelerate the senior V-12 Series 17's which, though their prototype weighed some 4400 lbs., tipped the scales at near 6000 lbs., thanks to the body lead required to smooth up the roughly-finished Franklin coachwork. Alas. Too little too late, and though at the time the Olympic was looked at as the staid old firm's salvation, only some 1500 were produced and Franklin went down the tube at the end of 1934. Engine design patents went to Air-Cooled Motors, Inc., (now the Franklin Engine Co.,) and years later they adapted a few 6-cyl. opposed engines to water cooling and supplied them for the 1947 Tucker.

1933 Franklin Olympic Convertible Coupe

Although we have noted that Jeep is beyond the qualifications for inclusion in this book, we must, out of deference to its legions of followers, include it here since it has been, and continues to be, so much a part of the U.S. motoring scene. Jeep as a make has been recognized only since the formation in 1963 of Kaiser-Jeep, but its roots lie in the Army's request for a "C&R Car" (Command

JEEP

and Reconnaisance) and which was built in prototype form by American Bantam, Willys-Overland, and Ford Motor Company. All were superbly adquate to meet the Army's specifications, but for complex reasons the Willys design was chosen and they produced 360,000 during the course of

WW II while Ford built 278,000 to Willys' design. The Jeep donned civilian clothes after 1946 and continued as a product of Willys-Overland, changing its name to Willys Motors, Inc., when Henry J. Kaiser interests purchased the facilities. A further change to Kaiser-Jeep Corp. was made in '63, the company continuing to build various versions of the ubiquitous 4X4's, as it has since 1970 under the AMC banner.

Gen. MacArthur at Leyte in 1944

1944 MB Jeep; exact Army issue

138/**SPECIAL INTEREST AMERICAN CARS**

Step right up, ladeez 'n gennlemen; wanna buy a franchise? Such was the cry of many a wheeler-dealer right after WW II had wound down. With the Big Three and leading independents short of steel and beset with supplier strikes, and with the public willing and able to buy anything on wheels (3 or 4, it scarcely mattered which), the time was ripe for an all-new car; one of low-cost and gas-stinginess. Rising to the opportunity came an ex-Chrysler engineer, John Liefeld, who interested a moneyed backer in scheming to produce what they would call the Bobbi-Kar. Some 800 investors/would-be dealers leaped at the franchises sold by the San Diego

KELLER

firm. As it turns out, the Securities & Exchange Commission took a dim view of all this and, to reduce an involved tale, Bobbi-Kar turned up again in Alabama in late '46 in no less than a run-down furniture factory which, at the time, seemed eminently suitable for car production—especially wood-bodied station wagons. Liefeld was gone by now, and George Keller, a Studebaker ex, gets in on the nefarious scheme although he had far higher hopes of manufacturing cars than the other Bobbi-Kar-ists. Things get confused here, but the firm winds up as George D. Keller Motors of Huntsville, and the prototype Bobbi-Kar became the Keller off the assembly line—at the rate of one car per month. To keep things simple, the Keller was built largely of proprietary parts—a Ford gizmo here, a Chrysler bit there, etc.—and it was of sound design. In the end, only about 18 Keller Super Chief wagons were built before Keller himself passed away unexpectedly late in '49. Things might have gone well had he survived, for the SEC was later to find everything 100% on the up-and-up even as Davis, Tucker and Playboy were proven to be merely stock schemes.

Keller Super Chief wagons

The least-known, least-publicized, yet the only car to survive the postwar mini-car boom was the redoubtable King Midget, whose star ascended so early in 1946 that Midget Motors Corp., of Athens, Ohio, was nearly the very first postwar production automobile. The brainchild of Claud Dry and Dale Orcutt, the King Midget survived through a surprising 23 years, quietly folding its doors in '69 after having manufactured some 5000 cars. At first the King Midget used for motive power an 8½-hp Wisconsin air-cooled engine driving

KING MIDGET

through a small but conventional manual transmission. Later versions employed a 9½-hp Kohler powerplant with a unique 2-speed automatic gearbox. The King Midget tipped the scales at 550 lbs., yet would hold a sustained 50-mph highway speed while delivering 60 mpg. The Midget's suspension was independent at all four wheels. It had an overall length of 102 ins., and a wheelbase of 72 ins. Total overall width was 48 ins., wheel tread was 42 ins., and seat width was 34 ins. Its turning radius was 11 ft. Obviously more akin to a golf cart or motorized grocery-getter than a passenger car, the one-body-style-only 2-seater was (at the time) highway legal and many were employed as commuter vehicles in addition to serving duty as around-town delivery units, mobile camera mounts, driver training aids, and other types of yeoman service. Nowhere else but at Midget Motors Corp., could one buy a brand-new American car with an f.o.b. price of $249.50!

King Midget 2-seater

King Midget 2-seater

Pictorial of minor marques

MUNTZ

Although it bears little resemblance to it, the Muntz Jet had its beginnings as the Kurtis Sport, a distinctive 2-seater based on Ford running gear and built in a quantity of only about 35 before manufacturing rights were sold to Earl Muntz in 1949. "Madman" Muntz, as he was popularly known for his zany promotional schemes and flamboyancy, stretched the 100-in. Kurtis wheelbase to 113 ins. to accommodate two back-seat passengers, but continued to use primarily aluminum for body panels as had Kurtis before him. Running changes, though, began to be made to the mostly-handbuilt cars to eliminate this costly and easily-dented material, and steel fenders and other parts began to appear over the production span of the first 28 Jets. All of these used the Cadillac ohv V-8 and HydraMatic transmission. Manufacturing was switched from Glendale, Calif., to Evanston, Ill., in late '50 where access to the suppliers of proprietary parts was more convenient, and an additional 366 Jets were turned out before the firm's demise in 1954. The Evanston Jets used the flathead Lincoln V-8, which required a wheelbase stretch to 118 ins., and which would also accommodate the later 1953 Lincoln ohv installed in the last few chassis produced. Muntz' time was continually divided among many enterprises, and though he lost a reported $1000 on each Muntz Jet produced, his other interests kept the marque alive—until his TV business suddenly lost several million dollars and he was obliged to quit the car-manufacturing business.

1949 Muntz Jet with Earl "Madman" Muntz

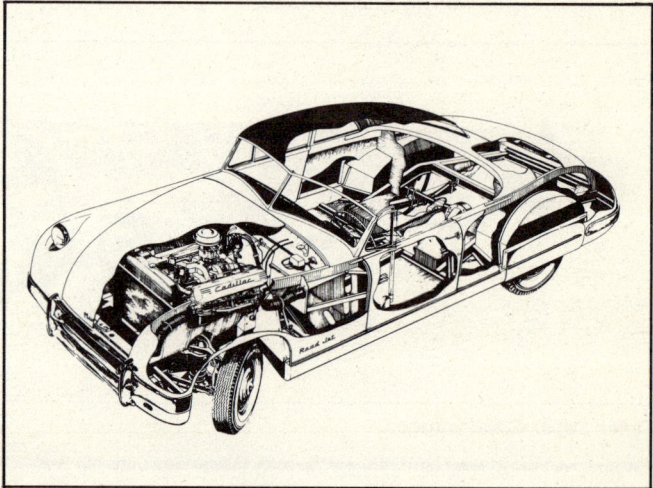
Cadillac-powered 1949 Muntz "Glendale" Jet

PLAYBOY

The Playboy, like many another postwar-baby, was conceived to fill an apparent gap left when the major manufacturers scrubbed their war-year plans to produce lightweight, economical, and low-priced cars. What the U.S., if not the whole world, needed, those involved with the Playboy reasoned, was a simple, basic-transportation automobile for primarily urban use yet with the stamina to stay with the full-size traffic on the open road. The prototype Playboy emerged as a small 3-seater, rear-engined, and stirred up great interest among both potential dealers and a car-starved public. Visionaries saw the Playboy with a retractable steel top, 4-wheel independent suspension, and an automatic transmission. Power would be via the Continental 4-cyl. engine; and all these innovations were indeed part and parcel of the prototype. But sanity prevailed when it came time to tool up for the special parts required for a car of this configuration, and later prototypes had the conventional front-mounted engine and, after some 17 pilot cars had been built with independent suspension, the following 80 (for a total of 97) used a standard rear end with semi-elliptic springs. Even a car that embodies many proprietary components still requires a lot of engineering and tooling, and it was figured that $20,000,000 was needed to put Playboy on the road. Then came the inevitable stock issue coincidentally with the failure of Tucker—which served to keep speculators away in droves—and the almost-successful, diminutive Playboy sunk into oblivion.

Reworked '47 Playboy speedster

Playboy emblem

140/SPECIAL INTEREST AMERICAN CARS

Reo is one of those major automotive firms whose dominance lies in the years well prior to our 1930–1960 coverage. But the marque qualifies for inclusion here since several models of interest were offered during the waning years of passenger car manufacturing and embodied certain mechanical innovations, notably an automatic 4-speed transmission known as the Self-Shifter introduced in 1933. Ransom Eli Olds, whose initials form the Reo name, had founded Oldsmobile Motor Works in Lansing, Mich., in 1896, and who became a mass-production pioneer. The great Curved Dash

REO

Oldsmobile appeared in 1902, but although it was an instant success, Olds left the firm to found Reo in 1904. Olds was an innovator and over the years his cars boasted many mechanical breakthroughs. The company's best year was 1928 with 29,000 cars sold, but it was only good enough for 19th spot on the popularity charts after having been within the top 10 during the pre-'Teens. By '30, Reo production settled on two versions of the Flying Cloud (the lower-priced Wolverine having been phased out in 1929), and the Royale which lived through '34. Forced to the bottom of their economic barrel through development of the Self-Shifter, the Depression, and development of the Royale, Reo, in '33, resorted to selling parts to other manufacturers in addition to making their own Flying Clouds. They supplied bodies and chassis to dying Franklin for '33 and '34, and let Graham use the body stamping dies of the Flying Cloud for just a few dollars per stamp. Reo went on in the truck business after 1936.

Record-setting 1930 Flying Cloud

1930 Reo Royale

If all the words ever written about Preston Tucker and his automobile were divided by the number of cars he built, the result would easily qualify for the *Guinness Book of Records*. Put another way, if all the money involved in the complex Tucker dealings was similarly divided, the per-car cost would be $560,000 apiece! This is based, of course, on the 49 Tuckers supposedly in existence. Suffice it to

TUCKER

say that everything possible to write about Tucker and his cars has been written, and no enthusiastic restorer is about to find one at an affordable price squirreled away in a barn. Nevertheless, it is fitting that the Herculean efforts that Preston Tucker put forth to mass-produce a 6-passenger, advanced-concept, middle-price car, (the initital target was $1500), is epitomized in this book. Most historians have "proven" that the Tucker clambake was a hoax, but though the demise of The Tucker Corp., caused by the SEC's intervention, came in 1948, Tucker was vindicated on all counts in 1950. He *had* intended to build the ultimate American car.

1948 Tucker Model 48 sedan

Special Interest Car Clubs

Clubs, groups and associations whose members are deeply enamored of specific automobiles are rampant, and their coverage of marques spans essentially every make ever produced. Some are obscure and so singular in interest, and of such probable short duration, as to be considered nebulous. Others have followers numbering in the thousands, their involvement bridging a car's entire model year lifespan, and with regional groups or chapters spread clear 'round the globe. In between are solidly founded but geographically centralized enthusiasts of a particular make, who offer the distant would-be-joiner only correspondence; as well as those whose club address changes whenever the corresponding secretary moves or is supplanted by someone else.

The following list of clubs, however, are those we found during compilation of this book, to be firmly rooted as far as mailing addresses go, as far as being able to offer assistance of all kinds goes, and as far as being capable of sharing same-car enthusiasm across the nation or across international boundaries goes. These are the clubs who responded to our plea for assistance in producing SPECIAL INTEREST AMERICAN CARS (1930 - 1960), and who volunteered photos and production numbers, and who supplied us with a flood of organization newsletters and material and data of a hard-to-find nature. At the time of publication, be aware, the addresses listed were accurate, and most groups will probably continue to be accessible as noted. But changing times, changing personnel and the switching of post office boxes may make certain of them tenuous at best.

Let us hasten to point out, though, that joining a group of enthusiasts with the self-same interest in the self-same cars as your own, is the best way to really enjoy—and locate information and parts for—your special interest car.

Mr. Bill Gordon, Treasurer
AIRFLOW CLUB OF AMERICA
2029 Minoru Dr.
Altadena, Calif. 91001
(Chryslers and DeSotos)

R. Cohoon
AMERICAN MOTORS OWNERS ASSOCIATION
924 N. Eagle St.
Naperville, Ill. 60540
(Nash, Hudson, Essex, Lafayette, Terraplane, Rambler, etc.)

CLASSIC CHEVY CLUB
P.O. Box 17188
Orlando, Florida 32810
('55, '56, '57 only)

NATIONAL CHEVROLET RESTORERS CLUB
Box 311
La Mirada, Calif. 90637
(devoted to all years)

NATIONAL NIFTY FIFTIES CLUB
227 So. Grove St.
Denver, Colo. 80219
(Chevrolets only)

VINTAGE CHEVROLET CLUB OF AMERICA
P.O. Box 1135
Bellflower, Calif. 90706
(superb monthly magazine)

V.C.C.A.
2359 W. Adams
Fresno, Calif. 93706
(for vintage Corvette lovers)

W.P.C. CLUB
Chrysler Product Restorers Club
17916 Trenton Dr.
Castro Valley, Calif. 94546
(for lovers of Chrysler products)

CROSLEY AUTOMOBILE CLUB
200 Ridge Road East
Williamson, New York 14589
(very enthusiastic and helpful organization)

DESOTO CLUB
105 E. 96th
Kansas City, Mo. 64114
(catering to enthusiasts)

THE EARLY FORD V-8 CLUB OF AMERICA
P.O. Box 2122
San Leandro, CA. 94577
(1932 - '48 Fords and Mercurys, regional groups across the nation)

THE FORD & MERCURY RESTORERS CLUB
P.O. Box 2133
Dearborn, Michigan 48123
(Fords and Mercurys from '32 thru '48)

MODEL "A" RESTORER'S CLUB
P.O. Box 1930 A
Dearborn, Michigan 48121
(large and well-organized-with chapters)

John Payton
NATIONAL CROWN VICTORIA ASSOCIATION
2807 S. High Street
Muncie, Indiana 47302
(Victoria models from '30's thru '50's)

INTERNATIONAL FORD RETRACTABLE CLUB
2530 Shakespeare Dr.
Indianapolis, Ind. 46227
('57, '58, '59 retractable hardtop)

PONTIAC—OAKLAND CLUB INTERNATIONAL
3298 Maple
Allegany, N.Y. 14706
(fantastic benefits for members)

CLASSIC THUNDERBIRD CLUB INT.
P.O. Box 2398
Culver City, Calif. 90230
(beautiful bi-monthly magazine for owners and admirers)

TUCKER AUTOMOBILE CLUB OF AMERICA
P.O. Box 1027
Orange Park, Florida 32073
(ownership not required)

WILLYS OVERLAND JEEPSTER CLUB
395 Dumbarton Blvd.
Cleveland, Ohio 44143
(dedicated to preserving the last phaeton)

NATIONAL WOODIE CLUB
5522 W. 140th St.
Hawthorne, Calif. 90250
(for all woodie lovers)

LINCOLN ZEPHYR OWNERS CLUB
P.O. Box 185
Middletown, Pa. 17057
(ownership not required)

Independent
Crosley
A compact born 30 years too soon

Once upon a time, there lived a man who had what in retrospect was not a half bad idea at all. In 1939 though, it seemed downright weird. His idea was that if you made a car small and basic enough, and cheap enough to operate, the world would beat a path to your showroom door.

No, it wasn't Henry Ford. It was Powell Crosley, Jr., and this wasn't the first time he'd had what seemed a weird idea. His first product had been radios. In the days when the average home radio cost $250 or more, Crosley came out with a radio that sold for only $25. Then, when his customers complained that they couldn't receive anything on the little sets, he put up a 500,000-watt broadcasting station, so that they could have something to listen to. Crosley radios were a success from that time on, and the Crosley Broadcasting System was a force in prewar radio.

He did it again with refrigerators. He patented a device called the Crosley Shelvador, which had shelves on the inside of the door. It may seem commonplace now, but it was revolutionary then. And other manufacturers couldn't do it until the Crosley patents ran out in the '50's.

Cars were Powell Crosley's favorite product, though. He had built one when he was a boy, and had designed and engineered another, only to be financially wiped out by a market panic. Thirty years later, in May of 1939, the Crosley car was introduced to the world. The press introduction was at the Indianapolis Speedway. The world was not exactly waiting with baited breath for a 2-door convertible that weighed under 1000 lbs., and sold for an f.o.b. price of $250. After all, you could buy a six-year-old Plymouth that still had a lot of life left in it for less than that, and look at how much iron you got for your money.

While no sales records were set that first model year, enough were sold to convince Crosley to go ahead with a 1941 model with an expanded line up of body styles.

What did you get for your approximately $300? A chassis with an 80-in. wheelbase, half elliptic springs with beam axle in front and quarter elliptics in the rear. Power was by a 2-cyl., Waukesha air-cooled engine, with the fan a part of the flywheel. A 9-in.-dia. clutch coupled this with the 3-speed transmission, and then the drive went through a torque tube to the rear axle. In the interests of simplicity, super soft engine mounts were used and universal joints were eliminated. All this basic transportation was covered with what was described in the press of the time as a "rakish" convertible body. The rear seat was an extra.

The major mechanical improvements for the 1941 model year included a universal joint in the driveline, larger engine bearings, and the use of the Bonderizing process to improve the body finish.

The single-barrel Tillotson carburetor designed for the engine was still sitting atop the cylinders, and the 4-gallon gas tank still lived under the hood along with the engine and battery.

Mechanical brakes operated on all four wheels. They were of an unusual design, in that the lining floated free between the shoes and the drum. The lining material wrapped around 350 degrees of the drum surface, and the

1. The man and his dream. Powell Crosley Jr. holds one of the first of the sheet metal COBRA engines that powered the post WW II models.

2. This perfect example of a 1941 convertible coupe resides in Harrah's Automobile Collection. Yellow paint was one of three available choices.

PHOTO COURTESY OF HARRAH'S AUTOMOBILE COLLECTION, RENO, NEVADA

Independent
Crosley

odd system had the advantage that a reline job could be done simply by slipping a lining into the drum, without having to remove any components.

For 1941, the line was expanded to include, besides the 2-and 4-passenger convertibles, a convertible sedan (it had windows for the rear seat passengers), a station wagon, a panel truck, a pickup, and two unique models called the "Parkway Delivery" and the "Covered Wagon." The parkway delivery was a mini-panel with no roof over the front seat, exposing the driver to the elements. This was considered quite elegant in the '30's, particularly if the driver was dressed in livery like a chauffeur. The covered wagon was a convertible pickup truck with a removable back seat. With the top in place, it could be used as a car, while with everything open and the seat out, it was a ¼-ton truck. Either of these two models is a real collector's item today, since most of the prewar production was confined to the convertible coupe and sedan.

One advantage claimed for the Crosley design was that it was narrow enough at 48-ins. to be moved through a standard commercial store door. This way it could be sold by the same dealers who already handled Crosley radios and refrigerators, with little or no modifications to their salesrooms. It was even small enough to be worked on in their back shops.

The author remembers seeing a full line on display in the appliance department of Macy's in New York, sometime in late 1940. During the same year, he was taken to the New York Automobile Show in Grand Central Palace, where, in a dim recess somewhere between the Studebakers and the Divco trucks, he found the Crosley display. This featured Cannonball Baker, live and in person, talking about his record setting run in a Crosley Covered Wagon. Unlike his previous cross-country runs, this one featured record setting gas mileage. Baker drove west from the factory in Cincinnati to Los Angeles then back via New Orleans, Jacksonville and New York. He covered 6517 miles, and averaged over 50 miles per gallon. Powell Crosley, where are you now?

Prices for the expanded 1941 line ranged from the 950 lb. 2-passenger convertible at $315 f.o.b. all the way up to the 4-place station wagon, tipping the scales at 1160 lbs. and costing $470. This was the year that a Cadillac Fleetwood cost $2195., and a Lincoln Continental convertible cost $2700.

A car like the original Crosley would seem to be a good thing for use in this day of soaring fuel prices, but unfortunately the Federally mandated safety and emission rules would bring the weight and complexity level up too high.

Instrumentation on the prewar models included an ammeter and oil pressure gauge, flanking a speedometer that read all the way up to 60 mph. A glove compartment just large enough for a pair of gloves was set into the right side of the dash, while above the steering column was the crank for the manual windshield wiper. Windows slid open for signalling and ventilation, while a standard summertime modification among Crosley owners was to remove the side glass entirely.

Less than 6000 of the prewar models were built, and any one of them would be a real treasure today. Not only are they a unique example of American automobile making, they're small enough to be restored in the comfort of one's livingroom.

World War II found the Crosley factory in Cincinnati turning out military equipment, and Powell Crosley think-

PHOTO COURTESY OF HARRAH'S AUTOMOBILE COLLECTION, RENO, NEVADA

ing of the improvements he would make in the postwar models. Gasoline rationing during the war had suddenly put Crosley ownership in a new light for many people. At 50 miles per gallon, even a 3-gallon "A" coupon went a long way. Crosley found one of the things he was looking for in the radically new 4-cyl. engine designed by Lloyd Taylor, of Taylor Engines in California. Taylor developed his engine under a Navy contract for a lightweight generating set for use on PT boats and for gun turrets on amphibious landing craft. The engine included such advanced features as an overhead camshaft, high compression and five main bearings. The most revolutionary feature, though, was the method of block construction. First of all, this was in unit with the cylinder head and detachable from the crankcase. Secondly, and more important, instead of being cast as all other engine blocks were and are, it was built up from an assembly of steel tubing and stampings. These parts were assembled in a jig, then copper brazed together at high temperatures, which also served to heat treat the cylinder walls and valve seats to bring them up to a high degree of hardness. Water jackets and passages were lined with a plastic material for anti-rust purposes, and all outside parts had some kind of stiffening ribs or fins cast into them for high rigidity. Machining operations consisted of trueing the bottom of the block where it meets the crankcase, boring the camshaft bearings and boring and honing of cylinder walls and cam follower guides. The block was bolted to the aluminum crankcase, with the hold-down bolts also serving as bolts for the main bearing caps.

The result of all this innovation was a 44-cu.-in. engine that weighed only 59 lbs. without accessories. It put out 26 hp at 5200 rpm, and had a compression ratio of 7.5:1. The copper brazing process gave it its unusual name, COBRA.

Crosley tested one of the generator sets for a continuous wide-open run of 1200 hours, or almost two months. The only problem that occured was in the exhaust valves due partly to the 100-octane unleaded aviation fuel it was running on. Carburetor was by Tillotson again, and still without an accelerator pump.

The postwar chassis into which this engine was dropped was essentially the same as the prewar chassis. On the chassis sat a "modern" envelope type body, which caused the car to grow 28 inches in length and 2 inches in width, even though the wheelbase and track were the same as before. The light weight of the engine kept the total weight below 1000 lbs., but just barely.

1. Illustration from owner's manual shows the 12 bhp. Waukesha engine of the prewar models. Cooling fan was integral with flywheel, starter motor stuck out in front.

2. Crosleys were still in production well into the war. This is 1942 Crosley Covered Wagon. Very rare indeed!

3. The credulous look on the model's face is because she's only looking at space. The factory artist airbrushed in a rendering of a 1946 model for a press handout in 1945.

4. Overhead camshaft design was considered radical at the time. Like the Vega engine today, low water level was the COBRA's greatest enemy.

5. Problems with the COBRA made Crosley abandon the sheet metal block and go to conventional cast iron, the CIBA engine. These proved more reliable, were only 12 pounds heavier.

6. Sports Utility, introduced in 1948, was postwar version of the Covered Wagon. Model is very rare.

PHOTO COURTESY OF CROSLEY AUTOMOBILE CLUB

Independent
Crosley

The transmission was the same three-speed as before, without benefit of silent-cut gears or synchromesh. Shifting this type of transmission quietly is an art, and was usually quickly learned by Crosley owners. Output from the transmission traveled down through the torque tube to the differential, where it drove the rear wheels through a set of 5.17:1 gears. The final drive ratio combined with the 4.50x12 tires to require the engine to turn 1000 rpm for every 12 mph in high gear. Peak horsepower came in at just about 65 mph., at which point the engine ran out of breath. This gearing also explained why all Crosleys sounded thrashed, even when new.

Shortages of materials and strikes made new car production a shaky thing at best in the months right after the end of the war, while at the same time a car hungry public was ready to buy anything with four wheels and an engine. Crosley leapt into the gap, and even though his suppliers couldn't provide nameplates for the first cars off the line, he had the name painted in red on the front and rear bumpers, 3-ins. high, and shipped the cars off to the dealers. Any color you wanted was available, so long as you wanted grey with red seats and wheels. Later, a convertible was added to the line. This was a European-style body, in which the sides and doors, including all glass, remained the same as in the sedan. Three removable bows supported the top fabric, which was simply snapped on at the rear, stretched over the bows and snapped on at the windshield. If the car was used open for any length of time, the top fabric would shrink slightly, and it became a considerable job to put the top up.

Instrumentation was contained in two circular dials in front of the driver, and included a 70-mph speedometer and all gauges. The starter button protruded from the dash above the ignition key on the driver's left, and on the far right, past the huge oval radio speaker grille, was a glove compartment large enough to hold *two* pairs of gloves. Rubber mats covered the floor, imitation leather covered the seats and nothing covered the inside of the doors. A long spindly gear lever came up from the top of the transmission, and the hand brake was a ring protruding through the floor in front of the driver's seat.

In 1949, a station wagon, a pickup truck, and a sports model called the HotShot were added to the line. The HotShot was the first real postwar sports car in America, and it lived up to its name by winning the first Sebring 12-hour race on index of performance. The winning car was absolutely stock, the same thing you could get for under $1000 at your local Crosley dealership, and it provided a little boost in sales. The HotShot had a dropped frame for a lower center of gravity, coil springs on the rear wheels for better handling, and genuine disc brakes on all four wheels, something no other American car had until the mid '60's. By 1949, certain deficiencies had shown up in the COBRA engine (automotive service put different strains on it than the generators it was originally designed for) and Crosley replaced it with a cast-iron block called the CIBA. In all other aspects the engine was almost the same if a little quieter. The HotShot had the CIBA engine, the 3-speed crash gearbox and removable doors and windscreen. In the interests of high performance, an accelerator pump had been added to the carburetor. A more deluxe version called the Super Sports was introduced in 1950, featuring real doors that opened on hinges, and a top that folded down instead of having to be dismantled and stowed. In many respects, the HotShot and the Super Sports were similar to the original "Bug-eye" Austin Healey Sprites. They were minimal sports cars that provided a lot of fun for little money.

Crosley was not having so much luck with the rest of the line, even though roll-up windows were now available, along with cloth upholstery on the sedans and wagons, and a more modern front end and dashboard. Standard-sized cars were easy to get by the early '50's, and Crosley couldn't keep his prices low enough to com-

PHOTO COURTESY OF CROSLEY AUTOMOBILE CLUB

PHOTO COURTESY OF CROSLEY AUTOMOBILE CLUB

pete. Production dwindled in 1951 to only 300 cars per month, and by 1952 Crosley sold out the automotive plant to General Tire and Rubber, who had no interest in making automobiles. The sale of the stock brought $68,000, and ended Crosley's dreams of becoming another Henry Ford.

Crosleys had a habit of wearing out fast, and being "disposable," in that they were thrown away rather than repaired. A good Crosley today is a rare thing indeed, although parts are not too terribly hard to get. Station wagons from 1948-50 seem to be the most commonly available. HotShots and Super Sports models would probably be the most desirable, as they were never anything more than fun cars and can still be that today. Look for a 1950 model, because Crosley succumbed to owners complaints about squealing brakes and dropped the disc brakes in favor of 9-in. hydraulic drums in 1951.

Any of the prewar models would be a find. They all survived the scrap metal drives of World War II because their fuel economy made them so desirable, but how many survived the Korean War is an unknown quantity. A 1941 Parkway Delivery in mint condition would probably be worth whatever (within reason) anyone would want for it.

The author's own favorite postwar model would be a 1950 convertible. It had the distinct Crosley look, could carry four people, and the soft top kept it a lot quieter.

The engines were used for many years after the demise of the company as motors for refrigeration units on big semi-trucks, so there is a more common availability of parts than a 14 year out-of-production date would normally indicate. There is also an active owner's club, furnishing information on hard-to-find parts and accessories, as well as restoration information.

With costs rising everywhere, it's just possible that the Crosley, with its fuel economy and efficient size, may become the special interest car to have in the future.

1. By 1950, some restyling had taken place on front and rear ends. This is the standard sedan, meaning it had sliding instead of roll-up windows, and leatherette instead of cloth upholstery.

2. Convertible, 1950 model, would be an ideal model to have today, combining economy with utility.

3. Crosley himself posed with the first of the HotShot models. This might have saved the company, had it come earlier.

4. This very clean 1950 Panel Truck was seen at a recent hot rod meet.

5. Probably the best selling model in the postwar series was the station wagon. This is a 1950 example.

6. Changes for 1951 included cloth upholstery, roll-up windows, and a propellor spinner on the front grille.

PHOTO COURTESY OF CROSLEY AUTOMOBILE CLUB

Independent

Graham

Ads stated: "Styled for sleek elegance and streamlined beauty".

Graham-Paige Motors Corporation is one of those members of the automobile industry whose history is intertwined with both preceding and following makes of cars. Some of those names are still around today, but several loomed on the horizon only to die a quick death. The genealogical tracing of the auto industry in general is an interesting study indeed, and anyone who delves into this sort of exercise quickly discovers that cars, automotive products, and individual people continue to pop up in unexpected places across a great span of time.

This continual shuffling of products and names has a single underlying reason; m-o-n-e-y, though each specific case of a merger or a failing is a story in itself. But if a generalization can be made, economic financing is the cause of all the automotive product uproar. Perhaps a company of long standing and with a solid reputation, to say nothing of sound production capabilities, finds itself short of ready money due to a strike, a general industry recession, or any of a hundred other causes. It thus may behoove the company to merge with another firm, say one with the long folding green but a little shy of facilities and production equipment. Or, a manufacturer with a strong dealer organization, but whose products are slow sellers, may receive an offer to link up with a company having a good product line but a weak dealer chain.

Graham-Paige suffered such complexity, and Hupmobile, Chandler, Ruxton, Moon, Kissell, Willys, Nash, Paige, Cord, Kaiser and Frazer are but some of the names that come to light during a study of this very interesting company.

It is not within the scope of this book, with its concentration on American cars produced between 1930 and 1960, to reach back and detail a company's prior history. But briefly, what was known as Graham-Paige Motors came into being in 1927 when the three Graham brothers bought a controlling interest in the Paige-Detroit Motor Car Co.—using capital they gained from their association with Dodge. The old Paige had had a solid reputation and, equally important to the moneyed Graham brothers, extensive production facilities; extensive enough that in the fledgling firm's first year of 1928 78,000 Graham-Paiges were produced—obviously merely a continuation of the '26-'27 Paige.

The Graham brothers wisely retained the Paige name (for dealer and customer identification) but thoughtfully preceded it with their own family surname. The corporation continued until its demise in 1941 with the hyphenated appelation, but the cars themselves bore only Graham on their emblems after mid-'30. Thus do names come and go.

Grahams (as we shall henceforth refer to the marque), continued for a time as yearly-updated extensions of the old Paige, and were solid, reliable cars in the upper medium price range. They offered internal expanding hydraulic front brakes and 4-speed gearboxes. Five models—three with 8-cyl. engines and two with 6's—were offered on three wheelbases. All offered safety glass as an option.

The only open car of this era was the Standard Six roadster, but 12 closed cars were available; a rumble seat coupe, a low-production limousine, and 10 versions of the 4-door sedan.

The first pure Graham emerged for

148/SPECIAL INTEREST AMERICAN CARS

1932 and all models were dubbed Blue Streaks. They incorporated advanced-concept streamlining and pioneered the use of skirted front fenders. The gracefully sweeping rear of the body concealed the gas tank which had previously been much in evidence on American cars. Graham also offered its external equipment in pairs—dual taillights, dual windshield wipers, etc.—which was considered quite a novelty at the time. The chassis mounted the springs outside of the frame side rails, providing a low center of gravity and a remarkably stable ride. Eight-cylinder versions rode on a 123-in. wheelbase and boasted 90 hp. The smaller 6's claimed 70 hp.

Followers of Grahams of this vintage aren't exactly legion due to the relative scarcity of restorable examples and the lack of parts in any condition at flea markets. However, all the models are deemed collectable. The would-be restorer, though, should be aware of the difficulty and cost of obtaining body or chassis components. If any Grahams are particularly noteworthy, the Blue Streaks certainly get the nod. Milestone cars they are, thanks to their advanced styling. Sweeping and graceful, they are often taken as cars of a much later era.

The Blue Streaks went on into '33 with minor improvements, including an attractive V'd and split front bumper. Sixes and eights shared the same body shells.

Graham burst its bombshell in '34 with the announcement of a centrifugal supercharger which boosted the 8's hp rating to 135 at 4000 rpm! The device was mounted between the intake manifold and the carburetor and was whirled at 5.5 times crankshaft speed. Graham made much of this revolutionary concept and sales of the option were brisk. The blown 8's were claimed to have a 95-mph top speed and they sold for $1295. The 6's cost $750, but were reduced to $700 in mid-year. Body and trim changes in all models for '34 were minimal, an indication that the swoopy styling introduced for '32 could afford to stand pat.

Despite all the hurrah generated by the optional supercharger on the 8, no more were produced after 1935, from which point Graham continued with their 6-cyl. engine—blown and unblown, take your choice—until the very end in '41.

This would make the scarce '34 and '35 8's valuable today, more so than the 6's—even though Grahams of any type or vintage are scarcely common.

Even though the 8 was relegated to the scrap heap by '36, Grahams were touted ever after as relatively powerful (considering their 213.5 cu. ins. and flathead configuration). Unblown, the engine produced 80 hp, while with the optional supercharger they put out 112 hp—a hefty 40% increase.

The advanced styling that Graham exhibited beginning in 1932 remained little changed, allowing other manufacturers to "catch up," as it were, so they became less appealing or innovative as they continued with the original Blue Streak styling. In 1938, however, Graham exhibited another all-new design, terming it "Spirit of Motion." Though not as inspired in execution as the earlier Blue Streaks, they featured a "futuristic" pointed-nose concept which was either copied or accidentally paralleled by several other makers. From the cowl back the Graham's appeared Chrysler-ish, except for inset fender skirts with a "speed line" pressed into the fender metal and streaming aft. Forward of the cowl, the hood jutted ahead of everything but the bumper. The grille, which formed the foremost part of the hood, angled *back* and down, a motif also carried over to the front fenders where the squared headlights formed the foremost part. Graham offered four models for '38 (Special, Custom Special, Super-

1. The first pure Graham came along in 1932; the previous two years were simply carry-overs of earlier Paiges. This was the first of the Blue Streak series. The milestone car in styling makes it a desirable item, though there is some artistic license here.

2. Comparison of this to the previous photo shows difference between an artist's rendition and the real thing. Nonetheless, design was advanced for the time and flaunted deeply skirted fenders. Basic lines would remain little-changed for several years.

3. The Graham centrifugal supercharger, debuted for 1934, was an option on the 8-cyl. engine only.

4. The powerful, blown 8-cyl. engine disappeared after the '35 model year, but the 'charger could still be had on the 6's. Blue Streak styling was beginning to become outdated as this '36 4-door reveals, but it remained contemporary with other makes.

5. The Series 110 Supercharger Six for 1936 was inspiring with its V'd bumper, long hood and low roofline. It was $895 out the door and rode on a 115-in. wheelbase; boasted 112 hp at a frenetic 4000 rpm.

SPECIAL INTEREST AMERICAN CARS/149

Independent
Graham

charger, and Custom Supercharger), which were all trim levels (and with or without blower) of its three basic bodies—a 2-door sedan, a 4-door sedan, and a coupe.

Changes for '39 were merely refinements; Graham introduced its column shift lever and did away with running boards. Model series and body types remained the same as in '38, but the 6-cyl. engine grew to 217.5 cu. ins. and produced 116 hp with supercharger, increasing again for 1940 with 120 hp at 4000 rpm.

Though the forward-looking (literally) Grahams were touted as being essentially all-new, sales began to plummet from already low levels. Over 16,000 Blue Streaks had found buyers in '36, and another 12,000-plus in '37. The pointy nose cars, though, went to little more than 4000 people in '38, then dropped below even this for '39. The handwriting was obviously on the wall and the end was nearing, but Graham would yet pull another rabbit out of the hat—or try to.

Production of the "sharknose" mod-

1. The lower-level Cavalier in coupe form had five odd-shaped hood side vents, sat bolt upright in profile compared to the senior line of cars. This is the '37 Series 95.

2. Top-of-the-line Graham Series 120 Custom Supercharger with sidemounted spares and on 120-in. wheelbase, is distinctive, yet is Chrysler-ish from the cowl back.

3. The '37 Series 120 Custom as a coupe featured a rumble seat, is a model worth seeking out today—especially with the optional supercharger and 116 hp.

4. The "Spirit of Motion" came in '38 when the sharknose frontal treatment was announced. Grille slants rearward from peak of hood, a line duplicated in the fenders fronted with bold, square headlights.

5. The Custom Supercharger Combination Coupe was termed a "style setter," had a folding rear seat for an extra passenger. Backseat-less business coupe was also available. "Speed lines" streamed from wheel openings, rear fenders had skirts as standard.

6. Even as Graham's fortunes were on the wane, a deal was made to use the body dies from the defunct Cord to breathe new life into the marque. The result was the famed Hollywoods, produced during 1940 only, but left-overs were later sold with '41 registration. Prospects of company survival quickly flamed out, and the Graham was gone.

7. One of the only 2000 Hollywoods built undergoes rejuvenation.

3

4

5

6

7

els continued into '40, though sales dwindled to near zero with only some 1800 finding a home. This year, however, a curious thing happened. Norman deVaux who had purchased leftover Cord machinery, dies, and equipment for a tiny fraction of their worth, when manufacture of the great Cord 810 series was discontinued, had taken his "treasure" to the foundering Hupp company. Hupp was in dire straits at the time, in company with a host of other manufacturers, and deVaux was able to parlay his outlay of less than $50,000 for the Cord equipment into the general manager's position of the company. The plan was to quickly utilize the Cord tooling for a new car to be called the Hupp Skylark which would utilize the basic Cord sedan body shell but with an all-new front end; not so much to disguise the older Cord heritage—Hupp boasted of its Cord body—but to add a distinctively new Hupp appearance that would resemble neither the forerunning Hupps *nor* the Cord. For problems beyond the scope of an article on Graham, but mainly involving the trials and tribulations of trying to produce a relatively inexpensive Hupp from the costly Cord (which required much hand labor), Hupp was about to fold completely after building only a few dozen cars.

The enterprising deVaux, on the brink of losing not only his title but the Hupp firm, went to call on Graham. Brother Joseph was more than a little interested. He saw in deVaux the chance to save the company he and his brothers had formed. Moreover, not only could Graham come up almost instantly with a new car, but they had a built-in market for additional body sales back to Hupp, who could then continue to market the Skylark. What deVaux had seen in Graham was production capacity as well as the need for a new design, so the egg was hatched and the Graham Hollywood/Cord was announced early in '40 and the older Hupp Skylark (but with its "own" Cord body) soon followed. Graham's Hollywood and Hupp's Skylark virtually defied differentiation and the twin plans to save the two companies bombed out. Graham eventually disposed of its some 2000 Hollywoods and Hupp its some 350 Skylarks, and Graham-Paige Motors went out of the car-making business in 1941—until its then-chairman and president Joseph Frazer held the famous July 1945 meeting with Henry Kaiser. Kaiser had a dream and money. Frazer (Graham) had car-building facilities. So. . . .

SPECIAL INTEREST AMERICAN CARS/151

Independent
Hudson

A standout performer of independent brilliance

Like so many other marques, Hudson was born out of a desire to offer a motorcar for the masses—more performance and better quality for less money. Thus, the Hudson Motor Car Company was formed in the spring of 1909 as a subsidiary of Chalmers-Detroit. Those involved included: Hugh Chalmers, George Dunham, Roy Chapin, Howard Coffin, Roscoe Jackson, and Detroit department store magnate, J.L. Hudson, who was Jackson's relative by marriage. The emblem that guided Hudson was a triangle signifying *performance, service, ... and value.* It manifest itself in their first offering, a maroon and black roadster with a $900 price tag. Its quality of finish, level of performance, and modest cost made it an immediate sales success.

In December 1909, Hudson Motor Car Company broke away from Chalmers-Detroit—with George Dunham choosing to remain with Hugh Chalmers and the parent company. In the reorganization, J.L. Hudson curtailed his involvement by becoming Chairman of the Board. Roy Chapin took over the reins as president. Coffin, who like Jackson, Chapin and Dunham had come from Oldsmobile, continued as chief engineer.

The 1911 model year saw Hudson with a new design and a new factory. The former was a new model engineered by Coffin and dubbed the "33," while the latter was designed by Albert Kahn and occupied the corner of Jefferson and Conner Avenues. The Model 33 lent added significance to the Hudson triangle and credo, but 1913 and the 6-cyl., Model 54 added the polish. This decision by Hudson Motor Car Company, to market a moderately priced car with a 6-cyl. engine was a very bold one. Sixes were normally quite costly and fitted into cars that had more in common with yachts for land use than with transportation vehicles. However, the combination of high power output and low overall weight gave the Model 54 performance that put it in a class by itself.

Its successor debuted in 1916. It was named the Super Six and featured a one-piece cast block. With this engine and the newly designed chassis that cradled it, Hudson began their dominance of stock-car performance trials. The great Ralph Mulford used a Hudson Super Six to nail the measured mile record several notches up the wall with a 102.5-mph clocking at Daytona Beach, Florida. He likewise gave Hudson victories at Pike's Peak, Sheepshead Bay (75.8 mph for 24 hours), across America (from San Francisco to New York in 5 days, 3 hours, 18 minutes), and twice across America (other half of the San Francisco to New York run with the same car).

The Super-Six engine was Hudson's mainstay through the Twenties and gave creedence to their claim as"... the world's largest manufacturer of six-cylinder cars," as stated in their advertising. This slogan and their reputation for pioneering sixes in moderately priced cars gave birth to the Essex in 1919. Roy Chapin realized that the end of WW I would create a huge market for inexpensive automobiles—and that was something that Hudson and its Super Six engine had drifted away from during its 10-year life. So Hudson, like Chalmers-Detroit before it, created a separate company, with separate finances and leadership, to tap the low-price market.

Thus, the 4-cyl. Essex—with its targeted $1000 price swelled to just over $1300—drove into the postwar marketplace. Its hexagon emblem was backed by Hudson and fronted a vehicle of good value. It managed to retain the 4-cyl. engine and a reasonable slice of the automotive market thanks to competition successes and clever innovations. Not the least of these was an all-steel closed body with an under-$1500 price tag. Needless to say, today's price for one of those 1921 forerunners of the sedan is about 10 times that original cost. By the mid-Twenties', however, the price of the Essex Coach was brought to well under $1000 and prompted the family who needed all-weather transportation to abandon Ford's Model T.

The year 1929, found Hudson and companion Essex riding a wave of incredible popularity and sales. Essex, in fact, was in the Top Five sales leaders, and offering both 4- and 6-cyl., cars. But the wave broke with a crash. A stock market crash!

In 1930, Hudson introduced the

152/SPECIAL INTEREST AMERICAN CARS

"Greater Eight" engine. It was a logical extension (by two cylinders) of the Essex 6-cyl. powerplant. The Greater Eight's 214-cu.-in. displacement was achieved with a 2¾-in. bore and 4½-in. stroke. To compensate for smaller displacement, the lower and sleeker 1930 models were also shorter and lighter. Considering the deepening Depression, Hudson and Essex both offered a staggering array of body styles, but the contract with Biddle and Smart to supply custom bodies was terminated. LeBaron continued to utilize Hudson products to the delight of connoisseurs of classic coachwork, however. The factory coachwork was of good quality and tastefulld done, but moneyed collectors today lean toward any Murray, LeBaron, or Biddle and Smart-bodied Hudson or Essex. Hence, the special interest aficionado with burning desire,

1. The Model 20 Hudson of 1909 is where it all began. In the driver's seat is the soon-to-be President of Hudson Motor Car Co., Roy D. Chapin.

2. Custom coachwork on 1931 Hudson helps explain why they are sought-after collector's items today.

3. Also eagerly pursued by avid collectors are the Hudson boat-tail roadsters. This '32 standard roadster is a better (less expensive) choice for special interest Hudson fans.

4. Amelia Earhart poses proudly with 1933 Terraplane sporting wires and dual sidemounted spare wheels. Find a Terraplane roadster or coupe and you've got a real winner.

5. Terraplane's coupe-pickup was a grocer's delight, and helped Hudson augment the 1937 line of Dover commercial vehicles. The "bulbous" look introduced in '36 is in evidence.

but burned-out wallet, is well-advised to pass up the basket-case Essex boat-tail roadster (known as the Speedabout), or LeBaron-bodied Hudson club sedan for the almost-as-desirable Essex Sunsedan or Hudson town sedan. Don't overlook a phaeton, roadster or a sporty coupe in either the Hudson or Essex line. Parts are scarce, but not premium, and do-it-yourself restoration is not (if carefully accomplished and thoroughly researched) going to send the final selling price plunging.

The 1931 offerings from Hudson and Essex were only cosmetically different, but Hudsons were only available with 8-cyl. engines (again on 119-in. and 126-in. wheelbases), while Essex inherited the Super Six designation. Briggs and Murray supplied the custom coachwork on a continuing basis (sunsedans, phaetons and roadsters) with LeBaron doing an occasional masterpiece. The factory produced brougham bodies on the long wheelbase Hudson chassis. These superb models boasted landau irons for the fabric top, dual sidemounted spares, and large trunk on a rear-mounted rack.

Hudson's sport roadster (with boat-tail styling) and the Essex boat-tail Speedabout are the collector's picks from all the 1931 factory offerings, but prices for restorable examples are high. Should you stumble across a bargain-priced sedan that's complete and strikes your fancy, don't pass it up because it won't appreciate as much as one of the more exotic models. If you like it, buy it! You'll gain experience during the restoration that will be most beneficial should the chance to "trade up" present itself later on.

Unlike the poor sales of 1930, Hudson's 1931 figures were in the form of a huge debit ($2,000.000) and Roy Chapin's thinking turned for the third time toward a low-price car embodying quality and performance to help the 1932 sales picture.

The Hudson/Essex lineup was enriched in the spring of '32 by the release of a new model in the Essex line: Terraplane! Amelia Earhart christened the new model, and none other than Orville Wright took delivery of the first Essex Terraplane. Fanfare announcements promised that the Essex Terraplane would be to land, what the aeroplane was to the air and the hydroplane was to the water. *And it was, too!*

The Essex Terraplane utilized the Super Six engine which had been modified by, among other things; a 4 ¾-in. stroke and cylinder bore enlarged to almost 3-ins., improved manifolding, a new Carter downdraft carburetor, and careful machining and assembly. This 193-cu.-in. engine (producing 70 hp at 3200 rpm) was then fitted to a short (106-in. wheelbase) chassis that was extremely strong and light. To pare additional weight for a more favorable power/weight ratio, the all-steel body took advantage of semi-unitized construction. The result was an immediate sales hit bolstered by talk of 80-mph cruising speeds, 25-mpg economy, and incredible acceleration—aided by light weight and low (high numerically) rear axle ratio. Of course the low prices (from $425) didn't hurt, and neither did news of the Essex Terraplane's racing successes—which made them as talked-about as the V-8 Fords.

Collectors place high value on these Essex Terraplanes of '32, with the

Independent
Hudson

roadster topping the list. It was, after all, the roadster model that posted a new stock car record in the Pike's Peak hillclimb—a breathtaking 21-minute, 21-second charge to the top.

The '33's don't enjoy quite the following despite the tasteful incorporation of skirted fenders. The 8-cyl. engine was offered in some Essex Terraplane models and identification is aided by the fact that 8-cyl. powered cars incorporated vent doors in the hood side panels whilst 6-cyl. equipped Hudsons had a row of long vertical louvers and Essex Terraplanes with 6-cyl. engines displayed a double row of shorter vertical louvers.

Hudson Motor Car Company showed a loss in '33 of 2¼-million dollars, but the 1934's showed new optimism with fresh styling across the board and semi-independent front suspension. It was a Baker-designed parallelogram mount using leaf springs and I-beam axle stubs. It was dubbed "Axle-Flex." Essex was disassociated with Terraplane in '34. The latter being quite capable of standing alone, and the former being dropped all together. Essex was gone, but Hudson was still viable and Terraplane was immensely popular—a popularity that would later threaten to overshadow the Hudson itself. Besides, the sales incentive was the modern styling which, from the back-slanted grille to the pleasantly rounded and sculptured fenders that flowed liquidly into the rear deck, bespoke good taste. And the good taste of the public was reflected in impressive sales—more than double '33's figures. But the losses were a staggering 3.2-million dollars. Price, performance, and quality were there, but so were heavy restyling costs and the spectre of a deepening Depression.

America was slowly regaining its feet, however, and the 1935 Hudson/Terraplane lineup, though little changed visually from the '34's, turned a modest profit and gave the company its first 100,000-plus sales year since 1930. Thusfar, the Thirties had not been kind to the Hudson Motor Car Company, but at least they hadn't joined the many independent manufacturers who were carried under by the currents of the Depression. Hudson's 1935 sales no doubt received some help from songstress Kate Smith, whose radio show was sponsored by Hudson. Then too, those who basked in Hudson's performance image were aided by the trip a '35 Hudson Eight sedan made to Muroc Dry Lake in southern California—it came away with 35 new AAA records on the books.

The $5.5 million loss of 1932 had been offset by Roy Chapin's resuming the presidency of Hudson in '33, and negotiating for a $6 million loan in '35. The future was looking better—much better—as the 1936 Hudson and Terraplane models made their debut. It was a new look for '36, characterized by some sages as the "bulbous" look. The separate grille shell had given way to a rounded, insect-like, nose of thin vertical bars tapering into the front end sheetmetal and adorned with overlay strips delineating the famous Hudson triangle. On the Terraplane, chevron strips were added inside the triangle. The performance image was further enhanced by luminaries such as Indy 500 driver, Wilbur Shaw, and World Land Speed Record king, Sir Malcolm Campbell. 1936 was marred for Hudson by the passing of Roy Chapin in February. Picking up the reins as president was A.E. Barit, who had been with Hudson since 1910. But Chapin left a legacy. 1936 closed with Hudson announcing a $3.4-million profit.

The "bulbous" look was continued for 1937, but rumble seats were no longer offered. Those desiring fresh air and seating for more than two could purchase Hudson's convertible Brougham. Sad to say, not too many people did, so add it to the list of ultra-desirable special interest Hudsons. With swoopy yellow finish and full rear wheel skirts, it can still turn a few heads today. Actually, any '37 Hudson with the "Electric Hand" option is of special interest. This vacuum-operated, solenoid-controlled shifter developed by Bendix, took the shift lever off the floor and replaced it with a selector lever on the steering column (the '36 Cord 810 put theirs on the dashboard).

The popularity of the Terraplane continued to overshadow Hudson (Madison Avenue overkill?). So in 1938, the threat was ended with the introduction of the Hudson Terraplane—a prestige model, not as costly as a Mod-

el 87 Hudson, but no longer inexpensive. Like many small, fast cars, the Terraplane had grown over the years—and so had the price. Thus, Hudson debuted the Hudson 112 (112-in. wheelbase) as their new low-price model. Unfortunately, the 112 lacked one thing: Performance! Dating all the way back to the company's founding, Hudson's price-leaders had been performers. The Hudson 112 broke this tradition, and 1939 saw the last of the Hudson 112s. Hurrying into 1939 is a good idea since the recession of 1938 put Hudson over $4.5 million in the red, and '38 isn't notable insofar as special interest Hudsons is concerned.

The 1939 model year is hardly better, but it was the 30th anniversary year and Hudson celebrated by producing their 2,614,165th car on May 4. '39 also witnessed the end of the Terraplane name. The basic lineup consisted of the 112, Hudson Six, Country Club Six and Eight on wheelbases of 117-ins., 122-ins., and 129-ins., respectively. The 6-cyl. engine in the 112 had been coaxed up to 86 hp in '38 and remained at that figure for '39. The larger 6-cyl. engine featured 110 hp, while the Sraight Eight boasted 122 hp. Hudson's convertible brougham model with dual sidemounted spares is a desirable special interest "find" from this era.

Even before 1940 was officially ushered in by Guy Lombardo and his Royal Canadians, the '40 Hudsons were making news. Under AAA sanction and with British speed king John Cobb at the wheel, a '40 Hudson 8-cyl. sedan posted a 93.9-mph record on the Bonneville Salt Flats in Utah. In fact, before Hudson left the salt, they had put 121 speed and endurance records in the book. So along with their new styling, '40 Hudsons also had performance. Not that their legendary durability had been forsaken, it hadn't. One of the records that Hudson posted was averaging 70.5 mph for 20,327 miles! Hudson produced five models (in various body styles) for 1940, as well as continuing their line of commercial vehicles. In place of the discontinued 112, Hudson offered the low-priced Hudson Six. In acending order was the Super Six, Country Club Six, Hudson Eight and Country Club Eight. The Country Club Eight designation (initiated in '39) is the one to seek out if you're shopping for a special interest

1. Also among the most desirable of prewar Hudson models is this 1939 convertible brougham with dual sidemounted spares. This was leadoff of Hudson's Country Club series.

2. In '48, Hudson introduced the "step-down" design and Monobilt construction. Note how frame wraps around back end and outside the rear wheels. Its safety is obvious.

3. Safety, roadability, and comfort of "step-down" Hudsons saw many of the nation's law enforcement agencies adopt them as pursuit vehicles. Hudson helped by offering special pursuit packages for police work.

4. The list of special interest postwar Hudsons is topped by the '51 Hornet convertible, though any of the Hornet series is collectable.

5. Interior of '51 Hornet (instrumented for MOTOR TREND Magazine road test) was quite roomy.

6. Dick Rathman (shown here winning the Langhorne 150-mile stock car race) was one of many drivers who made Hudson Hornets a legend in stock car racing. Others included Marshall Teague, Tim Flock, Lee Petty, and Herb Thomas. In '52, Hornets won 27 NASCAR races.

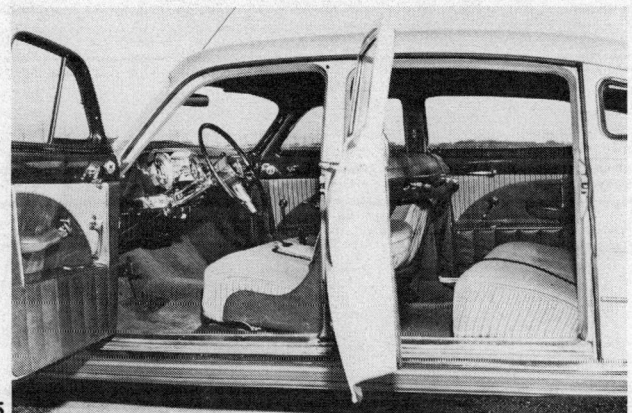

Independent
Hudson

Hudson from the Forties. Despite improved sales figures over '39, Hudson's year-end tally for 1940 showed they had lost over $1.5 million.

In 1941, Hudson divided time between manufacturing ack-ack guns and aircraft components in a Naval ordinance facility outside Detroit and warmed-over 1940 models at its Detroit plant. The Country Club models were replaced with a new (and more lasting) designation: Commodore. So the '41 lineup of models included the Six and Super Six (now up to 102 hp) plus the Commodore and Custom Commodore (either 6- or 8-cyl. powered). Factory shipments dropped fractionally over 1940, but profits soared to $3,756,418.

Only 5396 cars and 67 commercial Hudsons carry the 1942 designation. Critical materials such as steel, copper, chromium, etc., were being diverted for the war effort. Much of the material was going to help embattled Britian, but on December 7, 1941, Japan attacked Pearl Harbor, Hawaii, and on that same day, Congress declared war (interestingly, Japan and Germany didn't officially declare war on the U.S. until four days later). Hudson's contributions to the war effort increased and auto production decreased until on February 5, 1942, the last Hudson rolled off the assembly line for the duration. The Detroit facility being given over completely to producing instruments of victory. Among the items manufactured or assembled by Hudson during the war, were; ailerons and cabins for P-39s, folding wings for Helldivers, Hudson Invader engines for landing craft, sections for B-29 Superfortresses and miscellaneous fighter aircraft.

Every manufacturer was keenly anticipating a return to peacetime auto production, but few made the changeover as quickly as Hudson. Japan surrendered August 14, 1945, and the first Hudson was built 16 days later. Hudson shipped 5005 cars in 1945, but only 93,870 in '46 (all were '46 models—differing from the prewar offerings by virtue of new front-end styling). Shortages of critical materials, supplier strikes, and other factors had manufacturers against the ropes, and the situation had changed but little when the '47 models made their debut. Again, the "symphonic styling" touted in 1940 was still in evidence and looked "dated." Especially in comparison to the new-look '46 Kaiser-Frazer line and the sensational Lowey-designed '47 Studebakers.

The 1948 new car showings ushered in what collectors consider to be Hudson's golden years. The '48-'52 Hudsons are prima facie special interest cars. Strangely, the prototype was born in 1941; the brainchild of Frank Spring, Hudson's chief stylist, and Sam Frahm, their chief engineer. It was wide, it was low, and it was beautiful. But it was too much for Hudson's president, A.E. Barit—at least in 1941 with the profit picture still on the bleak side and certainly no money available for tooling up a radical design. The lowness, which Barit objected to, was achieved by channeling the body over the frame and mounting the floorboards beneath the frame rails. A Hypoid rear end permitted a lower driveshaft so the drive tunnel didn't encroach too much upon the interior. To achieve the necessary strength and light weight, the body and frame were welded together into a single unit. Thus, not only was it a strong, rattle-resistant, roomy design, but the low center of gravity produced a car with great road-holding ability. It was this latter feature that convinced A.E. Barit to order it into production.

In late '47, then, Hudson stole the show with the announcement of their revolutionary "Monobilt" '48 models featuring "step-down" design. Their totally new styling, however, masked the tried and true 6- and 8-cyl. engines. Still in all, the '48's were fast, economical, roomy, and handled like no other car in America. America responded by purchasing 142,454 Hudsons making

1

2

1948 the most profitable year for Hudson since 1929. The "step-down" design produced a $13-plus million profit.

Hudson left well enough alone and with merely a change of side trim and clean-up of the bumper, the '49 "step-down" Hudsons made their debut. Profits were not quite as good; just over $10 million on sales of 144,685 units.

Re-entering the low-price field in 1950, Hudson initiated the Pacemaker series with 221-cu.-in., 6-cyl. engine rated at 112 hp, on a 119-in. wheelbase (5-ins. shorter than the Super and Commodore's). Overall length was less, too, by 6 ins. Total sales decreased slightly (143,586), but profits increased to 13-plus million dollars.

Hudson opened the 1951 model year with a brand new (sort of) engine. An L-head, 308-cu.-in., 145-hp 6-cyl. engine with aluminum high-compression head. Dubbed the "H-Power" engine, it was exclusive to the new Hornet series. In '52, the low-priced series was known by the name, Wasp. Only the name was new, however, since the body was the same basic "step-down" design introduced in '48. But in '53, Hudson brought out a new "light" car. The Jet stressed economy of purchase and operation with its 104-cu.-in. 6-cyl. engine and 105-in. wheelbase. Despite the Hudson Jet, the company lost in excess of $10 million in '53. The '54 line displayed extensive sheetmetal changes, but the traces of the '48 design were unmistakeable. Then on January 14, 1954, came the announcement that had been rumored for more than a year. Hudson Motor Car Company merged with Nash-Kelvinator. The new combine was to be known as American Motors Corporation. It was the beginning of the end for Hudson. From 1955, until the Hudson name was dropped in 1958, it was more akin to the Nash line. So the Nash-bodied Hudsons of '55, '56, and '57 can be dismissed insofar as collectables are concerned.

Among the offerings of Hudson's golden years, the '51 through '54 Hudson Hornets top the list. The convertibles, of course, are most desired and prices of pristine examples run upward of $5000. The Hornet hardtops are second on the list, with a well-restored '54 Hollywood hardtop fetching $4000 and others slightly less. Other Hornet models bring up to $3500 depending upon accessories. Before losing heart, however, bear in mind that these prices are for restored examples only. It is possible to obtain an unrestored or incomplete Hornet for a tenth of these prices. And this definitely favors the do-it-yourselfers, as does the solid construction and basic simplicity of these cars.

Should you desire to own a pioneer example of a "step-down" Hudson, the experts' choice is the 1948 convertible brougham. This simply means that this model has been shown to appreciate more in value than comparable models of the same year, or the same model in '49 or '50 versions. The prime reason for purchasing a Hudson (or any special interest car, for that matter) should be the appreciation of an affordable piece of America's motoring history and not the potential of great profits. It is thanks to those who feel that the triangle of *performance, service* and *value* is is worthy of preservation that the marque hasn't faded into oblivion in the almost 20-years since its demise.

1. The 1953 Hudson Hornets indulged in toothy hood scoop. Their record in stock car racing this year was an impressive 45 first-place victories.

2. Also in '53, Hudson returned to the small car philosophy with the Hudson Jet.

3. Restyled 1954 Hudson Hornets boasted Twin H-Power (dual carb) engines, but total Hudson production dropped to 32,293 units. A merger with Nash-Kelvinator signaled the beginning of the end.

4. Before lamenting Hudson's passing, mention should be made of the super-rare Touring-bodied Hudson Italia with Hudson's triangle proudly up front. Doors opened into roof.

5. The completely restyled 1955 Hudson line looked suspiciously like Nashes. The merger created American Motors Corporation, who voted in favor of Rambler and against Hudson.

Independent
Hupmobile
A star of the medium-priced field

The Hupp Motor Car Co., was one of the many fledgling firms to enter the automobile manufacturing business in its early infancy, opening its doors in 1908 and producing buggy-like runabouts but powered by large, for the time, 4-cyl. engines. Within three years a more contemporary touring car appeared and Hupp brothers Robert and Luis were safely embarked on a career which would prove successful for a number of years but fade coming out of the Depression and reach a final car-building halt just prior to World War II.

The Hupps were endeared to the medium-priced field, wisely leaving the low-price market to, most notably, Ford, and the higher price or luxury class to such as Packard, Lincoln and Cadillac. This wise decision may be the clue to the Hupps' relative longevity as auto manufacturers, at least for as long as it lasted, since the competitors above and below their market target were prone to fall by the wayside like proverbial flies. Although the Hupmobiles were scarcely innovative or visually exciting through the 'Teens and '20's, the make developed a reputation for reliability and by '13 some 12,000 were made. Within ten years, though, output had risen to a satisfying 38,000. (By comparison, Ford shoved 1,800,000 Model T's out the door in 1923). But the Hupps remained content with their own little niche in the industry and continued, even without much inspiration, serving the faithful following they had raised.

Hupmobile stayed with a mediocre but trustworthy 4-cyl. engine through the early years but announced a straight-8 for '25. Then with a reversal of the trend of the time, they announced a 6-cyl. engine one year later which replaced the 4-cyl. engine.

Hupmobile entered the '30's decade with a line-up that tended toward the highest parameter of the medium-priced field. Five models were introduced with the top-line Custom Eight series or Model H's priced at a steep $1945. The in-line 8, however, embodied a sizeable 365.5 cu. ins., put out 133 hp, and was said to easily pass 60 mph in second gear and 90 mph in high. The car was a bargain for the price, even though it nearly overshot its market bracket. Only Duesenberg, the V-16 Cadillac and one or two others achieved a higher horsepower figure. The Hupmobile also pioneered an oil *cooler* via a separate section of the radiator, and an in-line oil filter was included.

Other models for '30 were the low-level 70-hp Century Six (which garbed as a business coupe sold for $995 and which allowed Hupp to bracket the price range), a 90-hp Century Eight, a 100-hp Eight, a 133-hp Eight and the big Custom Eight already mentioned. Changes for the '31 model year were minimal but freewheeling became an option and this was controlled by a button on top of the shift lever. Over 16,000 of all models finally reached '31 buyers.

Restyling and innovation blanketed the 8-cyl. Hupp line for '32. Advertising at the time proclaimed, "... added flash, dash, beauty, and power!" Though the front fenders of these senior cars were somewhat shorter than Hupp customers may have been used to, they boldly carried sidemount

1

158/SPECIAL INTEREST AMERICAN CARS

spares. The grille was daringly if only slightly V'd, the hood was long by contemporary standards, and the rearward sloping windshield was thankfully rid of the customary visor. A total of eight series were available for '32; from a 6-cyl. Model 214 (6's retained the '31 styling but shared the V'd radiator) to the big 8-cyl. Model 237. Despite the overhaul of Hupps' offerings, prices were substantially reduced as the company fought for their fair share of the market during the end of the Depression era which had caused so many makers to fold up their tents and steal away. Hupp body types boringly concentrated on 4-door sedan versions and a few coupes, but an attractive convertible was offered.

Extravagant as it may seem now (but more so then), Hupp actually offered seven different engines during the early '30's. This expensive nonsense may have lead to Hupmobile's approaching demise, for the capital investment needed to produce so many powerplants might well have been saved as a hedge against the future, but that was admittedly distant at this point.

The Hupps retrenched in '33, narrowing their number of series models. Styling remained pat for the 8-cyl. offerings but now the 6's embodied the new styling introduced on the senior cars the previous year. This was Hupmobile's 25th anniversary and the appellation "Silver Anniversary Hupmobile" was loudly proclaimed in company advertisements. A financial statement made public at the end of the '32 fiscal year reported, "... no indebtedness, no outstanding loans, and seven times as much in assets as in liabilities." Prospects looked good as the Depression began to wane, but trouble lay not far ahead for what appeared to be a well-entrenched enterprise.

Unique, streamlined styling advancements were in vogue during the mid-'30's and with no little bravado Hupp brought forth their advanced "Aerodynamic" model in '34, along with carried-forth '33's for those more conservative buyers. A first for Hupp was the customer's option of an 8 or a 6 in otherwise identical cars—the Aerodynamics. Previously, the 6- and the 8-powered Hupps differed markedly. Startling to on-lookers was this model's faired-in headlights whose tapered housings flowed back to nearly the cowl and faded into the hood sides. Front fenders were broad and were skirted to leave cutouts neatly circling the tires. The real standout, though, was the highly unusual windshield treatment which, more than any other

1. Uniformed policeman with rifle is perhaps guarding a bank delivery from runningboard of a 1930 Hupmobile phaeton. Its straight-eight delivered 133 hp from 365.5 cu. ins., and was good for an easy 90 mph—a superb example of a cops/robbers vehicle.

2. The Series 222 Cabriolet Roadster for '32 was one of eight series, and this was only soft-top offered. Sidemounts seemed to force shortening of the front fenders, might have looked better deeply sunk into longer fender line.

3. The Aerodynamics came out in time for the '34 model year, were bold in design with headlights faired into the hood sides and odd-appearing attempt to provide panoramic vision for driver with 3-piece, flat-paned windshield. Carry-overs from previous year were kept in the other series, but the unfortunate Aerodynamic began a decline which Hupp couldn't survive.

Independent
Hupmobile

design feature, gave these models its unpopular appearance—but we should remember that real innovation, whether considered good or bad either at the time or now, makes a car a special interest candidate, and the Aerodynamic Hupps rank high here.

The unusual windshield was an attempt to achieve wrap-around visibility, which GM mastered by the early '50's. But instead of utilizing curved glass, which was a technological possibility at the time and indeed had been pioneered as early as 1915 by Cadillac, Hupp used three pieces of flat glass; a wide central pane flanked by half-round, rearward-angling sections. Though the idea was hardly new, for some Lincolns had tried it ten years earlier, it was a homely standout in '35 and made the Aerodynamics singularly Hupps which could be mistaken for nothing else.

The Aerodynamics (produced as 2- and 4-door sedans, a Victoria and a coupe), *might* have caught on, but the public was perhaps understandably reluctant to try on such a "breakthrough," especially when way-out designs of the times, notably in the Chrysler and DeSoto Airflows, were showing a meager following. Sales of Hupmobiles, not the Aerodynamics alone but all Hupps, fell to record lows and by mid-'36 the old Chandler plant in Cleveland, which Hupp had acquired in 1929, closed its doors.

But because the Hupmobile as a make still had a following of sorts—certainly not enough to sustain its once-high volume of output but sufficient to keep the firm alive—the plant was reactivated in '37 but less than 3000 cars were built during this and the following year. These were simply carry-overs (luckily minus the Aerodynamic line) and undistinguished. The only feature worth noting is that overdrive became standard on all the 8's.

If ever handwriting could be read on the wall, this was it as far as Hupp was concerned. Nevertheless, a brave and noteworthy attempt was once more made to save the Hupp name and its facilities (said to be capable of producing 100,000 cars a year if properly managed) late in '38, and more details are given in the chapter on Graham-Paige for at this point the once-competitive firms became intriguingly entangled. But briefly, and at the risk of some repetition, Cord had just gone out of business and sold off most of its assets which included some equipment and, most importantly, the body dies for the wonderful but now-lamented 810 series. This "scrap" was picked up for a song by one Norman deVaux (lately of the defunct De Vaux-Hall automobile which failed after little more than a year), and he carted everything over to Hupp, who he knew to be in severely dire straits, and offered it all up to the gasping company in exchange for a chunk of stock. The upshot of this complex deal was an attractive car to be known as the Hupmobile Skylark and which used the basic Cord body but had its own distinctively pointed nose and a shorter wheelbase. Hupp thought it had it made when the first few prototypes met with great approval, not only by its own dwindling dealership chain but by rivals as well, and deVaux was enjoying the exalted position of general manager. But there was a problem, a serious one, in that the Cord had been a high-priced car but could be built at a modest profit even though lack of adequate steel-stamping equipment necessitated much hand labor, especially since eight small dies (instead of one large one) were used to punch out various portions of the turret top which then had to be welded together, soldered, and finished by nothing less

1. Flat-back shape of the '35 Victoria had bottom-hinged trunk lid with very limited opening and accessibility.

2. Heavy eyebrow effect of the top above the "wraparound" windshield did little to enhance the '35 Aerodynamic's lines, but designers can't be faulted since the car was a break-through in streamlining at the time. Front-opening forward doors carried "knee-room" lines for long-legged people. Since windshield pillars were brought rearward, it would appear that driver visibility is impaired, rather than improved, by its proximity.

3. Much was made of the "sensational" Skylark, produced as a last-ditch attempt to save the Hupp firm, which utilized Cord body tooling but with an outstanding new hood and grille. Hupp actually built only some 35 of them, then let Graham-Paige use the equipment on a "sharsies" basis. The Skylarks both came and went in 1940.

4. Cord heritage was much in evidence, and Hupp didn't hide the fact. Still, the Skylarks were the sensation of the day (especially since they preceded the nearly-identical Graham Hollywood). The expensive Cord had required much hand labor for fitting the body pieces together, but assembly was too costly for Hupp which had a target price, at least for the inexpensive Flagship, of only $895. About 350 Skylarks were built, command a high price today.

than old fashioned elbow grease.

The all-new Hupp wasn't ashamed—in fact it was proud—of the heritage of its body, and early announcements heralded the introduction of no less than 5 models; the Flagship ($895), the Mainliner ($975), the Cruiser ($1075), and two convertibles, the Sportster ($1145) and Corsair ($1175). Custom models were also listed (but not defined), beginning at $2000, but all Skylarks were in fact customs in view of the laborious assembly procedures.

This valiant start finally boiled down to only some three dozen Skylarks being built *by Hupp*, but now the ever-active deVaux wandered over to failing Graham-Paige. Acting on behalf of Hupp on one hand and himself on the other, he struck a deal. *Graham-Paige could use the Hupmobile/Cord tooling and equipment if they also assembled the complicated bodies for Hupp's use!* So, for a time, both Hupp and Graham were back in business. Unfortunately, Hupp completed only about 350 Skylarks for '39 and '40. Graham enjoyed a somewhat larger production, making nearly 2000 Hollywoods—as they called their nearly identical model—by the end of '40. A left-over supply of a few hundred were actually sold in early '41, but these were merely '40's with the later registration.

Luckily for both Hupmobile as well as Graham-Paige, the government was by now beginning to dole out defense contracts and both companies, though no longer in the automobile business, were alive and healthy after the war though into diverse lines of products. Graham, by the way and through lengthy complexities dealt with elsewhere in this book, got back into cars via Kaiser-Frazer, but all that has nothing to do with Hupp.

It is obvious from this necessarily brief discourse of an interesting carmaker that the Hupp Motor Car Co., turned out few vehicles that properly fit within our definition of Special Interest, with the exceptions of course of the Aerodynamics and the Skylarks but which are extremely scarce due to low initial volume. But buffs who simply can't resist a bargain price for an old '30's—any car, but more specifically an old Hupmobile—shouldn't turn their backs on a Hupp product if it is relatively sound and, most importantly, complete.

3. POWER AND POISE PERSONIFIED—THE HUPMOBILE SKYLARK FLAGSHIP

4.

Independent
Kaiser-Frazer
And don't forget the Henry J and DKF-161

Shortly after the start of World War II, Joe Frazer and Henry J. Kaiser were telling each other how ignorant they were. But by 1945, the pair united to bring America some very exciting postwar cars which, temporarily at least, made Kaiser-Frazer the fourth largest American automobile producer.

Both men were well respected in their fields. Frazer had a brilliant sales and automotive background, while the aggressive Kaiser had established a huge construction and shipbuilding empire through hard work, ingenuity and determination.

Joe Frazer was the gentlemanly Southerner, whose lineage went back to George Washington. Though well educated, he was enamored with the automobile, and began his career as a lowly mechanic's apprentice. He soon made his mark, however, by creating the auto industry's first technical school. Later, as treasurer of General Motors' Export Division, he organized General Motors Acceptance Corporation, and later was loaned to Pierce to set up a similar credit agency for that company.

Teaming with another ex-GM man, Walter Chrysler, he went to Maxwell to head the sales department and pull the company out of the red. When Chrysler built his own automobile, Frazer helped promote it to eighth place in the industry in only a couple of years. He also named the Plymouth and helped organize DeSoto.

Always dissatisfied with success, Frazer moved to the presidency of troubled Willys-Overland. He quickly increased sales from $9 million to $170 million and is responsible for coining the name "Jeep."

With the end of World War II in sight, he gained control of Graham-Paige in late 1944. He knew the postwar automobile demand would be staggering, so he wanted to be ready. But financing loomed as the big stumbling block.

A friend, Amadeo P. Giannini, founder and president of Bank of America in California, set up a meeting between Frazer and Henry J. Kaiser, who wanted to set up an automobile factory in California.

Unlike Frazer, Kaiser didn't have the sophisticated, comfortable childhood enjoyed by his partner. Through nerve and determination, he set up a West Coast construction company and, through the 1920's, was the Pacific Coast's sand and gravel king.

Kaiser not only was an innovator, he was a doer—known to always complete projects well ahead of schedule without sacrificing quality. After completing 200 miles of highway in Cuba, his business burgeoned. He helped build Hoover Dam (now Boulder Dam) to hold back the waters of the Colorado River, then supervised construction of Bonneville Dam on the Columbia and Grand Coulee upper dam.

His businesses continued on a grand scale. His company helped build the substructure for the San Francisco-Oakland Bay Bridge, tunnels in Colorado and Maryland, aqueducts in New York, canals and subways in Chicago, jetties at Grays Harbor and along the Columbia River, dry docks at Pearl Harbor and a third set of locks for the Panama Canal. Always ahead of scheduled completion date.

With the obvious need for merchant vessels in World War II, Kaiser converted a mud flat in Richmond, Calif., into a shipyard. Although never before in the shipbuilding business, the amazing Kaiser built more than a quarter of America's merchant vessel tonnage during the war, and was the first to prefabricate ship sections.

For Henry J. Kaiser, nothing was impossible. And nothing couldn't be done quickly.

Even with all his war ventures, Kaiser set aside a small factory in 1942 to design, build and experiment with automobiles. Henry wanted another "people's car" similar to the Model T Ford. And he knew the market would be ripe once the war ended.

So, when Henry J. and Joe met, the decision came quickly. They would build cars together.

In July 1945, the Kaiser-Frazer Corporation was formed by the Henry J. Kaiser Company (a family concern) and Graham-Paige Motors. Each was to share half the expenses. Incorporation was in Nevada on Aug. 9, 1945, for tax purposes.

Now Kaiser-Frazer was ready to wade into the greatest selling market in automotive history. It was estimated that immediate postwar demand couldn't be met until 1948, not to mention those vehicles that would need to be replaced through the attrition of wear and destruction. If anyone was to break into the automobile industry, this was the time to do it.

As soon as the war ended, everything had to be done fast. Kaiser-Frazer leased the giant Willow Run aircraft

1. The battle was joined when Henry Kaiser and Joe Frazer dared challenge GM, Ford and Chrysler in the 1947 marketplace. Smooth envelope body style was continued through 1950 model year although '47 and '48 saw only 4-door sedans produced.

2. Both Kaiser and Frazer utilized the same chassis, body and engine components with exterior trim and interior providing delineation.

3. The L-head 6-cyl. engine (seen here in a '51 Frazer Manhattan) was continually refined but never replaced during the entire life of the company.

162/SPECIAL INTEREST AMERICAN CARS

factory outside Detroit, abandoning its idea to build cars in California. Willow Run was the largest building in the world under one roof, and K-F built into it the world's longest continuous automotive assembly line—9754 ft.

Fortunately, Joe Frazer had gotten more than 3000 dealers committed during the war and had a vehicle designed by Howard A. "Dutch" Darrin. It was a model of this design that Frazer used to lure Kaiser into partnership.

Although the integral-fender-designed model was meant as a demonstration showpiece only, Kaiser wanted to move fast. With only slight modifications, the mockup was tooled for production. Darrin was so infuriated that, when the car was produced with tiny "Darrin-Styled" logos on the trunk lids, Dutch asked that they be removed. When the supply of pre-punched trunk lids was gone, so was the Darrin logo.

Kaiser-Frazer really had an advantage when production began in May 1946. It was the only totally new car in the industry, not a rehash of a previous model. Although the public scoffed at the radical styling ("You can't tell whether it's coming or going!"), it was quickly accepted by the car-hungry populace.

Kaiser, of course, was the "baby" of the Henry J. Kaiser Company, while Graham-Paige was responsible for Frazer. Both cars were mechanically the same. Drivetrain and chassis were basically conventional. A ladder frame instead of the accepted X-frame of the day was used. Wheelbase was 123.5 ins.

After much searching and deliberation, the engine used was a 226.2-cu.-in., L-head 6 from Continental. The "Red Seal" engine produced 100 bhp and provided acceptable performance with good fuel economy in the 20-30 mpg range, with an optional overdrive offering even better mileage.

It was quickly evident, however, that Henry wasn't going to get his "people's car." Even after discarding front-wheel drive (which Henry wanted for the Kaiser), the car still couldn't fit into the low-priced field. A $1868, it was a medium-priced vehicle.

Two Kaiser models were built for the 1947 model year: the K100 Special 4-door sedan and the K101 Custom 4-door sedan.

The K100 was the initial Kaiser model. It was austere by today's standards, but compatible with cars of its generation. With Frazer, it shared "Cradle Ride," whereby passengers sat between the axles. Both cars gave an excellent ride. A no-draft ventilation system was used, with ducts directing air from the grille area instead of via the traditional cowl vent. Seats were exceptionally wide for the day, and soon earned Kaiser-Frazer a good name for comfort.

The K101 Custom was introduced later, with a color-coordinated interior similar to that of the trend-setting Frazer. However, only 5412 Customs were sold, compared with 65,062 Specials.

Frazer was the high-priced model, competing in the high-middle range with Oldsmobile, Buick, Chrysler, Hudson and Packard. A lot of tough opposition.

At this point, however, Graham-Paige ran into financial problems, unable to meet its 50/50 responsibility to the Kaiser-Frazer Corporation. So Graham-Paige was bought out by K-F. Only 6476 basic Frazers were produced under the G-P name.

In all, the basic Frazer model was sold to 36,120 customers. With a price tag of $2053, it differed from Kaiser in exterior trim, used more luxurious colors inside and out, had more seat padding and insulation was better.

The Frazer Manhattan, which probably was not produced until the 1947 calendar year, was the showpiece for K-F. Even though it was priced at $200 more than the basic Frazer, it's exterior colors were shockingly magnificent, even as indicated by their names—Parakeet, Doeskin, Arena Yellow, Flax, Claypipe Gray. And the Manhattan was the only K-F car to have two-toned exterior colors.

Inside, upholstery never looked so good. Rich formal shades and warm pastels had previously been unknown in the automobile industry. But Frazer borrowed decorator colors and designs from the home. Full leather was also available as an option. Dashboards and even steering wheels were color-coordinated. Like the Kaiser, Frazer also used push-button door handles inside. Hailed as a safety innovation, these buttons proved bothersome to those accustomed to handles.

Those first-year cars were not without problems, as was expected. Changes were made continuously during the production run. Predominant sore spots were suspension-caused tire wear, air and water leaks, vapor locks and occasional lapses in fit and finish quality.

With the 1948 model year, the cars were pretty good. K-F had begun building its own engines through an agreement with Continental. The same four models appeared, with no appreciable visual change.

2

3

Independent
Kaiser-Frazer

Engine life was greatly improved when Kaiser-Frazer took over that aspect of production. Some powerplants, however, were still furnished from Continental's Muskegon plant. It's said that a standing policy among K-F employees was never to buy a car with a 5-digit (Muskegon) engine serial number. They'd always pick the 6-digit (Kaiser-Frazer) number.

Modifications included an increased compression ratio to 7.3:1, improved oil pressure sending unit for better oil flow, stiffened block, oil-less pilot bearing on rear crank bushing, new crankshaft vibration damper and reengineered engine mounts.

In May 1948, a dual intake and exhaust manifold option was offered for Kaiser Customs and Frazer Manhattans that raised horsepower to 112. The tire wear problem was corrected by redesigning the steering linkage layout. Heavier shock absorbers and springs were added, along with new super cushion tires.

This turned out to be the second biggest year in Kaiser-Frazer history. Kaiser Specials produced totaled 90,588, Kaiser Customs 1263, Frazers 29,480, and Frazer Manhattans 18,591.

By 1949, other manufacturers all had new body styles. And instead of cutting back to retrench, Henry borrowed $40 million to push out the now almost-obsolete cars of 1947. This created a giant rift between Kaiser and Joe Frazer, who eventually left the company.

The 1949 lineup was introduced in September 1948, with some startling but ill-accepted models. The only exterior changes were new grilles, bumpers and side trim. Fender skirts were optional on the Kaiser Deluxe (which replaced the Custom) and Frazer Manhattan. The entire instrument panel was changed from horizontal gauges to circular instruments. Chassis alterations included redesigned frame crossmembers permitting more ground clearance and increased height, longer front coil springs and altered rear leafs.

Kaiser-Frazer was still unable to afford either the purchase or construction of its own V-8. Power was needed, however, to keep up with the opposition. So the dual manifold became standard on Kaiser Deluxe and all Frazers. Since cooling had been a problem all along, shrouding was added. But vapor lock continued to plague the L-head 6, a problem that wouldn't be cured until 1952.

Taxicabs were introduced for the first time, fitted with dual manifold, heavy-duty suspension and drivetrain parts, vinyl interior, grab handles and aluminum kickpads. This model was dropped, however, early in 1951.

Again K-F resigned itself only to 4-door models. But three totally new designs were introduced.

The first were the Kaiser Traveler (Special series) and Vagabond (Deluxe series). These were forerunners of today's hatchbacks. The rear deck opened, as on station wagons, and the seats folded flat on the floor. The spare was mounted against the left rear door, which was welded shut.

As the story goes, Henry and his wife used a station wagon to reach their Lake Tahoe retreat, but neither liked it because it was rattly, rode like a pickup truck and the removable seats had to be manhandled. By drawing lines on a dust-covered Kaiser, he explained what he wanted for this "utility" model. It proved to be a stroke of luck, because these vehicles accounted for a quarter of K-F production in 1949.

The real special interest items for 1949 and 1950 were the Kaiser and Frazer convertibles and Kaiser Virginian. Introduced in January 1949, the convertible was little more than a cut-down 4-door sedan. An X-frame was necessary to help rigidity, and body braces were added wherever necessary. It's not the way a convertible should be built, but they turned out to be fairly solid automobiles.

These were the only 4-door converti-

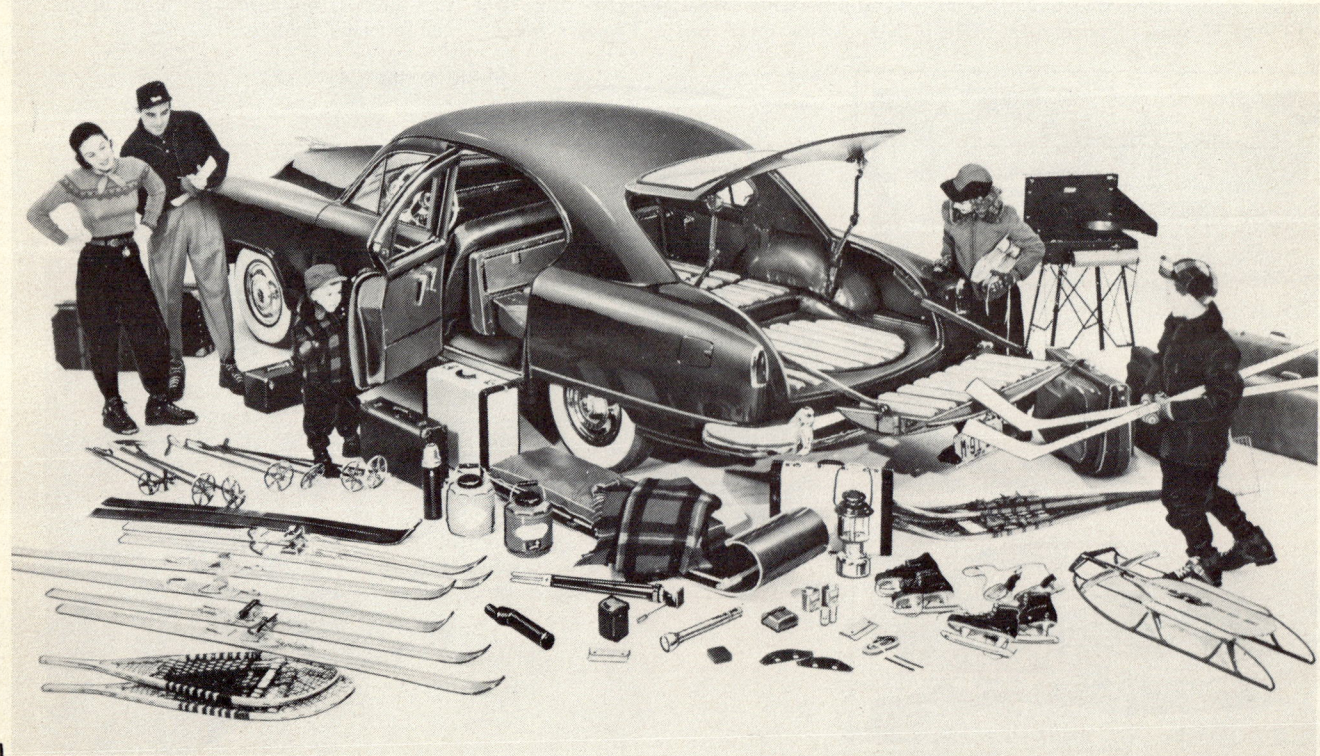

bles being offered on the market. To help support the soft top and frame, a permanently fixed glass pillar was installed between front and rear doors. It looked quite awkward with the top and windows down. Perhaps that's why so many convertible owners drove with all the windows up. Only 124 of these 1949 and 1950 convertibles were built,

1. 1951 saw the final utilization of the original K-F body style, which was cosmetically restyled to its ultimate. This '51 Kaiser Traveler is the predecessor of today's hatchbacks and a very collectable model.

2. The 1952 Kaiser entered a much more competitive marketplace with Darrin styling in 12 different models. All are eminently collectable.

3. Even from the rear, the '53 Kaiser Manhattan tricks casual observers with subtle 'V' combined with Kaiser emblem, but they were still powered by the 6-cyl. engine.

4. Most obvious difference between the '52 and '53 (shown) Kaiser is the unusual headlight trim rings. The back end also displayed trim changes.

5. Dashboard layout in the '54's was a bit on the exotic side, but hinted at the safety consciousness to come with padded dashboards and seat belt option.

6. In a last ditch effort to keep the 6-cyl. engine competitive, Kaiser fitted McCulloch superchargers. These '54's are of very special interest.

which make them real collectors' items.

The Kaiser Virginian was a very interesting car. It was K-F's attempt at a hardtop. Although equipped with the convertible's permanent center-post glass pillar, it didn't completely qualify as a hardtop. More Virginians were sold than convertibles, but the 1949-50 production remained a low 1376 units.

The Virginian featured a lighter top than sedans, and was strengthened by crease lines designed to resemble convertible top bows. It used the X-frame as on the convertible. To further give the effect of a closed convertible, padded nylon or cotton was applied over the roof. A wide, 3-section rear window was used for better visibility. A Custom version of the Virginian was also made, but in low volume. It featured quality cloth and carpeting, plus additional interior brightwork.

The 1950 model year was a real bummer. The 1949's hadn't sold well, and the company was faced with tens of thousands of leftover cars. So, the 1950's merely became renumbered 1949's, Kaiser-Frazer personnel actually went to dealers' lots to change the serial number plates. Fortunately, it was a short model year, which ended on March 15, 1950. When production stopped to tool for the phenomenal 1951's, not only were dealers stuck with these white elephants, but Willow Run was left with some 10,000 vehicles at the factory that they couldn't sell. A stroke of genius on the part of the K-F styling staff, however, turned

SPECIAL INTEREST AMERICAN CARS/**165**

Independent
Kaiser-Frazer

these leftovers into the 1951 Frazer with some real macho looks.

This was to be the last year for Frazer. It was preordained, since there really was no reason to carry on the name of a man no longer with the company. All this despite the fact that orders were more than five times greater than production, which totaled 10,214.

Though the 1951 Frazer was basically no more than a 1949, you couldn't tell by looking. The elements that made the last Frazer striking in appearance were strictly bolt-ons: fenders, airfoil grille assembly and identification script. The quality of interiors remained in Frazer only. The car was also using the larger 123.5-in. wheelbase, making it the largest and best riding product in the line that year. Trunk space also was K-F's largest for 1951. Prices started at $2220 for the sedan and went up to $3075 for the Manhattan. And Hydra-Matic was now offered.

The four models offered by Frazer were the most in its brief history, with the utility Vagabond and Hardtop added to the sedan line.

The Vagabond and Convertible are best bets for special interest cars in 1951. Especially since this was the only year for the utility-bodied Frazer, a body style termed "beneath the dignity of Frazer" by its namesake.

Although the model year was the greatest in K-F history, it was also the longest. And it was a time for important decisions concerning the future.

It was apparent that the public felt K-F had let them down in the 1949-1950 model years. They hadn't kept pace. In 1951 they had a chance to reverse that feeling, especially with the introduction of the new Kaiser, which has to be one of the great styling examples ever to come out of Detroit. Even today this Darrin-designed automobile remains one of the most beautiful cars ever conceived.

The styling was clean and revolutionary. For the first time, K-F accepted Dutch's so-called Darrin Dip at the rear door, which accentuated front and rear fenderlines and added sleekness to the design. A 2-piece widow's peak windshield gave the appearance of the classical V-shaped windscreen. Also, the windshield was canted more severely and was the largest in the industry. In fact, glass area all around was greater than any car of its day.

Darrin called the design "Speed Styling," because the car not only looked as if it were moving when parked, but also had good aerodynamic characteristics for its day. Everything about the car was beautiful. It had the lowest beltline in the industry and the lowest weight of any competitive vehicle. The 6-in. ground clearance was also daringly low for its day. The wheelbase was shortened to 118 ins. The spare was hidden in a well in the trunk. The circular instrument panel was easily legible in front of the driver. And, unlike the later Studebaker Starliner, the 1951 Kaiser looked great in all body styles.

An interesting story surrounds the selection of Darrin's design. When final selection was being made for the 1951 Kaiser, the company had its own styling department, said to be envious of outsiders. When the full-size clay mockups were presented to Henry J, company stylists gathered around Darrin's car to hide it from the boss. Seeing he might get politicked out by the residents, Darrin resorted to attention-getting trickery. He loosened the belt on his trousers, so that when he approached Kaiser, his pants fell down, making him the immediate center of attraction. Amid the laughter, Darrin got Kaiser's attention and instant approval to put the car into production.

The spring introduction of the 1951 Kaiser certainly must have influenced the buying public, since that's normally a good time for selling automobiles. Twelve models were offered in the Kaiser line, including 2-doors for the first time. The series names remained the same—Special and Deluxe. And prices were down $100 from the previous year.

The Special was nothing more than a de-trimmed Deluxe. The more expensive, flashy Deluxe, in fact, was the best seller that year. It offered stainless steel belt molding, rub rail (optional on the Special), bright window mold-

ings, foam rubber seat pads under upholstery, carpeting, padded vinyl dash and a chrome-plated lower dash panel.

The Frazer was gone by November 1950, but it was quickly replaced by the fascinating Kaiser Dragon. Three series were produced that year. This was Kaiser's answer to the Manhattan.

The first series, regardless of color scheme, was called the Golden Dragon. The Golden Dragon was not actually a separate model, but a trim package offered on the Deluxe. Although primarly an option on 4-door sedans, some 2-door sedans and club coupes carried the Dragon package.

The backbone of the Dragon was a new material called vinyl. K-F preferred to call it—believe it or not—Dragon Vinyl. It was textured to look like alligator skin and was extremely durable. Thick carpeting was used throughout and certain mandatory options were part of the package, including Hydra-Matic and whitewall tires. The Golden Dragon came with a painted top, while later versions used vinyl tops.

The second series was introduced on Feb. 6, 1951, and superseded the first series. This time the new, durable material was called Dinosaur Vinyl! There were now three versions—Golden Dragon, Silver Dragon and Emerald Dragon.

On April 27, 1951, yet another Dragon appeared. It was the Jade Dragon and featured Tropical Vinyl, which had the color and appearance of woven straw.

The utility Traveler didn't become available until after January 1951. It was now a true 4-door vehicle without the welded-shut door. The spare was moved to the well under the floor to make it more pleasing to passengers,

1. Awaiting loving owners, four '55 Kaisers are loaded up for a trip to the showroom floor. These were among the last Kaisers sold. Buick XP-300 showcar styling is obvious in front end treatment of the last Kaisers.

2. Chassis of the DKF-161 came from the Henry J's and featured independent front suspension and 6 cyl. engine with three carburetors.

3. The ads extolled '51 Henry J's as being "new without being radical..." and even claimed the two-door sedan was "sleek and racy..." What it really was, was an attempt at inexpensive, reliable, compact transportation.

4. One of the choicest Kaisers is the Kaiser-Darrin sports car. The DKF 161 had slide-open rather than swing-open doors and fiberglass bodies.

SPECIAL INTEREST AMERICAN CARS/167

Independent
Kaiser-Frazer

but the floor was no longer flat as in earlier models.

The 1951 Kaiser was peppier than the previous year, only because of the weight cutback. The Supersonic Six now came with a dual-throat Carter carburetor on a dual manifold system, which was standard on all models. Yet, vapor lock and overheating were still common. Handling had been improved with the shortened wheelbase and altered spring rates.

Kaiser's "people's car" finally appeared on Sept. 28, 1950. It didn't have the front-wheel drive Henry had advocated for so many years, and it didn't have the ridiculously low price he had strived to achieve. In fact, it was only slightly cheaper than Chevrolet's cheapest model.

A contest was held to name the car, and it's been said the winning name was predetermined—Henry J.

Kaiser's future hinged on this new compact automobile. It was to be the new Model T. And it was more important than the V-8, which Kaiser needed desperately to keep its bigger cars competitive at the marketplace. It's true that a large market existed for a low-priced economy car. But it wasn't to be Henry J with its controversial, almost embarassing, styling. As one owner put it, "She's nice to have around, but I wouldn't want to be seen in public with her."

By now, Kaiser had become involved with Willys, and it was Willys engines that were used in the two Henry J models for 1951—a 134.2 cid, 68-bhp 4-cylinder and a 161 cid, 80-bhp 6. The engines were not interchangeable.

The 6-cylinder Henry J Deluxe turned out to be a sparkling performer. Zero to 60 in 14 secs. was pretty hot in those days. Besides, with optional overdrive, over 30 mpg was possible.

The Henry J was relatively low (5 ft. high), although it looked taller because of its stubby 100-in. wheelbase. There was good legroom in the front, but somewhat limited at the rear. The basic dashboard contained warning lights for oil and amps—then a novelty and praised.

There were some strange things about the little car. There was no trunk lid, no glovebox, no ventilation system and its appearance was far too spartan in the days of chrome and luxury trim.

Henry J production was slightly more than 80,000. A disappointing figure for what was to be the salvation of K-F.

Something else loomed ominous—the Korean War. The federal government decreed cutbacks, and K-F was awarded defense contracts that took precedence over building cars.

Yet, when the 1952's came out, it still looked as though Kaiser might come out pretty well. A beautiful bit of maneuvering by Edgar Kaiser, then president in place of Joe Frazer, involved Sears with the Henry J program. For the first time in 40 years, Sears would sell an Allstate automobile.

Sears, apparently, had more integrity about its automobile than Kaiser. They tried to brighten up the car a bit. A quilted Saran plastic interior was available in three series of plaid. A variety of interior combinations included smooth vinyl and occasional leather. A glovebox was standard, and interior seat and door-panel trim were upgraded as well as armrests and sun visors. Even the trunk lid opened.

Appearance differences from the Henry J included a blue-painted engine with orange "Allstate" lettering, smooth hubcaps or wheel covers without the "K," blank horn button and instrument panel bezel without the "K," special grille assembly, parking lights, front fenders, Allstate nameplates, special hood ornaments and taillights.

Sears also fitted each Allstate with its own tires, inner tubes, batteries and spark plugs. Sears also promoted the "Triple Gurantee"—18 months against road hazards on tires, 24 months on battery and 90 days or 4000 miles on Kaiser's new car warranty.

The agreement between K-F and Sears didn't last long, however. In 1952 only 1566 cars were sold, with a dismal 797 in 1953 when Sears backed out. The Henry J didn't fare much better in 1952, with total model production down to a mere 23,568, even with a trunk lid and glovebox and more economical rear-end gearing.

The first of the 1952 Henry J's were renumbered 1951's. They were called Vagabonds, using some leftover script and leftover Continental spare-tire kits to make them look a bit different.

The genuine '52's appeared on Feb. 20, 1952, with minor modifications. Names were changed to Corsair and Corsair Deluxe. A new grille and fender taillights now appeared. Even the real '52's borrowed from the past. A backlog of 1949 model heaters with automatic temperature control and full fresh air or recirculating heat fit Henry J's, and were offered in August.

The Kaiser, too, carried over 1951 models with a different name—Virginian. Again, leftover nameplates and Continental kits were used.

When the 1952 Kaisers did emerge, more chrome trim was used then before. And it wasn't distasteful, except for one thing—the "V" emblem on the hood. It falsely implied V-8 might be in the works for the following year. A truly gross misrepresentation, as far as the public was concerned, and another nail in the coffin.

There were some nice small touches in the Kaiser Deluxe and new Kaiser Manhattan series. The windshield was now of 1-piece design and the trunk handle was eliminated in favor of a pop-up deck spring which automatically flipped open the trunk when unlocked.

Not only were sales down drastically in a shortened model year, but in 1952, Kaiser's defense contracts were cut off because of the government's fear for the company's solvency.

Still, early 1953 models sold well. At this point, however, it would have taken a miracle to pull the company out. Apparently Kaiser believed in miracles, because in April 1953 he merged Kaiser Motor Company with Willys.

It was the Dragon that breathed fire this year. Vinyl was used liberally inside, even to line the glovebox. Over 200 lbs. of insulation made it quieter. And dig this... 14-carat gold was used to plate the hood ornament, front and rear "V" medallions, deck and fender script and the trunk lid keyhole cover. Real gold! Later in the model run, an occasional Dragon order was filled by pulling a low-priced Deluxe off the line and giving it the Dragon treatment. These later models had enamel paint, while the real Dragons used lacquer. Standard equipment was tinted glass, oversize whitewall tires, Hydra-Matic, 8-tube radio with rear speaker, heater/defroster, windshield washer and center armrests front and rear.

An effort to bolster showroom traffic in the spring of 1953 was attempted with the Kaiser Carolina, an unchromed, stripped-down line. Dealers were instructed not to sell them, if possible, but to move buyers into more expensive Deluxe and Manhattan models. Only 1812 Carolinas were built in 4-door and 2-door form.

A rare Kaiser option appeared in May 1953—power steering. Only 733 were sold in 1953 and 107 in 1954.

One thing you've got to say about old Henry... he really had guts. His company was teetering, he had to sell Willow Run, yet he was willing to try Darrin's new idea—an expensive, 2-seat sports car.

Only 435 of these sleek, elegant cars were built. They were only 50 ins. high to the top and had a lower center of gravity than any other American automobile. They were firmly sprung and used the Henry J chassis and engine. The engine developed 125 bhp with three carburetors and had a top speed of about 100 mph.

Again the famed Darrin Dip was very much in evidence. Landau irons were used as a folding mechanism, and the top dropped into its own storage compartment. The car also had a trunk. Doors rolled into the front fenders rather than opening conventionally. More important, the body was built of fiberglass.

The Kaiser-Darrin interior was of pleated vinyl, with luxurious carpeting from the Dragon. The dashboard was thickly padded, and seatbelts were optional. Standard equipment included overdrive, turn signals, tinted windshield and wind wings, windshield washers and electric wipers, side curtains, white sidewalls, dual horns, tachometer, stainless steel wheel covers, exhaust deflector, bumper guards and cigar lighter. Heater and wire wheel covers were optional.

Production stopped in mid-1954, with some 100 Kaiser-Darrins left unsold. Darrin himself bought 50 and sold them all through his Los Angeles showroom. Some were equipped with 304-bhp Cadillac V-8's and claimed a top speed approaching 140 mph. And eight were equipped with Darrin's own design for a removable hardtop.

The 1954 Kaiser Special and Manhattan were ugly masses of chrome. An attempt was made to copy the Buick XP-300 showcar with concave grille and bulky trim. The wraparound rear window and crash pad at the back of the front seat for rear passengers were nice touches.

With the Dragon now gone, the appealing car of interest was the supercharged Manhattan. The Special retained the 118-bhp version of the 6, but since no V-8 was available, Kaiser was badly in need of power, so a McCulloch supercharger was added. It was V-belt driven from th crankshaft pulley through a planetary ball drive. It was activated by a solenoid built into the accelerator linkage. Called "Power on Demand," it freewheeled economically at 60 mph, delivering 1.5 psi boost. A push on the accelerator pedal advanced it to 5.0 psi. It was the first production supercharged car since the Graham Hollywood of prewar years.

In 1955, Kaiser had it. Only the Manhattan was offered, and those were renumbered cars. After 1291 were produced, Kaiser closed its doors for good.

Frazers continue to be the most desirable of the K-F line of sedans, although all Kaisers, Frazers, Henry J's, Allstates and Kaiser-Darrins must be considered of special interest.

Kaiser-Frazer offered styling and daring to a postwar American buying public. And to the industry, it offered innovations in interior design.

As Richard M. Langworth aptly put it in his recent book on Kaiser-Frazer: It was "The Last Onslaught on Detroit."

1. Pointy rear fenders were serious attempt at "styling" a small car. The '51's, being the first model year are much sought after collector's items.

2. Spartan interiors of '51 Henry J's were dressed up a bit with reptile-textured vinyl. This makes restoration a bit sticky.

3. The 1952 Henry J's made the small tailfins useful by incorporating the taillights. The original mounting locations were concealed with buttons.

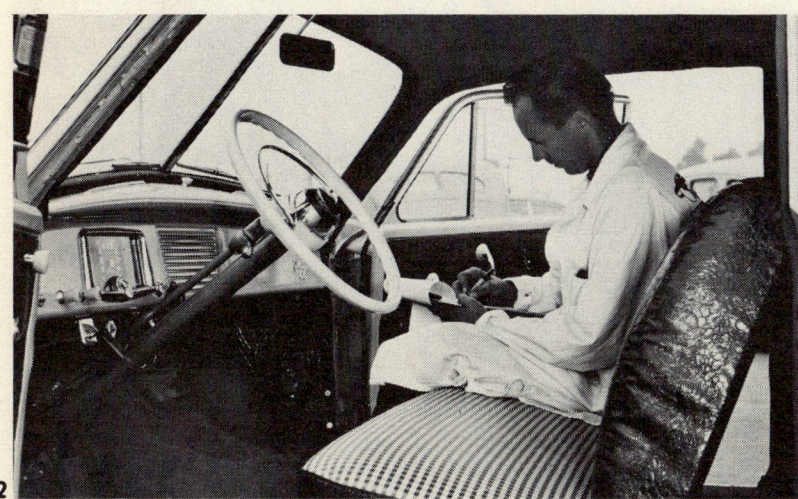

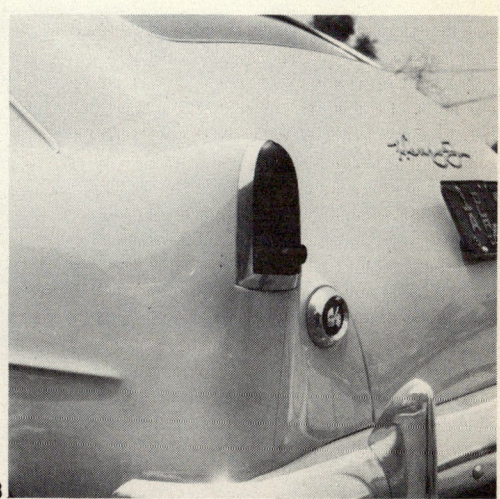

Independent
Nash
"Fill 'er up, . . . and make the bed!"

Charles W. Nash was president of General Motors in the summer of 1916, when he startled the business world by announcing he intended to resign to form a new company and build a car under his own name. As he was to observe decades later, it was merely a new challenge in a life of challenges.

Well acquainted with the many competitors then on the automotive scene, Nash elected to purchase the Thomas B. Jeffery Company, a pioneer in the auto industry.

For the remainder of 1916, the new Nash Motors Company marketed the Jeffery, but in 1917 the nameplate was changed to Nash. In September, 1917, the first Nash-designed car, powered by a 6-cyl. valve-in-head engine, made its bow as the 1918 Nash Model 681.

A roadster and sports car were added in 1919, with only minor appearance changes. In that year 31,108 cars and trucks were produced, and Nash Motors Company reported a profit of $5 million on sales of $41.7 million. Also in 1919, Nash bought a half-interest in the Seaman Body Corporation of Milwaukee, which was producing bodies for all Nash cars. (The remaining half was acquired in 1936.)

Nash cars continued to sell well and in 1924, when total Nash production was 53,626 units, Nash Motors acquired the Mitchell Motor Car Company in nearby Racine. In the following year, the Ajax car, built in Racine, made its bow. A low-priced automobile, it was short-lived and was superseded in mid-1926 by the Nash Light Six.

Nash sales passed the 100,000 mark in 1926 and reached a peak of 138,137 cars in 1928. When the Depression struck, Nash Motors Company was in sound financial condition with no debt, but sales fell sharply. The all-time low was 14,973 cars built in 1933.

Unlike many illustrious car makes that failed in this period, Nash survived, with its heaviest loss only $1.6 million in 1934, when the low-priced LaFayette series was introduced. Conditions began to improve by 1936, when 53,038 Nash cars were built and a net profit was realized for the first time in four years.

By this time, Charles Nash was 72 years old, and he began a search for a younger man to take over the company. At the suggestion of his friend, whom Nash had bought into the auto industry, Walter P. Chrysler, the presidency was offered to George W. Mason of Detroit, then president of Kelvinator Corporation, pioneer electric refrigerator manufacturer. Mason declined the offer but suggested a merger

of the two companies. Nash-Kelvinator Corporation was formed on January 4, 1937, with Mason as President and Nash as Chairman of the Board.

Mason immediately put his engineers to work developing an entirely new car to bolster Nash's share of the auto market. With the Edward G. Budd Manufacturing Company, they worked for four years and developed the "600" series which appeared in the fall of 1940. The "600" marked the first application in a mass-produced automobile of the unitized construction principle used successfully in aircraft design. The new car quickly raised Nash to second place among the independent producers, when World War II halted all U.S. car production.

Nash was among the first to resume postwar production, with 98,769 models built in 1946. Sales continued to climb and in 1949, when an all-new line was introduced, an all-time sales record of 142,592 cars was established. In March, 1950, Nash introduced the first modern compact car and for the new line, the nostalgic Rambler name was revived. In 1951, Nash brought out the Nash-Healey sports car which it marketed on a limited basis for four years. In 1952, Nash offered big cars styled by Pinin Farina, noted Italian designer.

While Rambler sales showed steady increases, overall sales were declining, and Mason decided to seek strength from merger with another company. On May 1, 1954, Nash-Kelvinator and Hudson Motor Car Company were merged to form American Motors Corporation. Mason was named chairman and president, with George Romney elected executive vice-president. On October 8, 1954, Mason died suddenly and four days later Romney succeeded him.

Bleak as the future looked, Romney saw a bright spot in the appeal of the Rambler and over the next eight years added many new models on two wheelbases. By late 1956 it was apparent that the company's future, beset by years of heavy losses, depended on concentration on the compact Rambler and an even smaller car, the Metropolitan, which was built in England to Nash specifications by Austin and which had bowed in 1954 just before the merger.

As demand continued to decline for the larger Nash Statesman and Ambassador during this period, the company decided after the 1957 model year to drop the Nash and Hudson names to concentrate on the Rambler's success.

But while the Nash name in 1957 joined hundreds of others that no longer grace the front ends of U.S. automobiles, it is only fair to emphasize a little-recognized fact. While the *name* was dropped, the *company* still exists ... as a strong contender in a highly-competitive automobile industry. In fact, American Motors Corporation is the sole surviving independent manufacturer.

Even though Nash Motors Company in 1930 built less than half as many cars as it did in 1929, it recorded a profit of $7.6 million on sales of $52 million in the first full Depression year. A record total of 32 different models was offered, with nearly all listed at prices above $1000 and seven selling for more than $2000.

It was a year of firsts for Nash. The company introduced its first 8-cylinder engine. Called the Twin-Ignition Eight,

1. This 1930 Nash Model 480 was known as the Twin-Ignition Six by virtue of dual coils.

2. A 1931 Nash delivery car with 2-door styling but quarter windows were blank and an access door added at the rear.

3. Nashes were not always the smallish cars we know today; this '32 Model 994 is big by any standards.

4. The 1932 Big Six model 971 rode on Nashes' smallest wheelbase; 116 ins. This convertible sedan, as it was called, is a good-looker.

5. For '33 the Advanced Eight convertible sedan (model 1183) was one of 34 models fielded by Nash in spite of the Depression era.

COURTESY AMC

Independent
Nash

it operated with two spark plugs to each cylinder, had nine main bearings. Twin-Ignition Six and Single Six models also were offered. The company touted clutch-pedal starting (avoiding accidental in-gear starts), and "automatic built-in radiator shutters." In all, 54,605 cars were built.

Dollar sales skidded in 1931, but the well-managed Nash Motors still reported a respectable profit and production of 38,616 cars.

The company identified the 24 models offered as "the greatest values in the medium and moderate price fields," with prices lowered from $140 to $360 from 1930 levels. The lowest-priced model that year was the Nash Six sedan or coupe at $795. In addition to the Nash Six, the company offered the Eight-70, the Eight-80 and the Eight-90. The top-of-the-line Ambassador sedan featured a detachable custom-built trunk.

Opening in the dismal climate of a deepening Depression, 1932 was destined to be the poorest auto production year since 1918. Many of the long-established U.S. auto companies failed, but Nash Motors almost unbelievably continued to operate in the black. Their profit was 6.2 times greater than that recorded by General Motors, the only other profitable U.S. car company in 1932.

Nash turned out only 17,696 automobiles, starting the year with 25 different models. To bolster sagging sales, Nash Motors in mid-year brought out a new line of cars called the "Second Series," with 28 6 and 8-cyl. models. Prices were adjusted only slightly, as the company directed its appeals to customers with eight new convertible roadster and sedan models with "lower, longer, wider control," and a "full-range dash-adjusted ride." Nash cars were available on wheelbases of 114, 116, 121, 128, 133 and 142 ins.

Nash Motors entered the 1933 model year still convinced that a wide range of models was the most effective answer to dwindling sales. Thirty-four distinct models were offered, with prices ranging from $695 for a Big Six town sedan to $2055 for a Nash Ambassador Eight limousine on a 142-in. wheelbase.

With the Kenosha main plant and Seaman Body plants in Milwaukee, closed down much of the time, sales fell for '33. The company produced only 14,973 years in calendar 1933, the lowest since its first year, 1917.

In 1934, Nash Motors Company elected to enter the low-priced field again (despite a rather unspectacular try with the Ajax in 1925-26) introduction of the LaFayette. Nash had acquired rights to the name in 1924 when it purchased the assets of the LaFayette Motors Corporation, originally of Indianapolis. This company, which produced only high-priced cars in limited numbers, was transferred by Charles W. Nash to Milwaukee in the early 1920's.

All eight Nash LaFayette models, built on a wheelbase of 113 ins., were powered by 75-hp. L-head engines. Price leader was the 2-door sedan, introduced at $645 and reduced in price on two occasions during the year, to $585.

In addition, the company offered four Big Six, six Advanced Eight and six Ambassador eight models in 1934. The company built its one-millionth Nash and virtually doubled sales over the preceding year.

The most significant changes made by Nash in 1935 involved marketing approaches. The number of models offered was sharply reduced to 14, with all 6-cyl. models priced below $1000. The LaFayette coupe remained the low-cost leader at $585. Horsepower of the LaFayette 6-cyl. engine was boosted to 80, and Nash advertising hailed the new "Aeroform" design of the complete line.

Nash Motors Company built 44,637 cars in 1935.

Economic recovery was slowly asserting itself as the 1936 model year began for Nash Motors. The company started the year with six LaFayette models ranging in price from $610 to $700, two Ambassador Sixes (sedan and victoria) and the new Nash "400" series comprising six models, priced from

1. We couldn't resist running this 1934 factory publicity photo, and we'll never know if the gentleman was able to get all that luggage into the trunk.

2. Fender-skirted, dual sidemounted '34 Ambassador Eight Model 1290 seems to be shunned by gentlemen examining the early-'20's Nash.

3. Nash styling for 1935 was termed Aeroform, offered in 2- and 4-door sedans as Advanced Six, Advanced Eight, and Ambassador Eight models.

4. Nash had entered the low-price field in 1934 with the LaFayette. This 1936 Model 3618 rode on 113-in. wheelbase and was billed as "the big car in the low-price field." No explanation is given for the admirer to the left.

5. The industry's first fresh air and heating ventilating system was introduced in 1938. This is the Nash Ambassador Eight 4-door sedan, Model 3888. Nash merged this year with Kelvinator.

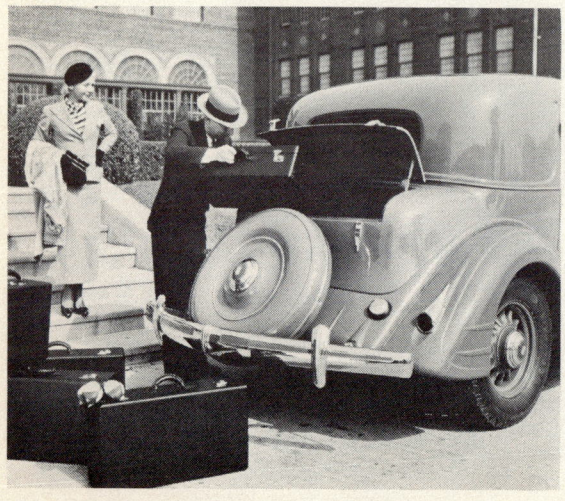

$665 for the coupe to $765 for the sedan.

Several months after introduction, however, because dealers in particular did not like the new front-end design, all "400" models after that date featured modified grilles (and each model number from that date carried the letter "A" after the number designation). Also offered in 1936 were Nash Ambassador Super Eight sedans and victorias, both priced just below $1000. Nash introduced the unique convertible bed feature, and a customer could order his sedan with or without a trunk.

Nash built 53,038 cars in 1936, generating a welcome profit.

The consolidation of Nash and Kelvinator became official on January 4, 1937. Headquarters of the new company were established in the Kelvinator administration building on Plymouth Road in Detroit, with George W. Mason, former Kelvinator chief executive who had made a name for himself in the automobile industry as Chrysler's first works manager in the mid-1920's, as President, and Charles W. Nash as Chairman of the Board.

Almost immediately, Mason put his engineers to work to design an entirely new car (the "600" series that was to bow in the fall of 1940). General confidence in the aggressive new company led to production during the year of 85,949 cars, highest since 1929. The "400" series was dropped, with the Ambassador broadened to include 12 models in addition to eight LaFayette models.

Nash Motors in 1938 introduced the industry's first fresh-air heating and ventilating system, now standard equipment in virtually every automobile built in the world. Called the "Weather Eye" conditioned-air system, it provided for the first time a unit that heated constantly moving fresh air.

It was a recession year, with auto industry sales down sharply from the previous year, and Nash sales dropped to only 32,017 cars.

The complete Nash line for 1939 underwent major styling changes, conceived by George W. Walker (who later was to become Ford's vice-president of styling). The new design was hailed in 1939 Nash literature as "so exquisitely modeled and streamlined that it gives the feeling of flight even while at rest."

The new line was well received, with sales for the year reaching 65,662 units, nearly twice as many as were sold in 1938. Twelve Ambassador models—six with 6-cyl. engines and six with 8's—were marketed in 2 and 4-door sedans, cabriolets and coupes. The same body style choices were available in the LaFayette series, with prices ranging from $770 to $950. All models featured a new steering column shift lever control.

For the model year 1940, Nash production reached 62,002, with 46,252 being LaFayette models, all built on a wheelbase of 117 ins.; 12,500 were Ambassador Sixes, on a 121-in. wheelbase, and 3250 were Ambassador Eights, on a 125-in. wheelbase. Calendar year production totaled 63,617.

In one of its rare excursions into custom car designs, Nash Motors commissioned Count Alexis de Sahknovsky, the noted stylists, to create a special cabriolet for the 1940 model year. Eleven custom-bodied cars were built, with five of them sporting copper-plated exterior trim. A low-cut door sill gave

3
COURTESY AMC

4
COURTESY AMC

5

Independent
Nash

the open model a racy appearance.

The long-awaited new car from Nash-Kelvinator made its bow in the fall of 1940—the low-priced Nash "600" (for 30 miles per gallon from a 20-gallon fuel tank). Not only was it a completely new offering, but it was also built in an entirely different way. The "600" became the first U.S. volume car to adopt unitized construction. On a wheelbase of 112 ins., the "600" replaced the LaFayette as the new Nash low-priced contender. Eight models, available in 2 and 4-door sedans, coupes and broughams, were priced between $710 and $870.

Nash Motors' production of 80,408 cars in 1941 helped the company generate a profit. With the tempo of war heightening in Europe, Nash-Kelvinator began defense production of cargo trailers in Racine, Wisconsin, and airplane propellers in Lansing, Michigan.

The momentum generated by the "600" had hardly begun when war halted all Nash production, as well as that of every other U.S. auto company for the duration. Nash-Kelvinator turned its attention completely to war production and in the next three and a half years produced more than $600 million worth of Pratt & Whitney aircraft engines, Sikorsky helicopters, aircraft propellers, bomb fuses, rocket motors and flying boat subassemblies.

Before auto production was halted in January, 1942, Nash had built 31,700 of the 1942 models (only 5428 in calendar 1942).

At war's end, Nash Motors was among the first to resume peace-time production of automobiles. The company produced 6148 cars in 1945 and 98,769 in the calendar year 1946. It was a seller's market, and every auto company scrambled to turn out as many cars as a limited supply of steel would permit. All firms were put on a steel allocation basis by government decree. So hungry for new cars were thousands of Americans that many accepted their cars from dealers with wooden bumpers in the back (later replaced with steel units), or other missing parts that also were in short supply because of raw-material shortages.

Nash made major changes in the front-end appearance of its postwar models, presenting a bright new grille on both the Ambassador and "600" for 1946. All models were powered by 6-cyl. engines. In anticipation of broader market opportunities, the company acquired a plant in Toronto for eventual production in Canada and purchased a tract of land near Burlington, Wisconsin, for a 204-acre proving ground.

In 1946, during the Automotive Golden Jubilee which celebrated the U.S. auto industry's 50th year, Charles W. Nash was among the 12 living pioneers to be honored.

Throughout the industry, styling and mechanical changes in 1947 were held to a bare minimum, except for Studebaker which introduced the first completely new postwar car. When Nash dealers convened in Detroit to see the 1947 models for the first time, a company official presenting the cars showed a large photographic blowup of the 1946 Ambassador sedan. As an orchestra played a loud fanfare, he ceremoniously reached up and stripped off a piece of chrome along the side of the body and thundered: "Gentlemen, here is the all-new 1947 Nash!" Continuing to be restricted by the national steel shortage, Nash nevertheless built 113,315 cars.

A canary-yellow Nash Ambassador driven by President George W. Mason paced the 1947 Indianapolis 500-Mile Race.

Refinement continued to be the styling byword as 1948 Nash models showed only slight changes. For the third consecutive year, a limited-edition Ambassador Suburban model with wood side panels was built (a total of 1000 were produced in the three-year period—275 in 1946, 595 in 1947 and 130 in 1948).

Nash also introduced in 1948 the only full-sized convertible it built in the postwar period. Exactly 1000 Ambassador convertible models were turned out. Production of all models for the year totaled 118,621 cars.

Nash Motors introduced its first all-new postwar car in 1949. Called the Nash Airflyte, it stressed aerodynamic

COURTESY AMC

design. (Today Nash enthusiasts affectionately call it the "bathtub" design.) The new Ambassador and "600" models featured the first use by Nash of one-piece curved windshields, the "Uniscope" cluster of instruments mounted on the steering column, enclosed front wheels, plastic inlaid instrument panel and a brougham model with rear seats that virtually faced each other. For the first time, the Ambassador was built on a unitized body.

Production and sales in 1949 were brisk, with 142,592 cars produced, an all-time Nash record. Also for the first time, Nash cars were produced outside Wisconsin as 1949 models were assembled in a newly-acquired plant in El Segundo, California.

Nash was a major automotive newsmaker in 1950. It was the year in which the company sounded a notice to the industry that it intended to become a dominant factor in an emerging trend toward smaller cars. The first modern Rambler was introduced in March, just two months after company executives toured the nation's major cities with a display of an even smaller experimental car to test public reaction. Called the N.X.I. (for Nash Experimental International), it was the forerunner of the imported Metropolitan, to be introduced four years later.

The first Nash Rambler model was a fully-equipped 100-in. wheelbase convertible with a top that was raised and lowered on unique side rails. Two months later a 2-door station wagon bowed. No effort was made to market them as low-priced cars as Nash stressed that they were fully-equipped luxury small cars that combined the advantages of big-car comfort and convenience with small-car superior economy and handling. In the calendar year 1950, the company built 20,782 Rambler models.

On its full-sized models, the new Statesman (replacing the "600") and Ambassador were the first U.S.-built cars to offer seat belts which came with models equipped with a new reclining front passenger seat. Automatic transmissions (GM's Hydra-Matic) were offered for the first time.

In May, Nash production began in the Toronto plant, with marketing emphasis on a new "Canadian Statesman" model. Nash produced 191,865 cars in the U.S. in 1950, with the 2,000,000th Nash being built on April 18 at Kenosha.

The smooth lines of the Airflyte design were interrupted by jutting fins as Nash kept pace with the trend in 1951 in facelifting its Ambassador and Statesman models. In June, a third new Rambler model—the hardtop Country Club—was introduced. Production for the year reached 161,140, including 57,555 Ramblers.

In February, Nash brought out the 2-passenger Nash-Healey, first sports car offered by a U.S. manufacturer in 20 years. The six-cyl. Ambassador engine was fitted with an aluminum head and dual carburetor. Overdrive was standard, as were leather upholstery, adjustable steering wheel and whitewall tires. The engine and driveline were shipped to Warwick, England, where a custom body was installed by the Donald Healey Company. In all, 104 of these 1951 models were produced.

1. All Nashes underwent complete restyling for 1939, masterminded by George W. Walker who would later become Ford's Vice President of Styling. This is the attractive LaFayette Deluxe Series convertible, Model 3911.

2. Count Alexis de Sanknovsky was commissioned in 1940 to execute this Special Cabriolet, Model 4081, and only 11 were built. This is probably the rarest of Nashes today.

3. Nash Ambassador Eight convertible for '41 is, like almost all open cars of the prewar era, a collectible item.

4. Several manufacturers offered '46 models with wood-over-metal panelling, including Nash with this Ambassador Model 4664, known as the Suburban.

5. Nash announced an all-new Rambler line in March of 1950. They bowed with just a station wagon, and the convertible shown here. Folding canvas top slid on unique side rails.

6. The first Nash-Healey appeared in February of 1951. A joint venture of Nash-Kelvinator and England's Donald Healey Co., resulted in 104 of this daring sports car built during the year.

3

4 COURTESY AMC

5

6 COURTESY AMC

Independent
Nash

In its 50th anniversary year, 1952, Nash Motors brought to the market a line of completely new cars styled by Pinin Farina, internationally-known Italian designer. The models included 2-door and 4-door sedans and hardtops in the Statesman and Ambassador series and 2-door suburbans, station wagons, convertibles and hardtops in the Rambler series.

Nash built 152,141 cars in 1952, of which 53,055 were Ramblers.

Beginning in January, 1952, an entirely new Nash-Healey sports car was introduced, featuring a roadster body built of aluminum by Pinin Farina in Turin, Italy. A total of 150 were produced.

A striking new front-end design distinguished the Nash Rambler series in 1953, while styling changes in the Ambassador and Statesman were held to a minimum. Total production for the year fell slightly from the previous year, to 135,389 cars, of which 41,885 were Ramblers.

A low-priced 2-door sedan was added to the Rambler line, and the popular continental spare tire mount was standard on all Rambler convertible and hardtop models. Power steering was offered for the first time, as an option, on Ambassador, which also introduced the LeMans Dual Jetfire engine.

A new LeMans hardtop was also added to the Nash-Healey series. Total Nash-Healey production in 1953 was 162.

The year 1954 was critical for Nash. Almost overnight, demand plunged and production for the entire year was only 67,192 cars, a 13-year low. This was despite a number of important product moves.

The Nash Rambler series was expanded to include 4-door sedans and 4-door Cross Country station wagon models on a longer 108-in. wheelbase. The Metropolitan small economy car was introduced in the United States and Canada in March. Built in England by Austin to Nash specifications, the 85-in. wheelbase Metropolitan was offered in 2-door hardtop and convertible models.

In 1954, Nash introduced the auto industry's first low-priced air-conditioning unit located entirely under the hood.

Early in the calendar year, Nash-Kelvinator and Hudson Motor Car Company began negotiations which led to the merger of the two companies on May 1. The new American Motors Corporation, headed by George W. Mason as President and Chairman, began immediately to consolidate its product offerings and dealer organizations to meet growing market opportunities and stiffer competition that was developing. In the calendar year, the company produced only 99,774 automobiles.

With the sudden death of Mason on October 8, 1954, the direction of the new American Motors was entrusted to George Romney, who was elected President and Chairman. Romney had joined Nash in 1948 and was executive vice-president at the time of the merger with Hudson.

In its first full year, American Motors in 1955 registered a $6.9 million loss on sales of $441.1 million. Production in Hudson's Detroit plants ceased, and a new line of 1955 Hudson models built on the Nash body shell was produced alongside Nash models in Kenosha.

In the 1955 model year, a total of 96,156 Nash cars were turned out; 56,023 were Nash Ramblers; 14,369 were Statesman models, 15,204 Ambassador Sixes and 10,560 Ambassador V-8's. New 208-hp. 8-cyl. engines, together with Ultramatic transmissions, were purchased from Packard.

The last cars to be built in the Nash assembly plant at El Segundo, California, came off the line on September 22.

With an all-new Rambler ready to capture a larger share of the developing compact-car market, American Motors elected to make the Rambler a marque on its own beginning with the 1956 model year, while continuing to market the series through both Nash and Hudson dealers. As a result, total Nash production for the model year was only 22,263 cars—7438 Statesman models, 5999 Ambassador Sixes, 4681 Ambassador V-8's with the Packard engine and 4145 Ambassador Specials powered by a new AMC-built 190-hp. V-8 introduced in April.

The popular little Metropolitan (which was to continue through the 1962 model year) underwent major changes for 1956, as the 1500 series replaced the original 1200. In addition to styling improvements, including two-tone paint treatments, the horsepower of the 4-cyl. engine was boosted 24 percent.

The final year for the Nash nameplate was 1957 as American Motors decided to drop both the Nash and Hudson names to concentrate on the compact Rambler. In the last Nash year, the Statesman was discontinued, with only four Ambassador models (sedans and hardtops) available. All were powered by the new American Motors V-8.

Thus, in its 40th anniversary year,

176/SPECIAL INTEREST AMERICAN CARS

the last Nash rolled from the Kenosha assembly line. Since the first model was produced in 1917, a total of 2,563,671 Nash cars had been produced for sale in the United States and throughout the world.

Singling out specific cars as being of Special Interest from the diversified models built by Nash, Nash-Kelvinator,

1. Noted stylist Pinin Farina was called on to redesign the Nash-Healey. Here Farina (right) shows off the first '52 to Nash president George W. Mason.

2. Pinin Farina's work for Nash was extended to the regular passenger car line, beginning in 1952, with what was called Airflyte styling. This is the Ambassador Custom Country Club, Model 5277, with pillarless hardtop design.

3. The Nash-Healey for 1953 saw the addition of a LeMans hardtop. Total N-H production for the year was 162, and the line would be dropped in '54.

4. The pint-sized Metropolitan came out in March of '54, was built by Austin in England. Wheelbase was only 85 ins., and body styles available were a 2-door hardtop and a convertible.

5. Here, for disbelievers, is what is officially known as a Hudson Rambler, Model 5518-2. Nash and Hudson had merged in mid-'54, and by 1955 all Hudsons were sharing body shells with Nash.

6. Under the hood beats a heart of Packard. AMC built 4681 Ambassadors with this engine for '56. This is the Country Club Hardtop, Model 5687-2.

American Motors and the final Hudsons, is difficult if production volume is a criterion. Even though Nash had risen to second place among the independents just before World War II, it failed to exceed 100,000 units for any year after 1929. And because of Nash's insistence that the way to approach marketing was through a wide array of model choices, (25 in 1932 at the height of the Depression, with only 17,696 cars sold!), it is easy to deduce that prewar Nashes are scarce today. Taking mechanical and styling innovations as the key to milestone cars, though, the American Motors Owners Association considers the following models as collectables:

1931 Nash Ambassador, because of its styling.

1934 LaFayette model 110, which introduced the low-priced line.

1938 LaFayette model 3813, due to the ventilating system.

1940 Nash cabriolet model 4081, with only 11 built.

1941 Nash Ambassador, with "unitized" construction.

1946 Nash Ambassador model 4664, for its wood side panels.

1951-1954 Nash-Healy, by virtue of styling.

1952 Nash Ambassador model 5277, with Pinin Farina styling.

1954 Hudson Italia, for styling and rarity; 26 built.

1954-1962 Nash Metropolitan, for size and economy.

1957 Hudson model 35787-2, the last of the breed.

1957 Rambler Rebel, for its high-performance V-8.

Independent
Packard
Why not be "... the man who owns one"

The image that a car enthusiast has of Packard, the corporation and its machines, depends upon his or her age. Those raised in the Twenties, Thirties recall with fondness the shining and silent monsters which transported the rich and powerful in naked splendor to work and play, and find it a little hard to believe that a company which produced so many magnificent automobiles has now vanished. Those raised in the '50's automatically think of Cadillac as the premier luxury car, and remember Packard as a rather fuddy-duddy company producing uninspired cars and patronized primarily by older folks. And, of course, since the last true Packard left Detroit 20 years ago, a whole generation has now grown up which does not remember Packard at all. The models we will arbitrarily define as special interest Packards are the medium-price cars made before the war, and all post war cars with the exception of the last two years.

Packard's first foray into the medium-price field occurred in 1932. Worried by declining sales as the deepening Depression took hold of the land, in January of that year Packard announced a new car which used the Standard Eight's engine and transmission in a short-wheelbase chassis cloaked in a new body. This was the Light Eight, and it was certainly a bargain. The original announced price was $1750, but when deliveries commenced in March, Packard realized that their manufacturing costs were higher than planned, and the price rose to almost $2000. This was still $500 cheaper than the Standard Eight, but the Light Eight didn't cost that much less to build, and Packard's profit margin was very slim. No wonder. The engine and transmission were the same, the new and stiffer frame had a wheelbase only 2 ins. shorter, it was offered in four body styles (coupe, roadster, 2-door sedan, 4-door sedan), and appointments and quality were typically Packard—lavish. The grille was new and different from any other Packard, with a pronounced sweep forward at the bottom like the prow of an old dreadnaught. Adjustable hydraulic shock absorbers were standard equipment, as was a clutch which could be set to be operated by engine vacuum. Examining a Light Eight and comparing it to the more expensive models makes it difficult to understand exactly where Packard expected to save so much money.

Viewed in a certain way, the Model 900 Light Eight was a success. It sold 6750 cars, well over half of Packard's 11,058 sales for 1932. But the profit margin was low and all sales were declining; Packard lost over $6 million in 1932. The problem with the Light Eight was that it was not really a medium-price car. It was a very slightly smaller version of a standard Packard, built the same way and using the same components. Packard did not know how to build down to a price. It had built only the finest luxury cars all of its corporate existence, and now found that simply scaling them down a wee bit didn't really save any money. To break into the medium-price field Packard would need a new car designed from the wheels up to be mass-produced. And it needed that car in a hurry, for its 1932 sales were down to a shocking 25% of what they had been only three years before. The luxury car market was disappearing like a snowball in an oven. The Light Eight was dropped at the end of the 9th series, and so was in production only one year. Interestingly, when the 10th series came out and Packard revised its model names (with Eight, Super Eight and Twelve replacing Standard Eight, Eight Deluxe and Twin Six), the new Eight was found to be much more similar mechanically to the orphaned Light Eight than to the Standard Eight, regardless of what Packard advertising wanted the public to believe.

Heavy planning for the true medium-price Packard began during the Light Eight's production. From the New York office president Alvan Macauley plucked Max Gilman of Sales, made him the Vice-President of Packard Distribution, and two years later moved him up again to general manager of the corporation. It was Gilman who decided what the price of the new car ought to be—under $1000 wholesale—and the general specifica-

tions necessary to achieve this. The engineering staff under the formidable Col. Vincent filled in the rest of the details, but the key man in this whole operation was George Christopher. Lured by Macauley and Gilman away from GM, Christopher was an engineer whose expertise was in stringent cost control, and he was made production manager for the project. And for the first time a Packard would be huckstered and ballyhooed in the press and on radio like any other car, an advertising job entrusted to former Chevrolet salesman Bill Packer.

The new Packard made its debut at the National Automobile Show in New York in January 1935, and it was the hit of the show. Called the model 120 from the length of its wheelbase, this was not considered a "series" Packard in time-honored company tradition, though it was introduced into the 12th series. Instead, it was its own independent model, not even produced in the same plant with the "classic" Packards. Together with the 6-cyl. model introduced two years later, it formed the so-called "junior series" to which Packard enthusiasts commonly refer.

The 120 offered tremendous value for its low price. Its engine was a new flathead straight eight with cylinder dimensions of 3¼x3⅞ ins., for 257 cu. ins., and 110 hp. It was a more modern design than the bigger eight used in the senior series, which had a 5-in. stroke. The chassis also had independent front suspension and hydraulic brakes, neither of which was on the senior series cars that year. The 120 was a complete line of seven body styles, ranging in price from the business coupe ($980) to the touring sedan ($1095). In between were the sport coupe (business coupe with a rumble seat), touring coupe (2-door sedan), convertible coupe, club sedan (4-door, blind rear quarter), and sedan (smaller trunk than touring sedan). The interiors were finished very well considering the price, but undoubtedly the most attractive feature of all was that the 120 looked nothing like any other medium-price car, but very much indeed like a larger Packard. It was a middle-class dream—a Packard that almost everyone could afford. The public flocked to the 120. Packard sold 24,995 of them the first year, and more than twice as many the following year. The 1936 120-B model was mechanically unchanged, but a convertible sedan was added to the line.

Now firmly established in the medium-price field, Packard looked around for new worlds to conquer. And at the National Automobile Show in October, 1936, came its new challenge to the low-price field. Called simply the Packard Six (internally called the 115-C, denoting the wheelbase and third year of body production), it used the 120's body and chassis components on a wheelbase of 115 ins., and the hood was shortened 5 ins. to match. Under that shorter hood was a shorter engine, the first 6-cyl. engine made by Packard since 1928. Very similar to the 120's eight, the Six's six had a flathead valve arrangement and cylinder dimensions of 3 7/16x4¼ ins., yielding 237 cu. ins., and 100 hp. Available were eight body styles, the same ones available in the 120 except for the convertible sedan, replaced by a station wagon. Prices were really low—$795 for the business coupe up to $910 for the convertible coupe and wagon, all of them cheaper than the cheapest 120. The public responded in record numbers, and 65,400 model 115-C Sixes were sold.

The 120 was not neglected during the year the Six was creating such a stir. Its engine stroke was lengthened to 4¼ ins. (same as the six), increasing the size to 282 cu. ins., and raising the

1. "Shovelnose" or "snowplow" grille is instant identification for the Light Eight, Packard's first foray into the medium-price field. Introduced in 1932, it was a beautifully detailed car which cost too much to make and was dropped after only one year.

2. The model 120 was Packard's entry into the medium-price field with a car especially designed for mass production. It had a 257-cu.-in. straight eight developing 110 bhp. An instant hit when brought out in 1935, the styling remained unchanged for three years except for variations on the hood louvers. This is a '37 touring sedan, the most popular body style. For this year the engine was stroked to yield 120 hp.

3. For 1938 the 120 received a 127-in. wheelbase, smoother fenders, and a larger split windshield. It remained basically unchanged for another three years, though the '40 facelift gave it a narrower grille, parking lights atop the fenders, and supplementary grilles below the headlights.

4. Over-restoration can sometimes hurt more than it helps. Neither the headlight shells nor the 1940 parking lights should be chromed on this otherwise-immaculate 1935 120 convertible coupe.

5. In its third year of production, this 1939 Six touring sedan looks much the same as it was first introduced, though the previous year it received a split windshield, longer wheelbase, and bored-out engine. The lowest-priced Packard ever built, the Six was renamed the 110 in 1940.

Independent Packard

power to 120 hp. A station wagon was added to the line, making nine body styles available, and in addition, two more model variations of the 120 made their appearance. One was the 120-CD, a plusher version available in touring sedan, club sedan, and touring coupe, and the other was the 138-CD, a special version set on a 138-in. wheelbase and available in limousine and 7-passenger sedan. Reflecting the economies of volume production, 120 prices for '37 were actually lower, body for body, than they had been in 1935. There was a substantial price rise, however, just before the revised models for '38 came out. The 50,000 cars of the 120 line produced this year, combined with the phenomenal sales of the Six and the recovering sales of the senior series, made 1937 the best year in all of Packard history.

There were major changes for 1938. The wheelbase of the Six was stretched 7 ins. to 122 ins., and its engine bore was opened up 1/16 ins. for 245 cu. ins., but the power rating remained the same at 100 hp. The styling was made subtly smoother, with more massive fenders and a larger windshield split in a V instead of a single pane of glass. The body lineup was juggled and reduced to five: business coupe, club coupe, convertible coupe, 2-door sedan, and 4-door sedan. The 120 now became known as the Eight, and it also received the new styling and a 7-in. longer wheelbase. Wait a minute, you may ask; if the 120 was now known as the Eight, what about the previous senior Packard with that designation? It was dropped. The junior cars now accounted for 95% of Packard's production, and there was no point in continuing three different senior lines; they were reduced to the Super Eight and the Twelve.

True Packard aficionados always refer to Packards by their series numbers, because in the early years the company (like Rolls-Royce) brought out a new model only when needed, and paid no attention to the calendar. By the mid-Thirties, however, Packard was bringing out a new series every year. The 120 and the Six, which shared so many parts with each other but had nothing in common with the senior cars, were at first not included in the series numbers denoting the larger cars. But in 1938 management relented, and the junior cars had their model numbers "integrated" with the senior cars. It was the year of the 16th Series, and the Six was denoted as the model 1600, the 120 as the model 1601, and the long-wheelbase 120 as the model 1602.

Only minor changes marked the next few years in the junior cars, although major changes occurred in the senior Packards. In 1939 (17th Series) the name 120 was reapplied to the Eight, and the senior Super Eight now became an interesting mixture of senior and junior parts. In a major cost-cutting move, Packard took the Super Eight's 319-cu.-in., straight eight, hooked it up to the 120's transmission, and slipped it into the 120's chassis and body. This enabled the Super Eight to be offered at much lower prices, but classic car enthusiasts frown upon this car today because of its hybrid parentage. Naturally, that makes it a prime special interest car; 3962 were produced. This was also the last year for Packard's mighty Twelve, as the great multi-cylinder race of the '30's came to an end.

For 1940 (18th Series), Packard completely revamped its model nomenclature. The Six was now called the 110, the 120 kept its name, and the senior series became two variations of one basic car. This was an all-new design, featuring a new straight eight with cylinder dimensions of 3½x4⅝ ins., which gave 356 cu. ins. and 160 hp. The lesser of the new seniors was called the Super Eight 160 (from the power rating), was available in three wheelbase lengths (127, 138, and 148 ins.) and seven standard body styles at moderate prices ($1524 to $2179). The 160 is not accepted by the Classic Car Club of America, and therefore makes a nice and handsome special interest car. The other new senior was the Custom Super Eight 180, and it had expensive custom bodywork on the 160 chassis. All 18th Series Packards, 110 to 180, carried new front-end styling with narrow grilles and catwalk supplementary grilles. It was a good year for Packard, as the 110, 120, and even the new 160 all sold in numbers second only to the great year of 1937.

In 1941 (19th Series) Packard styling was revised again, all models having headlights faired into the fenders, optional running boards, and more glass area. No major mechanical changes were made in either junior or senior series except for the introduction of the Electromatic clutch as an option. But major news was made with the debut of the Clipper on March 4, 1941, the most important new Packard since the 120. Wrapped around the 120's mechanicals was a spectacular streamlined body, a smooth 4-door sedan with beautifully integrated fenders. Flanking the delicate tall grille were horizontal bars, the first horizontal theme on any Packard. The Clipper was the first modern Packard, and customers went bananas over it. Despite the fact that it had only a 6-month production run and was available in only one body style, '41 Clipper production (16,600 cars) came very close to equalling the production for the entire '41 120 line (17,100 cars), which had eight different models!

It didn't take a marketing genius to see that the Clipper was a bell-ringer, and for 1942 (20th Series) Packard management was ready with a thorough model shakeup which brought

180/SPECIAL INTEREST AMERICAN CARS

Clipper styling to its entire range of cars. It also brought confusion to all but the most determined Packard enthusiast. Now a '41 Clipper is easy to remember; it was a standard 120 with a special body, and formed a supplement to the regular four lines of cars. But for '42 the regular 110 and 120 were dropped, replaced by a single Clipper which appeared in many guises. This car had a wheelbase of 120 ins. (that of the '41 Clipper was 127 ins.), and on it was a 4-door touring sedan, 2-door fastback club sedan, or business coupe (no rear seat). The first two of these three bodies were available in either Special or Custom trim, and any could be had with either the six or junior eight engine. If the six, it was called the Clipper Six 110; if the eight, it was known as the Clipper Eight 120. At least this kept alive the old series designations. These were the "junior Clippers," and can be identified externally by the short wheelbase, exposed rear wheel, and short front horizontal bars. The exception to the Clipper takeover of the junior series was the convertible coupe, which was continued in the old styling and on the old wheelbase lengths—122 ins. for the 110, 127 ins. for the 120.

But Clippers also got into the '42 senior act. Both the 160 and 180 offered a Clipper club sedan and touring sedan. The Clippers in these two series were mechanically identical, both using the big senior 356-cu.in. straight eight, but the 180 versions were plusher inside and cost about $500 more than the 160 versions. Unlike the junior Clippers, these senior Clippers were supplements to the regular senior cars, not replacements. They can be quickly distinguished from the junior Clippers by fender skirts, horizontal trim bars that wrap completely around the front fenders, and longer 127-in. wheelbase.

During World War II, Packard built their famous version of the Rolls-Royce Merlin V-12 for aircraft use and the marine V-12 used in the immortal PT boats. President Roosevelt personally asked Packard to sell its senior body dies to Russia during the war, and after some hesitation Alvan Macauley finally agreed. This was why the postwar Zis and Zil Soviet luxury cars looked so much like the Packard 160/180. It also meant, however, that when postwar production began Packard had only the Clipper body dies to use.

Production of the 21st Series began in October 1945 and lasted until September 1947. All the cars were Clippers, an unchanged continuation of the 1942 versions. There were the Six, Eight, and Deluxe Eight on the old junior chassis with its 120-in. wheelbase, with the Super Eight and Custom Super Eight on the senior chassis with its bigger engine. The distinction between "junior" and "senior" was blurring badly now, as both used the Clipper body which had started as a junior. All postwar Clippers used the wraparound front trim and fender skirts of the prewar senior Clippers, but can be distinguished by much thicker and more widely spaced bars in the grille. Of these, probably the most interesting to a modern enthusiast would be the luxurious Custom Super Eights, of which 7162 were produced.

In the latter part of 1947 the 22nd Series made its bow, the famous "pregnant" or "bathtub" Packard. This model has come in for a surprising amount of criticism, since it was actually one of the best-selling body styles in Packard history. Although the same wheelbases were kept, there was a major reshuffling of engines and model names. Gone was the Six, and the Eight and Deluxe Eight now used a brand new straight eight with a bore and stroke of 3½x3¾ ins. for 288 cu. ins. and 130 hp.

1. Like all '41 Packards, the 110 received handsome new styling with the headlights mounted in the fenders. This was the last year for this body style and separate 110 and 120 lines.

2. Introduced in 1941 as a variant of the 120 the Clipper proved to be enormously popular. The next year all the junior Packards were Clippers, and it was offered as a supplement to the senior Packards. This is a '42 senior Clipper sedan, identified by very narrow bars in the grille and trim bars that sweep around the front fender edges.

3. People throw rocks at the pregnant Packards now, but they outsold Cadillacs in their day. They were popular with movie personalities, such as young MGM star Marshall Thompson, giving his '48 Super Eight Victoria some totally superfluous polishing.

4. Here is a good view of Packard's 1951 line, which had all-new styling. In the foreground is the plush Patrician 400, which had a 327 9-bearing engine and Ultramatic as standard equipment. To the left is the lower-priced 300, which shared the Patrician's body, grille and 127-in. wheelbase, but had a 5-bearing engine and simpler trim. At the rear is the base 200 sedan, which had a 288 engine, a 122-in. wheelbase, a toothless grille and vertical taillights. The styling for 1952 was identical except for high-flying pelican which got its wings clipped.

SPECIAL INTEREST AMERICAN CARS/**181**

Independent

Packard

The Super Eight was demoted to the short 120-in. wheelbase, but received its own special engine of 327 cu. ins. and 145 hp. This engine was really our old friend the junior eight, which had been around since the 120's introduction in 1935 and hadn't been increased in size since 1937. It now received the rather substantial bore increase of ¼-in., which gave cylinder dimensions of 3½x4¼ ins. (same as the discontinued six) and raised its displacement from 282 to 327 cu. ins. The top-line Packard was now called the Custom Eight, and it was mechanically unchanged from the previous Custom Super Eight, so Packard was making three different straight-eight engines.

The pregnant Packards continued through 1950. However, 1949 was Packard's 50th anniversary, and to celebrate the company redesignated their cars the 23rd Series, the "Golden Anniversary" Packards. The only mechanical changes were the addition of five bhp to the ratings of the Eight and Super Eight engines, and the introduction of Ultramatic, Packard's automatic transmission. The Super Eight went back up again to the 127-in. wheelbase of the Custom Eight, but kept its 327-cu.-in. engine.

For 1951 (24th Series) there was a complete restyling of the entire line and a renaming of the models. Gone was any semblance of verticality in the styling, replaced by low wide lines. The base models were now called the 200 and 200 Deluxe, and had a 122-in. wheelbase with the 288-cu.-in. 135-hp engine. Next was the 300, which had the 127-in. wheelbase and the 327-cu.-in. 150-hp engine. And at the top was the 400 Patrician, also with a 127-in. wheelbase and a 327 engine, but this powerplant was rather special. Fighting a stubborn rear-guard action against the newer V-8's that every other luxury marque was now using, Packard put their 327 through a major redesign and gave it nine main bearings instead of five. It still had a flat-head valve arrangement, but the compression ratio was 7.8:1 and the engine was rated at 155 bhp. This engine replaced the older 356 engine, which was dropped. A little after the introduction of these models came the 250, a 2-door hardtop body style which had the 300's engine in the 200's shorter chassis.

The 1952 models (25th Series) were identical to the '51 cars, the only news being an improved Ultramatic and the introduction of optional power brakes, which Packard called Easamatic. A small but significant point was the passing of the high-winged pelican hood ornament, replaced by a much more stylized version with the wings streamlined back.

By 1953 Packard had a new president, James Nance, who was determined to shake up the company. Reflecting this energy, the 26th Series for '53 had only minor facelifting, but all the engines were uprated in power and all the model names were changed. The Clipper name was revived and applied to the previous 200, which now had 150 bhp from the 288-cu.-in. engine. Next up was the Clipper Deluxe, which had the Clipper's 122-in. wheelbase but 160 bhp from the 327 5-bearing engine. The 300 was now the Cavalier and at the top, the Patrician kept its 2-year-old name; both of these had the 127-in. wheelbase and 180-hp 327 engines with a 4-bbl. carburetor, but the Patrician was still the only one with the 9-bearing version. The in-between 2-door hardtop was now named Mayfair, and it had the Clipper wheelbase with the Cavalier's 180-hp engine. Sharing the Mayfair combination of short wheelbase and powerful engine were the convertible and a brand new model, the Caribbean. This was a spectacular convertible which looked like the Pan American, a show car of the previous year which had aroused great interest. Though the Caribbean had the same body and chassis as the convertible, it can be distinguished immediately by its fully exposed wire wheels, lack of side trim, and external spare wheel. Only 750 Caribbeans were made in '53. This

182/SPECIAL INTEREST AMERICAN CARS

model continued in limited production through 1956, and is today the most desired postwar Packard. Power steering made its appearance this year as an option on all models.

In 1954 chaos was developing in the corporate ranks—this was the year of the merger with Studebaker—but the only visible sign of this in the cars was the naming of them as the 54th Series, (for 1954) rather than the 27th. Body styling was unchanged, but '54 models can be spotted by the larger headlight rims with little caps on them. The 9-bearing engine came into its own this year, being both bored and stroked to 3 9/16x4½ ins. for 359 cu. ins., the largest in America. With an aluminum cylinder head and 8.7:1 compression ratio, it developed 212 hp and was the standard engine for the Patrician, Convertible, Caribbean, and Pacific, the last being a new 2-door hardtop replacing the Mayfair. The 327 5-bearing engine was rated at 185 bhp (4-bbl. carb) for the Cavalier and 165 bhp (2-bbl. carb) for the Clipper Deluxe and new Clipper Super, while the base Clipper Special stuck with its 150-hp 288 engine. The new Clipper Super promptly showed its worth by outselling every other model, even though this was a bad year for Packard; production was only one-third of the previous year, with a total of 31,290 cars.

As Packard fanciers know, 1955 was the year Jim Nance had been pointing towards, the year Packard was going to make its great comeback. The '55 cars had everything—new styling, brand new big V-8, Twin Ultramatic, Torsion-Level Ride, wraparound windshield—the works. The Clipper was more-or-less established as a separate make of car, and neither the name Packard nor the famous red hexagon appeared on the body. Instead, the Clipper steering wheel emblem was everywhere—grille, trunklid, hubcaps, roof pillars, dashboard. The Clipper Deluxe and Super sedans and Panama 2-door hardtop had the 122-in. wheelbase and a 320-cu.-in. (3 13/16x3½ ins.) version of the V-8 rated at 225 bhp. The Clipper Custom (sedan) and Constellation (hardtop) had the same wheelbase but a bored-out version (4x3½ ins.) of the V-8 rated at 245 bhp from its 352 cu. ins. The only cars called Packards this year were the Patrician sedan, 400 hardtop coupe, and Caribbean; the previous Cavalier and regular convertible were gone. These three all had 127-in. wheelbases and 352 V-8's, rated at 260 bhp for the Patrician and 400 and a healthy 275 bhp in the opulent tri-toned Caribbean. Torsion-Level Ride was a dramatic development which not only replaced conventional springs, but also provided automatic height compensation at the rear for heavy luggage or passenger loads. It was standard on the three Packard models, Clipper Custom and Constellation, while the other Clippers made do with conventional springs.

The last year for true Packards was 1956. There were several improvements, such as a limited-slip differential, push-button Ultramatic, and Torsion-Level Ride made standard for all models. All Clippers got the 352 engine, rated at 240 bhp in Deluxe and Super, and 270 bhp in the Custom. The top-line Packards had a bored-out 374-cu.-in. version (4⅛x3½ ins.), rated at 290 bhp in the Patrician and 400, and a whopping 310 bhp in the Caribbean. There were two Caribbeans this final year, the convertible being joined by a hardtop. Caribbean production was still very low; only 276 convertibles and 263 hardtops were made.

There is no point in discussing the '57-'58 Packards. They were warmed-over and uglified Studebakers, not worthy of the great name they carried. Production plummeted to pitiful levels, and the Studebaker-Packards remain curiosities, not special interest cars. 🐞

1. The rarest and most desirable '51 Packard is the 250, a very pretty 2-dr. hardtop. It had the 200's short wheelbase and taillights, the 300's engine and grille, and rear fender gimcracks from the Patrician. Only 4640 were made.

2. All postwar Packard straight eights are similar in appearance and design. This is a 327-cu. in. "Thunderbolt" engine in a '52 300 sedan.

3. Highlight of the '53 line was the Caribbean, a lush convertible with chrome wire wheels and full wheel cutouts. Like the Mayfair hardtop coupe, it had the Clipper's short wheelbase and the Cavalier's 180-hp engine.

4. Caribbean for 1954 shows slightly different styling at rear from its predecessor, still has wire wheels. It shared 212-hp engine with other top-line '54 models. Only 400 made.

5. The Caribbean for '55 was a magnificent brute a block long, three colors high and packed 275 hp. Only 500 were made, and many Packard lovers feel this is the best postwar Packard of all.

6. Patrician sedan shows revised '56 big-block grille it shared that year with Four Hundred and Caribbean. New push-button Ultramatic and limited-slip differential were standard on these models, as well as power brakes. Power steering, electric windows and seats were standard on Caribbean, optional on all other Packards and Clippers. This was the last year for true Packards.

7. The 1958 Packard Hawk was the last car of any interest made bearing the Packard name. A transparent modification of the Studebaker Golden Hawk, it had a fiberglass nose piece, fiberglass fins, a phoney spare tire cover, leather interior, and supercharged 289 V-8 rated at 275 bhp. Only 588 saw the light of day before the once-proud Packard name vanished forever.

Independent
Studebaker
America's oldest vehicle manufacturer

No other company described in this book has as long, if not as colorful, a history as does Studebaker. By the time even the early pioneering efforts of fledgling American automobile manufacturers were just beginning to bear four-wheeled fruit at the turn of the century, Studebaker had already been in business for almost half a century and was long established as the world's largest manufacturer of vehicles.

Many interesting pages could be spent on the first 50 years of Studebaker, but given our present parameters, we'll bring you up to our 1930 jumping-off point as briefly as possible. Descendants of a long line of wagon-makers and blacksmiths, Henry and Clem Studebaker established a wagon shop in South Bend, Indiana in 1852 with a total capital of $68. Migrations to the western territories, and the Indian Wars, brought them covered-wagon orders from settlers and the U.S. Army, and by 1867 they were grossing $350,000 annually. The Studebaker Brothers Manufacturing Company (two more of the brothers had entered the business) was formed in 1868, and within the next five years became the largest producer of wagons, buggies, harness, etc. Although Henry Ford is credited with establishing the moving assembly line over 40 years later, the brothers Studebaker must have been doing something right, for they were able to produce a completed vehicle every seven minutes!

By the turn of the century, sales were well over two million dollars and the company got into the new *horseless* vehicle field with their first electric cars in 1902, designed by no less a luminary than Thomas A. Edison. This proved successful enough that production of gasoline buggies was begun just two years later, in co-operation with the Garford Company, who supplied the chassis. The ever-expanding company acquired the Everett-Metzger-Flanders Company (formed by former Cadillac and Ford men) in 1908, and within a year 7960 E-M-F cars had been built. Due to rear-end problems with the E-M-F that had earned it such nicknames as "Every Morning Fixit," an improved car was brought out with the Studebaker name.

The engineering talents of Fred Zeder, Owen Skelton and Carl Breer, who later formed the nucleus of Chrysler's engineering staff, and the animated presidency of Albert Russel Erskine combined to make a viable automobile company that was third in production from 1912-1914. By 1920, Studebaker finally stopped production of horse-drawn vehicles and was firmly into the gasoline car business with a new line of all 6-cyl. cars that quickly built a reputation for durability. The company experimented in the low-price field with the Erskine model, brought out in 1926, but it still couldn't compete in price with Ford or Chevrolet, and it was geared so high, engine life suffered and likewise reputation.

About this time Delmar "Barney" Roos came into the Studebaker engineering picture, and his first contribution was to give the marque its first 8-cyl. engines, introduced in 1928 as the President Eight. He had designed engines for both Locomobile and Marmon, and the new Studebaker straight-eight was smooth, powerful, and quieter than any previous Studebaker engine.

Now at the early Depression beginning of this book's scope, the Studebaker line consisted of three names that would come to mean much in Studebaker history. The 1930 car-buyer could have his choice of the three different bodies, President, Commander and Dictator, (in descending price order), and each of these could be had with either a six or an eight, in varying sizes. These were all good-looking cars, built from hardwood framing covered with sheetmetal and with stamped fenders, a body-building technique Studebaker continued after many other manufacturers had gone completely to stamped steel panels. But then, you'd *expect* a company famous for building wagons and carriages for 80 years to continue to work with wood framing, even if some of the younger "upstart" vehicle manufacturers like Ford had gone to steel-stamping bodies.

Besides their good looks, Studebakers in 1930 also featured a double-drop frame for a lower silhouette, safety glass windshields, the first combination steering/ignition lock, thermostatic radiator shutters on the more expensive cars, and the newly-introduced feature of "free-wheeling." Although Studebak-

er hailed it as a great boon to the motorist and many other manufacturers jumped on the bandwagon right away, it was of questionable use for most normal driving, as coasting on hills was illegal in some states. While most carmakers dropped the idea as hastily as they had picked it up, Studebaker hung onto it for another five years. Something Studebaker really did have to brag about was their performance at the Indianapolis 500 race. Five of the Studebaker engineers got together in their unofficial spare time and fitted the 336-cu.-in. President straight-eights in two race cars, adding such goodies as four Winfield carbs, headers, magnetos and special high-compression heads they had built at work. The Indy rules had been opened up that year to allow stock-block engines to challenge the Miller supremacy there, and the two Studebaker-powered racers came in 8th and 18th that year. This was the best finish of any of the stock-block entries, which that year made up about half of the 33-car field, and Studebaker built a name for itself as a fast car.

By far the most impressive of the '30 Studebakers are the top-of-the-line President models, in the FH series with 125-in. wheelbase, and the FE series with another 10 ins. of wheelbase. Although not currently listed by classic car organizations as a true classic, the President was a large but well-proportioned car, whose smooth eight made it one of the best road cars in or out of its price class. Two of the nicest models to consider collecting today would be the President roadster and the "State Victoria," both of which had six wire wheels and rear-mounted luggage racks.

From 1928 on, Studebaker had been advancing its place in the production race compared to other manufacturers, but producing less cars every year. In fact, the only manufacturers still selling anywhere near their pre-Depression levels were the two cheapest makes, Ford and Chevrolet. Studebaker's 1930 production stood at 51,640, and was to drop slightly the next year, despite many improvements in the cars. The '31's had an attractive new V'd grille, *oval* headlights without a crossbar, fender lights, new bumpers with a drop in the center, and an 8-cyl. engine for all three models. Their lowest-price car was the Studebaker Six, the only one still with the six. Among the mechanical improvements offered on some of the '31 cars were an adjustable steering column, automatic choke, map light, air, oil and fuel filters, servo-mechanical brakes, and adjustable front seats. But by far the most important advance, in terms of cars we drive today, was the introduction of coated, steel-shell rod and crankshaft bearings. These easily-replaced, high load capacity bearings were a great step forward in engine durability and lower-end strength, and certainly didn't hurt Studebaker's chances in Indianapolis racing. In fact, the two Studebaker-eight-powered cars did even better in '31 than the year before, winning the pole position, leading much of the race, and finishing fourth, again ahead of any other stock-block entry.

The 1932 line featured new and larger bodies, and most body styles incorporated a lower percentage of window glass to body-area, giving them a "chopped-top" effect that adds a touch of classic coachbuilding to their profiles. In an attempt to bolster lagging sales during the depressed times, prices were lowered on all Studebaker models, and a brand new "economy" model was brought out. The Rockne Six, named after the famous Notre Dame football coach, was built on 110-and 114-in. wheelbases, with 66-and 72-hp engines. Priced much closer to the low-price competition than the Erskine had been, it couldn't beat the price of a Ford, which had two more cylinders to offer. Only a little over 23,000 Rocknes were built that year, and it was discontinued in '33. One of the most attractive and collectible of the '32 Studebaker body styles was the luxurious St. Regis Brougham. A 6-wheeler with accessory trunk at the rear, it had extremely long doors (stretching from cowl to rear fender) that allowed passenger entry to both front and rear seats, with only a small "formal" window following the doors.

With an output in 1932 of only 44,235 cars, Studebaker wasn't doing well, and in 1933 went into receivership, after a planned merger with White failed to materialize to save the company from $15 million worth of

1. Any of the early President models, as Studebaker's top of the line, are very desirable today, especially the open cars like this 1931 4-door phaeton with dual sidemounted spares.

2. Unlike many other-make roadsters, The President "Four Seasons" roadsters had roll-up windows. Opening in rear quarter is classic golf-bag door.

3. The '32 Studebakers had a choppedtop look as a result of lessening the glass area, as seen here on this '32 President coupe, with twin horns and "artillery" spoked wheels.

4. Stylish artist's conceptions like that of the '33 roadster here failed to capture the public's fancy in great numbers, and Studebaker went into a receivership period for two years.

Independent Studebaker

liabilities. Formerly dominating and hard-driving, Erskine felt crushed by the turn of financial events at the company and at home, and committed suicide—not an uncommon fate for big businessmen in the Depression. The new team assigned to take control of the company and bring it out of the doldrums were Ashton G. Bean (of White Motor Co.) Harold Vance, and Paul Hoffman, who would ultimately succeed in bringing the company back to a viable position in the market, although never into the "Big Three." After a production shutdown of several weeks, the new '33's came off the line and business, although not even as good as the year before in numbers, was profitable, partly because of Studebaker's many outside suppliers, who extended the company liberal credit terms to allow them to continue, and because the sale of Studebaker's interests in the Pierce-Arrow Company brought in a million dollars.

The '33 Studebakers are considered quite rare today, although not every collector is fond of the sweeping grille. The fenders of the '33-'34's were semi-skirted, and this company's first attempt at streamlining ("air-curve coachcraft") resulted in a beavertailed panel covering the fuel tank to improve airflow at the rear. Electric starting, reflector taillights, automatic choke, improved performance, and the Bendix vacuum-assisted power (mechanical) brakes were some of the other features in Studebaker's favor. Few cars on the road in the Thirties could match the big Studebaker eights for power, and the company still got good publicity for this aspect of their cars with their continuing efforts, and good showings, at the Indy 500. One of the advertising pitches of the period was "From the speedway comes their stamina... from the skyway comes their style!" While some manufacturers were starting to raise prices again in 1934, Studebaker kept lowering theirs to stay in business, and there were some sales improvement over the year before. The Dictator Six was now down to $645, and even the President Eight, with its engine now destroked and "debored" to 250 cu. ins. was around $1200, quite a drop from the year before, when the Speedway Presidents were priced between $1500 and $2000. The most interesting body style of the '34-'35 period would have to be the Land Cruiser (no, it didn't have four-wheel drive or come from Japan) with its streamlining. Fitted with rear fender skirts, fastback styling with flush-mounted rear trunk, and "wraparound" (four-piece) rear window, its styling was reminiscent of the Pierce Silver Arrow, for which Studebaker had been building bodies. Despite the company building a giant, 80-foot long replica to startle visitors to the Chicago Century of Progress Fair in 1934, its looks were described by some as ugly and fat, and they were sold in no great numbers.

Biggest of all Studebaker developments for 1935 was the introduction of independent front suspension and Borg-Warner overdrive. The "planar" front suspension, brainchild of Barney Roos, was a more truly independent system than any that their competitors were offering, except for Packard, GM and Chrysler, and consisted of upper and lower arms controlled by a transverse leaf spring. That year was also a Studebaker first for hydraulic brakes, and their 6-passenger sedan offering was a first for any company. A slight improvement in sales and the sincere efforts of the new management team brought the company out of receivership, and Hoffman became president, with Vance as chairman of the board.

The year 1936 became a bright one for Studebaker, with production up to 85,026, a whopping improvement of 73% over 1935. Breaking away from some of their conservatism in styling, outsider and famed industrial designer Raymond Loewy, a man destined to make considerable contributions to the company, was retained as a styling consultant. The new Studebaker bodies for '36 were the company's first all-steel-roofed cars, and the bodies were lowered by mounting them directly on the frame with no intermediate sills. The biggest mechanical improvement that year was the very practical "Automatic Hill Holder." When you depressed both the clutch and the brake pedals at the same time, the brakes would lock and hold the car. Thus you could get the throttle

1. Studebakers gradually declined in size through the Thirties as they got closer to the low-price field. This 1938 President sedan was one of the last of the big Studebakers. Note the unusual headlight lenses and rims.

2. Although not a stock design, this customized '38 convertible-sedan with fake outside pipes ala Auburn is neat. In this Paramount shot are (l. to r.) Eddie "Rochester" Anderson, Jack Benny and, leaning on rear door, Phil Harris. A customized Studebaker was probably "close enough" to a classic for the pennypinch character Benny portrayed.

3. Studebaker got into the low-price field for the first time successfully in 1939, with the introduction of the all-new Champion models. This President is extremely rare because of the few '39-'40 models equipped with sidemounts.

4. Note the unusual rear fenders on this '42 President Eight; they're a cross between post-war sleek and prewar round. Any '42 model is rare today.

5. The revolutionary 1947 Champion was the first of the truly new cars of the immediate post-war period. It was designed from the ground up with body by Loewy, improved chassis, wide passenger compartment and unparalleled rearward visibility with the very wide rear window, giving rise to comments that people didn't know "whether it was coming or going!"

and clutch to the right point to take off without any fancy footwork or clutch-popping. This must have appealed to the ladies of the day, especially in places like San Francisco.

Once Studebaker got its test track completed in 1926, and had loosened up its engineering department, a steady stream of automotive firsts came from South Bend. Not all of their achievements have been earth-shaking devices that revolutionized the industry (although the Studebaker-Clevite-developed bearing inserts were a giant leap forward in engine durability), but in their own way, Studebaker through the Thirties kept introducing features that we take for granted today, or that other manufacturers introduced many years later as "firsts." In 1937, for example, Studebaker was the first manufacturer to use non-scratch piston rings, variable-ratio steering gear, Hancock rotary door latches, and direct-acting tubular shocks. Of course, every car today has these features and we tend to forget their relative importance, but in 1937 the new steering and shocks represented a considerable improvement. With a 19.5:1 ratio when steering straight-ahead which had good road feel and response, the ratio turned to 24:1 when turned far enough, making parallel-parking your 3700-lb. State President a lot easier. The shocks, developed by Delco, made suspension designing simpler and servicing easier.

After two very good years, the business recession of 1938 found Studebaker production back down to a receivership-era level of 46,207, not a very good year at all, although the low production does make these cars more valuable today. The Studebakers still had very rounded fenders, "classic" side-mounted spares were still available on some models, and the park lights were still mounted at the crown of the front fenders. The grille retained the verticallity of the early Thirties, yet with thin, horizontal bars. The least attractive features of the '38's are the "bug-eyed" headlights. Caught in the transition from pod-mounted lights to fender-integrated lights, the '38 headlights sat in fairings that rose up from the fender, and were still tucked in close to the grille. Their unusual diamond-shaped lenses and fat chrome bezels didn't do much for the '38's front end looks.

The year 1939 was to be the beginning of a new and more glorious era for Studebaker, in which they gave up part of the fight for the middle-price-range and once again ventured into the profitable low-price field, only this time they were enormously successful compared to their experiences with the Erskine and the Rockne. After the brief flush of coming out of receivership in 1935 had worn off and the management took a good, hard look at the future, they decided to wade into the low-price field again, but this time equipped with a vehicle that had been designed *from the ground up* for that market. The result previewed in early 1939 after four years of development and strenuous testing, was the new, Loewy-designed Studebaker Champion. Priced at $740, it was less than $50 higher than a Ford or Plymouth, but at 2375 lbs. was 500-650 lbs. lighter than any other low-price car, and could claim 20% better performance and economy than its competitors. The all-new L-head six of 164 cu. ins. offered 78 hp, only giving away 4-6 hp to the other cars, and promised top speeds of 75-80 mph at over 20 mpg on the road. I wish I could buy one today to drive to work! The Champion had been totally wrung out, both on the test track where it managed to run a continuous 15,000 miles at over 60 mph, and on the road, where a cross-country run averaged 27 mpg with overdrive. The public responded to the new car by buying 72,791 Champions and bringing total 1939 production to 106,470, an incredible improvement of 230% over 1938, and there was joy again in South Bend, Indiana.

In 1940, the running boards all-but disappeared from Studebakers line, and the Champion kept on selling without any major changes in either '40 or '41, except for the usual annual grille changes. In 1942, however, war ended almost all automobile production and only 9285 civilian Studebakers were built before the plants were turned over to production of aircraft engines, military trucks and amphibious cargo carriers. Any of the '42 models would be considered quite rare today, especially the more expensive President styles.

During the latter part of the war, the most revolutionary Studebaker ever was in the works under two design teams, Raymond Loewy's and Virgil Exner's. Although Studebaker was not the first automobile manufacturer to resume production after the war, they were definitely the first to put true postwar *styling* into production. The '46 models were warm-overs of the '42, just as was the case with all of the other manufacturers, but in 1947, the new Champion came out and shocked the automotive world. Although Loewy is often given most of the credit, the final design of the '47 was basically Exner's. The incredibly-different '47 coupe had a four-piece wraparound rear window, and was the first American car whose body was as wide as the fenders. Only the rear quarter had any semblance of a fender; the fronts were totally integrated into the design. The new car was *seven* inches lower than the '46, and bringing the body out to the width of the fend-

3

4

5

SPECIAL INTEREST AMERICAN CARS/**187**

Independent
Studebaker

ers gave passengers an extra 6 inches of room up front and 10 inches in the rear seat. Except for the self-adjusting brakes, the rest of the car was not new, but the streamlined body with the Loewy-specified "airplane propellor" spinner nose must have seemed to 1947 car-buyers like a futuristic styling exercise that somehow made it to the production line. That production line, by the way, was up almost 60% over 1946, a trend that continued, as did the shape of the cars, for the next four years, the greatest production years in the company's history, culminating in 1950 with a Studebaker record level of 268,099 cars, many of these equipped with the new automatic transmission with the first air-cooled torque converter.

Unfortunately, the design that had been so clean, organized, functional and yet attractive when introduced had failed, as many designs before and after by Studebaker and other companies, to hold the interest of the fickle American consumer for more than a year or two. Clean as the "new look" was, it was growing old by 1950, and even the introduction of the automatic transmission, coil spring suspension, and the new overhead-valve V-8 ('51) couldn't keep up the sales record.

A new car was obviously necessary, and it would have to be a good one to continue competing with the giants of the Big Three. Some late 1940's doodlings of a European-flavored coupe by Studebaker designer Bob Bourke caught the eye of Loewy and a crash program was begun to get this handsome coupe into production. Studebaker had intended to come up with a new car for '52, their 100th anniversary, but it couldn't be completed in time. There's a long and interesting story behind the scramble to finalize the design and get it into production, but unfortunately we don't have the space in this present book. For our purposes, suffice it to say that the car did eventually make production, and although many complicated factors contributed to it not becoming the saviour Studebaker had been banking on, the important thing for car enthusiasts is that it became probably the finest design of the Fifties. Again it was radically different from the competition, it had very little chrome, rested on a new light-but-strong box frame, and sat much lower than the typical American car. The silhouette was never so sleek and futuristic as when parked next to any other make of Fifties vintage. It was a dramatically new car. Along with the V-8 engine and the automatic (with unusual anti-creep device reminiscent of the '36 hillholder), the '53 also offered power steering. Early cars off the line had an unusual Borg-Warner mechanical power steering unit, but this was later dropped in favor of GM Saginaw units (hydraulic). The clean profile of the Starliner hardtop (models with roof pillars were labeled Starlight) became the essence of all future Studebakers bodies, but few of the later designs would prove to be as pure as the '53 and '54. For 1954, the only real changes were different bumper guards and teeth added to the small grille openings on either side of the low drooping hood. The '53 coupe, although it never sold well enough to save the company (1953 production was 186,484, up over '52, but '54 went down to 85,252), is recognized today even by non-Studebaker fans as one of the true milestone cars.

Packard, another ailing independent, was brought into the Studebaker fold in 1954, and the alliance, while it probably hastened the end for Packard, at least provided Studebaker with some capital to keep going. The company even tried to capitalize on its rich heritage in '54, when it brought out a wagon model named the Conestoga. Nowhere near as nice as the coupe in styling, it is nevertheless a collectible Studebaker. In an unfortunate attempt to all at once chameleonize the clean body of the '53 Studebaker to look more like the "stylish" behemoths put out by Detroit, the front end was lavished with an abundance of chrome for '55. No more need be said about the '55's other than that the President series was revived to take the Land Cruiser's place, and the President Speedster models (with leather interior and special dash) are worth considering today.

Although '55 saw sales improve

1. The '48-52 Studebakers kept the basic post-war design, but by then the styling was no longer new and the other cars were also wide and slabsided. This collectable '51 soft-top lacks only a propellor on the front to taxi down the runway and off.

2. Many enthusiasts consider the '53 as Studebaker's finest hour, at least in terms of the design purity of the Bourke-Loewy European profile. At an amazing (for 1953) height of 56 ins., it was the lowest American passenger car. It's aerodynamics have always appealed to both collectors and racers.

3. The '54's were little changed but a new car into the lineup was this '54 Conestoga station wagon. Standing at left are Chairman of the Board Paul G. Hoffman, and president Harold S. Vance. Little did they know then what the next decade would bring.

4. Although the clean '53 design had been heavily gee-gawed by '55, this President Speedster model, with wirewheel hubcaps, leather interior and special dash, is still a good special interest model to look for today.

5. Based on further restylings of the '53 line, the Hawk series introduced in '56 is avidly sought by enthusiasts now. Top of the line in '56 was this Golden Hawk, with 275 hp Packard V-8 and Ultramatic, special dash and gauges, and other features designed to give a new "sports" image to Studebaker.

6. In 1957, the heavy Packard engine that had hurt handling was dropped in favor of a Studebaker engine with a Paxton blower for the Golden Hawks. The power was there, but now handling was there to match. This was a lot of car for the money in 1957. The Hawk line continues to be collectable right up to the last years of the company.

3

4

5

6

somewhat (to 112,392), Studebaker was still behind a dozen other manufacturers of automobiles, and it was an unlucky position. The '56 lineup saw the introduction of the *sporty* Studebakers, the Hawk restyling of the '53 with a more vertical, squared-off grille that was to remain the basic Studebaker feature for the company's next, and last, ten years. Powerful, road-holding cars, the Hawks descended in lineup from the top Golden Hawk (with Packard 324-cu.-in. V-8) to the Sky Hawk, Power Hawk, and the 6-cyl. Flight Hawk. The now-289-cu.-in. Studebaker V-8 was boosted to 275 hp by a McCulloch blower for the Golden Hawks of '57 and '58, and the Silver Hawk offered the 4 bbl. version. The Packard engine had been dropped from the Golden Hawk because its extra front-end weight adversely affected handling, so the blower was added to the Studebaker V-8 to stay in the Fifties horsepower race. The new performance potential never quite jibed with the public's image of Studebaker, however, and production in 1956 was down to 82,402, and had declined further to a low of 56,869 by 1958.

Since Studebaker had a 72,000 unit break-even point, it was obvious that things weren't going well. They weren't capturing the public's dollars with the models they had, and yet they didn't have the capital to invest in new tooling to change them. Harold E. Churchill, who became Studebaker President in 1956, was an automobile man who had some good plans for the future of the company. He foresaw the need for domestic compacts to fight the import tide, and actually got the new Lark into production for 1959 on a shoestring. While it temporarily brought production back up to 153,823 in '59 and the first Studebaker profit in five years, the arrival the next year of the competitors compacts, Falcon, Corvair, and Valiant, almost nullified the market impact of the Lark later on.

Poor management decisions, public apathy, Studebaker's hard-to-break image, aggressive selling by the Big Three, these and other complicated factors contributed to the demise of the nation's oldest vehicle manufacturer. For the later years, it's too easy today to lay the blame on the management or designers, they were caught between a rock and a hard spot, trying to come out with new cars when there was no budget for tooling or even designs, and the important decisions were being forced on them by the New York bankers and bean-counters who really called the shots. They wanted Studebaker to diversify and get out of the automobile business, and it happened, but not before some very memorable special interest cars were produced for the enthusiasts.

Independent

Willys

At one time, America's second largest car maker

The name Willys is another in a list of American automobile manufacturers which involved many take-overs, mergers, and marque discontinuations through its bumpy career, and which briefly loomed large on the auto industry's horizon only to fade with few laments. Many familiar (and some not-so-familiar) makes of cars are woven into the fabric that is the early Willys story, and further into the three-decade period that forms the parameters of this book Willys itself becomes firmly enmeshed with still other makes, some of which exist today. A detailed tracing of Willy's lineage brings one inescapably through such badges as Marion, Overland, Knight, Whippet, Americar, Kaiser, and, of course, the ubiquitous Jeep (which is now a trademark of American Motors Corporation).

It was hardly through chance that John North Willys acquired for himself, in 1907, the assets of the Standard Wheel Co., of Indiana which was suffering a financial muddle. Willys, the man, had been a Standard (and a Marion) dealer in Elmira, N.Y., and it behoove him to put the firm on its feet, if only to help sustain his own agency through continued sales of Standard's tiller-steered runabout which would eventually evolve into Willys, the car. By 1909 two models were offered, the Overland at $2000, and the higher-priced Willys at $2300. By 1910 Willys had managed to acquire the old Pope manufacturing facility in Toledo; a prophetic move since (historians take note) the Jeep which lay yet on a remote horizon would, 65 years later, be manufactured in the self-same buildings under the ownership of American Motors Corporation.

Willys-Overland, which title John North Willys bestowed when the Overland models were introduced, produced some 80,000 cars by 1914, making it a serious independent contender in the industry. The Edwards-Knight, a product of Edwards Motor Co. of New York, came into the Willys-Overland fold that year, bringing the famous double sleeve-valve Knight engine under Willys ownership but which was manufactured by Garford in Ohio, producers of their own car as well as Studebaker chassis from '04 to '11!

During the period of '12 to '18 Willys-Overland, through its various products, rated second only to Ford as America's largest producer of motor vehicles (though with approximately one-fifth of the leader's output; some 90,000 to 500,000 for '14, for example).

By 1923 Overlands climbed to 196,000 units sold, and in '26 the Whippet line was established as a low-cost Overland. Other Willys-Overland badges were the Model 70 Willys-Knight, Stearns-Knight and Falcon-Knight.

Willys as a single appelation fronted an all-new car in 1930, with both 6- and 8-cyl. engines, and Whippet became subserviant to it as a low-cost 4-cyl. The four was gone after '31, however, and the sleeve-valve engine disappeared quietly in '32. (The unique powerplant, incidentally was a development in 1906 of Charles Y. Knight who produced it as the Silent Knight!) It wasn't the fault of the passing of either of these engines that Willys-Overland began to flounder, but where once they had ranked 2nd in the industry, they slid to 10th in '32 (27,000 units); to 11th in '33 (though up to 30,000 units); to 15th in '34 (8000 units) and staying at the rating through '36 with 20,000 and 19,000 cars produced respectively. Willys fell into receivership and in '33 produced only a 4-cyl., 45-hp, 135-cu.-in. sidevalve engine and installed it in the "upside-down bathtub" model 77, which was anything but elegant but which eventually saved the firm from total bankruptcy.

Styling of the 77's, as indicated, was odd by American tastes, having an arched beltline which rounded down along the hoodline, and did the same in back. The headlights were un-elegantly flaired into the front fenders with sloping lenses which paralleled the angular but flat "waterfall" grille. Though the wheels were of pressed steel, spokes were simulated by embossing giving the unfortunate 77's a look of cheapness—but bravely offered for '33 at the astoundingly low cost of $445—America's lowest priced car!

The 77's quiet little engine—rubber-mounted via a license to the Chrysler patent—bears some detailing, since it would later play a vital role in World War II and become as familiar to countless GI's as the Model T engine had to rural Americans.

2

3

4

5

Cast en-bloc, the 4-cyl., L-head in-line developed (by 1936) 48 hp at 3200 rpm, had 5.7:1 compression, and spun in three main bearings. A single 1-bbl. Tillotson downdraft carburetor fed cylinders of 3.125-ins. bore and 4.375-ins. stroke through a conventional intake manifold. Exhaust was through a cast iron manifold with a single outlet. Its output went through a conventional single-plate clutch, a 3-speed transmission (floor-shifted), and back to a Hypoid rear end with semi-floating axles and a standard 4.3:1 ratio. It was a simple, forgiving, indestructable, system and would power the Willys Jeeps from the original prototype through production models to 1947.

The Model 77 succeeded in pulling Willys-Overland up by its bootstraps, even though the company was in receivership at the time and cars were built in batches of a few thousand at a time with creditor's permission. It was tough sledding for John North Willys and in late '34 and into '35 he directed the company from his bed after suffering a servere heart attack, no easy task for even a manufacturing genius in his 80's. Willys passed away in mid-'35 but only after he saw his firm begin to rise Phoenix-like from financial disaster.

New styling came to the old Model 77 in 1937. Still unmistakable from anything but the Willys that it was, the inverted bathtub shape was gone and the beltline was straight. The hood protruded out over the grille which was nothing more than a series of horizontal louvers in the forepart of the hood which rounded down and back to meet the juncture of the bulbous front fenders. The headlights were mounted in pods atop the fenders with their lenses thankfully vertical. Several body styles were offered; a 4-door sedan, a coupe, a roadster, and a tourer. Wheelbase of all models was 100 ins. Under the enveloping hood beat the heart of what was now termed the Go-Devil engine, the self-same motor of the Model 77, the basic design of which is traceable back to the old Whippets.

Design remained unchanged for 1938 and a total of nearly 27,000 were built. A facelift for what amounted to a U.S. compact car ahead of its time, was given the 100-in. wheelbase Willys for the 1939 model year. Willys followers today are not in agreement that the new front end was more attractive than the '37's and '38's, for the earlier '33 through '36's seem to enjoy a somewhat greater demand. Be that as it may, the '38's had a more sharply-pointed prow, still jutting ahead of the grille in profile. The grille still consisted of horizontal louvers punched into the hood, though the topmost was about at the hood's mid-point and they continued down onto a valance which separated the front fenders. The headlights were curious, having a decided eyebrow effect. To prove the economical operation that the little car could dish out, two were entered in the 1939 Gilmore-Yosemite Economy Run and came home in first and second places.

Another facelift occurred in 1940; the jutting hood was softened somewhat and the grille louvers eliminated. Air intake was now solely through the horizontally-louvered front valance and the headlights lost their pods to melt into the front fenders with oval-shaped lenses. Wheelbase grew 2 inches to 102 ins. to give a bit more legroom to long suffering drivers and passengers.

New for 1941 was the Model 441 on a 104-in. wheelbase and called the Willys-Americar, probably in the national spirit of this immediate prewar era. It was produced in the old Pope plant in Toledo like so many of its

1. The Willys-Knight Great Six was the leader of the Willys range for 1930 and, selling at $1850, it was aimed at the senior Chrysler's price range. This is the Model 66 sports roadster, with 120-in. wheelbase, and 87 hp.

2. The famous Model 77, in sedan form, reflected the endearment "upside down bathtub," but the appelation wasn't quite as deserved by the 4-door as by the coupe whose beltline rounded down at the rear. In its initial year of 1933, the 77's were advertised at a low $445, and though Willys-Overland was in receivership, this car managed to save the firm from bankruptcy.

3. The 77's were redesigned for '38 resulting in this appealing style. Advertising claimed as much as 36.5 miles per gallon. Four body versions were available, all on a 100-in. wheelbase and with the Go-Devil 4-cyl. engine that was later to power the World War II Jeeps.

4. Willys was updated for '39, and though carried a new hood, it still featured the jutting prow shape. Real news this year was the adoption of hydraulic brakes. Advertising claimed less than one cent per mile operating economy. 2-door was the Speedway Sedan.

5. A major facelift for '41 resulted in the 441 Model, on 104-in. wheelbase and officially tagged Americar. Willys output swiftly wound down in these immediate prewar days, for output was concentrated on MA Jeeps.

Independent
Willys

forebears, on a line which paralleled the Model MA Jeep which was now in production.

Willys manufactured the greater majority of the WW II Jeeps under a government agreement which also allowed Ford to produce the same vehicle, but in lesser numbers. All told, 361,349 Willys Jeeps were built but while these unique little machines have at least as large a following as all other Willys products combined, they are really a utility vehicle and thus beyond the scope of a book on passenger cars.

When civilian cars were again permitted, Willys stayed out of the conventional passenger car business for a while and concentrated their production of CJ's (for Civilian Jeep) not much unlike the military versions, but also adding an assortment of body styles as station wagons, a sportster, and others. Once more, however, these vehicles are unto themselves and while of special interest to their own enthusiasts, are not felt to be within this book's limitations.

Passenger car production was resumed at last for the 1952 model year, and two all-new lines were fielded; the Aero-Ace and Aero-Wing. Again, they were of compact design but featured unit construction and a 161-cu.-in. in-line, F-head 6-cyl. engine of 80 hp, and termed the Hurricane. The Aero-Ace and Aero-Wing were similar in most respects but the Ace was the top-line model and had a broader rear window with more luxurious trim and interior appointments.

Willys boldly broadened their model line-up for '53, terming the Aero models Ace, Wing, Lark and Falcon. Only 2- and 4-door sedans were available, but engine choices were the Lightning 6 with 75 hp, and Hurricane 6 with 90 hp. Also built, but for export only, was the faithful Hurricane 4, now up to 72 horsepower.

The year 1953 marks the merger of Willys with the Kaiser interests and our tale slows at this point to a stop. Although Aeros were produced until 1956, they were under the K-F banner and are delineated within that chapter.

The pre-'33 Willys and its derivatives were solid, reliable though mundane appearing cars and few except the sleeve-valve engined models are of particular interest for our purposes, although many are deemed true classics. However, since Willys had enjoyed sales second only to Ford until '31 most models are hardly scarce. But as production faltered and Willys slid down the rating charts, the cars become obviously in short supply today. The firm's salvation, remember, was the homely little Model 77 and all models through '36 are decidedly of special interest, as are the facelifted versions beginning in '37 and the later '39's. Production was low during these boot-strap years, and the fact that many of these quaint little machines saw active postwar duty as big-motored drag racing cars with only the basic body shell retained, few in anywhere near pristine condition survive today making one in virtually any condition a worthwhile restoration.

1. Pure passenger cars didn't roll from Willys' Toledo plant again until 1952. The new Aero lines featured welded unit construction and while a compact, it was really quite a contemporary automobile.

2. Plain-jane '52 Willys was the Aero-Lark. It had the Lightning 6, 72-hp. engine and listed at $1587.50.

3. Top-of-the-line Aeros were well embellished with exterior trim, comfort conveniences inside, and had a wider rear window than other models. Models were unchanged for '53, and in mid-year Willys merged with K-F.